Schriften zum Internationalen
und Europäischen Strafrecht

Edited by

Prof. Dr. Martin Heger, Humboldt-Universität zu Berlin
Prof. Dr. Florian Jeßberger, Humboldt-Universität zu Berlin
Prof. Dr. Frank Neubacher, M.A., Universität zu Köln
Prof. Dr. Helmut Satzger, LMU München
Prof. Dr. Gerhard Werle, Humboldt-Universität zu Berlin

Volume 82

Isabella Poewe

From Outlaws to Equal Players – Rebel Courts in International Law

Nomos

Onlineversion
Nomos eLibrary

The Deutsche Nationalbibliothek lists this publication in the Deutsche Nationalbibliografie; detailed bibliographic data are available on the Internet at http://dnb.d-nb.de

a.t.: Berlin, HU, Diss., 2025

Original title: "Rethinking the Administration of Justice by Non-State Armed Groups – Eligible for Recognition in International Law?"

ISBN (Print) 978-3-7560-3437-6 (Nomos Verlagsgesellschaft mbH & Co. KG, Baden-Baden)

ISBN (ePDF) 978-3-7489-6461-2 (Nomos Verlagsgesellschaft mbH & Co. KG, Baden-Baden)

ISBN (Print) 978-3-03891-881-3 (Dike Verlag, Zürich/St. Gallen)

1st Edition 2026

Dedicated to my parents and my beloved sister Lea

Acknowledgements

This book was accepted as a dissertation in the summer semester of 2025 by the Faculty of Law at Humboldt University of Berlin.

It marks the end of an exciting and enriching time as a law student, research assistant at the chair of Prof. Dr. Dr. h.c. Martin Heger, and ultimately as a doctoral candidate under the supervision of Prof. Dr. Florian Jeßberger. To him I am deeply grateful for his continuous support, his open ear, and his committed supervision of my work. His guidance, helpful remarks and, especially, his unwavering trust in my work have always encouraged me and were an invaluable help throughout the process.

My gratitude also goes to Prof. Dr. Dr. h.c. Martin Heger for kindly agreeing to review my thesis as a second supervisor as well as to Prof. Dr. Katrin Höffler for her interest and willingness to preside over the examination committee.

I would also like to thank Prof. Dr. Paola Gaeta who supervised my project during my time as a junior visiting fellow at the Geneva Graduate Institute. She provided me with invaluable and thought-provoking ideas which ultimately shaped the focus and perspective of this book. My time in Geneva not only was an academic enrichment but, above all, it was a personal one. I am deeply thankful to Dr. Liline Steyn and Dr. Rafael Carrano Lelis for the special moments we shared in Geneva and for their friendship.

Finally, I wish to thank my family and friends in Berlin who accompanied me throughout the entire process and without whom the realization of this dissertation would not have been possible. I am deeply grateful to my father for his constant proofreading and his helpful comments – especially as a judicial layman. My heartfelt thanks also go to Dr. Maren Lena Rixecker, Hoa Vuong and Dr. Nils Weinberg – three friends with whom I mastered the often challenging PhD-time. Their constant support was a major source of confidence and encouragement.

Last but not least, I would like to thank my godfather, Dr. Albert Heiss. His fascinating accounts of his work as a criminal lawyer were the origin of my desire to study law.

Berlin, September 2025 *Isabella Poewe*

Table of Contents

List of Abbreviations

Abbreviation	*Meaning*
AANES	Autonomous Administration of Northeast Syria
ACHPR	African Charter on Human and Peoples' Rights
ACHR	American Convention on Human Rights
AFSJ	Area of Freedom, Security and Justice
Al-Nusra	Jabhat al-Nusra li-Ahl al-Shām
BWC	Biological Weapons Convention
CCW	Convention on Certain Conventional Weapons
CISA	Convention Implementing the Schengen Agreement
CPS	Communist Party of El Salvador
CRC	Convention on the Rights of the Child
CWC	Chemical Weapons Convention
DFNS	Democratic Federation of Northern Syria
DRC	Democratic Republic of Congo
ECHR	European Convention on Human Rights
ECJ	European Court of Justice
ECtHR	European Court of Human Rights
ELN	National Liberation Army
ELP	Popular Liberation Army
ERP	People's Revolutionary Army
EUCFR	Charter of Fundamental Rights of the European Union
FAL	Armed Forces of Liberation
FARC	Revolutionary Armed Forces of Colombia
FMLN	Frente Farabundo Martí para la Liberación
FP	Tamil Federal Party
FPL	Popular Forces of Liberation-Farabundo Martí
FSA	Free Syrian Army
IAC	International Armed Conflict
IACHR	Inter-American Commission on Human Rights

IACtHR	Inter-American Court of Human Rights
ICC	International Criminal Court
ICC EoC	ICC Elements of Crimes
ICCPR	International Covenant on Civil and Political Rights
ICJ	International Court of Justice
ICL	International Criminal Law
ICRC	International Committee of the Red Cross
ICTR	International Criminal Tribunal for Rwanda
ICTY	International Criminal Tribunal for the former Yugoslavia
IHL	International Humanitarian Law
IHRL	International Human Rights Law
ISIL	Islamic State of Iraq and the Levant
LNA	Libyan National Army
LRA	Lord's Resistance Army
LTTE	Liberation Tigers of Tamil Eelam
NIACs	Non-International Armed Conflicts
NSAGs	Non-State Armed Groups
NSAs	Non-State Actors
ONUSAL	UN Observer Mission in El Salvador
PKK	Partiya Karkerên Kurdistaen
POW	Prisoners of War
PRTC	Revolutionary Party of Workers of Central America
PYD	Partiya Yekîtiya Dîmokratik
RN	Armed Forces of National Resistance
SDF	Syrian Democratic Forces
SNA	Syrian National Army
SPLA	Sudan People's Liberation Army
TULF	Tamil United Liberation Front
UNHRC	United Nations Human Rights Committee
UNSC	United Nations Security Council
YPG	Yekîneyên Parastina Gel

Chapter 1: An Introduction

This chapter will introduce the present research endeavor. It starts with outlining the aim and structure of the book (Section 1) and continues with presenting the focus of research and core assumptions which form the basis of this book (Section 2).

I. Aim and Structure of the Book

The aim of this book is to explore and assess whether courts of Non-State Armed Groups (**NSAGs**) which have been established and which operate during Non-International Armed Conflicts (**NIACs**) are eligible for recognition in the realm of international law. The question of recognition will be analyzed from two different perspectives: the establishment of such courts and the operation of such courts. These two perspectives are addressed in two corresponding legal analyses: firstly, the legality of the establishment of courts by NSAGs according to International Humanitarian Law (**IHL**) and secondly, the recognition of judicial decisions rendered by courts of NSAGs according to International Criminal Law (**ICL**).

This book seeks to contribute to a well-known debate in international law revolving around non-state actors, more precisely, NSAGs. NSAGs emerge during NIACs and consist of individuals, usually citizens of the state the group is fighting against. They usually aim at overthrowing an incumbent state government and replacing it or they may aim at secession and establishment of a new sovereign state. Hence, NSAGs are infringing upon states' sovereignty by challenging their monopoly over the use of force. At the same time, NSAGs are equal parties to NIACs, just as their – usually – state opponent(s). They are equal parties in the sense that IHL, the applicable legal framework in times of armed conflict, stipulates equal rights and equal obligations upon every party to a conflict. As far as NSAGs adhere to their obligations as postulated by IHL, they act in conformity with international law, hence, their actions can be considered legal according to international law. At the same time, their very existence as much as their actions infringe upon every state's sovereignty. This is particularly so regarding the establishment of parallel justice mechanisms – which is the focus of this thesis – as the provision of justice is considered the prerogative of states. Hence, NSAGs are *per se* illegal under domestic law. This reveals the area of tension which every scholarly work about recognition, legality or status of NSAGs in international law addresses: a constant friction between legality and illegality, lawfulness and unlawfulness, recognition and condemnation.

The book comprises three main themes and is divided into four main chapters. The three pillars comprise 'Rebel governance as a political and social science phenomenon in NIACs', 'NIACs and the applicable IHL', and 'The recognition of courts of NSAGs according to IHL and ICL'.

Chapter 2 will provide an overview of governance structures established by NSAGs during armed conflict. It will highlight the various forms of governance structures, assess the aims and objectives of so-called 'rebel governance' and provide an insight into, especially, 'rebel judicial governance'. It will combine a theoretical analysis of 'rebel governance' with an illustration of prominent historical examples of insurgent judiciaries to delineate the myriad ways in which NSAGs may engage in the administration of justice during armed conflict. Even though 'rebel governance' is a phenomenon primarily discussed and analyzed in political and social science literature, it carries implications for international law as well. In particular, it has implications for IHL applicable to NIACs.

Thus, Chapter 3 assesses the applicable IHL in times of NIACs. It will define NIACs according to pertinent IHL and ICL provisions before presenting an overview of the applicable treaty and customary law. This analysis will reveal that the applicable IHL to NIACs foresees the possibility for NSAGs to conduct 'penal prosecutions' and to convene 'regularly constituted courts' or 'courts offering the essential guarantees of independence and impartiality' pursuant to Common Article 3 (1)(d) to all four Geneva Conventions of 1949[1] (**Common Article 3**) and Art. 6 (2) Additional Protocol II[2] to all four Geneva Conventions (**Art. 6 (2) Additional Protocol II**).

---

1 Convention (I) for the Amelioration of the Condition of the Wounded and Sick in Armed Forces in the Field, UN Treaty Series Vol. 75 No. 970, 12 August 1949; Convention (II) for the Amerlioration of the Condition of Wounded, Sick and Shipwrecked Members of Armed Forces at Sea, UN Treaty Series Vol. 75 No. 971, 12 Augsut 1949; Convention (III) Relative to the Treatment of Prisoners of War, UN Treaty Series Vol. 75 No. 972, 12 August 1949; Convention (IV) Relative to the Protection of Civilian Persons in Time of War, UN Treaty Series Vol. 75 No. 973, 12 August 1949. Hereafter, the four Geneva Conventions of 1949.

2 Protocol Additional to the Geneva Conventions of 12 August 1949, and Relating to the Protection of Victims of Non-International Armed Conflicts, UN Treaty Series Vol. 1125 No. 17513, 8 June 1977. Hereafter, Additional Protocol II.

Nevertheless, the prevailing conventional thinking assumes that (members of) NSAGs are violent and acting in breach of IHL, thus, triggering criminal liability for committing international crimes under ICL.[3] This is also reflected in the fact that, up until now, the ICC has considered members of NSAG as perpetrators of IHL violations and international crimes rather than as enforcers of IHL and ICL.[4] Consequently, the exercise of criminal jurisdiction by NSAGs has been examined by the International Criminal Court (**ICC**) from the angle of individual criminal liability only. According to Art. 8 (2)(c)(iv) ICC Statute[5] 'the passing of sentences and the carrying out of executions without previous judgment pronounced by a regularly constituted court, affording all judicial guarantees which are generally recognized as indispensable' amounts to a war crime in NIACs. So far, there is only one case pending before the ICC – the *Al Hassan* case – which assesses whether the establishment of a court by a NSAG amounts to the war crime of Art. 8 (2)(c)(iv) ICC Statute[6]. What the ICC has not analyzed in greater depth yet, concerns the flipside of potential criminal

---

3 Ezequiel Heffes, 'Responsible Rebels: Exploring Correlations Between Compliance and Reparations in Non-International Armed Conflicts' (2022) 14 Journal of Human Rights Practice 415-433, 416.

4 Whereas scholars have endeavored the potential of NSAGs to enhance compliance with IHL in armed conflict. See, *inter alia*, Ezequiel Heffes, 'Generating Respect for International Humanitarian Law: The Establishment of Courts by Organized Non-State Armed Groups in Light of the Principle of Equality of Belligerents' (2016) 18 Yearbook of International Humanitarian Law 181-201; Ezequiel Heffes, 'The Responsibility of armed opposition groups for Violations of International Humanitarian Law: Challenging the State-Centric System of International Law' (2013) 4 Journal of International Humanitarian Legal Studies 81-107; Heike Krieger (ed), Inducing Compliance with International Humanitarian Law - Lessons fron the African Great Lakes Region (1st edn, Cambridge University Press 2015); Cedric Ryngaert and Anneleen Van de Meulebroucke, 'Enhancing and Enforcing Compliance with International Humanitarian Law by Non-State Armed Groups: an Inquiry into some Mechanisms' (2012) 16 Journal of Conflict and Security Law 443-472; Marco Sassòli, 'Taking Armed Groups Seriously: Ways to Improve their Compliance with International Humanitarian Law' (2010) 1 Journal of International Humanitarian Legal Studies 5-51.

5 Rome Statute of the International Criminal Court, UN Treaty Series Vol. 2187 No. 38544, 1 July 2002. Hereafter, ICC Statute.

6 See ICC, Prosecutor v Al Hassan Ag Abdoul Aziz Ag Mohamed Ag Mahmoud, Rectificatif à la Décision relative à la confiramtion des charges portées contre Al Hassan Ag Abdoul Aziz Ag Mohamed Ag Mahmoud, 13 November 2019, Case No. ICC-01/12-01/18-461-Corr-Red. The case concerns the committed crimes against humanity and war crimes by Mr. *Al Hassan*, a member of the coalition of the armed groups Ansar Eddine and Al-Qaeda in the Islamic Maghreb ('AQUIM'), in the context of the Islamic court in Timbuktu, Mali. On 26th of June 2024, Mr. *Al Hassan* was convicted of some of the charges brought against him. See ICC, Prosecutor v Al Hassan Ag

liability for the establishment of courts by NSAGs, namely, the potential recognition of courts established by NSAGs. It remains to be seen which implications the ICC's deliberations regarding the term 'regularly constituted court' in the *Al Hassan* case will carry for the possible recognition of non-state courts in the realm of ICL.

Therefore, Chapter 4 and Chapter 5 assess the recognition of courts of NSAGs from two different angles: the legality of such courts according to IHL, and the recognition of judicial decisions rendered by such courts according to ICL. The latter question will focus on the applicability of the ICC Statute's *ne bis in idem* principle to judgments rendered by courts of NSAGs during armed conflict.

The last part of this books presents final conclusions resulting from the preceding chapters. These conclusions will be formulated as theses.

II. Focus of Research and Basic Assumptions

The present work is based on the following thesis: The administration of justice by NSAGs naturally takes place during armed conflict. ICL, in turn, relates to conduct which is usually committed during armed conflict. Hence, ICL is a particular fruitful forum to assess the recognition of insurgent administered justice. So far, the ICC has considered courts of NSAGs irrelevant in assessing the admissibility of a case.[7] Bearing in mind that IHL foresees the possibility for NSAGs to convene courts and to prosecute and punish criminal offences in times of armed conflict[8], one is confronted with the unconvincing result that a NSAG might legally convene a court and exercise criminal jurisdiction, but the judgments rendered by such courts do not enjoy legal recognition or legal effect. In more abstract words, one is confronted with the unreasonable scenario where one exercises a right according to one realm of international law, namely IHL, whilst the result of exercising this very right is not recognized in another realm of international law, namely ICL. The phenomenon of having norms of different bodies of international law addressing one conduct and resulting in – at times – inconsistent outcomes, has been described as a problem of 'systemic in-

Abdoul Aziz Ag Mohamed Ag Mahmoud, Trial Judgment, Case No. ICC-01/12-01/18, 26 June 2024.

7 See under Chapter 4: The Legality of Courts of NSAGs, IV. 1.

8 See Common Article 3 (1)(d) and Art. 6 (2) Additional Protocol II.

tegrity' in international law.[9] To resolve this dissonance in the present case, courts of NSAGs should be granted a *locus standi* in ICL for the limited purpose of the exercise of criminal jurisdiction in times of armed conflict presumed this exercise of criminal jurisdiction adheres to the standards stipulated in pertinent IHL and ICL provisions. In other words, judgments and decisions rendered by courts of NSAGs should find recognition in the upward *ne bis in idem* pursuant to Art. 20 (3) ICC Statute, presumed the respective NSAG-court has been legally established according to Common Article 3 (1)(d), and has been operating in a manner consistent with the requirements stipulated in Art. 6 (2) Additional Protocol II. Hence, the present research concentrates on the issue of 'systemic integrity' in international law and seeks to promote it by focusing on two principle issues:

Firstly, it assesses the recognition of 'rebel' administered justice solely according to international law and solely in relation to the ICC's jurisdiction. Hence, the analysis of the legality of insurgent courts focuses on the pertinent IHL provisions applicable to NIACs. Thus, it does not assess the legality of 'rebel courts' according to the domestic law of the territorial state.

Additionally, the analysis of whether judgments rendered by courts of NSAGs should be recognized in the *ne bis in idem* principle focuses on the vertical relation between the ICC as an international institution and courts of NSAGs during armed conflict. Thus, it does not assess how such judgments relate to the jurisdiction or the *ne bis in idem* principle of the respective territorial state or third states.

Secondly, the book assesses the recognition of non-state administered justice during NIACs irrespective of the legal classification of the underlying criminal conduct the respective insurgent court is penalizing. Hence, regarding the issue of legality, the assessment and its findings apply to any insurgent court which operates during an ongoing NIAC, regardless of whether the respective 'rebel court' prosecutes and penalizes ordinary

9 This term has been established by Katharine Fortin, 'The Procedural Right to a Remedy When the State has Left the Building? A Reflection on Armed Groups, Courts and Domestic Law' (2022) 14 Journal of Human Rights Practice 387-414, 405, who refers to Alessandra Spadaro, 'Punish and Be Punished?' (2020) 18 Journal of International Criminal Justice 1-30 and highlights the paradoxical alternatives of a commander of either punishing their subordinates for having committed international crimes according to Art. 28 ICC Statute but simultaneously running the risk of being hold accountable for the war crime of Art. 8 (2)(c)(iv) ICC Statute or not punishing their subordinates and then being held accountable under the doctrine of command responsibility according to Art. 28 ICC Statute.

crimes or crimes with a nexus to the armed conflict in the sense of war crimes as enshrined in Art. 8 ICC Statute. Ultimately, and regarding the question of recognition within the ICC's *ne bis in idem* principle, the assessment and its findings apply only to those judgments rendered by insurgent courts concerning conduct which falls under the subject matter jurisdiction of the ICC.

Chapter 2: Non-State Armed Groups and Judicial Governance

This chapter will introduce and discuss the pertinent terms and phenomena.

It starts with defining the term Non-State Armed Group (Section 1) by, firstly, assessing the term's constituent elements and, secondly, by delineating various types of Non-State Armed Groups. Subsequently, the chapter elaborates on the phenomenon of 'rebel governance', its scope and, particularly, its aim of building legitimacy (Section 2). It then turns to the specific phenomenon of 'judicial governance' by Non-State Armed Groups before it finally provides an overview of prominent examples where Non-State Armed Groups engaged in the administration of justice during armed conflict (Section 3).

I. Non-State Armed Groups: Understanding the Term

The focus of the thesis rests on NSAGs as actors in IHL and ICL. For the purpose of the present work, the term NSAG is used as referring to and including 'armed opposition groups', 'organized armed groups', 'insurgent groups' or 'rebel groups'. These terms will be used interchangeably and are used to refer to a group of individuals whose members engage in protracted violence with the intention to gain control over all or parts of a pre-existing state's territory in order to overthrow a state government, to force the incumbent state to reform or to gain secession.[10] Likewise, the terms 'insurgent', 'non-state', and 'rebel' are used interchangeably to refer to the nature of NSAGs. Furthermore, the term 'NSAG' is used in the context of NIACs pursuant to the definitions set out in Common Article 3 and in Art. 1 (1) Additional Protocol II.

Terms such as NSAG, 'armed opposition groups', 'insurgents' or 'belligerents' are not defined in international law, neither in treaty nor in

10 Nelson Kasfir, 'Rebel Governance - Constructing a Field of Inquiry: Definitions, Scope, Patterns, Order, Causes' in Zachariah C. Mampilly, Nelson Kasfir and Ana Arjona (eds), Rebel Governnace in Civil War (1st edn, Oxford University Press 2015) 21-46, 24.

customary law.[11] Not even IHL defines the term NSAG.[12] However, Common Article 3 (1) mentions 'members of armed forces'. Articles 43 (1) and (2) of Additional Protocol I of 1977[13] define the term of 'armed forces'. However, this definition is applicable to situations of International Armed Conflicts (**IACs**) only. Additionally, Art. 1 (1) Additional Protocol II applicable in times of NIACs also uses the term of 'armed forces' and 'organized armed groups' without further defining the term.

Against the background of a missing definition and due to the term's centrality to the thesis' elaborations, it is crucial to explain and define the term NSAG. This will be done by analyzing its constitutive elements and by assessing different types of NSAGs.[14]

1. Non-state vs. state

Starting with the first constitutive element of the term NSAG, namely 'non-state', the question arises how to best describe an adjective which displays a negative feature. Most scholars conceptualize and define the element of 'non-state' by applying the 'not-a-cat' syndrome, hence, by carving out what NSAGs are not rather than by what they are.[15] The term 'non-state' can be understood formally as well as functionally. Accordingly, a 'NSAG' can be an entity 'other than a fully recognized state'[16], an entity

11 Annyssa Bellal, 'What Are ‚Armed Non-State Actors'? A Legal and Semantic Approach' in Ezequiel Heffes, Marcos D. Kotlik and Manuel J. Ventura (eds), International Humanitarian Law and Non-State Actors: Debates, Law and Practice (1st edn, Asser Press 2020) 22-42, 23; Heike Krieger, 'International Law and Governance by Armed Groups: Caught in the Legitimacy Trap?' (2018) 12 Journal of Intervention and Statebuilding 563-583, 566.

12 Tilman Rodenhäuser, Organizing Rebellion: Non-State Armed Groups under International Humanitarian Law, Human Rights Law, and International Criminal Law (1st edn, Oxford University Press 2018) 9.

13 Protocol Additional to the Geneva Conventions of 12 Augsut 1949, and Relating to the Protection of Vicitims of International Armed Conflicts, UN Treaty Series Vol. 1125 No. 17512, 8 June 1977. Hereafter, Additional Protocol I.

14 Annyssa Bellal, 'What Are ‚Armed Non-State Actors'? A Legal and Semantic Approach' in Ezequiel Heffes, Marcos D. Kotlik and Manuel J. Ventura (eds), International Humanitarian Law and Non-State Actors: Debates, Law and Practice 24 ff.

15 Cedric Ryngaert, 'Non-State Actors: Carving out a Space in a State-Centred International Legal System' (2016) 63 Netherlands International Law Review 183-195, 183.

16 Jan Klabbers, '(I Can't Get No) Recognition: Subjects Doctrine and the Emergence of Non-State Actors' in Andrea Bianchi (ed), Non-State Actors and International Law (1st edn, Routledge 2016) 37-55, 43.

'not acting under the lawful authority of any state'[17], or an entity being 'distinct from the armed forces of any state'[18].[19] The term non-state actor could also be interpreted by referring to the aims and objectives of the respective actor. Then, 'non-state' could also be understood as being *against* [emphasis added] a state. This interpretation holds true for especially one type of non-state actor, namely armed opposition groups fighting a state in an armed conflict. Regarding armed opposition groups, the element of non-state also refers to their stance towards the state, which is characterized by a counter element.[20] Thus, the term 'non-state actor' can include a wide range of entities.[21]

2. Armed vs. non-armed

The second constitutive element of 'NSAG' is the characteristic of being 'armed'. According to common parlance, 'armed' refers to 'carrying weapons' or 'using weapons', hence, referring to the means of achieving a certain goal. In the realm of IHL, the adjective 'armed' additionally refers to the organizational nature of a group and is captured by terms, such as, 'armed forces'. The notion of 'armed forces' is defined in Art. 43 (1) Additional Protocol I as follows:

> 'armed forces to a conflict consist of all organized armed forces, groups and units which are under a command responsible to that Party for the conduct or its subordinates, even if that Party is represented by a government or an authority not recognized by an adverse Party.'

17 Tilman Rodenhäuser, Organizing Rebellion: Non-State Armed Groups under International Humanitarian Law, Human Rights Law, and International Criminal Law 9.

18 Art. 1 of the African Union Convention for the Protection and Assistance of Internally Displaced Persons in Africa (Kampala Convention), 6 December 2012.

19 Annyssa Bellal, 'What Are ‚Armed Non-State Actors'? A Legal and Semantic Approach' in Ezequiel Heffes, Marcos D. Kotlik and Manuel J. Ventura (eds), International Humanitarian Law and Non-State Actors: Debates, Law and Practice 34.

20 The term 'counterstate' is rarely used in this context. References of it can be found, for example, in Zachariah C. Mampilly, Rebel Rulers Insurgent Governance and Civilian Life during War (1st edn, Cornell University Press 2011) 49 at fn 1 or in Timothy P. Wickham-Crowley, 'The Rise (and Sometimes Fall) of Guerrilla Governments in Latin America' (1987) 2 Sociological Forum 473-499, 478.

21 Annyssa Bellal, 'What Are ‚Armed Non-State Actors'? A Legal and Semantic Approach' in Ezequiel Heffes, Marcos D. Kotlik and Manuel J. Ventura (eds), International Humanitarian Law and Non-State Actors: Debates, Law and Practice 34.

The definition enshrined in Art. 43 (1) Additional Protocol I relates to the nature of the actor and is linked to certain rights, such as, the right to directly participate in hostilities and enjoy combatant status.[22] Additional Protocol I applies to situations of IACs only, hence, to conflicts between states, to situations of belligerent occupation pursuant to Common Article 2 and to national liberation movements according to Art. 1 (4) and Art. 44 (3) Additional Protocol I. Consequently, even though Common Article 3 (1) refers to 'armed forces' as well, the definition set out in Art. 43 (1) Additional Protocol I cannot be used to define 'armed forces' as stipulated in Common Article 3 (1).[23]

In the context of NIACs, Art. 1 (1) Additional Protocol II similarly refers to the concepts of 'dissident armed forces or other organized armed groups', albeit without defining these terms. The International Committee of the Red Cross' (**ICRC**) interpretative guidance on the notion of Direct Participation in Hostilities suggested to define the terms as follows:

> 'organized armed groups constitute the armed forces of a non-state party to the conflict and consist only of individuals whose continuous function it is to take a direct part in hostilities.'[24]

According to this definition, a so-called 'continuous combat function'[25] is considered a prerequisite for any individual to be considered as a member of an armed group. Hence, persons with political, administrative, or other non-fighting functions are considered civilians and not members of the organized armed group protected by the principle of distinction. Hence, in the realm of IHL the adjective 'armed' primarily refers to the nature of an actor and is known from concepts like 'armed forces' or 'organized armed groups'. Nevertheless, the use of 'armed violence' as means to achieve certain goals, is an inherent feature of NSAGs.

22 See Art. 43 (2) Additional Protocol I; ibid 25.

23 Ibid.

24 Nils Melzer, ICRC Interpretative Guidance on the Notion of Direct Participation in Hostilities under International Humanitarian Law (1st edn, International Committee of the Red Cross 2009) 27.

25 Ibid 27.

3. Group vs. individual

Turning to the third and final constitutive element of the term NSAG, the term 'group' displays the collective nature. Collectivity is one of the necessary conditions for the applicability of IHL.[26] The use of armed force and violence by individuals is not regulated by IHL but by other bodies of law such as International Human Rights Law (**IHRL**) or domestic criminal law. IHL binds NSAGs as collective entities only and also only if the entity possesses a specific level of organization.[27] Whereas IHL regulates actions by entities - presumed they are a party to the conflict - only, accountability for violations of this regulatory framework only exists in the form of individual (criminal) responsibility according to ICL.[28] *Bellal* refers to this as 'the paradox of NSAGs accountability'[29]. To what extent NSAGs possess a legal personality according to international law, and can be held accountable for their actions as an entity is a different debate which this work will not elaborate on.[30]

---

26 Annyssa Bellal, 'What Are ‚Armed Non-State Actors'? A Legal and Semantic Approach' in Ezequiel Heffes, Marcos D. Kotlik and Manuel J. Ventura (eds), International Humanitarian Law and Non-State Actors: Debates, Law and Practice 40.

27 See, ICTY, Prosecutor v Dusko Tadić aka „Dule", Decision on the Defence Motion for Interlocutory Appeal on Jurisdiction 2 October 1995, Case No. IT-94-1-AR72 para 70; see on this, e.g., Tilman Rodenhäuser, Organizing Rebellion: Non-State Armed Groups under International Humanitarian Law, Human Rights Law, and International Criminal Law 15 ff.

28 Annyssa Bellal, 'What Are ‚Armed Non-State Actors'? A Legal and Semantic Approach' in Ezequiel Heffes, Marcos D. Kotlik and Manuel J. Ventura (eds), International Humanitarian Law and Non-State Actors: Debates, Law and Practice 40.

29 Ibid.

30 On this see, e.g., Ilya Nuzov, 'Post-Conflict Justice: Extending International Criminal Responsibility to Non-State Entities' in Ezequiel Heffes Marcos D. Kotlik Manuel J. Ventura (ed), International Humanitarian Law and Non-State Actors: Debates, Law and Practice (1st edn, Asser Press 2020) 230-258, 230; Jann K Kleffner, 'The collective accountability of organized armed groups for system crimes' in Harmen van der Wilt André Nollkaemper (ed), System Criminality in International Law (1st edn, Cambridge University Press 2009) 238-269, 238-264; Andrew Clapham, 'Corporations and Armed Opposition Groups' (2008) 6 Journal of International Criminal Justice 899-926.

4. Typology of other Non-State Actors

Typologies can be useful to bring clarity to general concepts. One can distinguish certain types of Non-State Actors (**NSAs**), those with a formally recognized status under international law and formal participation in armed violence, such as, 'national liberation movements, '*de facto* entities, 'belligerents' and 'insurgents', and others which lack a formally recognized status in international law but which still participate in armed violence.[31] Examples of the latter category would include, *inter alia*, terrorist groups or organized criminal groups. The conceptual lines are often blurry and types of NSAGs may overlap since one type of NSAG may borrow characteristics from another.[32]

a. National liberation movements

National liberation movements enjoy special treatment under IHL. According to Art. 1 (4) Additional Protocol I, national liberation movements are considered a party to an IAC if 'they are fighting against colonial domination and alien occupation and against racist regimes in the exercise of their right to self-determination' and providing that the state they are fighting against is a party to Additional Protocol I as well.[33] Members of national liberation movements may also enjoy combatant and prisoners of war (**POW**) status presumed they fulfill the requirements laid out in Art. 44 (3) Additional Protocol I. Additionally and according to Art. 96 (3) Additional Protocol I, national liberation movements can also undertake a unilateral declaration by which Additional Protocol I and the four Geneva Conventions of 1949 become applicable. Once again, neither treaty nor customary international law define the term. Art. 1 (4) and Art. 96 (3) Additional Protocol I only speaks of 'peoples' without further clarification.[34] To what extent national liberation movements can be defined as a 'non-state'

31 For this differentiation, see Jordan J. Paust, 'Armed Opposition Groups' in Math Noortmann, August Reinisch and Cedric Ryngaert (eds), Non-State Actors in International Law (1st edn, Bloomsbury 2017) 274-292, 274.

32 Annyssa Bellal, 'What Are ‚Armed Non-State Actors'? A Legal and Semantic Approach' in Ezequiel Heffes, Marcos D. Kotlik and Manuel J. Ventura (eds), International Humanitarian Law and Non-State Actors: Debates, Law and Practice 28.

33 Ibid 37.

34 Ibid.

entity is debatable due to their state-like aspirations and status but also since they may be recognized as state members in certain regional or inter-governmental organizations.[35]

b. De facto entities

De facto entities differ from national liberation movements in so far as they do not necessarily strive for the liberation of oppressed people.[36] The term has neither been defined in treaty nor customary international law. *De facto* entities usually exercise effective authority over at least some territory within a state, irrespective of the fact whether they are engaged in warfare against the incumbent state government or whether they are subsisting in times of peace.[37] They do so without being recognized as an independent state or a government of an already existing state.[38] They may exercise all the functions of a sovereign government, *inter alia*, maintaining law and order, convening courts or adopting and imposing laws regulating the relations of the territory's inhabitants to one another or to the government.[39] *De facto* authorities usually occupy and administer a significant portion of territory, are usually highly organized and act under a responsible chain of command. The term '*de facto* authority' has recently gained renewed prominence with the withdrawal of the US troops in Afghanistan in August 2021 and the takeover of the Taliban, exercising effective control[40] over

35 Ibid 36; Andrew Clapham, Human Rights Obligations of Non-State Actors (1st edn, Oxford University Press 2006) 273.

36 Annyssa Bellal, 'What Are ‚Armed Non-State Actors'? A Legal and Semantic Approach' in Ezequiel Heffes, Marcos D. Kotlik and Manuel J. Ventura (eds), International Humanitarian Law and Non-State Actors: Debates, Law and Practice 38; Jonte van Essen, 'De Facto Regimes in International Law' (2012) 28 Utrecht Journal of International and European Law 31-49, 33.

37 Jonte van Essen, 'De Facto Regimes in International Law' 33; Michael Schoiswohl, '*De Facto* Regimes and Human Rights Obligations - The Twilight Zone of Public International Law?' (2003) 6 Austrian Review of International and European Law Online 45-90, Jochen A Frowein, 'De Facto Regime', Max Planck Encyclopedia of Public International Law (MPEPIL) 2013) accessed 9 March 2022, 50.

38 Michael Schoiswohl, '*De Facto* Regimes and Human Rights Obligations - The Twilight Zone of Public International Law?' 50.

39 See House of Lords, Government of the Republic of Spain v Arantzazu Mendi, Judgment, 23 February 1939, Case No. L.R. 1939 A.C. 256.

40 ICJ, Military and Paramilitary Activities in and against Nicaragua (Nicaragua v United States of America), Jurisdiction of the Court and Admissibility of the Application, Judgment, 26 November 1984, ICJ Reports 1984.

the country's territory and population.[41] Recognition of the Taliban as Afghanistan's official government is dependent upon the recognition of third states[42] and highly unlikely.

De facto authorities should be distinguished from *de facto* states. A *de facto* state is a geographical and political entity which seeks secession or independence from the incumbent state and recognition as a sovereign state by the international community.[43]

Just like a *de facto* authority, a *de facto* state lacks recognition of the international community and therefore remains illegitimate in the eyes of latter.[44] In the course of the annexation of Crimea through the Russian Federation in 2014[45], for example, the pro-Russian separatist regions in eastern Ukraine, Donetsk and Luhansk, have declared themselves as self-autonomous and independent People's Republics in 2014. A few days before the Russian armed attack on the Ukraine, the Russian Federation has recognized those regions as independent states.[46] The Russian Federation attempts to justify the attack by referring to the right of collective self-de-

---

41 For an insightful overview on (non)-recognition of a government of a state in the case of the Taliban and Afghanistan, see Lukas Kleinert, 'Recognition of a Taliban Government ?: A Short Overview on the Recognition of Governments in International Law' (Völkerrechtsblog, 8 September 2021) <https://voelkerrechtsblog.org/recognition-of-a-taliban-government/#> accessed 29 October 2021.

42 James Crawford and Ian Brownlie, Brownlie's principles of public international law (9th edn, Oxford University Press 2019) 142; Helmut Philipp Aust, 'Die Anerkennung von Regierungen: Völkerrechtliche Grundlagen und Grenzen im Lichte des Falls Venezuela' (2020) 80 ZaöRV 73-99, 84 ff.

43 Scott Pegg, International Society and the De Facto State (1st edn, Ashgate 1998) 26; Jonte van Essen, 'De Facto Regimes in International Law' 33.

44 Scott Pegg, International Society and the De Facto State 26.

45 See United Nations General Assembly Resolution 68/262 (on the territorial integrity of Ukraine), UN Doc. A/RES/68/262, 1 April 2014.

46 See Deutsche Welle, 'Russia recognizes independence of Urkaine separatist regions' Deutsche Welle (21.02.2022) <https://www.dw.com/en/russia-recognizes-independence-of-ukraine-separatist-regions/a-60861963> accessed 8 March 2022; see also the United Nation's press release declaring Russia's recognition as a violation of the territorial integrity and sovereignty of Ukraine and inconsistent with the principles of the Charter: UN, 'Secretary-General Says Russian Federation's Recognition of ‚Independent' Donetsk, Luhansk Violate Ukraine's Sovereignty, Territorial Integrity'(United Nations, 23 February 2022).. The recognition of Dontesk and Luhansk as independent states amounts to a violation of the principle of non-intervention. Supporting non-state actors is unlawful under international law as the ICJ held in its famous Nicaragua decision, see, ICJ, Military and Paramilitary Activities in and against Nicaragua (Nicaragua v United States of Amercia), Judgment, 27 June 1986, ICJ Reports 1986 para 246.

fence pursuant to Art. 51 UN Charter[47] and the accusation of a purported genocide taking place in Eastern Ukraine.[48] On March 16th , 2022, the International Court of Justice (**ICJ**) ruled on this matter and indicated the following provisional measures:

> 'The Russian Federation shall immediately suspend the military operations that it commenced on 24 February 2022 in the territory of Ukraine; the Russian Federation shall ensure that any military or irregular armed units which may be directed or supported by it, as well as any organizations and persons which may be subject to its control or direction, take no steps in furtherance of the military operations referred to in point (1) above.'[49]

Hence, while a *de facto* state aims at secession and independence from the parent state and pursues to build a 'new' sovereign state, a *de facto* authority or *de facto* regime 'merely' seeks to be recognized as the official government of an already existing state, leaving the parent state intact.[50] In terms of legal consequences, the qualification or classification of an entity as a '*de facto* authority' can trigger the applicability of different norms, *inter alia*, those relating to self-defence under the UN Charta – normally only applicable to and for states[51] – or arguably human rights.[52] For these reasons it is

47 Charter of the United Nations, UN Treaty Series Vol. XV, 24 October 1945.

48 For an insightful illustration on Russia's claim of self-defense see Marko Milanovic, 'What is Russia's Legal Justification fur Using Force against Ukraine?' (EJIL:Talk!, 24 February 2022) <https://www.ejiltalk.org/what-is-russias-legal-justification-for-using-force-against-ukraine/> accessed 8 March 2022 and Ralph Janik, 'Putin's War against Ukraine: Mocking International Law' (EJIL:Talk!, 28 February 2022) <https://www.ejiltalk.org/putins-war-against-ukraine-mocking-international-law/> accessed 8 March 2022.

49 ICJ, Allegations of Genocide Under the Convention on the Prevention and Punishment of the Crime of Genocide (Ukraine v Russian Federation), Order, 16 March 2022 para 86.

50 Jonte van Essen, 'De Facto Regimes in International Law'.

51 See on the justification of self-defense by the USA against the Taliban in 2001, Rüdiger Wolfrum and Christiane E. Philipp, 'The Status of the Taliban: Their Obligations and Rights under International Law' (2002) 6 Max Planck Yearbook of United Nations Law 559-601, 586 ff.

52 On the applicability of human rights law to ANSAs, see Liesbeth Zegveld, The Accountability of Armed Opposition Groups in International Law (1st edn, Cambridge University Press 2002); Katharine Fortin, The Accountability of Armed Gorups under Human Rights (1st edn, Oxford University Press 2017); Darragh Murray, Human Rights Obligations of Non-State Armed Groups (Hart Publishing 2016).

crucial to accurately determine the nature of an entity since it results in fundamental consequences concerning the applicable legal regime.[53]

c. Insurgents

The term 'insurgents' or 'insurgent group' is probably the category of NSAs which is most associated with the term NSAG.[54] 'Insurgent groups' typically aim at challenging and destroying the power of an incumbent government of a state[55], at the secession of a region or at the end of an occupational or colonial regime.[56] 'Insurgents' is a *terminus technicus* under the laws of war.[57] Under traditional international law[58], a so-called 'insurgency' amounted to the lowest level of recognized warfare and triggered the applicability of only a few humanitarian norms.[59] Today, the concept of 'insurgents' or 'insurgent group' equals the notions of 'armed opposition group', 'organized armed group', 'belligerent group' or 'rebel group'.[60] Hence, it refers to NSAGs as a party to a NIAC. Therefore, it triggers the applicability of Common Article 3 and may trigger the applicability of Additional Protocol II as well. Unlike members of the armed forces of a party to an IAC, members of 'insurgent groups', 'non-state armed groups' or

53 Annyssa Bellal, 'What Are ‚Armed Non-State Actors'? A Legal and Semantic Approach' in Ezequiel Heffes, Marcos D. Kotlik and Manuel J. Ventura (eds), International Humanitarian Law and Non-State Actors: Debates, Law and Practice 38.

54 Ibid 28.

55 Ibid; Richard H. Shultz, Douglas Farah and Itamara V. Lochard, Armed Groups: A Tier-One Security Priority, Report (USAF Institute for National Security Studies, September 2004), INSS Occasional Paper 57, 18.

56 In the case of a fight against colonial domination and alien occupation and against racist regimes in the exercise of the right of self-determination, Art. 1 (4) Additional Protocol I speaks of 'national liberation movements' to which the law of international armed conflicts is applicable.

57 Jordan J. Paust, 'Armed Opposition Groups' in Math Noortmann, August Reinisch and Cedric Ryngaert (eds), Non-State Actors in International Law 280.

58 The term 'traditional international law' has been used by scholars to refer to the laws of war prior the 1949 codifications.

59 Anthony Cullen, The Concept of Non-International Armed Conflict in International Humanitarian Law (1st edn, Cambridge Unversity Press 2010) 12 f.; Heather Wilson, International law and the use of force by national liberation movements (1st edn, Clarendon Press 1990) 24.

60 Annyssa Bellal, 'What Are ‚Armed Non-State Actors'? A Legal and Semantic Approach' in Ezequiel Heffes, Marcos D. Kotlik and Manuel J. Ventura (eds), International Humanitarian Law and Non-State Actors: Debates, Law and Practice 28.

'armed opposition groups' are not entitled to combatant status, combatant immunity or POW status when captured.[61]

d. Militias

Another type often referred to in the context of NSAs is the category of 'militias', also referred to as 'paramilitaries' or 'vigilantes'. The term 'militias' could be described as 'a recognizable irregular armed force operating within the territory of a weak and/or failing state.'[62] Notably, it does not equal the term 'militias' as stipulated in Art. 4 (A) (1) and (2) Convention (III) Relative to the Treatment of Prisoners of War.[63]

Members of 'militias' are often composed of young males who are drawn into the milieu because it grants them access to money, resources, and power.[64] 'Militias' often represent specific ethnic, religious, tribal, clan or other communal groups and may operate under the control and authority of a factional leader, a clan or an ethnic group but also on their own. They generally lack any formal military training.[65] 'Militias' can act in furtherance of a state government as well as they can act in the absence of an incumbent government. A common difficulty with pro-government militias concerns the establishment of state responsibility[66] for their unlawful actions since their allegiance to a state may vary and often their main motivations are not politically driven.[67] A prominent example for 'militias' which act in the absence of a central government and are more autonomous, are the 'war

61 Dieter Fleck, 'The Law of Non-International Armed Conflict' in Dieter Fleck (ed), The Handbook of International Humanitarian Law (4th edn, Oxford Universtiy Press 2021) 634-663, 643; see also Common Article 3.

62 Richard H. Shultz, Douglas Farah and Itamara V. Lochard, Armed Groups: A Tier-One Security Priority, Report (USAF Institute for National Security Studies, September 2004), INSS Occasional Paper 57, 23.

63 Annyssa Bellal, 'What Are ‚Armed Non-State Actors'? A Legal and Semantic Approach' in Ezequiel Heffes, Marcos D. Kotlik and Manuel J. Ventura (eds), International Humanitarian Law and Non-State Actors: Debates, Law and Practice 28.

64 Richard H. Shultz, Douglas Farah and Itamara V. Lochard, Armed Groups: A Tier-One Security Priority, Report (USAF Institute for National Security Studies, September 2004), INSS Occasional Paper 57, 23.

65 Ibid.

66 According to Art. 8, Art. 9 or Art. 10 Draft Articles on Responsibility of States for Internationally Wrongful Acts, 2001.

67 Peter G. Thompson, Armed Groups - The 21st Century Threat (1st edn, Rowman & Littlefield 2014) 71.

lord' militias that are involved in various armed conflicts in Africa, such as the Lord's Resistance Army (**LRA**) in Uganda.[68] A common difficulty with this type of 'militias' lies in establishing the required degree of organization to trigger the applicability of IHL.[69]

e. Terrorist groups

Some authors also include 'terrorist groups' into the category of NSAs. Defining 'terrorism' is not a simple task. 'Terrorist groups" main strategy is the use and spread of indiscriminate violence and force and the creation of fear among a civil society to achieve a certain political, ideological or religious goal.[70] To date, states have been unable to agree upon a universally recognized definition.[71] This is owed to, *inter alia*, the circumstance that terrorism is an offence which constantly evolves in nature and its means and methods. It also is a highly politized crime. Due to the diversity of the crime and its political nature, it appears doubtful that a checklist definition will uniformly capture its essential components. Thus, the international community's approach towards defining terrorism as a crime or prohibited act has focused on establishing treaties to combat terrorism without explicitly defining it.[72] For instance, the UN Convention for the Suppression of the Financing of Terrorism[73] focuses on criminalizing certain acts of financing terrorism and, to this end, describes 'terrorism' as:

> 'any other act intended to cause death or serious bodily injury to a civilian, or to any other person not taking an active part in the hostilities in a situation of armed conflict, when the purpose of such act, by its nature or

68 See https://www.globalsecurity.org/military/world/para/lra.htm accessed 15 September 2021.

69 Annyssa Bellal, 'Central African Republic: From Conflict to Chaos and Back Again?' in Stuart Casey-Maslen (ed), The War Report - Armed Conflict in 2013 (1st edn, Oxford University Press 2014) 411-428.

70 Annyssa Bellal, 'What Are ‚Armed Non-State Actors'? A Legal and Semantic Approach' in Ezequiel Heffes, Marcos D. Kotlik and Manuel J. Ventura (eds), International Humanitarian Law and Non-State Actors: Debates, Law and Practice 30.

71 See Beth Van Schaack, 'Finding the Tort of Terrorism in International Law' (2008) 28 Review of Litigation 382-478, 407.

72 Gilbert Guillaume, 'Terrorism and International Law' (2004) 53 International and Comparative Law Quarterly 537-548, 539.

73 International Convention for the Suppression of the Financing of Terrorism, UN Doc. 38349, 10 April 2002.

context, is to intimidate a population, or to compel a government or an international organization to do or to abstain from doing any act.'[74]

Another attempt at defining 'terrorism' was made with the UN Security Council Resolution 1566[75] which described 'terrorist acts' as:

> 'criminal acts, including against civilians, committed with the intent to cause death or serious bodily injury, or taking of hostages, with the purpose to provoke a state of terror in the general public or in a group of persons or particular persons, intimidate a population or compel a government or an international organization to do or to abstain from doing and act [...]'[76]

However, to date, this resolution has not contributed to a uniform definition and convergence at a national level.[77] Since 2000 and until present, the UN Draft Comprehensive Convention on Terrorism has been in negotiation and aims at establishing an international definition of terrorism.[78]

Discussing 'terrorist groups' in the context of NSAs is a delicate matter since the label of 'terrorist' entails serious legal consequences with regard to national criminal proceedings of individuals charged with terrorist offences according to domestic jurisdiction. It is especially states which are likely to label any NSAG that opposes their regime as a 'terrorist group'. This tends to blur the line between acts that comply with the applicable law in times of armed conflict and actual acts of terrorism which can also occur in times of peace.[79]

---

74 See, Art. 2 (1) (b) of the International Convention for the Suppression of the Financing of Terrorism.

75 United Nations Security Council Resolution 1566 (concerning threats to international peace and security caused by terrorism), UN Doc. S/RES/1566, 8 October 2004.

76 See ibid para 3.

77 Ben Saul, 'Legislating from a Radical Hague: The United Nations Special Tribunal for Lebanon Invents and International Crime of Transnational Terrorism' (2011) 24 Leiden Journal of International Law 677-700.

78 Draft Comprehensive Convention on International Terrorism, UN Doc. A/C.6/56/WG.1/CRP.3, 19 October 2001.

79 Annyssa Bellal, 'What Are ‚Armed Non-State Actors'? A Legal and Semantic Approach' in Ezequiel Heffes, Marcos D. Kotlik and Manuel J. Ventura (eds), International Humanitarian Law and Non-State Actors: Debates, Law and Practice 30.

f. Organized criminal groups

Organized criminal groups consist of individuals involved in organized crime such as human trafficking, drug trafficking, corruption, slavery etc. Such groups often display a hierarchal structure and leadership whose primary purpose is to operate outside the law in a particular criminal enterprise.[80] Often, these groups are built upon a strong sense of membership or family alignments which ensures the security of its members.[81] They frequently engage in more than one type of criminal behavior and can operate over large areas, even globally.[82] Unlike NSAGs which are party to a NIAC, criminal organization groups do not oppose a state to either replace the incumbent government or to gain secession.[83] However, in the rare case of sufficient organization, power and strength, organized criminal groups which engage in armed violence against a state could considered a party to an armed conflict and trigger the applicability of IHL.[84]

5. Conclusion

There exist various types of NSAs. The present work revolves around NSAGs.

A NSAG is a group of individuals whose members engage in protracted violence with the intention to overthrow a state government, to force the incumbent state to reform or to gain secession. The term 'NSAG' includes 'armed opposition groups', 'organized armed groups', 'insurgent groups' or 'rebel groups'. These terms will be used interchangeably. Likewise, the terms 'insurgent', 'non-state' and 'rebel' will be used interchangeably to refer to the nature of NSAGs. Furthermore, the term 'NSAG' will be used in the

80 Richard H. Shultz, Douglas Farah and Itamara V. Lochard, Armed Groups: A Tier-One Security Priority, Report (USAF Institute for National Security Studies, September 2004), INSS Occasional Paper 57, 29.

81 Ibid.

82 Ibid.

83 Annyssa Bellal, 'What Are ‚Armed Non-State Actors'? A Legal and Semantic Approach' in Ezequiel Heffes, Marcos D. Kotlik and Manuel J. Ventura (eds), International Humanitarian Law and Non-State Actors: Debates, Law and Practice 29.

84 Julie Lambin, 'Mexico: Armed Gang Violence Sliding Into Armed Conflict?' in Annyssa Bellal (ed), The War Report - Armed Conflicts in 2017 (1st edn, Geneva Academy of International Humanitarian Law and Human Rights 2018) 83-91, 87.

context of NIACs pursuant to Common Article 3 and pursuant to Art. 1 (1) Additional Protocol II.[85]

A note of clarification: NSAGs are highly dynamic entities. Their goals, their structure, their level of organization, their resources, their level of control, etc. can change and evolve during armed conflict. Thus, it is difficult to refer to a single uniform template applicable to all NSAGs at all times for the legal analysis which follows in Chapter 3 and Chapter 4.

II. Governance by NSAGs: Understanding a Phenomenon

This section highlights a widespread phenomenon of internal armed conflicts, namely, the provision of governance structures by insurgent groups, also referred to as 'rebel governance'. NSAGs do not only participate in armed violence, but they often also challenge the state by establishing parallel structures and attempting to govern. In the following, the concept of 'rebel governance' will be delineated by describing its scope, its patterns as well as its immediate purposes. This analysis will lead into unravelling a prominent long-term aim of 'rebel governance': establishing legitimacy. Despite the myriad ways in which NSAGs may govern, they unite in their pursuit to build legitimacy vis-à-vis their desired target group.

1. Rebel governance: conceptual clarifications

Insurgent behavior need not necessarily be limited to violent conduct on the battlefield, it can also include non-violent interaction with the civilian population which may take the form of an organized and structured governance scheme.[86] This section elaborates on the phenomenon of 'rebel governance', firstly, by defining the term, secondly, by assessing the features of NSAGs which engage in 'rebel governance', thirdly, by illustrating different types of 'rebel governance' and, finally, by highlighting the immediate purposes and functions of governance in times of armed conflict.

---

85 Nelson Kasfir, 'Rebel Governance - Constructing a Field of Inquiry: Definitions, Scope, Patterns, Order, Causes' in Zachariah C. Mampilly, Nelson Kasfir and Ana Arjona (eds), Rebel Governnace in Civil War 24.

86 Ana Arjona, Nelson Kasfir and Zachariah Mamiplly, 'Introduction' in Zachariah C. Mampilly, Nelson Kasfir and Ana Arjona (eds), Rebel Governance in Civil War (1st edn, Cambridge University Press 2015) 1-20, 1.

Social science literature defines governance as institutionalized modes of social coordination to establish and implement collectively binding norms and/or to provide collective goods for human society.[87] The term 'rebel governance' refers to governance structures established by NSAGs in times of armed conflict. The term 'rebel' refers to the governor, hence, it refers to NSAGs. Social science literature which elaborates on governance practices by entities other than the state describe this phenomenon as governance in areas of limited statehood.[88] Areas of limited statehood are defined as areas where the state lacks the ability to establish and implement central decisions and rules or where it lacks the capacity to uphold its monopoly over the use of force.[89] In the context of armed conflict, areas of limited statehood emerge due to insurgent revolt. Limited statehood can refer to parts of a country's territory as well as to specific policy areas.[90] Regarding the absence of state authorities, the defence in the *Al Hassan* case before

87 Thomas Risse and Eric Stollenwerk, 'Legitimacy in Areas of Limited Statehood' (2018) 21 Annual Review of Political Science 403-418; Heike Krieger, 'International Law and Governance by Armed Groups: Caught in the Legitimacy Trap?' 569; Tanja A. Börzel, Thomas Risse and Anke Draude, 'Governance in Areas of Limited Statehood: Conceptual Clarifiactions and Major Contributions of the Handbook' in Anke Draude, Tanja A. Börzel and Thomas Risse (eds), The Oxford Handbook of Governance and Limited Statehood (1st edn, Oxford University Press 2018) 1-25, 9.

88 Tanja A. Börzel, Thomas Risse and Anke Draude, 'Governance in Areas of Limited Statehood: Conceptual Clarifiactions and Major Contributions of the Handbook' in Anke Draude, Tanja A. Börzel and Thomas Risse (eds), The Oxford Handbook of Governance and Limited Statehood 2; Cord Schmelzle and Eric Stollenwerk, 'Virtuous or Vicious Circle? Governance Effectiveness and Legitimacy in Areas of Limited Statehood' (2018) 12 Journal of Intervention and Statebuilding 449-467; Eric Stollenwerk, 'Measuring Governance and Limited Statehood' in Anke Draude, Tanja A. Börzel and Thomas Risse (eds), The Oxford Handbook of Governance and Limited Statehood (1st edn, Oxford University Press 2018) 106-128.

89 Tanja A. Börzel, Thomas Risse and Anke Draude, 'Governance in Areas of Limited Statehood: Conceptual Clarifiactions and Major Contributions of the Handbook' in Anke Draude, Tanja A. Börzel and Thomas Risse (eds), The Oxford Handbook of Governance and Limited Statehood 4 ff; Stephen D. Krasner and Thomas Risse, 'External Actors, State-Building, and Service Provision in Areas of Limited Statehood: Introduction' (2014) 27 Governacne: An International Journal of Policy, Administration, and Institutions 545-567, 549; Heike Krieger, 'International Law and Governance by Armed Groups: Caught in the Legitimacy Trap?' 563; Cord Schmelzle and Eric Stollenwerk, 'Virtuous or Vicious Circle? Governance Effectiveness and Legitimacy in Areas of Limited Statehood' 449.

90 Thomas Risse and Eric Stollenwerk, 'Legitimacy in Areas of Limited Statehood' 406.

the ICC, for example, referred to a situation where 'the state has left the building'.[91]

In the field of political and social science literature, rebel governance is described and defined as a phenomenon with primarily three implicit features:[92]

Firstly, the entity who governs must hold some territory within the state against which it is fighting. Territorial control comes in stages and may vary spatially.[93] Hence, it may change during the state of war.[94] Additionally, territorial control can be contested or dominant.[95] Dominant or stable control over territory means that the rebel group is able to keep to enemy outside the area and is able to prevent the incumbent state or a competing insurgent group from installing its own governmental structures within that territory.[96] Holding stable control over territory may enable rebel groups to establish formal – as opposed to *ad-hoc* – governance structures.[97]

Secondly, the presence of a civilian population in that territory, although, rebel-held territory may also be uninhabited. Civilians may flee upon the group's arrival or the government of the incumbent state may force them to resettle.[98] Additionally, NSAGs might prefer an unpopulated area since it creates less of a threat from the incumbent state.[99] Hence, holding unpopulated terrain may be beneficial to a rebel group if the group lacks the

91 ICC, Prosecutor v Al Hassan Ag Abdoul Aziz Ag Mohamed Ag Mahmoud, Transcript of Confirmation of Charges, 17 July 2019, Case No. ICC-01/12-01/18, 27.

92 Nelson Kasfir, 'Rebel Governance - Constructing a Field of Inquiry: Definitions, Scope, Patterns, Order, Causes' in Zachariah C. Mampilly, Nelson Kasfir and Ana Arjona (eds), Rebel Governnace in Civil War 25.

93 Stathis N. Kalyvas, The Logic of Violence in Civil War (1st edn, Oxford University Press 2006) 132-138.

94 Nelson Kasfir, 'Rebel Governance - Constructing a Field of Inquiry: Definitions, Scope, Patterns, Order, Causes' in Zachariah C. Mampilly, Nelson Kasfir and Ana Arjona (eds), Rebel Governnace in Civil War 27.

95 Stathis N. Kalyvas, The Logic of Violence in Civil War 210-220.

96 Nelson Kasfir, 'Rebel Governance - Constructing a Field of Inquiry: Definitions, Scope, Patterns, Order, Causes' in Zachariah C. Mampilly, Nelson Kasfir and Ana Arjona (eds), Rebel Governnace in Civil War 28.

97 Megan A. Stewart, 'Civil War as State-Making: Strategic Governance in Civil War' (2017) 72 International Organization 205-226, 207; Megan A. Stewart and Yu-Ming Liou, 'Do Good Borders Make Good Rebels? Territorial Control and Civilian Casualties' (2017) 79 The Journal of Politics 284-301.

98 Nelson Kasfir, 'Rebel Governance - Constructing a Field of Inquiry: Definitions, Scope, Patterns, Order, Causes' in Zachariah C. Mampilly, Nelson Kasfir and Ana Arjona (eds), Rebel Governnace in Civil War 29.

99 Ibid 29.

resources and structures to govern civilians or if the group has not gained sufficient military power yet. On the other hand, choosing a populated area might give a weak group the opportunity to increase its resources by organizing civilians to generate material gain.[100]

Thirdly, the group must commit an initial act of violence to become a rebel group and then either continue those hostilities or threaten with them.[101] The initial act of violence against the incumbent state or another rebel group is the starting point of a rebellion and demonstrates the group's intent to opposition.[102] Violence may be an underlying feature of rebel governance, inflicted on civilians either by the opposing party to the conflict or the governing rebel group itself. Where the opposing party to the conflict causes the civilian violence, rebel governance structures may be of benefit and may offer protection, especially in the realm of the provision of collective goods and services such as shelter and medical care.[103] Where the rebel group itself is the preponderant actor of violence, there either is no governance system or it is a highly coercive one.[104]

Meeting the three conditions, however, does not mean that every rebel group necessarily decides to install governance structures.[105] Once a NSAG gains and secures control over inhabited territory, it needs to decide, foremost if, and secondly, how to interact with the civilian population living on the territory. Insurgents may have no interest in interacting with the civilian population living on the territory they have control over. They may even consider them as a burden or commit atrocious crimes against them.[106] However, insurgents may also view civilians as a resource to gain material enrichment for military ends or utilize them to gain and maintain stable control over territory. If a NSAG decides to interact and organize relations with civilians, they engage in 'rebel governance'. One can distinguish three different types of governance contributions: the direct delivery of collective goods and services, the formulation and implementation of collectively binding rules and thirdly, the establishment of institutions which regulate

100 Ibid 29.
101 Ibid 25.
102 Ibid 30.
103 Ibid 31.
104 Ibid 31.
105 Ibid 26.
106 Ibid 26.

the rule-making itself.[107] Rebel governance usually starts informally and often is based on an *ad hoc* decision-making.[108] However, it can also become formal and hierarchically structured throughout time when the respective NSAG gets more sophisticated in structure and organization and establishes its own formal rules and institutions.[109]

Rebel governance may be holistic, hence, attempting at covering a variety of social areas, such as health, education, employment, security or justice. However, rebel governance may also operate fragmentally, covering only certain areas. This often correlates with the respective insurgent goal of a group. NSAGs which aim at secession of the territorial state usually follow state-building aspirations, and consequently, may invest their resources in governing all areas of social life. In contrast, NSAGs which aim at overthrowing the incumbent state government may make use of preexisting state institutions or establish new structures in those areas only which need reform according to the group's ideology and social beliefs.[110]

Despite the myriad ways of how NSAGs govern, they usually govern for the same purposes. The immediate purposes and functions of 'rebel governance' relate to, especially, civilian participation and support and organization of civilians for material gain.[111]

Usually, rebel groups install governance structures to solicit support and acceptance from the civilian population for ideological reasons, or to gain foreign assistance of third states to improve their chances of winning.[112] *Mao Tse-tung* claimed that the adoption of governance structures by armed opposition groups is natural since insurgents want to win the hearts and

107 Tanja A. Börzel, Thomas Risse and Anke Draude, 'Governance in Areas of Limited Statehood: Conceptual Clarifiactions and Major Contributions of the Handbook' in Anke Draude, Tanja A. Börzel and Thomas Risse (eds), The Oxford Handbook of Governance and Limited Statehood 11 f.

108 Nelson Kasfir, 'Rebel Governance - Constructing a Field of Inquiry: Definitions, Scope, Patterns, Order, Causes' in Zachariah C. Mampilly, Nelson Kasfir and Ana Arjona (eds), Rebel Governnace in Civil War 23.

109 Ibid 23.

110 Ibid 40.

111 Ibid 24; Regine Schwab, 'Insurgent courts in civil wars: the three pathways of (trans)formation in today's Syria (2012-2017)' (2018) 29 Small Wars & Insurgencies 801-826, 803.

112 Nelson Kasfir, 'Rebel Governance - Constructing a Field of Inquiry: Definitions, Scope, Patterns, Order, Causes' in Zachariah C. Mampilly, Nelson Kasfir and Ana Arjona (eds), Rebel Governnace in Civil War 34.

minds of the population, and governance is one way to achieve this.[113] Civilian support and acceptance often is rooted in the sense of belonging and the perception of having a right to say and a right to participate. Hence, the establishment of representative institutions and procedures, such as, the creation of legislatures, civilian advisory boards or local councils may consolidate civilian support and acceptance of the respective group.[114] Civilian support and acceptance may either be based on coercion and threat of punishment or on voluntary involvement.[115] It my run through formal or informal, through organized or through *ad-hoc* procedures.

Secondly, 'rebel governance' often aims at generating income, especially, for the respective NSAG's military agenda. Since every rebel group needs funds to support and execute military operations, all of them must invest at least some resources towards this purpose.[116] Hence, NSAGs may focus on governing and organizing the local population to produce a steady income through, *inter alia*, taxation practices, purchase, seizure, kidnapping or extortion schemes.[117]

In summary, 'rebel governance' exists where an insurgent group exercises control over territory, decides to manage relations with the civilian population living on that territory, and consequently, either invests in establishing its own processes and institutions or makes use of preexisting state mechanisms and institutions.[118] 'Rebel governance' varies greatly according to the group's capacity and resources.

---

113 See Zedong Mao, Selected Military Writing of Mao Tse-Tung (Foreign Languages Press 1963); Regine Schwab, 'Insurgent courts in civil wars: the three pathways of (trans)formation in today's Syria (2012-2017)' 803.

114 Nelson Kasfir, 'Rebel Governance - Constructing a Field of Inquiry: Definitions, Scope, Patterns, Order, Causes' in Zachariah C. Mampilly, Nelson Kasfir and Ana Arjona (eds), Rebel Governnace in Civil War 34.

115 Ibid 34.

116 Ibid 37.

117 Nelson Kasfir, 'Rebel Governance - Constructing a Field of Inquiry: Definitions, Scope, Patterns, Order, Causes' in Zachariah C. Mampilly, Nelson Kasfir and Ana Arjona (eds), Rebel Governnace in Civil War 23.

118 Jeremy M. Weinstein, Inside Rebellion: The Politics of Insurgent Violence (1st edn, Cambridge University Press 2006) 165; Zachariah C. Mampilly, Rebel Rulers Insurgent Governance and Civilian Life during War 51.

2. Rebel governance and the aim of legitimacy

'Without empirical legitimacy, there is no successful governance.'[119]

The previous section referred to immediate purposes of rebel governance, such as, gaining civilian support or generating material gain. Additionally, many NSAGs which engage in governance pursue a specific, long-term purpose: building legitimacy. Legitimacy is necessary to transform violent power into durable political positions. Hence, gaining legitimacy through governance is especially important for NSAGs which pursue long-term political goals.[120] Hence, it is essential for NSAGs which, for example, either aim at secession of the territorial state or which aim at overthrowing the incumbent state government and replacing it.[121] Such NSAGs seek to gain legitimacy by mainly two audiences: the domestic audiences and/or the international audience.[122]

Discussing legitimacy in the context of governance by NSAGs warrants clarification as regards the distinction between legal legitimacy - that is the right to rule based on legal norms[123] - and empirical legitimacy - that is the right to rule based on social acceptance.[124]

119 Stephen D. Krasner and Thomas Risse, 'External Actors, State-Building, and Service Provision in Areas of Limited Statehood: Introduction' (2014) 27 Governance 545-567, 547.

120 Ana Arjona, 'Civilian Cooperation and Non-Cooperation with Non-State Armed Groups: The Centrality of Obedience and Resistance' (2017) 28 Small Wars & Insurgencies 755-778; Zachariah C. Mampilly, 'Performing the Nation-State: Rebel Governance and Symbolic Processes' in Zachariah C. Mampilly, Nelson Kasfir and Ana Arjona (eds), Rebel Governance in Civil War (1st edn, Cambridge University Press 2015) 74-97; Sukanya Podder, 'Understanding the Legitimacy of Armed Groups: A Relational Perspective' (2017) 28 Small Wars & Insurgencies 686-708; Klaus Schlichte and Ulrich Schneckener, 'Armed Groups and the Politics of Legitimacy' (2015) 17 Civil Wars 409-424; Megan A. Stewart, 'Civil War as State-Making: Strategic Governance in Civil War' 210.

121 Benedetta Berti, 'Violent and Criminal Non-State Actors' in Anke Draude, Tanja A. Börzel and Thomas Risse (eds), The Oxford Handbook of Governance and Limited Statehood (1st edn, Oxford University Press 2018) 272-289, 277.

122 Klaus Schlichte and Ulrich Schneckener, 'Armed Groups and the Politics of Legitimacy' 409.

123 Tanja A. Börzel, Thomas Risse and Anke Draude, 'Governance in Areas of Limited Statehood: Conceptual Clarifiactions and Major Contributions of the Handbook' in Anke Draude, Tanja A. Börzel and Thomas Risse (eds), The Oxford Handbook of Governance and Limited Statehood 12.

124 Thomas Risse and Eric Stollenwerk, 'Legitimacy in Areas of Limited Statehood' 404.

For state actors, legitimacy means legal legitimacy and is derived from legality or legal recognition.[125] The concept of legal legitimacy makes it difficult to discern between legitimacy and legality as distinct concepts. Hence, for states, NSAGs are qua their nature as non-state actors and qua their conduct of challenging and opposing a state's sovereignty through the use of force, illegal and illegitimate.[126] In line with this, international law denies NSAGs legal status or legal recognition unless they are recognized as 'national liberation movements' according to Art. 1 (4) Additional Protocol I. Similarly, Common Article 3 (4) clearly states that the application of the Convention's provisions does not affect the legal status of the parties to the conflict.

Thus, NSAGs must derive legitimacy from other sources than legality or legal recognition, namely, from *de facto* recognition and acceptance. *De facto* recognition and 'social acceptance' of an insurgent group's governance structures relate to the concept of empirical legitimacy.[127] Following the definition of *Weber*[128], scholars in political science literature define empirical legitimacy as the 'right to rule'[129], the 'license to govern'[130] or the 'shared belief in the rightfulness of actions'[131]. It also refers to a population's sense of obligation or willingness to obey the authority of a governance actor

125 Klaus Schlichte and Ulrich Schneckener, 'Armed Groups and the Politics of Legitimacy' 414; Heike Krieger, 'International Law and Governance by Armed Groups: Caught in the Legitimacy Trap?' 566.

126 Armed opposition to the incumbent state government infringes on every state's integrity and usually amounts to a violation of domestic law and amounts to the crimes of rebellion and/or insurrection which are regulated at a national level. Heike Krieger, 'International Law and Governance by Armed Groups: Caught in the Legitimacy Trap?' 565.

127 Thomas Risse and Eric Stollenwerk, 'Legitimacy in Areas of Limited Statehood' 404; Margaret Levi and Audrey Sacks, 'Legitimating beliefs: Sources and indicators' (2009) 3 Regulation & Governance 311-333.

128 See Max Weber, 'Die drei reinen Typen der legitimen Herrschaft' in Johannes Winckelmann (ed), Gesammelte Aufsätze zur Wissenschaftslehre (7th edn, Mohr Siebeck 1988) 475-488.

129 Bruce Gilley, The Right to Rule: How States Win and Lose Legitimacy (1st edn, Columbia University Press 2009).

130 Tanja A. Börzel, Thomas Risse and Anke Draude, 'Governance in Areas of Limited Statehood: Conceptual Clarifiactions and Major Contributions of the Handbook' in Anke Draude, Tanja A. Börzel and Thomas Risse (eds), The Oxford Handbook of Governance and Limited Statehood 10.

131 Klaus Schlichte and Ulrich Schneckener, 'Armed Groups and the Politics of Legitimacy' 413.

or a governance institution[132] and to the belief in the justification or the moral validity of a political organization and its activities.[133] NSAGs may build legitimacy through symbolic-based means or through performance-based means.[134] Symbolic sources of legitimacy are important for bolstering discourses and speeches of NSAGs whereas performance-based sources of legitimacy are important for the conduct and behavior of NSAGs.[135]

Regarding symbolic-based politics of legitimacy, NSAGs often follow typical lines of narratives and arguments to justify their actions and to bolster their insurgent agenda.[136] Oftentimes, they embed their claims and actions in communal belief systems, the sense of ethnic and religious belonging and shared traditions and cultures, hence, in a socio-cultural setting.[137] Claims can be also based on the socio-economic and political aspirations of the local community. Such claims are often linked to ideologies such as social-revolutionary, ethno-nationalist or religious ideas of political leaders.[138] NSAGs may utilize disappointments and grievances to portray themselves as the community's representative and giving the community's concerns a voice. Another, common symbolic-base mean is the so-called construed 'enemy image' which often benefits a group's claim that it needs to protect, defend and liberate the local community from this threat.[139] In this context, portraying the enemy – be it the state government or another opposing non-state armed group – as especially brutal and evil suits the group's purpose in justifying its violent actions and measures as necessary and appropriate.[140]

A group's legitimacy may also be based on certain performances. This relates, especially, to the provision of services to the local population such as the distribution of jobs, supply of food, water and medical care, the establishment of taxation systems or the provision of security and justice.

132 Margaret Levi and Audrey Sacks, 'Legitimating beliefs: Sources and indicators' 314.
133 Klaus Schlichte and Ulrich Schneckener, 'Armed Groups and the Politics of Legitimacy' 413.
134 Ibid 417.
135 Ibid 413.
136 Ibid 417.
137 Ibid; Thomas Risse and Eric Stollenwerk, 'Legitimacy in Areas of Limited Statehood' 410; Cord Schmelzle and Eric Stollenwerk, 'Virtuous or Vicious Circle? Governance Effectiveness and Legitimacy in Areas of Limited Statehood' 462.
138 Klaus Schlichte and Ulrich Schneckener, 'Armed Groups and the Politics of Legitimacy' 417.
139 Ibid.
140 Ibid.

So-called 'delivery-based legitimization'[141] is particularly apparent in situations where insurgent groups are in stable control over territory.[142] This also includes the use of formal procedures such as regular meetings and elections, and might enhance a group's perceived legitimacy.

Pursuing legitimacy in armed conflict, comes with challenges for many NSAGs: They need to reconcile the continuing use of force in armed conflict with legitimacy, and they often need to satisfy multiple audiences of legitimacy with often considerably diverging expectations and demands.[143]

Firstly, the persistent use of violence may have diminishing effects on the legitimacy of a group's governance.[144]. This is especially the case where violence is exerted vis-à-vis the local population and over a long period of time in an indiscriminate way.[145] Mass killings, sexual violence, and other atrocities may considerably undermine a group's credibility and legitimacy.[146] One can often observe a downward spiral where more violence leads to less legitimacy and vice versa.[147] By contrast, the use of violence vis-à-vis the adversary may contribute to a group's legitimacy as it demonstrates power and military strength. Often, NSAGs try to minimize the negative effects of violence for their legitimacy through adopting counter-measurements, such as the establishment of military training and education or the adoption of code of conducts.[148] Code of conducts are a useful tool in communicating a NSAG's willingness to contain the use of violence within their own ranks and to abide by international law applicable to

141 Ibid 418; Antonio Giustozzi, Empires of Mud: Wars and Warlords in Afghanistan (1st edn, Hurst 2009) 193 f.

142 Klaus Schlichte and Ulrich Schneckener, 'Armed Groups and the Politics of Legitimacy' 418.

143 Ibid 415 ff.

144 Nelson Kasfir, 'Rebel Governance - Constructing a Field of Inquiry: Definitions, Scope, Patterns, Order, Causes' in Zachariah C. Mampilly, Nelson Kasfir and Ana Arjona (eds), Rebel Governnace in Civil War 25; Klaus Schlichte and Ulrich Schneckener, 'Armed Groups and the Politics of Legitimacy' 416; Heike Krieger, 'International Law and Governance by Armed Groups: Caught in the Legitimacy Trap?' 569.

145 Klaus Schlichte and Ulrich Schneckener, 'Armed Groups and the Politics of Legitimacy' 416; Zachariah C. Mampilly, Rebel Rulers Insurgent Governance and Civilian Life during War 53-55.

146 Klaus Schlichte and Ulrich Schneckener, 'Armed Groups and the Politics of Legitimacy' 416.

147 Ibid 416.

148 Heike Krieger, 'International Law and Governance by Armed Groups: Caught in the Legitimacy Trap?' 571 f.

armed conflicts.[149] In addition to that, some NSAGs also issue unilateral declarations to demonstrate their recognition of international humanitarian law.[150] In this vein, Geneva Call, a non-governmental organization which is engaged in enhancing compliance with IHL by NSAGs in times of armed conflict, established so-called Deeds of Commitments which NSAGs can sign and thereby express and demonstrate their intention to comply with certain norms enshrined in the Deeds.[151]

The second challenge in the pursuit of gaining legitimacy stems from the multiplicity of legitimacy audiences which need to be addressed.[152] NSAGs need to reconcile mainly three different audiences at two different levels: its members, the local, regional or national population which they seek to govern (domestic level) and the international community, comprising third states, international organizations, transnational NGOs and the media (international level).[153] For a NSAG which seeks to replace the incumbent state government, support, obedience and acceptance by the local population living on the territory of control as well as by the regional and national population is of crucial importance.[154] For a NSAG which, especially, aims at secession, recognition and support by third states and the international community become elementary as well. This means that NSAGs often must communicate their agenda to different audiences and try to reconcile possibly diverging legitimacy beliefs and expectations.[155] However, having

149 Ibid 572. For an overview of prominent examples of condes of conducts by NSAGs, see Olivier Bangerter and Nelleke van Amstel, 'A collection of codes of conduct issued by armed groups' (2011) 93 International Review of the Red Cross 483-500.

150 Art. 93 (3) Additional Protocol I, for example, foresees the possibility for 'national liberation movements' to issue unilateral declarations whereby the four Geneva Conventions of 1949 become applicable to the parties.

151 Heike Krieger, 'International Law and Governance by Armed Groups: Caught in the Legitimacy Trap?' 572.

152 Klaus Schlichte and Ulrich Schneckener, 'Armed Groups and the Politics of Legitimacy' 419; Heike Krieger, 'International Law and Governance by Armed Groups: Caught in the Legitimacy Trap?' 567 f.; Cord Schmelzle and Eric Stollenwerk, 'Virtuous or Vicious Circle? Governance Effectiveness and Legitimacy in Areas of Limited Statehood' 463.

153 Heike Krieger, 'International Law and Governance by Armed Groups: Caught in the Legitimacy Trap?' 567; Klaus Schlichte and Ulrich Schneckener, 'Armed Groups and the Politics of Legitimacy' 419.

154 Klaus Schlichte and Ulrich Schneckener, 'Armed Groups and the Politics of Legitimacy' 419; Heike Krieger, 'International Law and Governance by Armed Groups: Caught in the Legitimacy Trap?' 567.

155 Zachariah C. Mampilly, 'Performing the Nation-State: Rebel Governance and Symbolic Processes' in Zachariah C. Mampilly, Nelson Kasfir and Ana Arjona (eds),

to respond to multiple legitimacy audiences with different, often conflicting beliefs can hinder the NSAG in gaining legitimacy. Actions and strategies that contribute to enhanced legitimacy within one audience may at the same time decrease it with another audience.[156] Especially challenging is the pursuit of building legitimacy vis-à-vis the international community, be it third states or international organizations. Here, international law creates legal-normative obstacles.[157] Armed groups as violent non-state actors do not enjoy legal personality, they are not entitled to conclude treaties with other states or international organizations.[158] In other words, their ability to formally communicate with the international community is limited *per se*. However, NSAGs can use their obligations under IHL as a starting point to engage and communicate with the international community by respecting the substantive law. Since the international community has a legally induced interest in maintaining compliance with IHL during armed conflict and in limiting humanitarian casualties, there might be a willingness on behalf of the international community to engage in dialogue with armed groups which in turn might contribute to a group's legitimacy.[159]

To conclude, particularly NSAGs with long-term political and military goals seek to establish legitimacy and may invest in establishing governance structures to further this purpose. Whereas states argue that legitimacy derives from legality solely, NSAGs must argue that legitimacy derives from other sources, such as 'social acceptance', as well.

Rebel Governance in Civil War 84-87; Heike Krieger, 'International Law and Governance by Armed Groups: Caught in the Legitimacy Trap?' 569; Klaus Schlichte and Ulrich Schneckener, 'Armed Groups and the Politics of Legitimacy' 421.

156 Cord Schmelzle and Eric Stollenwerk, 'Virtuous or Vicious Circle? Governance Effectiveness and Legitimacy in Areas of Limited Statehood' 463.

157 Klaus Schlichte and Ulrich Schneckener, 'Armed Groups and the Politics of Legitimacy' 419.

158 Heike Krieger, 'International Law and Governance by Armed Groups: Caught in the Legitimacy Trap?' 567.

159 Ezequiel Heffes and Jonathan Somer, Inviting non-state armed groups to the table - Report (ODI, December 2020); Cedric Ryngaert and Anneleen Van de Meulebroucke, 'Enhancing and Enforcing Compliance with International Humanitarian Law by Non-State Armed Groups: an Inquiry into some Mechanisms' 443 f.; Marco Sassòli, 'Taking Armed Groups Seriously: Ways to Improve their Compliance with International Humanitarian Law' 29 ff.; Bridget L. Coggins, 'Rebel Diplomacy: Theorizing Violent Non-State Actors' Strategic Use of Talk' in Nelson Kasfir Ana Arjona, and Zachariah Mamiplly (ed), Rebel Governance in Civil War (1st edn, Cambridge Universtiy Press 2015) 98-118, 114 ff.; Heike Krieger, 'International Law and Governance by Armed Groups: Caught in the Legitimacy Trap?' 567.

In pursuing legitimacy NSAGs are often caught in a so-called 'legitimacy trap': firstly, due to the multiple legitimacy audiences with varying demands and secondly, due the state-centered design of the international legal order which promotes states' claims to legitimacy on the one hand and contests NSAGs' claims to legitimacy on the other. Since governance by NSAGs serves their legitimacy whilst it simultaneously infringes on the sovereignty of the state on whose territory they establish and execute their governance structures,[160] the affected state has a strong interest in opposing and fighting an armed group's attempts and efforts in gaining legitimacy. This is also referred to as 'legitimacy war'[161].

3. Conclusion

'Rebel governance' is a widespread phenomenon of internal armed conflicts. At a minimum, it relates to the organization of a civilian population within rebel held territory for a public purpose.[162] 'Rebel governance' is evolving and transitory, and a reflection of an insurgent group's strength and correlating capacity to invest resources into the governance of the civilian population.[163] The establishment of governance structures by NSAGs occurs especially in situations where the respective NSAG has established a certain degree of control over territory and/or population and possesses a certain degree of organization.[164] Rebel governments vary considerably

160 Heike Krieger, 'International Law and Governance by Armed Groups: Caught in the Legitimacy Trap?' 574.

161 Jo Hyeran, Compliant Rebels: Rebel Groups and International Law in World Politics (1st edn, Cambridge University Press 2015) 257.

162 Nelson Kasfir, 'Rebel Governance - Constructing a Field of Inquiry: Definitions, Scope, Patterns, Order, Causes' in Zachariah C. Mampilly, Nelson Kasfir and Ana Arjona (eds), Rebel Governnace in Civil War 24; Tanja A. Börzel, Thomas Risse and Anke Draude, 'Governance in Areas of Limited Statehood: Conceptual Clarifiactions and Major Contributions of the Handbook' in Anke Draude, Tanja A. Börzel and Thomas Risse (eds), The Oxford Handbook of Governance and Limited Statehood 9; Reyko Huang, The Wartime Origins of Democratization - Civil War, Rebel Governacne, and Political Regimes (1st edn, Cambridge University Press 2016); Zachariah C. Mampilly, Rebel Rulers Insurgent Governance and Civilian Life during War 51.

163 René Provost, Rebel Courts: The Administration of Justice by Armed Insurgents (1st edn, Oxford University Press 2021) 40.

164 Heike Krieger, 'International Law and Governance by Armed Groups: Caught in the Legitimacy Trap?' 564; Zachariah C. Mampilly, Rebel Rulers Insurgent Governance and Civilian Life during War.

in their structure and level of organization.[165] NSAGs may decide to not govern at all, they may install *ad hoc* and informal governance structures or they may invest in elaborate bureaucracies.[166] NSAGs may regulate the economic, social and political life of civilians through the provision of public goods, the management of economic affairs and regulation of security and justice affairs.[167] Depending on the desired effect, NSAGs may attempt at governing holistically as well as deciding to govern selectively only. Notably, providing for law and order through a group's own police force and/or judiciary is a frequent element in the realm of 'rebel governance'.[168] Besides the immediate effects of soliciting civilian support and producing material gain, governance by NSAGs may also aim at building legitimacy. Legitimacy in the context of 'rebel governance' refers to empirical legitimacy, hence, the right to rule and to govern based on social acceptance and is especially important for NSAGs with long-term political goals, such as overthrowing the incumbent government and replacing it or building a new state. In this regard, the multiplicity of different legitimacy audiences often poses a challenge to NSAGs.

III. Judicial Governance by NSAGs: From Theory to Practice

This section elaborates on a specific branch of 'rebel governance': 'rebel judicial governance'. This relates to the establishment and operation of judicial institutions and mechanisms by NSAGs during armed conflict. The provision of judicial instruments is an important tool for many NSAGs in claiming authority and power. It is the ultimate denial of every state's sovereignty and monopoly over the use of force.[169]

165 Nelson Kasfir, 'Rebel Governance - Constructing a Field of Inquiry: Definitions, Scope, Patterns, Order, Causes' in Zachariah C. Mampilly, Nelson Kasfir and Ana Arjona (eds), Rebel Governnace in Civil War 23.

166 Ana Arjona, Nelson Kasfir and Zachariah Mamiplly, 'Introduction' in Zachariah C. Mampilly, Nelson Kasfir and Ana Arjona (eds), Rebel Governance in Civil War 1.

167 Ibid.

168 Heike Krieger, 'International Law and Governance by Armed Groups: Caught in the Legitimacy Trap?' 569; Nelson Kasfir, 'Rebel Governance - Constructing a Field of Inquiry: Definitions, Scope, Patterns, Order, Causes' in Zachariah C. Mampilly, Nelson Kasfir and Ana Arjona (eds), Rebel Governnace in Civil War 36; Corinna Jentzsch, 'Auxiliary Armed Forces and Innovations in Security Governance in Mozambique's Civil War' (2017) 19 Civil Wars 325-347, 326.

169 Frank Ledwidge, Rebel Law - Insurgents, Courts and Justice in Modern Conflict (1st edn, Hurst&Company 2017) 16 f.

After mapping out general features of insurgent judiciaries (Sub-section 1), the theoretical framework of insurgent judiciary will be illustrated by highlighting prominent examples of insurgent administered justice during armed conflict from past and presence (Sub-section 2).

1. Insurgent judiciary in theory

Why do rebels govern through the provision of judicial mechanisms? According to *Anderson*, insurgent groups adjudicate disputes as 'revolutionary rehearsals of the exercise of the power they hope to wield one day on a larger scale'[170].

The provision of judicial institutions plays an important role in the attempt of insurgent groups to govern.[171] The administration of justice by NSAGs can take various shapes. Insurgent administration of justice can comprise different types of judicial mechanisms, it can aim at different effects (functions), can cover different areas, and can be directed towards different audiences.

Firstly, the establishment and operation of judicial institutions by NSAGs during armed conflict can be in parallel to continuing state institutions, often as a direct challenge to the state judiciary, as well as it can fill a legal void where state institutions ceased to operate due to insurgent dominance.[172]

Secondly, insurgent administration of justice can be directed vis-à-vis different addressees. NSAGs may invest in the provision of judicial mechanisms to regulate inter-civilian relations and to secure order within the civilian population living on rebel-held territory. Accordingly, the adjudication of disputes may range from civil law to criminal law matters. The latter scenario may comprise ordinary crimes as well as it may relate to crimes

170 Jon Lee Anderson, Guerrillas (1st edn, Abacus 1992) 172.

171 See Regine Schwab, 'Insurgent courts in civil wars: the three pathways of (trans)formation in today's Syria (2012-2017)' 801. Note of clarification: not all NSAGs engage in the provision of judicial mechanisms. According to a dataset on rebel use of judiciaries established by Cyanne Loyle, it is only around 18% of all NSAGs. See Cyanne E. Loyle, 'Rebel courts and rebel legitimacy' (2023) International Politics 1-18, 4.

172 Cyanne E. Loyle, 'Rebel courts and rebel legitimacy' 6. In the Al Hassan Case before the ICC, the Defence referred to a situation where 'the state has left the building'. See ICC, Prosecutor v Al Hassan Ag Abdoul Aziz Ag Mohamed Ag Mahmoud, Transcript of Confirmation of Charges 27.

specifically linked to the armed conflict. Likewise, NSAGs may establish judicial mechanisms to maintain law and order within the ranks of the group's own fighting force.[173] This relates to the adjudication of conduct committed during armed hostilities in the battlefield, be it violations of the group's own code of conduct or breaches of international law applicable in times of armed conflict. Such processes are often military and disciplinary in nature. Hence, they fall outside the remit of civilian-oriented judicial governance in armed conflict.

Thirdly, the immediate effect or function of administering justice is dispute resolution and securing social control in insurgent-held territory.[174] Dispute resolution involves resolving problems between two opposing parties and amounts to a universal precondition for social order.[175] Beyond this immediate effect of administering justice, many NSAGs invest in the provision of judicial mechanisms to achieve a mediate, yet even more important, effect: namely, to secure cooperation and compliance by the civilian population, to gain its support and trust and, thus, to build legitimacy among the civilian population – all during armed conflict with continuous 'on-side' fighting.[176]

There are different types of judicial mechanisms established by NSAGs during armed conflict. NSAGs may administer justice through traditional judicial instruments, such as courts, which conduct trials and pass binding judgments or through quasi-judicial mechanisms, such as truth commissions, commissions of inquiry or reparation mechanisms, which focus on the mediation and arbitration of disputes.[177] Courts as institutions can rely on coercive power enforcement which may render them more effective than alternative mechanisms of dispute resolution.[178] The choice of justice instruments indicates whether civilian support shall be achieved through 'fear and sympathy'[179], meaning that judicial processes can be deployed in a coercive or in a conciliatory manner.[180] Accordingly, insurgent judicial

173 Cyanne E. Loyle, 'Rebel courts and rebel legitimacy' 6.
174 Tom Ginsburg, 'Rebel Use of Law and Courts' (2019) 15 Annual Review of Law and Social Science 495-507, 497; Martin Shapiro, Courts: A Comparative and Political Analysis (1st edn, The University of Chicago Press 1981) 1.
175 Tom Ginsburg, 'Rebel Use of Law and Courts'.
176 Cyanne E. Loyle, 'Rebel courts and rebel legitimacy' 2; Cyanne E. Loyle, 'Rebel Justice during Armed Conflict' (2021) 65 Journal of Conflict Resolution 108-134, 108.
177 Cyanne E. Loyle, 'Rebel Justice during Armed Conflict' 111.
178 Tom Ginsburg, 'Rebel Use of Law and Courts' 497.
179 Stathis N. Kalyvas, The Logic of Violence in Civil War 91.
180 Cyanne E. Loyle, 'Rebel Justice during Armed Conflict' 116.

processes may have two functions: either to co-opt support from the local population by addressing grievances resulting from insurgent behavior or government behavior in the hope to increase sympathy and trust towards the insurgent group or to co-opt support from the local population by demonstrating power and authority through coercion and direct punishment.[181]

Coercive judicial processes are designed to demonstrate the group's capability to hold people accountable for their wrongdoings. They amount to instruments that are put in place with the intention of securing (civilian) compliance through intimidation and fear. Coercive judicial processes would include trials in order to address a wrongdoing within a formalized legal context and legal structure.[182] Trials held through courts of NSAGs amount to a formal examination of an alleged wrongdoing within a legal structure.[183] They bear a coercive potential because they demonstrate a group's ability to identify, capture and hold individuals accountable for their actions through punishment.[184] Courts of NSAGs can be established to try civilians, to try fighters of the respective armed group or to try fighters of the opposing party/parties. The crimes which may be tried by such courts may also range widely from ordinary crimes to specifically conflict related crimes.

By contrast, conciliatory judicial processes are designed to publicly address grievances through other means than prosecutions and punishments, namely, through mechanisms such as truth commissions, commissions of inquiry, reparation schemes or amnesty offers. These instruments amount to a strategy of co-optation by which a NSAG tries to sustain civilian support through rewarding supporters and showing its willingness to properly address the grievances and interests of the civilian population, also possibly in the future.[185] According to *Loyle*, conciliatory judicial processes are more likely to be established if the respective rebel group enjoys a reasonably high degree of acceptance and support within the local population it exercises control over whereas coercive judicial mechanisms are more likely

181 Ibid.
182 Ibid.
183 Ibid.
184 Mark J. Osiel, 'Why Prosecute - Critics of Punishment for Mass Atrocity' (2000) 22 Human Rights Quarterly 118, 141-144; Cyanne E. Loyle, 'Rebel Justice during Armed Conflict' 118.
185 Cyanne E. Loyle, 'Rebel Justice during Armed Conflict' 117.

to be installed in situations where the respective group faces low levels of support from the civilian population.[186]

One may conclude that – although varying in their nature, structure, and functioning – the umbrella objective of insurgent judicial mechanisms lies in adjudicating disputes that have occurred or are occurring during armed conflict in 'rebel'-controlled territory to cultivate and consolidate support from the local population through coercive or conciliatory judicial processes.[187]

2. Insurgent judiciary in practice: prominent examples

This section illustrates historical and contemporary examples of judicial mechanisms established by NSAGs during armed conflict. The aim of the present case analyses is to shed light on the phenomenon of 'insurgent judicial governance' and to give an impression of the myriad ways of how NSAGs deploy judicial mechanisms, the reasons why NSAGs establish judicial mechanisms, what law they apply and which crimes they prosecute. The cases chosen for analysis are the judicial system of the Frente Farabundo Martí para la Liberación Nacional in El Salvador, the judicial system of the Revolutionary Armed Forces of Colombia in Colombia, the court system of the Liberation Tigers of Tamil Eelam in Sri Lanka as well as Kurdish courts operating in Northeast Syria.[188] The selection of cases is descriptive and follows a diverse approach. It is motived by the attempt of covering the diversity of insurgent judiciaries during armed conflict. Hence, the present case selection covers past conflicts as well as present conflicts. It comprises two-party conflicts with one dominant insurgent group fighting against a state regime as well as multiparty conflicts with an array of NSAGs fighting against a state regime and/or fighting each other. The highlighted examples of insurgent judiciaries cover well-structured and highly advanced court systems as well as *ad hoc* and rudimentarily structured judicial systems. The following case analyses each start with a brief overview of the respective armed conflict before assessing the governance systems of the respective insurgent group(s) with a special focus on the provision of judicial mechanisms.

---

186 Ibid 118; see also Cyanne E. Loyle, 'Rebel courts and rebel legitimacy' 4 f.

187 Cyanne E. Loyle, 'Rebel Justice during Armed Conflict' 109, 111.

188 For an overview on these court systems see also Sandesh Sivakumaran, 'Courts of Armed Opposition Groups: Fair Trials or Summary Justice?' (2009) 7 Journal of International Criminal Justice 489-513, 491ff.

a. FMLN judiciary in El Salvador[189]

The first example relates to the armed conflict in El Salvador and the provision of insurgent administered justice by the dominant NSAG, called Frente Farabundo Martí para la Liberación Nacional (**FMLN**).

aa. Background of the conflict

Throughout the period of 1980-1992, an armed conflict between the government of El Salvador and the armed opposition group FMLN took place on the territory of El Salvador.[190]

The civil war in El Salvador was the first conflict which triggered the applicability of Additional Protocol II.[191] It rooted in diverging ideologies stemming from political instability following decades of colonialism, and in the overall economic inequality within the country with a small elite unwilling to redistribute its wealth to the impoverished majority of population.[192] The conflict lasted 12 years and amounts to one of the twentieth century's longest-lasting civil wars in Latin America.[193] It was a multi-party armed conflict characterized by multipolarity amongst the involved insurgent groups in the beginning but later evolved towards hegemony with the FMLN being the dominant group.[194] Armed forces of the Salvadoran government and of the economic elite – also referred to as coffee bour-

189 Sandesh Sivakumaran, The Law of Non-International Armed Conflict (1st edn, Oxford University Press 2012) 552 ff.; Zachariah C. Mampilly, Rebel Rulers Insurgent Governance and Civilian Life during War.

190 Sandesh Sivakumaran, 'Courts of Armed Opposition Groups: Fair Trials or Summary Justice?' 491.

191 Jonathan Somer, 'Jungle justice: passing sentence on the equality of belligerents in non-international armed conflict' (2007) 89 International Review of the Red Cross 655-690, 679.

192 Michael E. Allison and Alberto Martín Alvarez, 'Unity and Disunity in the FMLN' (2012) 54 Latin American Politics and Society 89-118, 92; Steve Hobden, 'El Salvador: Civil war, civil society and the state' (2000) 3 Civil Wars 105-120, 106; Harald Jung, 'The Civil War in El Salvador' (1982) Boletín de Estudios Latinoamericanos y del Caribe 5-13, 5.

193 Lise M. Howard, 'United Nationals Observer Mission in El Salvador (ONUSAL)' in Joachim A. Koops et al. (eds), The Oxford Handbook of United Nations Peacekeeping Operations (1st edn, Oxford University Press 2015) 352-360, 351.

194 For terminology, see Regine Schwab, 'Insurgent courts in civil wars: the three pathways of (trans)formation in today's Syria (2012-2017)' 802.

geoisie – formed an alliance and governed El Salvador.[195] In response to this alliance, several armed opposition groups have emerged during the Cold War period, amongst others, the Popular Forces of Liberation-Farabundo Martí (**FPL**), the People's Revolutionary Army (**ERP**), the Armed Forces of National Resistance (**RN**), the Revolutionary Party of Workers of Central America (**PRTC**) or the Armed Forces of Liberation (**FAL**) which arose from the Communist Party of El Salvador (**CPS**).[196] Those insurgent groups formed throughout the 1970s and followed different political and military agendas and strategies. While some of them had a stronger focus on prolonged armed violence and insurrection, others concentrated more on political work and political participation.[197] In 1980, the FMLN emerged out of five former armed opposition groups following the military coup against the then president Carlos Humberto Romero.[198] The FMLN defined itself as a South-/Central American Marxist liberation movement.[199] They followed an agenda of armed violence as means of revolution, shared the view that social democracy, reformism and elections were not a viable strategy, and believed that it was impossible to achieve democracy and social justice.[200]

The civil war started with the so-called 'final offensive' launched in January 1981 by the FMLN.[201] In this course, the FMLN gained control of approximately 30 percent of the land and over 20 percent of the Salvadoran population. In the so-called 'zones of operation', which were the areas under control of the FMLN, the FMLN engaged in building a new infrastructure and social organization.[202] Throughout the armed conflict, the FMLN fought for four main objectives: the end of military dictatorship,

195 Michael E. Allison and Alberto Martín Alvarez, 'Unity and Disunity in the FMLN' 92; Steve Hobden, 'El Salvador: Civil war, civil society and the state' 107; Harald Jung, 'The Civil War in El Salvador' 5.

196 Michael E. Allison and Alberto Martín Alvarez, 'Unity and Disunity in the FMLN' 92 f.; Harald Jung, 'The Civil War in El Salvador' 9.

197 Michael E. Allison and Alberto Martín Alvarez, 'Unity and Disunity in the FMLN' 93 f.

198 Ibid 94 f.; Hugh Byrne, El Salvador's civil war : a study of revolution (1st edn, Lynne Rienner Publishers 1996) 54.

199 Frank Ledwidge, Rebel Law - Insurgents, Courts and Justice in Modern Conflict 57; Harald Jung, 'The Civil War in El Salvador' 12.

200 Michael E. Allison and Alberto Martín Alvarez, 'Unity and Disunity in the FMLN' 95.

201 Steve Hobden, 'El Salvador: Civil war, civil society and the state' 107.

202 Harald Jung, 'The Civil War in El Salvador' 12.

the democratization of the country, the respect for human rights and the unification of the civil society.[203]

In April 1990, the signing of the so-called Geneva Agreement of April 4th, 1990 formed the basic framework for peace negotiations. It documents first consultations between the government of El Salvador and the FMLN concerning the format and mechanisms for bringing a definite end to the armed conflict.[204] After that, the San José Agreement on human rights of July 26th, 1990 followed.[205] It expresses the parties willingness and commitment to ensure respect and protection of fundamental human rights during the ongoing conflict, *inter alia*, the right to life, the right to liberty, the right of freedom of expression or the prohibition of torture or other cruel, inhumane or degrading treatment or punishment.[206] In May 1991, the United Nations Security Council (**UNSC**) established the so-called UN Observer Mission in El Salvador (**ONUSAL**) to monitor the compliance with and adherence to international humanitarian law and international human rights commitments of and agreements between the FMLN and the Salvadoran government.[207] In January 1992, the government of El Salvador and the FMLN signed a negotiated ceasefire agreement which resulted in the rebel group's re-emergence as a political party.[208] In February 1992 the cessation of the armed conflict formally entered into force.[209]

---

203 See Esther Portillo-Gonzales, 'FMLN Reflections, 20 Years Later: An Interview With Nidia Díaz' (2012) NACLA Report on the Americas 55-57. María Marta Valladares, also known as Nidia Díaz, has been one of the most prominent commanders of the FMLN.

204 United Nations Security Council, Geneva Agreement, UN Doc. A/46/551/S/23128, 9 October 1991.

205 United Nations Security Council, Agreement on Human Rights (San Jose Agreement), UN Doc. A/44/971/S/21541, 16 August 1990.

206 Ibid.

207 United Nations Security Council Resolution 693 (on the establishment of the United Nations Observer Mission in El Salvador), 20 May 1991.

208 See United Nations General Assembly, Peace Agreement (between the Government of El Salvador and the FMLN), UN Doc. A/46/864, 30 January 1992; Michael E. Allison and Alberto Martín Alvarez, 'Unity and Disunity in the FMLN' 89; Esther Portillo-Gonzales, 'FMLN Reflections, 20 Years Later: An Interview With Nidia Díaz' 55.

209 ONUSAL, Third report of the United Nations Observer Mission in El Salvador (United Nations Observer Mission in El Salvador 19 February 1991) 2.

bb. The FMLN's judicial system

The FMLN did not have state-building aspirations, nor did the group aim at providing the civilian population with an alternative governance system. The group's agenda was a militant one. The group aimed at revolting the incumbent government. The narratives of discipline and compliance with international law were a constant scheme.[210] The administration of justice served the purpose of demonstrating strength and control, and of ensuring discipline and order. The FMLN invested in the provision of judicial mechanisms to enforce the narratives of discipline and order, especially, within the group's own fighting cadre but also within the civilian population.

The group claimed that IHL presupposes that either of the parties to the conflict has the authority to try and sanction violations committed in relation to the armed conflict.[211] The group also stressed compliance with international law.[212]

There is only little accessible literature as to how the FMLN administered justice towards the civilian population. Apparently, the insurgent group primarily conducted prosecutions of its own forces for violations of IHL and for breaches of internal rules.[213] Amongst the sanctions were expulsion, admonishment, demotion, detention and removal of rank.[214] The FMLN also conducted prosecutions for espionage and collaboration with the government.[215] One prominent example concerns the shooting of two US military fighters[216] by members of the FMLN's fighting unit who then had to face trial for allegedly committing a war crime in breach of

210 Frank Ledwidge, Rebel Law - Insurgents, Courts and Justice in Modern Conflict 57.

211 FMLN Secretariat for the Promotion and Protection of Human Rights, The Legitimacy of Our Methods of Struggle (Inkworth Press on behalf of FMLN 1988) 6 and 17; see also Jonathan Somer, 'Jungle justice: passing sentence on the equality of belligerents in non-international armed conflict' 679.

212 Frank Ledwidge, Rebel Law - Insurgents, Courts and Justice in Modern Conflict 57.

213 Jonathan Somer, 'Jungle justice: passing sentence on the equality of belligerents in non-international armed conflict'; Sandesh Sivakumaran, 'Courts of Armed Opposition Groups: Fair Trials or Summary Justice?' 491.

214 Frente Farabundo Martí para la Liberación Nacional. Secretariat for the Promotion and Protection of Human Rights, The Legitimacy of Our Methods of Struggle (FMLN 1988) 6; Sandesh Sivakumaran, 'Courts of Armed Opposition Groups: Fair Trials or Summary Justice?' 491.

215 Sandesh Sivakumaran, The Law of Non-International Armed Conflict 552.

216 US forces supported the Salvadoran government.

the FMLN's own code of conduct and the Geneva Conventions.[217] In a communication of the FMLN about this incident, they stated to act with 'all rigor, in accordance with our standard war time judicial procedures' and to prepare the conditions for a 'clear and impartial' judicial process.[218] The insurgent group claimed that it endeavored to assure its compliance with fundamental fair trial guarantees stipulated by both the Geneva Conventions of 1949 as well as its Additional Protocol II of 1977.[219] However, the FMLN's courts were criticized by, *inter alia*, ONUSAL for not providing the requisite due process guarantees, namely, for the lack of impartiality, the lack of legal training on part of the decision makers and the failure to afford all necessary rights and means of defence.[220] Especially, ONUSAL pointed out that the principle of legality was violated since the FMLN's legal code called 'Principios, Normativos y Medidas Dispuestoe por el FMLN en el transcurso de la guerra' does not ensure the basic norms of a penal code as required by Art. 6 (2)(c) Additional Protocol II and fails in establishing procedural guarantees.[221] ONUSAL also criticized the summary nature of proceedings.[222] Americas Watch, which also observed the trial concerning the shooting of the two US servicemen, also viewed the court system critically. It criticized the FMLN's courts for failing to provide legal training to those administering justice, for not disclosing the identity of the defense counsel to the accused and for its overall lack of impart justice.[223] The FMLN, on the other hand, defended its system by pointing out that the statutory requirements of Additional Protocol II must be adapted to the

217 Frank Ledwidge, Rebel Law - Insurgents, Courts and Justice in Modern Conflict 58; Sandesh Sivakumaran, The Law of Non-International Armed Conflict 552; IACHR, Annual Report of the Inter-American Commission on Human Rights 1990-1991 (Inter-American Commission on Human Rights, 22 February 1991), OEA/Ser.L/V/II.79.rev.1 Doc. 12, Chapter VI.

218 "Communique of the FMLN about the Circumstances in which the Death of the Northamerican Crew Occurred", January 8, 1991; see <https://www.hrw.org/reports//pdfs/e/elsalvdr/elsalv.913/salrptspe.pdf> accessed 11 February 2022.

219 Jonathan Somer, 'Jungle justice: passing sentence on the equality of belligerents in non-international armed conflict' 679; see also ICTY, Prosecutor v Dusko Tadić aka „Dule", Decision on the Defence Motion for Interlocutory Appeal on Jurisdiction para 107.

220 ONUSAL, Third report of the United Nations Observer Mission in El Salvador (United Nations Observer Mission in El Salvador 19 February 1991) paras 112-114.

221 See ibid para 113.

222 Ibid para 114.

223 AW, Violations of Fair Trial Guarantees by the FMLN's Ad Hoc Courts, Report (Americas Watch, 1990) 21.

conditions and capacities of the NSAG and adjusted to the real possibilities during the time of armed conflict.[224] Additionally, the group claimed that its procedural law did afford fair trial guarantees, such as the presumption of innocence, the prohibitions on retroactive trials, coerced testimony, and enforced guilty pleas.[225]

The FMLN's investment in judicial mechanisms is a sound example for illustrating that many NSAG engage in judicial activity during armed conflict to impose order and discipline and to demonstrate power and strength group vis-à-vis its own members.[226] Their courts served the group's wider narrative of discipline and compliance with international law.[227]

b. FARC judiciary in Colombia

The second example relates to the long-lasting armed conflict in Colombia and the establishment of parallel judicial mechanisms by the dominant insurgent group, the Revolutionary Armed Forces of Colombia (**FARC**).

aa. Background of the conflict

The armed conflict in Colombia belongs to one of the most brutal and longest-lasting conflicts of the last century. It included multiple actors, especially an array of different 'guerrilla' and paramilitary groups, fighting both the respective state regimes throughout the years as well as fighting each other for territorial dominance.

The roots of the Colombian conflict go back to a period of domestic unrest following the assignation of the presidential candidate *Jorge Eliécer Gaitán* in 1948.[228] What followed were single violent outbursts between

224 Sandesh Sivakumaran, 'Courts of Armed Opposition Groups: Fair Trials or Summary Justice?' 492; Jonathan Somer, 'Jungle justice: passing sentence on the equality of belligerents in non-international armed conflict' 680.

225 Sandesh Sivakumaran, The Law of Non-International Armed Conflict 492 and 552.

226 Jon Lee Anderson, Guerrillas 187; Frank Ledwidge, Rebel Law - Insurgents, Courts and Justice in Modern Conflict 57.

227 Frank Ledwidge, Rebel Law - Insurgents, Courts and Justice in Modern Conflict 57.

228 René Provost, Rebel Courts: The Administration of Justice by Armed Insurgents 31; Catherine C. Le Grand, 'The Colombian Crisis in Historical Perspective' (2003) 28 Canadian Journal of Latin American and Caribbean Studies / Revue canadienne des études latino-américaines et caraïbes 165-209, 172.

1948 and the early 1960s, rooting in diverging political agendas between the leading parties, the Liberals and the Conservatives as well as in diverging ideologies concerning access to land.[229] This violence provisionally decreased when the political parties' leaders concluded a political pact which foresaw an alternation of presidency and political offices until 1974.[230] However, each subsequently following incumbent government failed to address the continuous problems of inequality, rural development and access to land.[231] This led to increasing strikes and protest throughout the country by all kinds of people, students, peasants and workers.[232] Eventually, this continuous unrest converted into a long-lasting armed conflict (almost five decades) between the government and several armed opposition groups including right-wing paramilitaries and left-wing guerrilla groups with a communist agenda, such as the FARC, the National Liberation Army (**ELN**), the Popular Liberation Army (**ELP**) or the April 19 Movement (**M19**).[233] They sought to bring about social justice and socialism.[234] The most rapidly growing insurgent group was the FARC. It proclaimed itself to be the revolutionary army of Colombia, fighting against poverty and improving peasants' life.[235] It was the longest-lasting 'guerilla group' in Latin-America and unique in the sense that its leadership was exclusively composed of lower-class peasants.[236] The FARC started as a loose rural peasant movement, executing mostly self-defence and eventually declared

229 Ana Arjona, Rebelocracy - Social Order in the Colombian Civil War (1st edn, Cambridge University Press 2016) 89; Catherine C. Le Grand, 'The Colombian Crisis in Historical Perspective' 172.

230 Catherine C. Le Grand, 'The Colombian Crisis in Historical Perspective' 173.

231 Ana Arjona, Rebelocracy - Social Order in the Colombian Civil War 89; Catherine C. Le Grand, 'The Colombian Crisis in Historical Perspective' 173.

232 Ana Arjona, Rebelocracy - Social Order in the Colombian Civil War 89.

233 Ibid 89; René Provost, Rebel Courts: The Administration of Justice by Armed Insurgents 31.

234 Ana Arjona, 'Wartime Institutions: A Research Agenda' (2014) 58 Journal of Conflict Resolution 1360-1389, 1365.

235 Norman Offstein and Carolina Aristizábal, 'An Historical Review and Analysis of Colombian Guerrilla Movements: FARC, ELN and EPL' (2003) Revist Desarrollo y Sociedad 99-142, 107.

236 René Provost, Rebel Courts: The Administration of Justice by Armed Insurgents 31; Catherine C. Le Grand, 'The Colombian Crisis in Historical Perspective' 176; Bilal Y. Saab and Alexandra W. Taylor, 'Criminality and Armed Groups: A Comparative Study of FARC and Paramilitary Groups in Colombia' (2009) 32 Studies in Conflict & Terrorism 455-475, 459 f.

itself a revolutionary army in 1964.[237] In the beginning, the FARC operated in the rural areas which were geographically and socially cut off from the centers of Colombia.[238] The group's popularity and power decreased in the 1960s and mid-1970s due to governmental improvements and investments in the agricultural sector.[239] Consequently, the FARC – like other 'guerrilla groups' as well – engaged in drug trafficking and other criminal behavior such as kidnapping and extortion to extract resources and maintain financial autonomy.[240] Throughout the mid-1970s and 1980s, the FARC's membership increased tremendously. At its peak in the early 2000s, the group comprised about 20.000 fighters.[241] Interim attempts of peace negotiations in the 1980s between the government and several guerrilla groups failed. What followed was a bloody period of armed violence between various guerrilla groups, paramilitaries and the Colombian armed forces in the late 1980s and early 1990s.[242] During the 1990s, the FARC became the most powerful guerrilla group.[243] It showed dominant presence in 40 to 50 percent of the Colombian municipalities.[244] Due to the parallel growth of guerrilla and paramilitary presence throughout the country, the conflict reached its peak in the late 1990s.[245]

Peace negotiations between the incumbent government and the FARC continued but never lead to a full ceasefire. Between 1998 and 2002, the government agreed on demilitarizing a huge part of territory in the south of Colombia as an attempt to boost peace talks. This left the FARC to take over all governance structures, in the political, economic and social realm.[246] Final peace talks with the FARC commenced again in 2012 which

237 HRW, War Without Quarter: Colombia and International Humanitarian Law, Report (Human Rights Watch, 1998) 136.

238 René Provost, Rebel Courts: The Administration of Justice by Armed Insurgents 32.

239 Norman Offstein and Carolina Aristizábal, 'An Historical Review and Analysis of Colombian Guerrilla Movements: FARC, ELN and EPL' 103.

240 Catherine C. Le Grand, 'The Colombian Crisis in Historical Perspective' 181; Ana Arjona, Rebelocracy - Social Order in the Colombian Civil War 98.

241 René Provost, Rebel Courts: The Administration of Justice by Armed Insurgents 29 and 35; René Provost, 'FARC Justice: Rebel Rule of Law' (2018) 8 UC Irvine Law Review 227-274, 228; HRW, War Without Quarter: Colombia and International Humanitarian Law, Report (Human Rights Watch, 1998) 136.

242 René Provost, Rebel Courts: The Administration of Justice by Armed Insurgents 33.

243 Ana Arjona, 'Wartime Institutions: A Research Agenda' 1365.

244 René Provost, Rebel Courts: The Administration of Justice by Armed Insurgents 47.

245 Ibid 33.

246 Ana Arjona, Rebelocracy - Social Order in the Colombian Civil War 91; René Provost, Rebel Courts: The Administration of Justice by Armed Insurgents 31.

led to the General Agreement for the Termination of the Conflict and Building of a Stable and Long-Lasting Peace ('Havana Accord').[247] A general ceasefire agreement was reached in June 2016 signed by the government of Colombia and the FARC in November 2016, designating the former guerrilla group a political party.[248] The final peace agreement includes, *inter alia*, a section on the enforcement of solution programs to the illicit drug problem and a big section on restorative justice mechanisms for the victims of the conflict. Part of the comprehensive system of truth, justice, reparation and non-recurrence is the so-called Special Peace Jurisdiction which is comprised of a Judicial Panel for Amnesty and Pardon and a Tribunal of Peace whose mandate it is to administer justice and investigate, prosecute and punish serious human rights violations and serious infringements of international humanitarian law.[249]

In 2018, the FARC took part in the decommissioning of its last remaining accessible weapons which formed part of the UN Verification Mission in Colombia.

In October 2021, ICC Chef Prosecutor, Mr. *Karim A.A. Khan*, concluded the Court's preliminary examination in Colombia which has been conducted since 2004, stating that the ongoing transitional justice process in Colombia satisfies the principle of complementarity.[250] In addition to that, Mr. *Karim A.A. Khan* and the incumbent president of Colombia signed a cooperation agreement whereby the government of Colombia commits to continuously support the judiciary's effort in prosecuting those responsible for crimes under the jurisdiction of the ICC.[251]

In November 2021, the United States revoked its designation of the FARC as a 'foreign terrorist organization', a lift which recognizes the laying down of arms by the FARC according to the Final Agreement and which allows the United States to contribute to the implementation of peacebuilding mis-

247 René Provost, Rebel Courts: The Administration of Justice by Armed Insurgents 34.

248 Final Agreement to End the Armed Conflict and Build a State and Lasting Peace - Colombia Peace Agreement, 24 September 2016; see <https://www.aljazeera.com/news/2021/11/30/us-lifts-colombias-farc-foreign-terrorist-designation> accessed 28 January 2022.

249 Ibid 138, 153 ff.

250 See <https://www.icc-cpi.int/itemsDocuments/20211028-OTP-COL-Cooperation-Agreement-ENG.pdf> accessed 28 January 2022.

251 See UN, Verification Mission in Colombia, Report (United Nations Secretary General, 27 December 2021) 2; The official document of the cooperation agreement can be viewed under <https://www.icc-cpi.int/itemsDocuments/20211028-OTP-COL-Cooperation-Agreement-ENG.pdf>.

sions involving the FARC.[252] To date, Colombia is still not free of violence. Dissident armed groups that have emerged from the FARC and other rebel groups still engage in violence throughout the country.[253]

bb. The FARC's judicial (governance) system

The FARC was a highly structured group with an advanced hierarchy and a highly centralized command structure.[254] The group tried to infiltrate state institutions and to influence measures in a way which would improve the population's well-being while at the same time try to impede the state's functionality and legitimacy by demonstrating the state's lack of capacity to govern independently and impartially.[255] The establishment of parallel governance structures took place in many areas but especially in the domain of justice.

The FARC's justice system had two ramifications: the internal, military component and the external, civilian component of justice.

Like man NSAGs when engaging in law-making and law enforcement, the FARC started to engage in the administration of justice internally, with establishing a code of conduct and enforcing disciplinary measures against its own fighting forces.[256] These internal disciplinary rules were more elaborate and uniform than the initial set of rules applicable to the civilian population.[257] The FARC's code of conduct – including the Statute, the Disciplinary Regulations and the Internal Norms of Commandment – was first approved in 1966 but revised several times.[258] It was an elaborate document which was divided into different chapters. Chapter 1 of the Statute, for example, contained sanctions applicable to all members of the

252 See <https://www.aljazeera.com/news/2021/11/30/us-lifts-colombias-farc-foreign-terrorist-designation> accessed 28 January 2022.

253 See <https://www.aljazeera.com/news/2021/11/30/us-lifts-colombias-farc-foreign-terrorist-designation> accessed 28 January 2022.

254 René Provost, Rebel Courts: The Administration of Justice by Armed Insurgents 34.

255 Ibid 35.

256 Ibid 47.

257 Mario Aguilera Pena, 'Claves y Distorsiones Del Régimen Disciplinario Guerrillero' (2013) 26 Análisis Político 45-62, 52.

258 Mario Aguilera Pena, 'Las guerrillas marxistas y la pena de muerte a combatientes. Un examen de los delitos capitales y del "juicio revolucionario": An Analysis of Capital Crimes and "Revolutionary Courts-martial"' (2014) 41 Anuario Colombiano de Historia Social y de la Cultura 201-236, 211.

group – irrespective of the rank – in case of a disciplinary breach. The Disciplinary Regulations contained provisions prohibiting various acts, such as a prohibition to kill fellow FARC members or to kill men and women from the civilian population.[259] In case of a violation of these disciplinary rules, a fighter was at risk to lose their position in the group or to conduct forced labour or any other penalty which was agreed on by a special body.[260] For the most serious crimes, such as treason, spying, sexual violence, killing, and looting, the FARC established a special mechanism, called 'Revolutionary court-martial', which was in charge of determining the appropriate sanction and which was called up by the respective FARC unit commander who reported the allegedly committed crime.[261]

The FARC's administration of justice in relation to civilian matters evolved during the conflict with enhanced control over certain areas and a corresponding demand to organize the local civilian population.[262] It took place especially in areas where governmental control was largely absent, such as in the demilitarized zone in the south of the country during 1998 and 2002. In this 'demilitarized zone', the government withdrew not only all its troops but all its governance structures including its law apparatus which left the FARC being a *de facto* authority of that area. Besides the 'demilitarized zone', the FARC has never exclusively controlled territory. Rather, did the group often co-exist and co-govern next to the incumbent state regime. In areas where state institutions were still present, the FARC did not always dismantle these state institutions but infiltrated them, for example, by instructing state judges and state prosecutors to act accordingly to the group's interests.[263] In areas of mixed control, justice mechanisms of the community, of the government and of the FARC sometimes operated variably and interactively.[264]

In this course of the conflict, especially in the late 1990s, the FARC adopted many state-like structures and started applying its own set of law which was deeply influenced by local customs and far from uniform and

259 René Provost, Rebel Courts: The Administration of Justice by Armed Insurgents 43.
260 Ibid 43.
261 Ibid 43 f.
262 Ibid.
263 Nicolás Espinosa, 'Entre la justicia guerrillera y la justicia campesina ¿Un nuevo modelo de justicia comunitaria? La Macarena, Meta, estudio de caso' (2003) 0 Revista Colombiana de Sociología 117-145, 128-131; René Provost, Rebel Courts: The Administration of Justice by Armed Insurgents 50.
264 René Provost, Rebel Courts: The Administration of Justice by Armed Insurgents 50.

formal.[265] The applicable law rooted in traditions of peasant life and was often unwritten.[266] In the beginning, the rules were simple: do not steal, do not kill, do not rape.[267] Over the years, however, the rules formulated by the FARC became more and more sophisticated.[268] The group adopted a set of written law, called 'Manual de Convivencia ciudadan' which translates to 'a manual for living together'. This manual contained all sorts of provisions aiming at regulating a good functioning of the community, *inter alia*, provisions regulating the ownership of property, restrictions on movement of persons and goods, a basic driving code, regulations on the economic life, penalties for crimes, such as assault and murder, and regulations concerning fishing and hunting etc.[269]

In criminal matters, the FARC conducted so-called popular trials in rural areas, mostly for ordinary crimes such as murder, rape, theft or tax related crimes.[270] Human Rights Watch, for example, criticized those criminal trials for disregarding fundamental judicial rights such as the presumption of innocence, the right to a defence or the right to be duly informed about the charges as stipulated in Art. 6 Additional Protocol II.[271] Fieldwork conducted by *Provost* indicates that the crimes committed against the security and authority of the FARC as a group, such as spying or informing on behalf of the government or alleged ties to paramilitary groups were prosecuted with very little due process and amounted to summary justice.[272] However, when it came to ordinary crimes, such as theft or domestic violence occurring within the civilian population, the trials conducted by the FARC displayed

265 Arturo Carrillo-Suarez, 'Hors De Logique: Contemporary Issues in International Humanitarian Law as Applied to Internal Armed Conflict' (1999) 15 American University of International Law Review 1-150, 94 who refers to the application of 'some primitive law'.

266 René Provost, Rebel Courts: The Administration of Justice by Armed Insurgents 48.

267 Mario Aguilera Pena, 'Las guerrillas marxistas y la pena de muerte a combatientes. Un examen de los delitos capitales y del "juicio revolucionario": An Analysis of Capital Crimes and "Revolutionary Courts-martial"' 209; René Provost, Rebel Courts: The Administration of Justice by Armed Insurgents 40.

268 Mario Aguilera Pena, 'Las guerrillas marxistas y la pena de muerte a combatientes. Un examen de los delitos capitales y del "juicio revolucionario": An Analysis of Capital Crimes and "Revolutionary Courts-martial"' 211.

269 René Provost, Rebel Courts: The Administration of Justice by Armed Insurgents 48.

270 Ibid 53; HRW, War Without Quarter: Colombia and International Humanitarian Law, Report (Human Rights Watch, 1998) 142.

271 HRW, War Without Quarter: Colombia and International Humanitarian Law, Report (Human Rights Watch, 1998) 142.

272 René Provost, Rebel Courts: The Administration of Justice by Armed Insurgents 55.

more fair trial standards, sometimes even including restorative justice elements such as acknowledging the harm done vis-à-vis the victim(s).[273] Penalties ranged from financial penalties to community service to even the death penalty for grave crimes such as murder or rape.

Overall, the FARC's provision of justice mechanisms amounted to an *ad hoc* adaption to current needs of the civilian population rather than it offered a well-structured and institutionalized justice alternative to existing state institutions.[274] The FARC's practice of administering justice was not uniform nor was it institutionalized. In contrast, the group instrumentalized existing state institutions by means of influencing and controlling them according to the group's policy and ideology.[275]

c. LTTE judiciary in Sri Lanka

The third example relates to the internal armed conflict which occurred in Sri Lanka in the 1980s between the incumbent government and the dominant NSAG, the Liberation Tigers of Tamil Eelam (**LTTE**), and to the corresponding emergence of insurgent governance structures, including the provision of justice.

aa. Background of the conflict

The roots of the conflict go back to times of Portuguese, Dutch and British colonialism between the 16th and 19th century which contributed to ethnic, religious and socio-economic differentiations and ultimately resulted in societal divisions.[276] The armed conflict in Sri Lanka[277] lasted between 1983 and 2009 and rooted in Tamil state-building aspirations as a result

273 Ibid.

274 Ibid.

275 Ibid 51.

276 Niels Terpstra and Georg Frerks, 'Governance Practices and Symbolism: De facto sovereignty and public authority in 'Tigerland'' (2018) 52 Modern Asian Studies 1001-1042, 1010; Kingsley De Silva, A History of Sri Lanka (1st edn, C. Hurst & Company 1981).

277 Back then the country's name was Ceylon. It changed to Sri Lanka in 1972 when the then dominant Sinhalese political party SLFP adopted a new constitution which also rendered Sinhala the sole official national language. See Zachariah C. Mampilly, Rebel Rulers Insurgent Governance and Civilian Life during War 99-102.

of Sinhalese nationalism, oppression, and internal colonialism of the Tamil minority.[278] The armed conflict was waged between the government of Sri Lanka and, amongst other militant Tamil groups, the dominant LTTE which were fighting for a separate Tamil state (Tamil Eelam) in the North and East of Sri Lanka.[279]

After decades of colonialism, Sri Lanka gained independence in 1948.[280] By that time, Sri Lanka was marked by a variety of ethnic, religious, and linguistic groups.[281] Around 74,9% were Sinhalese, 11,1% were Sri Lankan Tamils (predominantly in the North and East), 9,3% were Muslims and 4,1% were Indian or Estate Tamils.[282] Sinhalese politics implemented instruments which oppressed the Tamil population brought to Sri Lanka under the British colonial power by, *inter alia*, denying the Indian Tamils membership and adopting the Ceylon Citizenship Act of 1948 which rendered the Indian Tamil stateless and denied them political rights.[283] Additionally and under the administration of the Sri Lanka Freedom Party (**SLFP**) in the 1950s, the Official Language Act of 1956 was adopted which declared Sinhala the official national language. The SLFP followed a Sinhalese ethno-nationalist agenda which resulted in discrimination of the Tamil population and an almost total exclusion from positions in the military, civil service and academic sector by the early 1970s.[284] The discriminatory policies adopted by the SLFP caused turmoil within the Tamil Federal Party (**FP**) which, at the time of the SLFP's regime, had little electoral success and little political influence. Even though, the FP soon advocated the establishment of a separate state for the Tamil people in the North and East of Sri Lank as part of their political agenda, the party proved itself unable to achieve any meaningful parliamentarian success/in-

---

278 Amita Shastri, 'The Material Basis for Separatism: The Tamil Eelam Movement in Sri Lanka' (1990) 49 The Journal of Asian Studies 56-77; see also Nira Wickramasinghe, Sri Lanka in the Modern Age: A History of Contested Identities (2nd edn, Hurst and Company 2015) 265 ff.

279 Sandesh Sivakumaran, The Law of Non-International Armed Conflict 553; René Provost, Rebel Courts: The Administration of Justice by Armed Insurgents 220.

280 Kingsley De Silva, A History of Sri Lanka 489 ff.

281 Kristian Stokke and Anne Krisit Ryntveit, 'The Struggle for Tamil Eelam in Sri Lanka' (2000) 31 Growth and Change 285-304, 288.

282 René Provost, Rebel Courts: The Administration of Justice by Armed Insurgents 220.

283 Zachariah C. Mampilly, Rebel Rulers Insurgent Governance and Civilian Life during War 99.

284 Ibid 101.

fluence.[285] Therefore, various Tamil parties formed a new alliance with a more militant alignment, called the Tamil United Liberation Front (**TULF**). In 1976, the TULF adopted a resolution demanding the establishment of a separate and sovereign state for the Tamil people, namely Tamil Eelam, based on the right of self-determination in order to safeguard and represent the rights and aspirations of the Tamil nation.[286] Soon, the initial non-violent political resistance turned into violent resistance with various militant Tamil groups fighting for a separate state. In the beginning, there have been around 30 different militant groups, each of the claiming to represent the Tamil peoples of Sri Lanka.[287] By 1983, the LTTE succeeded in eliminating other Tamil militant groups and claimed to be the sole representative of the Tamil speaking nation in Sri Lanka.[288] 1983 is also the year which marked the shift from sporadic riots and violent outbursts to the beginning of a steady armed conflict.[289] In the early 1990s, the LTTE was able to establish stable and extensive control over parts in North and East Sri Lanka (North and East Province).[290] During the 1990s, the conflict zone in the country could be divided in three different zones of military control: 'cleared areas', 'uncleared areas' and 'grey areas'.[291] 'Cleared areas' have been in control of the Sri Lankan military. The territory referred to as 'uncleared' has been in control of the LTTE and in the territory referred to as 'grey area' both LTTE as well as the Sri Lankan military exercised control. There has been no clear demarcation between those areas but rather overlapping governance

285 Amita Shastri, 'The Material Basis for Separatism: The Tamil Eelam Movement in Sri Lanka' 60; Kristian Stokke and Anne Krisit Ryntveit, 'The Struggle for Tamil Eelam in Sri Lanka' 296.

286 Niels Terpstra and Georg Frerks, 'Governance Practices and Symbolism: De facto sovereignty and public authority in 'Tigerland'' 1011; Nira Wickramasinghe, Sri Lanka in the Modern Age: A History of Contested Identities 258.

287 Zachariah C. Mampilly, Rebel Rulers Insurgent Governance and Civilian Life during War 108 ff.; Niels Terpstra and Georg Frerks, 'Governance Practices and Symbolism: De facto sovereignty and public authority in 'Tigerland'' 1012.

288 Niels Terpstra and Georg Frerks, 'Governance Practices and Symbolism: De facto sovereignty and public authority in 'Tigerland'' 1012.

289 Asoka Bandarage, The Separatist Conflict in Sri Lanka: Terrorism, Ethnicity, Political economy (1st edn, Routledge 2009) 77-109.

290 Niels Terpstra and Georg Frerks, 'Governance Practices and Symbolism: De facto sovereignty and public authority in 'Tigerland'', 1013 f.

291 Timmo Gaasbeek, 'Bridging troubled waters? Everyday inter-ethnic interaction in a context of violent conflict in Kottiyar Pattu, Trincomalee, Sri Lanka' (Thesis, Wageningen University 2010) 132 f.

structures whereby the LTTE exercised influence on state institutions in government-controlled territories and vice versa.[292]

In total, the LTTE waged four major wars ('Eelam Wars') against the government between 1983 until the ultimate defeat of the LTTE by the government on May 18th, 2009.

bb. The LTTE's judicial system

The LTTE's state building process was inherently linked to the aim of representing the Tamil nation and providing a functioning framework for the realization of the Tamil people's rights and aspirations.[293] Thus, the LTTE attempted at governing holistically, also investing in social welfare for the civilian population and economic development of Tamil Eelam.[294]

The insurgent group adopted an advanced administration with a so-called Central Governing Committee at its heart, comprising a political wing, a military wing, an international secretariat and a peace secretariat.[295] The civil administration, called the Tamil Eelam Secretariat, emerged under the political wing and comprised several departments including a finance and tax department, a justice and police section as well as a ministry for health and one for economic development.[296] The LTTE's main focus in the pursuit to build a separate state for the Tamil people rested on maintaining internal and external security through police and judicial institutions. The establishment of a parallel judicial system by the LTTE was key in the pursuit of maintaining law and order in the areas they controlled and in demonstrating the capacity to provide for an autonomous administration for the Tamil people.[297] The group's justice system rooted

292 Niels Terpstra and Georg Frerks, 'Governance Practices and Symbolism: De facto sovereignty and public authority in 'Tigerland'' 1026; see Kristian Stokke, 'Building the Tamil Eelam State: Emerging State Institutions and Forms of Governance in LTTE-Controlled Areas in Sri Lanka' (2006) 27 Third World Quarterly 1021-1040, 1022-1024 who speaks of a 'de-facto dual state structure'.

293 Kristian Stokke, 'Building the Tamil Eelam State: Emerging State Institutions and Forms of Governance in LTTE-Controlled Areas in Sri Lanka' 1027.

294 Ibid 1024; Niels Terpstra and Georg Frerks, 'Governance Practices and Symbolism: De facto sovereignty and public authority in 'Tigerland''.

295 René Provost, Rebel Courts: The Administration of Justice by Armed Insurgents 225.

296 Ibid 225.

297 Kristian Stokke, 'Building the Tamil Eelam State: Emerging State Institutions and Forms of Governance in LTTE-Controlled Areas in Sri Lanka'.

in the perceived oppression of the Tamil population by the Sinhala dominant and discriminatory regime and the constitution of 1972 which denied minority rights and aspirations to the Tamil people.[298]

At the beginning of the conflict, in the early 1980s, the LTTE did not have stable control over large areas, was not organized well enough and did not have the necessary resources to establish a thorough judicial system.[299]

Like many insurgent groups, the LTTE's initial aim was to maintain law and order as well as to ensure obedience among the population living on 'rebel'-held territory. Hence, in the beginning of the conflict, the group's first priority was to maintain social order and to ensure that the people living on the territory under the group's control would follow their rules.[300] The initial institution was the Tamil Eelam police which was properly formed in 1991 and which was responsible for, *inter alia*, preventing and detecting crime, regulating traffic and transport, and for communication and intelligence matters.[301]

Throughout the 1980s, the group started with so-called mediation boards operating at the village level.[302] These mediation boards proved controversial since they were lacking a legal code as a basis for adjudication as well as adequately trained personnel.[303] At that time, the LTTE used its sporadic established judicial system mainly as a source to generate revenue from the local population living in the areas under the group's control. With the help

---

298 Illayathamby Pararajasingham, 'Thamil Eelam - a de facto State: Tamil Eelam Legal System' (TamilNet, 30 October 2003) <https://www.tamilnet.com/art.html?catid=79&artid=10277#> accessed 27 May 2021; Kristian Stokke, 'Building the Tamil Eelam State: Emerging State Institutions and Forms of Governance in LTTE-Controlled Areas in Sri Lanka' 1027.

299 Illayathamby Pararajasingham, 'Thamil Eelam - a de facto State: Tamil Eelam Legal System'; Sandesh Sivakumaran, 'Courts of Armed Opposition Groups: Fair Trials or Summary Justice?' 489-513.

300 Zachariah C. Mampilly, Rebel Rulers Insurgent Governance and Civilian Life during War.

301 Kristian Stokke, 'Building the Tamil Eelam State: Emerging State Institutions and Forms of Governance in LTTE-Controlled Areas in Sri Lanka', 1028; Niels Terpstra and Georg Frerks, 'Governance Practices and Symbolism: De facto sovereignty and public authority in 'Tigerland'' 1015.

302 Joanne Richards, An Institutional History of the Liberation Tigers of Tamil Eelam (LTTE), Working Paper (Graduate Institute of International and Development Studies - Centre on Conflict, Development and Peacebuilding, November 2014) 44; Kristian Stokke, 'Building the Tamil Eelam State: Emerging State Institutions and Forms of Governance in LTTE-Controlled Areas in Sri Lanka' 1027.

303 Kristian Stokke, 'Building the Tamil Eelam State: Emerging State Institutions and Forms of Governance in LTTE-Controlled Areas in Sri Lanka' 1027.

of so-called land courts, the LTTE managed to establish a source of steady income by means of imposing annual taxes on land property particularly from rather wealthy members of the Tamil diaspora.[304]

Throughout the 1990s and alongside the gain of stable control over territories mainly in North and partly in East Sri Lanka, the LTTE set up a well-functioning court system as part of their process of parallel state building.[305] The group also adapted its own written law.[306] In 1994, the Tamil Eelam penal code and civil code were enacted. They combined elements of British, Indian and Sri Lankan criminal law and took into consideration customary practices based on the LTTE's interpretation of cultural norms as stipulated in the Thesavalamai Code.[307]

At its peak, the LTTE's judicial system consisted of a total of 17 courts, structured in a hierarchical manner. The court system consisted of six District Courts, two High Courts with civil and criminal divisions, a Special Court, three Courts of Appeals and a Supreme Court which was sometimes referred to as 'Special Bench'.[308] The District Courts (criminal and civil) had primary jurisdiction over minor criminal and civil cases. The High Courts had jurisdiction over most serious crimes which were passable of capital punishment such as treason, murder, rape and arson.

According to the chief of the judicial division of the Civil Administration of the LTTE at that time, the establishment of the LTTE's own court system pursued various aims and objectives[309] but, primarily, the LTTE aimed at maintaining and upholding law and order in the areas under their control. In addition to that, the convention of the LTTE's own judicial system also followed the notion of 'serving the poor'. Further, the court system also

---

304 Zachariah C. Mampilly, Rebel Rulers Insurgent Governance and Civilian Life during War 116 f.; Joanne Richards, An Institutional History of the Liberation Tigers of Tamil Eelam (LTTE), Working Paper (Graduate Institute of International and Development Studies - Centre on Conflict, Development and Peacebuilding, November 2014) 45.

305 Zachariah C. Mampilly, Rebel Rulers Insurgent Governance and Civilian Life during War.

306 Sandesh Sivakumaran, The Law of Non-International Armed Conflict 553.

307 Zachariah C. Mampilly, Rebel Rulers Insurgent Governance and Civilian Life during War 117.

308 René Provost, Rebel Courts: The Administration of Justice by Armed Insurgents 233; Kristian Stokke, 'Building the Tamil Eelam State: Emerging State Institutions and Forms of Governance in LTTE-Controlled Areas in Sri Lanka' 1027.

309 See Chris Kamalendran, 'The inside story of „Eelam Courts"' Sunday Times (Sri Lanka) (8 December 2002) <https://sundaytimes.lk/021208/news/courts.html> accessed 24 June 2021.

served the aim to run a smooth administration of the areas in the North and East and to strengthen the rule of law which has been subverted by the GoSL according to the LTTE's perception.[310]

Hence, the LTTE's participation in administering justice focused on regulating everyday life in the areas under their control by providing ordinary dispute resolution through an advanced and structured court system and by applying its own written set of law. This reflects the group's primary aim of building legitimacy vis-à-vis Sri Lankan Tamils.

d. Kurdish judiciary in Northeast Syria

The final example relates to Kurdish judicial procedures and mechanisms established by the self-proclaimed regime in Northeast Syria, affiliated with the Democratic Union Party/Partiya Yekîtiya Dîmokratik (**PYD**) and its corresponding military wing, the People's Protection Unit/Yekîneyên Parastina Gel (**YPG**) which formed during the multi-party armed conflict in Syria and its neighboring countries since 2011.

aa. Background of the conflict

Even though hostilities decreased in the las couple years, the armed conflict in and near Syria is still ongoing with continuously deteriorating economic and social conditions.

The Syrian armed conflict is difficult to decipher, and its nature not blatant. Its complexity is mostly owed to the involvement of many different actors in the armed conflict, ranging from the Syrian regime, an array of different armed insurgent groups – both domestic and foreign – to multiple third states, such as the United States, Turkey, Russia, or Iran.[311] Hence, the conflict is characterized by a series of simultaneously ongoing inter-surgent conflicts and an internationalized evolvement due to the participation of many external players.

---

310 Illayathamby Pararajasingham, 'Thamil Eelam - a de facto State: Tamil Eelam Legal System'.

311 Eyal Zisser, 'Syria - from the six day war to the Syrian civil war' (2017) 44 British Journal of Middle Eastern Studies 545-558, 555; Matthew Krause, 'Northeastern Syria: Complex Criminal Law in a Complicated Battlespace' (Just Security, 28 October 2019) <https://www.justsecurity.org/66725/northeastern-syria-complex-criminal-law-in-a-complicated-battlespace/> accessed 20 October 2021.

Led by ethno-religious representation and a sectarian narrative, the Syrian armed conflict started in 2011 and still has not ceased.[312] The religious and ethnic demography of the country at the outburst of the conflict pictured as follows: Most of the population is (Sunni) Arab with the majority being Muslims and some of them being Christians or of a different gnostic religious group. Next are the Kurds, followed by other minority groups such as Armenians, Assyrians, or Chechens.[313]

Single violent outbursts have heralded the so-called 'Arab spring' in March 2011 which marked the start of a systematic and organized armed opposition against the *al-Assad* regime, culminating in a brutal armed conflict throughout the whole territory of Syria and parts of neighboring countries, such as Turkey and Iraq. Under the presidency of *Bashar al-Assad*, Syria experienced an economic and social crisis fueled by demographic trends[314] which led to discontent among the country's population.[315] Economic reforms under *Bashar al-Assad* led to 'crony capitalism' and a decrease in economic growth.[316] At the same time, Syria experienced an increase in its population with considerably more young than elder people.[317] The demographic development and an imbalance in age distribution, combined with a decrease in youth employment, led to an increasing rate of unemployment resulting in social unrest.[318] The already weak economic state worsened when Syria experienced environmental hardship related

312 Most recently, since the attack of Hamas against Israel on October 7, 2023, and the subsequent outbreak of violence, Syria is involved in cross-border shelling against Israel and its Israel Defence Forces (IDF) due to Palestinian factions and Lebanese Hezbollah filiates in Syria. Additionally, Syria has been part of the so-called 'axis of resistance' for decades and in a state of war against Israel since 1948. See ACLED, 'Middle East Regional Overview: The Regional Implications of the Israel-Gaza Conflict' (Armed Conflict Location & Event Data Project (ACLED) 2023) <https://acleddata.com/2023/11/08/regional-overview-middle-east-october-2023-the-regional-implications-of-the-israel-gaza-conflict/> accessed 25 November 2023.

313 Lucas Swinnen, The Syrian Civil War: A Never-Ending Story?, IFF Working Paper Online (Institute of Federalism, March 2023) 10 f.

314 See Melani Cammett et al., A Political Economy of the Middle East (4th edn, Routledge 2018) 125 f.

315 See Lucas Swinnen, The Syrian Civil War: A Never-Ending Story?, IFF Working Paper Online (Institute of Federalism, March 2023).

316 Ibid 5.

317 Ibid 7 f. See also The World Bank Data on the Syrian Arab Republic https://data.worldbank.org/country/syrian-arab-republic accessed 14 November 2023.

318 See presentation by Farzaneh Roudi of the Population Reference Bureau, 'Youth Population & Unemployment in the Middle East &North Africa', July 2011 <https://www.un.org/development/desa/pd/sites/www.un.org.development.desa.pd/files

to a severe era of drought which resulted in water and food shortage, destruction of crops and a large migration from rural to urban areas, which in turn caused an unexpected need for employment. What started in rural areas, soon travelled throughout the whole country, and resulted in nation-wide discontent and upset with the *al-Assad* regime, culminating in violent and non-violent protests. The state's armed forces vigorously and violently repressed these protests which ultimately led to the outburst of protracted and organized armed violence within the country.[319] Multiple armed opposition groups have emerged and organized themselves. Amongst them, the Free Syrian Army (**FSA**), later Syrian National Army (**SNA**) – backed by Turkish armed forces and aiming at overthrowing the incumbent regime – the Syrian Democratic forces (**SDF**) and the YPG which both represent the Kurdish population within Syria, and which aim at autonomy within a federal state of Syria. In addition, radical Islamist insurgent groups emerged, including the infamous Jabhat al-Nusra li-Ahl al-Shām (**Al-Nusra**) and the Islamic State of Iraq and the Levant (**ISIL**). The emergence of multiple NSAGs with diverging political agendas throughout the conflict mirrors the ethno-religious composition of the country. Many of the armed groups followed an Islamic-based approach to governance, with some being more radical than others.[320] Whereas ISIS and al-Nusra, for example, follow a radical interpretation of Islamic texts, the PYD and other Kurdish parties in Syria follow a secular approach.

Despite their unified opposition to the regime, the involved insurgent groups differ greatly in their ideological and political agendas which caused an array of intra-insurgent conflicts for territorial and ideological dominance throughout the last decade.[321]

Kurdish politics in Syria started in 2003, with the formation of the PYD which started to advocate for the recognition of Kurdish rights. The PYD's social- and ideological agenda was modelled on Kurdish political movements in Syria of the early 20th century such as the Partiya Karkerên

---

/unpd_egm_072011_roudi_youth_population_and_employment.pdf> accessed 14 November 2023.

319 See Regine Schwab, 'Insurgent courts in civil wars: the three pathways of (trans)formation in today's Syria (2012-2017)' 805.

320 Eyal Zisser, 'Syria - from the six day war to the Syrian civil war' 355.

321 Syed Huzaifah Bin Othman Alkaff and Nurulhuda Binte Yussof, 'An Overview of the Syrian Conflict' (2016) 8 Counter Terrorist Trends and Analyses 8-11; Olivier Walther and Patrick Steen Pedersen, 'Rebel fragmentation in Syria's civil war' (2020) 31 Small Wars & Insurgencies 445-474.

Kurdistaen (**PKK**)[322], although today the PYD denies any affiliation with the PKK.[323] Until the 'Arab spring' in 2011, the PYD was the largest Kurdish opposition party in Syria. This role evolved with the outburst of the armed conflict, and the PYD together with its military counterpart, the YPG, gradually became the strongest NSAG.

In 2013, Kurdish political movement on and near Syrian soil flourished, and the YPG established stable control in the northern-east parts of Syria. The YPG/PYD managed to establish territorial and social control in a sustainable manner due to their important role in the fight against radical Islamist groups. Together with other allied groups, the YPG/PYD formed the so-called 'transitional autonomous government in the area of West Kurdistan', also referred to as 'Rojava' which geographically relates to Northeast Syria.[324] The term 'Rojava' is rooted in Kurdish nationalism and literally means 'western'. The usage of this term implies a notion of cross-border Kurdish identity.[325]

Representing the Kurdish population in Syria, the PYD/YPG is striving for a recognized autonomous Kurdish region within a federal state of Syria. The group's political agenda relates to federalism and democratic autonomy.[326]

---

322 Filiz Katman and Dilshad Muhammad, 'Tracing Kurdish Politics in Syria and its Prospects' in Jasemine K. Gani and Raymond Hinnebusch (eds), Actors and Dynamics in the Syrian Conflict's Middle Phase - Between Contentious Politics, Militarization and Regime Resilience (1st edn, Routledge 2022) 236-251, 241-243; René Provost, Rebel Courts: The Administration of Justice by Armed Insurgents 367.

323 Aldar Khalil, 'Syrian Kurds Are Not the PKK' Foreign Policy (15 May 2017) <https://foreignpolicy.com/2017/05/15/syrias-kurds-are-not-the-pkk-erdogan-pyd-ypg/> accessed 18 November 2023.

324 The three cantons which comprise 'Rojava' are Afrin, Ain-al-Arab (Kobani), and Jazira.

325 Thomas McGee, ''Rojava': Evolving Public Discourse of Kurdish Identity and Governance in Syria' (2022) 15 Middle East Journal of Culture and Communication 385-403.

326 Filiz Katman and Dilshad Muhammad, 'Tracing Kurdish Politics in Syria and its Prospects' in Jasemine K. Gani and Raymond Hinnebusch (eds), Actors and Dynamics in the Syrian Conflict's Middle Phase - Between Contentious Politics, Militarization and Regime Resilience 246; Eva Savelsberg, 'The Kurdish PYD and the Syrian Civil War' in Michael Gunter (ed), Routledge Handbook on the Kurds (1st edn, Routledge 2018) 357-365, 359; Lucas Swinnen, The Syrian Civil War: A Never-Ending Story?, IFF Working Paper Online (Institute of Federalism, March 2023) 16.

By the middle of 2016, the *de facto* governmental landscape in Syria was fragmented with different insurgent groups holding territorial control over different parts of the country. Notwithstanding interim territorial setbacks by Turkish-led military operations, the YPG is still in stable control of parts in Northeast Syria.[327]

Today, after more than ten years of armed violence, the Syrian armed conflict has cooled down with most of the insurgent groups having been defeated and the al-Assad regime having regained power over most of the country's territory.[328] The Kurds, despite having attained a certain level of autonomy in Northeast Syria are still facing military attacks from the Turkish army.[329]

bb. The PYD/YPG's judicial system

As the Syrian armed conflict is characterized by inter-insurgent contestation for territorial control and power in and near the territory of Syria, many NSAGs invested in the establishment of parallel governance structures, including the administration of justice through own courts. Kurdish entities, such as the PYD/YPG, did so as well.[330]

As stated above, the YPG has been generally considered an important ally of third states as well as of the Syrian government in the fight against radical Islamist NSAGs. Especially, during and after the 'Battle of Kobani' in late 2014 and early 2015, the PYD enjoyed international support by

---

327 Mikael Ekman and William D. Meyer, Rule of Law Assessment Report: Syria 2021 (International Legal Assistance Consortium, 2021) 112 f.

328 See the latest map of Armed Conflict Location & Event Data Project (ACLED) mapping key developments in the armed conflict in Syria regarding the second and third quarter of 2022: Muaz Al-Abdullah, 'The State of Syria: Q2 2022 - Q3 2022' (Armed Conflict Location & Event Data Project (ACLED), 2022) <https://acleddata.com/2022/12/01/the-state-of-syria-q2-2022-q3-2022/> accessed 16 November 2023.

329 See ACLED, 'Conflict Watchlist 2023 - Kurdish Regions: High Risk of Violent Escalation and Domestic Turmoil' (Armed Conflict Location & Event Data Project (ACLED), 2023) <https://acleddata.com/conflict-watchlist-2023/kurdish-regions/> accessed 14 November 2023. Turkey views the YPG as an extension of the PKK.

330 This section focuses on the *de facto* provision of judicial mechanisms by PYD/YPG albeit criticism regarding gross violations of human rights committed by the group's institutions and appointed personnel. See AI, Amnesty International Report 2022/23: The state of the world's human rights (Amnesty International, 27 March 2023), 350 ff. and HRW, Under Kurdish Rule - Absuses in PYD-run Enclaves of Syria, Report (Human Rights Watch, 18 June 2014).

third states such as the United States as a recognized anti-ISIS ally.[331] This international support and acceptance contributed to consolidated *de facto* control of the PYD in Northeast Syria and was utilized by the group to explain and justify their legitimization and recognition.[332] What followed was the steady and advanced provision of parallel structures in 'Rojava' culminating in a *de facto* administration. Striving for an autonomous region within a federal Syria, the 'Rojavan' *de facto* administration aims at building legitimacy towards the local population as well as towards third states and the international community.

From 2014 onwards, the *de facto* administration in 'Rojava' advanced little by little. This resulted in the establishment of local councils, ministries, courts as well as a police force responsible for law enforcement and internal security.

As of today, the self-proclaimed regime comprises a so-called General Council competent for drafting and issuing laws, an Executive Council regulating the economic development, and a Social Justice Council organizing the judicial institutions.[333] The governance system allegedly follows a bottom-up, democratic process and provides for education, employment, health care and security.[334]

In 2014, the *de facto* administration in 'Rojava' adopted a 'Social Contract'[335] which functioned as their provisional constitution, proposing a system of democracy, self-governance, minority rights and secularism for the self-proclaimed autonomous cantons of 'Rojava'. It is considered a set of theoretical and practical foundations, laws, and organizational rules to determine the relationship between the administration and the people. Based on the 'Social Contract', several judicial and administrative institutions have been established. In 2016, the 'Social Contract' was revised and, amongst other amendments, replaced the name of 'Rojava' with the 'Demo-

331 Thomas McGee, ''Rojava': Evolving Public Discourse of Kurdish Identity and Governance in Syria' 394.

332 René Provost, Rebel Courts: The Administration of Justice by Armed Insurgents 365.

333 See the official website of AANES <https://aanesgov.org/?page_id=344> accessed 25 November 2023.

334 Rana Khalaf, Governing Rojava - Layers of Legitimacy in Syria, Research Paper (Chatham House, The Royal Institute of International Affairs, December 2016) 17.

335 An online version can be found on the website of the Rojava Information Center (RiC): <https://rojavainformationcenter.org/storage/2021/07/2014-Social-Contract-of-the-Autonomous-Regions-of-Afrin-Jazira-and-Kobane-1.pdf> accessed 21 November 2023.

cratic Federation of Northern Syria' (**DFNS**).[336] Since 2018, the official name of the self-proclaimed regime is the 'Autonomous Administration of Northeast Syria' (**AANES**) and the 'Social Contract' has been complemented by the 'Charter of the Social Justice System of the Autonomous Administration of North and East Syria'.[337] The latest modification of the 'Social Contract' – sometimes also referred to as 'Charter' – took place in 2023.[338]

The AANES' justice system comprises multiple institutions, resulting in a complex organizational structure. It follows the principle of 'social justice', according to which problems shall be resolved by means of dialogue, negotiation, and mutual consent.[339] There are Peace and Consensus Committees, People's Courts – also called Social Justice Courts – with separate divisions for prosecution, trial, and cassation stage, a Supreme Constitutional Court and Judicial Councils. Peace and Consensus Committees are competent for mediating minor disputes in both civil and criminal law matters by means of reconciliation.[340] In contrast, the Social Justice Courts are dedicated to serious matters which cannot be mediated at the Peace and Consensus Committees, comprising a trial and appeal level. There also exists a Court of Cassation in Qamishli.[341] At the People's Courts, the judges appointed must be trained in law.[342] The Supreme Constitutional Court, then, oversees the conformity of decisions rendered by the People's courts with the 'Social Contract'.

There is a prevailing confusion as regards the applicable law before courts in the AANES. Judges at the People's Courts primarily apply Syri-

336 An online version of the 2016 'Social Contract' can be found on the website of RiC: <https://rojavainformationcenter.org/storage/2021/07/2016-Social-Contract-of-the-Democratic-Federation-of-Northern-Syria.pdf> accessed 21 November 2023; see also Mikael Ekman and William D. Meyer, Rule of Law Assessment Report: Syria 2021 (International Legal Assistance Consortium, 2021), 115.

337 See ibid 116.

338 Zana Al-Ali, 'New Social Contract establishes one region in northeast Syria' North press agency (Raqqa 28 August 2023) accessed 22 November 2023.

339 See Article 68 (1) of the 2016 'Social Contract'.

340 Michael Knapp, Anja Flach and Ercan Aybôga (eds), Revoultion in Rojava: Democratic Autonomy and Women's Liberation in Syrian Kurdistan (1st edn, Pluto Press 2016) 164 f.; Mikael Ekman and William D. Meyer, Rule of Law Assessment Report: Syria 2021 (International Legal Assistance Consortium, 2021), 131.

341 René Provost, Rebel Courts: The Administration of Justice by Armed Insurgents 369.

342 Michael Knapp, Anja Flach and Ercan Aybôga (eds), Revoultion in Rojava: Democratic Autonomy and Women's Liberation in Syrian Kurdistan 166.

an national law whenever it does not contradict the law adopted by the AANES. Sometimes, recourse is held to legal systems of third states, such as the United Kingdom, Switzerland or France. Additionally, 'local customs' also apply.[343] There is little publicly available information regarding the prosecuted crimes before AANES courts but, allegedly, they range from minor ordinary crimes, such as theft, to more serious crimes, such as drug trafficking or murder.

The 'Social Contract' dedicates many articles to fundamental rights and freedoms akin to the Universal Declaration of Human Rights of 1948[344] and the International Covenant on Civil and Political Rights[345] (**ICCPR**). Allegedly, the 'Social Contract' proclaims the independence and impartiality of the judiciary[346] and other fundamental judicial guarantees, such as, the presumption of innocence or the right to a defence.[347] However, international organizations like Amnesty International and Human Rights Watch, have criticized the AANES' judicial procedures for violating fundamental and due process guarantees, such as the prohibition of arbitrary detention, ill-treatment during detention or the right to adequate and expedite information about the charges and adequate means of defence.[348] Lawyers operating at the People's Courts have also contested the AANES' claim to provide independent and impartial justice by stating that most courts are staffed with PYD-appointed personnel, serving the group's interests.[349] The AANES, in turn, claims that international organizations have confirmed the

---

343 See Mikael Ekman and William D. Meyer, Rule of Law Assessment Report: Syria 2021 (International Legal Assistance Consortium, 2021) 117-119; HRW, Under Kurdish Rule - Absuses in PYD-run Enclaves of Syria, Report (Human Rights Watch, 18 June 2014) 25.

344 United Nations General Assembly Resolution 217 A (III), Universal Declaration of Human Rights, 10 December 1948.

345 International Covenant on Civil and Political Rights, UN Treaty Series Vol. 999 No. 14668, 16 December 1966.

346 See Article 63 of the 2014 'Social Contract'.

347 See Articles 64 and 66 of the 2014 'Social Contract'.

348 See AI, Amnesty International Report 2022/23: The state of the world's human rights (Amnesty International, 27 March 2023), 352 f. and HRW, Under Kurdish Rule - Absuses in PYD-run Enclaves of Syria, Report (Human Rights Watch, 18 June 2014) 19 ff.

349 HRW, Under Kurdish Rule - Absuses in PYD-run Enclaves of Syria, Report (Human Rights Watch, 18 June 2014) 14 f.

conformity of local prisons and detention camps with international human rights standards.[350]

The AANES also established a special anti-terrorism court, called 'People's Defence Court'.[351] There, they focus on holding foreign and Syrian ISIS fighters accountable for crimes committed during the armed conflict, albeit limited to crimes with 'terrorist' characteristics based on the Anti-Terrorism Law adopted by the AANES in 2014 and 'in accordance with international laws related to terrorism'[352].[353] The AANES claims to provide 'public, fair and transparent trials' at the People's Defence Court. The judicial bench comprises both male and female judges equally.[354] In the aim of trying foreign ISIS fighter, the AANES not only addressed third states to repatriate and try former ISIS fighters, they also called for assistance by the international community and proposed the establishment of an international tribunal in Northeast Syria to specifically address international crimes committed by former ISIS fighters.[355] By participating in the adjudication of international crimes, the AANES seeks to build legitimacy towards the international community and to earn recognition by third states.

Overall, the Kurdish parallel justice system in Northeast Syria offers a contemporary example of parallel insurgent justice during armed conflict. Even though the AANES claims to adhere to international fair trial guarantees and to provide independent, impartial and expedite justice to the population living in 'Rojava', international organizations have documented otherwise. Amnesty International and Human Rights Watch, for example, have reported severe shortcomings of the local insurgent judiciary, especially regarding the independence of the judicial bodies from the political and military wing and the provision of fundamental judicial guarantees. In the

350 RIC, Bringing ISIS to justice - Towards an international tribunal in North East Syria (Rojava Information Center, 14 March 2019) 12.

351 Mikael Ekman and William D. Meyer, Rule of Law Assessment Report: Syria 2021 (International Legal Assistance Consortium, 2021) 143 ff.

352 See official statement of the AANES on their website: <https://aanesgov.org/?p=4567> accessed 22 November 2023.

353 Mikael Ekman and William D. Meyer, Rule of Law Assessment Report: Syria 2021 (International Legal Assistance Consortium, 2021) 144.

354 Jane Arraf, ‚Revenge Is For The Weak': Kurdish Courts In Northeastern Syria Take On ISIS Cases' NPR (20 May 2019) <https://www.npr.org/2019/05/29/727511632/revenge-is-for-the-weak-kurdish-courts-in-northeastern-syria-take-on-isis-cases> accessed 20 October 2021.

355 See RIC, Bringing ISIS to justice - Towards an international tribunal in North East Syria (Rojava Information Center, 14 March 2019) 17 ff. and 35 ff.

first place, the judiciary of the AANES responds to everyday social needs, disputes, and criminality among the local population in rebel-held territory. Little is known regarding the prosecution and punishment of international crimes, such as war crimes or crimes against humanity. However, the AANES prosecutes conflict-related crimes with a focus on 'terrorist' elements in the so-called 'Peoples' Defence Court'.

e. Interim conclusion

The present case selection illustrated the heterogeneity of how NSAGs deploy judicial mechanisms, including differences in purposes and target populations.

The LTTE's judicial system is probably the most prominent example for a court system established by an insurgent group during armed conflict.[356] It is an example for a highly sophisticated and comprehensive court system which was well-structured with fully articulated written laws, a law school, and a working constitution.[357] The LTTE aimed at building legitimacy towards the civilian population by primarily adjudicating everyday disputes, such as land or financial disputes of the local population living in 'rebel'-held territory.[358] The LTTE did not aim at enforcing IHL or at administering international criminal justice through, *inter alia*, punishing international crimes.

The FMLN's investment in judicial mechanisms, in turn, was less elaborate and mainly aimed at demonstrating power and discipline vis-à-vis the group's own fighting cadre. Thus, the group's administration of justice focused on holding the group's own fighting members accountable for breaches of IHL.

The FARC's provision of justice is a sound example of an insurgent group which attempted at administering justice equally vis-à-vis its own fighting force as well as vis-à-vis the civilian population. The NSAG started its judicial activity with regulating military-related conduct by applying its own code of conduct and enforcing disciplinary measures. Throughout the conflict, the FARC also adopted its own set of law and conducted civil as

356 Sandesh Sivakumaran, 'Courts of Armed Opposition Groups: Fair Trials or Summary Justice?' 489-513.

357 Frank Ledwidge, Rebel Law - Insurgents, Courts and Justice in Modern Conflict 61.

358 Sandesh Sivakumaran, 'Courts of Armed Opposition Groups: Fair Trials or Summary Justice?' 494.

well as criminal trials in relation to punishable conduct committed by the civilian population. In sum, the FARC administered justice on an *ad hoc* basis, in response to the needs of the local population. Correspondingly, the group made use of preexisting state institutions and administered justice in parallel to continuing state institutions.

Finally, the Kurdish example in Syria demonstrates the evolution of a contemporary insurgent justice system. Until today, the armed conflict in and near Syria has not ceased – despite the transitional government convened by Mr. *Ahmed al-Sharaa*. The then PYD and now self-proclaimed administration of Northeast Syria, AANES, has established and sustained stable territorial control over parts in North and East Syria. Similar to the LTTE, Kurdish entities in Northeast Syria follow state-building aspirations as they seek an autonomous Kurdish region within a federal state of Syria. Hence, the judiciary of the AANES attempts at responding to everyday social needs, disputes, and criminality among the local population in rebel-held territory. Additionally, the Kurdish example demonstrates that insurgent groups may also invest in the establishment of parallel justice mechanism to claim acceptance and recognition from third states and the international community.

3. Conclusion

As shown by the above analysis of different examples, insurgent administration of justice during armed conflict has many facets. The provision of judicial mechanisms by NSAGs during armed conflict can range from *ad hoc* and loose mechanisms to advanced and well-structured institutions. Judicial mechanisms may be deployed in a coercive manner to demonstrate power and control or in a conciliatory manner to generate respect and support. The provision of judicial mechanisms can range from alternative justice mechanisms, such as mediation processes, truth commissions or commissions of inquiry, to traditional justice mechanisms, such as prosecutions and trials conducted in courts. Insurgent justice can be addressed towards different audiences: towards the civilian population, the group's own ranks or towards both groups. Insurgent justice can range from regulating everyday life in 'rebel' held territory to specifically regulating conduct relating to armed conflict. Accordingly, it can relate to ordinary dispute resolution, be it criminal or civil law, to addressing conduct specifically linked to armed hostilities.

NSAGs can apply written law and/or unwritten law, such as local customs. The applicable law can range from the group's own law to the law of the territorial state or of third states. The applicable law can also be IHL.

Besides the immediate effect of dispute resolution, the provision of justice by NSAGs can aim at different effects. A common objective is building legitimacy. NSAGs usually aspire to build legitimacy towards the civilian population, the group's own members, towards third states or towards the international community.

As much as there exists variation with regard to the concrete operation of insurgent justice during armed conflict, certain features are common to all NSAGs that engage in the administration of justice during armed conflict: Such groups are usually in (stable) control over territory, they usually hold (effective) control over the civilian population living on that territory, and they possess such a level of organization and structure as to enable them to engage in the provision of governance structures, including the administration of justice.

Chapter 3: Non-International Armed Conflicts and International Humanitarian Law

This chapter concentrates on defining Non-International Armed Conflicts and provides an overview of the applicable humanitarian law. It starts with elaborating on the different statutory definitions of NIACs according to Common Article 3, according to Additional Protocol II as well as according to the definitions which emerged through the jurisprudence of international criminal tribunals, namely, the ICTY and the ICC (Section 1). The chapter continues by mapping out the applicable humanitarian law in times of NIACs (Section 2). It does so by, firstly, sketching the historical evolution of IHL applicable to NIACs and, secondly, by outlining the applicable humanitarian treaty- and customary law as of today.

I. Defining Non-International Armed Conflicts: The Arena of NSAGs

NIACs are the military and political arena of NSAGs. The term 'NIAC' is also a legal term, determining the scope of applicable IHL norms. Like the term 'NSAG', it is defined in a negative fashion and termed as what it is *not*, namely, an International Armed Conflict (**IAC**).[359] This simplistic terminology is misleading. An armed conflict which is not international in character is not automatically non-international in the legal sense. As the present section will show, the designation of a NIAC is dependent upon certain prerequisites.

IHL does not define the term 'NIAC' or 'conflict not of an international character'.[360] However, international humanitarian treaty law clearly distinguishes between IACs on the one hand and NIACs on the other. With respect to the four Geneva Conventions of 1949 and its two Additional Protocols of 1977 – as the main sources of international humanitarian treaty law – this becomes clear from the explicit language in its pertinent

359 Being remindful of Philip Alston's 'not-a-cat' syndrome.

360 Eric David, 'Internal (Non-International) Armed Conflict' in Andrew Clapham and Paola Gaeta (eds), The Oxford Handbook of International Law in Armed Conflict (1st edn, Oxford University Press 2014) 353-364, 355.

provisions. According to Common Article 2 to all four Geneva Conventions of 1949 (**Common Article 2**), the Conventions 'shall apply to all cases of declared war or any other armed conflict which may arise between two or more of the High Contracting Parties even if the state of war is not recognized by one of them. The Convention shall also apply to all cases of partial or total occupation of the territory of a High Contracting Party, even if the said occupation meets with no armed resistance'. High Contracting Parties in the sense of Common Article 2 can only be states and their official governments.[361] Hence, Common Article 2 refers to IACs, fought between two or more states, and to occupation which qualifies as an IAC. Common Article 3 includes 'armed conflicts not of an international character occurring in the territory of one of the High Contracting Parties' into the Conventions' scope. Likewise, does Additional Protocol II stipulate additional humanitarian treaty law, exclusively applicable to 'armed conflicts [...] which take place in the territory of a High Contracting Party between its armed forces and dissident armed forces or other organized armed groups'[362].

Theis section assesses different statutory definitions of NIACs stipulated by Common Article 3, Additional Protocol II as well as by the Rome Statute of the ICC. It will also assess the *Tadić*-definition of NIACs developed by the International Criminal Tribunal for the former Yugoslavia (**ICTY**). Determining the nature of the conflict, international or non-international, is a fundamental preliminary step in specifying the applicable humanitarian law to NIACs which follows in Section 2.[363]

1. Definition according to Common Article 3 to all four Geneva Conventions of 1949

Common Article 3 was the first substantive provision in international law to explicitly address NIACs. The *chapeau* of Common Article 3 starts with the words:

---

361 See Art. 2 (1)(a) and Art. 3 Vienna Convention on the Law of Treaties, UN Treaty Series Vol. 1155 No. 18232, 27 January 1980. Hereafter, the Vienna Convention on the Law of Treaties (**VCLT**).

362 See Art. 1 (1) Additional Protocol II.

363 Jelena Pejić, 'Status of armed conflicts' in Elizabeth Wilmshurst and Susan Breau (eds), Perspectives on the ICRC Study on Customary International Humanitarian Law (1st edn, Cambridge University Press 2007) 77-100, 77 and 85.

> 'In the case of an armed conflict not of an international character occurring in the territory of one of the High Contracting Parties'. The provision, even when reading it in its full length, does not define an 'armed conflict not of an international character'.

Pursuant to Common Article 3, a NIAC is an armed conflict fought either between organized armed groups themselves or between an armed group and a state. However, the drafting history sheds light on what the drafters have envisaged with the chosen term 'armed conflict not of an international character'.

Common Article 3 came into existence during the Diplomatic Conference which was held in Geneva between April 21st and August 12th, 1949. The provision – as it stands now – has been the result of lengthy debates about whether and how to regulate internal strife through international law, a field of law considered to be apt to regulate inter-state conflicts only. 'Rebels' were considered criminals, and internal strife was considered to fall under the merit of domestic law. Albeit the general acceptance to regulate internal armed conflicts also through international law, there was a prevailing hesitance and fear amongst many state representatives as to how to regulate them. States were especially concerned about any encroachment on their sovereignty.

At the Diplomatic Conference, Draft Article 2 paragraph 4, which foresaw the inclusion of internal armed conflicts into the scope of the four Geneva Conventions of 1949, was subject of much debate and criticism. Draft Article 2 paragraph 4 has laid the foundation for Common Article 3 and read as follows:

> 'In all cases of armed conflict not of an international character which may occur in the territory of one or more of the High Contracting Parties, each of the adversaries shall be bound to implement the provisions of the present Convention. The Convention shall be applicable in these circumstances, whatever the legal status of the Parties to the conflict and without prejudice thereto.'[364]

The language of Draft Article 2 paragraph 4 raised concerns that it would cover all forms of insurrection, rebellion, anarchy, and plain brigandage

364 ICRC, Draft Revised or New Conventions for the Protection of War Victims (International Committee Red Cross, May 1948) 10 and 32.

wars.[365] There was reluctance and fear on behalf of states to confer any sort of belligerent status or even a certain degree of legal recognition to insurgent groups.[366] Many states feared that it would hamper their right to repression and that they would need to compromise their rights as states.[367] Other states, in turn, supported the inclusion of civil wars into the scope of the Geneva Conventions.[368]

This disagreement led to many amendments, suggesting to limit the scope of application of the Conventions to internal conflicts which exhibited features of real war. In other words, many delegates sought to render the application of the Conventions dependent on certain conditions.[369] Some of the introduced criteria which referred to the distinction between 'rebellion' and 'uprising'[370], to the 'organization' of a group or the '*de facto* authority of the insurgent group over persons within a determinate territory'[371], to the 'recognition of belligerency of the rebels by the lawful Government'[372] or even to the requirement that 'the dispute had been admitted to the agenda of the Security Council or the General Assembly of the United States as being a threat to international peace'[373].

The question of defining the phrase 'armed conflict not of an international character' remained throughout the Diplomatic Conference and has not been solved during the drafting process.

---

365 Jean S. Pictet, Commentary on the Geneva Convention (I) for the Amelioration of the Condition of the Wounded and Sick in Armed Forces in the Field (International Committe of the Red Cross 1952), Article 3, 43.

366 Ibid 44.

367 See, e.g., Delegate of France (Mr. Lamarle): Federal Political Department Bern, Final Record of the Diplomatic Conference of Geneva of 1949 Vol. II, 16 October 1978, Section B, 10; see also the Mexican Delegate (Mr. De Alba) who stressed that 'rights of the states shall not be placed above all humanitarian considerations' ibid, Vol. II, Section B 11.

368 See, for example, the Norwegian Delegate (Mr. Castberg) who considered civil war 'a form of conflict resembling international war, but taking place inside the territory of a State': ibid, Vol. II, Section B, 11.

369 See ibid, Vol. II, Section B 44; Jean S. Pictet, Commentary on the Geneva Convention (I) for the Amelioration of the Condition of the Wounded and Sick in Armed Forces in the Field, Article 3, 45.

370 Delegate of Monaco (Mr. De Geouffre De La Pradelle): Federal Political Department Bern, Final Record of the Diplomatic Conference of Geneva of 1949 Vol. II, Section B 45.

371 Delegate of the United States of America, Mr. Harrison: ibid, Section B 12.

372 This was proposed by, *inter alia*, the Delegate of Canada (Mr. Wershof), see ibid Section B 13.

373 See ibid Section B 121.

Thankfully, the ICRC commentary of 1952 provided helpful criteria in defining a NIAC as stipulated in Common Article 3 based on the aforementioned criteria suggested by delegations during the drafting process. These so-called convenient criteria read as follows:

> '(1) That the party in revolt against the *de jure* Government possesses an organized military force, an authority responsible for its acts, acting within a determinate territory and having the means of respecting and ensuring respect for the Convention.
> (2) That the legal Government is obliged to have recourse to the regular military forces against insurgents organized as military and in possession of a part of the national territory.
> (3)(a) That the de jure Government has recognized the insurgents as belligerents; or
> (b) that it has claimed for itself the rights of a belligerent; or
> (c) that it has accorded the insurgents recognition as belligerents for the purposes only of the present Convention; or
> (d) that the dispute has been admitted to the agenda of the Security Council or the General Assembly of the United Nations as being a threat to international peace, a breach of the peace, or an act of aggression.
> 4(a) That the insurgents have an organisation purporting to have the characteristics of a State.
> (b) That the insurgent civil authority exercises de facto authority over persons within a determinate territory.
> (c) That the armed forces act under the direction of the organized civil authority and are prepared to observe the ordinary laws of war.
> (d) That the insurgent civil authority agrees to be bound by the provisions of the Convention.'[374]

The list was not intended to be obligatory but to stipulate guiding criteria for distinguishing a 'genuine armed conflict from a mere act of banditry or an unorganized and short-lived insurrection'.[375] The aim was to hold the scope of application of Common Article 3 as wide as possible and to ensure minimum humanitarian standards while at the same time not limiting a

374 Jean S. Pictet, Commentary on the Geneva Convention (I) for the Amelioration of the Condition of the Wounded and Sick in Armed Forces in the Field 49 f.

375 Jean S. Pictet, Commentary on the Geneva Convention (IV) relative to the Protection of Civilian Persons in Time of War (International Committee of the Red Cross 1958) 35 f.

state's right to put down rebellion and not conferring any authority rights or status to the insurgent group.[376]

The failure to specify the term NIAC in the *chapeau* of Common Article 3 bears testimony to the overall concern amongst states of conferring any status to insurgents or treating them equal to states, the archetype subjects of international law.[377] This concern is reflected in paragraph (4) of Common Article 3.

2. Definition according to Additional Protocol II of 1977

Adopted in 1977, Additional Protocol II aimed at elaboration and completion of Common Article 3.[378] It offers greater precision and detail regarding its scope of application.

Additional Protocol II supplements Common Article 3 without modifying its existing conditions or application. Hence, Common Article 3 continues to apply in every NIAC regardless of whether Additional Protocol II applies as well.[379]

Art. 1 (1) Additional Protocol II defines a NIAC as an armed conflict

> 'which takes place in the territory of a High Contracting Party between its armed forces and dissident armed forces or other organized groups which, under responsible command, exercise such control over a part of its territory as to enable them to carry out sustained and concerted military operations ant to implement this Protocol.'

Compared to Common Article 3, Art. 1 (1) Additional Protocol II establishes a higher threshold, requiring a high level of organization on behalf of the armed group, introducing an element of territorial control and excluding conflicts which solely take place between armed groups *inter se* without the

---

376 Jean S. Pictet, Commentary on the Geneva Convention (I) for the Amelioration of the Condition of the Wounded and Sick in Armed Forces in the Field 50.

377 See, for example, Delegate of Italy (Mr. Maresca) who was concerned to give the impression that 'rebels already constitute a subject in international law' Federal Political Department Bern, Final Record of the Diplomatic Conference of Geneva of 1949 Vol. II, Section B.

378 Lindsay Moir, 'The Concept of Non-International Armed Conflict' in Andrew Clapham, Paola Gaeta and Marco Sassòli (eds), The 1949 Geneva Conventions - A Commentary (1st edn, Oxford University Press 2015) 391-414, 393.

379 Yoram Dienstein, Non-International Armed Conflicts in International Law (2nd edn, Cambridge University Press 2021) 182.

involvement of state armed forces as well as conflicts between an organized armed group and the state taking place outside the territory of the latter.[380] Hence, the scope of application is very limited and much narrower than the one of Common Article 3.[381] According to the ICRC's commentary on Additional Protocol II, the purpose was to retain Common Article 3's independent existence and relevance, while providing more precise rules.[382] This means that once a NIAC exists, Common Article 3 is always applicable, while Additional Protocol II only in those sub-cases where the organized armed group fulfills the specific requirements of Art. 1 (1) Additional Protocol II, namely, the requirements of 'responsible command', 'territorial control', and the 'ability to plan and carry out sustained and concerted military operations'.[383]

a. Responsible command

The criterion of 'responsible command' implies that the group must possess *such* [emphasis added] a degree of organization *which enables it to carry out sustained and concerted military operations* [emphasis added]. At first glance, the criterion of 'responsible command' appears to be similar to the second criterion of the *Tadić*-formula relating to the organization of

380 Dieter Fleck, 'The Law of Non-International Armed Conflict' in Dieter Fleck (ed), The Handbook of International Humanitarian Law 640; Jelena Pejić, 'Status of armed conflicts' in Elizabeth Wilmshurst and Susan Breau (eds), Perspectives on the ICRC Study on Customary International Humanitarian Law 88.

381 Lindsay Moir, 'The Concept of Non-International Armed Conflict' in Andrew Clapham, Paola Gaeta and Marco Sassòli (eds), The 1949 Geneva Conventions - A Commentary 393; Jelena Pejić, 'Status of armed conflicts' in Elizabeth Wilmshurst and Susan Breau (eds), Perspectives on the ICRC Study on Customary International Humanitarian Law 88.

382 ICRC, Commentary of 1987 Protocol Additional to the Geneva Conventions of 12 August 1949, and relating to the Protection of Victims of Non-International Armed Conflicts (Protocol II), 8 June 1977 (International Committee of the Red Cross 1987) para 4454; Lindsay Moir, 'The Concept of Non-International Armed Conflict' in Andrew Clapham, Paola Gaeta and Marco Sassòli (eds), The 1949 Geneva Conventions - A Commentary 394.

383 ICTR, Prosecutor v Jean-Paul Akayesu, Trial Judgment, 2 September 1998, Case No. ICTR-96-4-T para 607; ECtHR, Korbely v Hungary, Judgment, 19 September 2008, Application No. 9174/02 para 87; Lindsay Moir, 'The Concept of Non-International Armed Conflict' in Andrew Clapham, Paola Gaeta and Marco Sassòli (eds), The 1949 Geneva Conventions - A Commentary 394.

the group to engage in 'protracted violence'.[384] The ICRC Commentary does not provide any guidance or insights in terms of how the 'responsible command'-criterion stipulated in Art. 1 (1) Additional Protocol II differs from the 'organization of the parties'-criterion established by the ICTY in the *Tadić* case.

However, since Additional Protocol II imposes a higher threshold than Common Article 3, it is reasonable to interpret the 'responsible command'-criterion pursuant to Art. 1 (1) Additional Protocol II restrictively, thus, demanding a higher level of command structure and organization than is required pursuant to the corresponding *Tadić*-criterion in relation to Common Article 3.

b. Territorial control

According to Art. 1 (1) Additional Protocol II, the organized armed group must exercise 'such control over a part of its [the High Contracting Party's] territory as to enable them to carry out sustained and concerted military operations and to implement this Protocol'. 'Territorial control' is an explicit requirement in Art. 1 (1) Additional Protocol II. As stated above, territorial control is not required for the existence of a NIAC under the scope of Common Article 3. At the Diplomatic Conference of 1974-1977, the requirement of 'territorial control' was criticized for being too narrow and not matching the modern, particularly guerrilla warfare which often is characterized by a high mobility where territorial control continuously changes hands, and levels and areas of control sometimes shift overnight.[385] Many delegations criticized this requirement for excluding then from the ambit of Additional Protocol II many, if not most of contemporary types of internal armed conflict.[386]

The size of the territory under control and the level of control are not explicitly mentioned in Art. 1 (1) Additional Protocol II. Proposals made during the Diplomatic Conference of 1974-1977 to include more narrow

384 See ICTY, Prosecutor v Dusko Tadić aka „Dule", Decision on the Defence Motion for Interlocutory Appeal on Jurisdiction para 70.

385 Federal Political Department Bern, Official Records of the Diplomatic Conference on the Reaffirmation and Development of International Humanitarian Law Applicable in Armed Conflicts 1974-1977, 2 February 1979, Vol VIII, CDDH/I/SR. 24 para 32.

386 Ibid para 32.

yardsticks, such as a 'substantial part of the territory' or a 'non-negligible part of the territory' were rejected.[387] However, the word 'such' in Art. 1 (1) Additional Protocol II reasonably suggests that the size of territory and level of control must be sufficient as to enable the group to satisfy the other requirements of planning and carrying out 'sustained and concerted military operations' and to 'implement this Protocol'. The ICRC Commentary on Additional Protocol II recognizes that territorial control can rapidly change over the course of an armed conflict and suggests an assessment of territorial control in relation to the level of control exerted by the opposing party to the conflict.[388]

In order to meet the threshold of Additional Protocol II, it suffices if the organized armed group established control over territory at some point during the conflict. Most NIACs are characterized by rapid movement, fluctuations regarding the intensity and geographical reach of violence and changes regarding the level and reach of territorial control. Hence, there may be situations which at any given time satisfied the threshold of Art. 1 (1) Additional Protocol II and its requirement of 'territorial control' but later slide back to a NIAC covered only by the lower threshold of Common Article 3 because the respective armed group loses control over territory.[389]

c. Sustained and concerted military operations

Art. 1 (1) Additional Protocol II further stipulates that the organized armed group must be capable of carrying out 'sustained and concerted military operations'. In fact, it often is these sustained and concerted military operations which result in territorial control of the group. Hence, there is a close correlation between these two criteria.

The word 'sustained' means that the military operations must be conducted in a continuous and persistent manner. However, the ICTY held

387 ICRC, Commentary of 1987 Protocol Additional to the Geneva Conventions of 12 August 1949, and relating to the Protection of Victims of Non-International Armed Conflicts (Protocol II), 8 June 1977 para 4465; see also Yoram Dienstein, Non-International Armed Conflicts in International Law 63.

388 ICRC, Commentary of 1987 Protocol Additional to the Geneva Conventions of 12 August 1949, and relating to the Protection of Victims of Non-International Armed Conflicts (Protocol II), 8 June 1977 para 4467.

389 Yoram Dienstein, Non-International Armed Conflicts in International Law 63.

that occasional intervals of several days in the actual fighting are common and part of a conflict's dynamic and, therefore, cannot be ruled out.[390]

The term 'concerted' means that the military operations must be carried out in agreement or according to a commonly agreed upon plan.[391]

It appears unlikely that a NIAC will fulfill the criteria of 'territorial control' and 'sustained and concerted military operations' from the very beginning of the conflict. Rather will most NSAGs fulfill these criteria over the course of the conflict.

d. Capacity to implement the Protocol

The preceding criteria of 'responsible command', 'territorial control' and the 'ability to carry out sustained and concerted military operations' determine the last and ultimate criterion: the group must be able to implement the Protocol. A group which depicts a command structure more likely is well equipped to carry out sustained and concerted military operations which in turn will result in control over some territory which ultimately enables the group to implement the Protocol and adhere to its obligations.

In sum, Art. 1 (1) Additional Protocol II list a chain of mutually dependent criteria for the existence of a NIAC.

e. Not internal disturbances and tensions

Finally, Art. 1 (2) Additional Protocol II stipulates that the Protocol does not apply to 'situations of internal disturbances and tensions, such as riots, isolated and sporadic acts of violence and other acts of a similar nature'.

According to the ICRC, 'internal disturbances and tensions' are situations which do not amount to a NIAC as such but which amount to confrontations within the country which involve armed violence of a certain seriousness and duration.[392]

---

390 ICTY, Prosecutor v Fatmir Limaj et al., Trial Judgement, 30 November 2005, Case No. IT-03-66-T para 168; Yoram Dienstein, Non-International Armed Conflicts in International Law 64.

391 See ICRC, Commentary of 1987 Protocol Additional to the Geneva Conventions of 12 August 1949, and relating to the Protection of Victims of Non-International Armed Conflicts (Protocol II), 8 June 1977 para 4469.

392 Ibid paras 4471 ff.

Violence can take different forms, from being spontaneous to more systematic acts of armed struggle between organized armed groups and the authorities in power.[393]

'Internal disturbances and tensions' include situations, such as demonstrations without a concerted plan from the outset, sporadic and isolated acts of violence or other acts of similar nature such as large scale arrests of people for their activities and opinions.[394]

The Inter-American Commission on Human Rights (**IACHR**), for example, held that internal disturbances include 'large scale violent demonstrations, students throwing stones at the police, bandits holding persons hostage for ransom, or the assassination of government officials for political reasons.'[395] In theory this might be a definable category but in practice the delineation of 'mere' 'internal disturbances and tensions' and proper 'NIACs' proves difficult.

The relationship between Common Article 3 and Additional Protocol II is set out in Art. 1 (1) Additional Protocol II according to which Additional Protocol II develops and supplements Common Article 3 without modifying its existing conditions or application.[396] Since Common Article 3 amounts to customary IHL in its entirety, it remains appliable in NIACs which do not reach the threshold of Additional Protocol II.[397] Vice versa, in NIACs which do satisfy the higher threshold of Art. 1 (1) Additional Protocol II, Common Article 3 continues to be applicable alongside the more specified regulations of Additional Protocol II.

3. Definition according to the Tadić-formula of the ICTY

The ICTY played an important role in defining the term 'NIAC' pursuant to Common Article 3. In doing so, the tribunal orientated itself towards the

---

393 Ibid para 4475.

394 Ibid paras 4474-4476.

395 Inter-American Commission on Human Rights, Juan Carlos Abella v Argentina, 18 November 1997, Case No. 11.137 OEA/Ser.L/V/II.98 doc. 6 rev. para 154.

396 Federal Political Department Bern, Official Records of the Diplomatic Conference on the Reaffirmation and Development of International Humanitarian Law Applicable in Armed Conflicts 1974-1977, Vol. VIII, CDDH/I./SR. 22, 201.

397 ICTY, Prosecutor v Dusko Tadić, Appeals Judgement, 15 July 1999, Case No. IT-94-1-A paras 23 and 70; ICTR, Prosecutor v Jean-Paul Akayesu, Trial Judgment para 608; Yoram Dienstein, Non-International Armed Conflicts in International Law 181.

text and drafting history of Common Article 3. In its *Tadić* jurisprudence, the ICTY developed a detailed definition of 'armed conflict' in general, and of 'non-international' in particular. Accordingly, an armed conflict exists whenever there is 'any resort to armed force between states or protracted armed violence between a governmental authority and organized armed groups or between such groups within a state'[398].

The Trial Chamber in the *Tadić* case further developed this definition and established two criteria to determine the existence of 'protracted armed violence' in internal armed conflicts: (i) the intensity of the conflict and (ii) the organization of the parties to the conflict.[399]

It found that these two criteria are useful for 'distinguishing an armed conflict from banditry, unorganized and short-lived insurrections, or terrorist activities, which are not subject to international humanitarian law'[400]. It also referred to the 'convenient criteria' set out in *Pictet's* commentary on Common Article 3, noting that they serve as relevant factors in determining 'protracted violence' although they do not form part of Common Article 3's final text.[401]

Turning to the first criterion, the violence must reach a certain level of intensity to be considered 'protracted violence'.[402] Criteria which have been used by the ICTY jurisprudence to determine the intensity of the conflict are the gravity of hostilities and the duration of hostilities.[403] These criteria are used to exclude isolated and sporadic acts of violence.[404] Factors which have been taken into account regarding the gravity of hostilities include, *in-*

398 ICTY, Prosecutor v Dusko Tadić aka „Dule", Decision on the Defence Motion for Interlocutory Appeal on Jurisdiction para 70.

399 ICTY, Prosecutor v Dusko Tadić aka „Dule", Trial Judgment, 7 May 1997, Case No. IT-94-1-T para 562; see also ICTY, Prosecutor v Ljube Boškoski and Johan Tarculovski, Trial Chamber Judgment, 10 July 2008, Case No. IT-04-82-T para 175; ICTY, Prosecutor v Fatmir Limaj et al., Trial Judgement para 84.

400 ICTY, Prosecutor v Dusko Tadić aka „Dule", Trial Judgment para 562.

401 Ibid para 562; Jean S. Pictet, Commentary on the Geneva Convention (I) for the Amelioration of the Condition of the Wounded and Sick in Armed Forces in the Field 49 f.

402 ICTY, Prosecutor v Ljube Boškoski and Johan Tarculovski, Trial Chamber Judgment para 177.

403 Eric David, 'Internal (Non-International) Armed Conflict' in Andrew Clapham and Paola Gaeta (eds), The Oxford Handbook of International Law in Armed Conflict 356.

404 ICTY, Prosecutor v Dusko Tadić aka „Dule", Trial Judgment para 562.

ter alia, the seriousness of attacks, increase in armed clashes[405], the spread of clashes over territory and over a period of time[406], the distribution of weapons among both parties to the conflict[407], whether the conflict has attracted the attention of the UN Security Council[408], the number of civilians forced to flee from the combat zones[409], the type of weapons used[410] – in particular the use of heavy weaponry[411], the extent of destruction[412], the number of casualties caused by shelling or fighting[413], the quantity of troops and units deployed[414] or the occupation of territory[415]. The ICC, for example, has adopted this approach, reiterating that it is appropriate.[416]

---

405 Ibid para 565; ICTY, Prosecutor v Mucić et al., Trial Judgement, 16 November 1998, Case No. IT-96-21-T para 189; ICTY, Prosecutor v Ramush Haradinaj et al., Trial Judgement, 3 April 2008, Case No. IT-04-84-T paras 91 and 99.

406 ICTY, Prosecutor v Ljube Boškoski and Johan Tarculovski, Trial Chamber Judgment para 177; ICTY, Prosecutor v Dusko Tadić aka „Dule", Trial Judgment para 566; ICTY, Prosecutor v Dario Kordić and Mario Čerkez, Appeals Judgement, 17 December 2004, Case No. IT-95-14/2-A paras 340 f.; ICTY, Prosecutor v Fatmir Limaj et al., Trial Judgement paras 168 f.

407 ICTY, Prosecutor v Mucić et al., Trial Judgement para 188.

408 ICTY, Prosecutor v Ljube Boškoski and Johan Tarculovski, Trial Chamber Judgment para 177; ICTY, Prosecutor v Dusko Tadić aka „Dule", Trial Judgment para 567; ICTY, Prosecutor v Ramush Haradinaj et al., Trial Judgement para 49.

409 ICTY, Prosecutor v Dario Kordić and Mario Čerkez, Appeals Judgement para 340 where civilians have been evacuated; ICTY, Prosecutor v Dusko Tadić aka „Dule", Trial Judgment para 139 where civilians were expelled; ICTY, Prosecutor v Fatmir Limaj et al., Trial Judgement paras 139 and 167 where civilians were threatened or displaced.

410 ICTY, Prosecutor v Fatmir Limaj et al., Trial Judgement, para 166; ICTY, Prosecutor v Ramush Haradinaj et al., Trial Judgement para 49.

411 ICTY, Prosecutor v Dusko Tadić aka „Dule", Trial Judgment, para 565 speaking of 'artillery bombardment'; ICTY, Prosecutor v Fatmir Limaj et al., Trial Judgement para 166 referring to the use of 'landmines'.

412 ICTY, Prosecutor v Dusko Tadić aka „Dule", Trial Judgment para 565; ICTY, Prosecutor v Dario Kordić and Mario Čerkez, Appeals Judgement paras 337 ff.; ICTY, Prosecutor v Fatmir Limaj et al., Trial Judgement para 142.

413 ICTY, Prosecutor v Dusko Tadić aka „Dule", Trial Judgment para 565; ICTY, Prosecutor v Dario Kordić and Mario Čerkez, Appeals Judgement paras 339; ICTY, Prosecutor v Ramush Haradinaj et al., Trial Judgement para 49.

414 ICTY, Prosecutor v Ramush Haradinaj et al., Trial Judgement para 49.

415 ICTY, Prosecutor v Fatmir Limaj et al., Trial Judgement paras 146 and 158.

416 ICC, Prosecutor v Jean-Pierre Bemba Gombo, Decision Pursuant to Article 61(7)(a) and (b) of the Rome Statute on the Charges of the Prosecutor Against Jean-Pierre Bemba Gombo, 15 June 2009, Case No. ICC-01/05-01/08-424 para 244; ICC, Prosecutor v Thomas Lubanga Dyilo, Judgment pursuant to Article 74 of the Statute, 14 March 2012, Case No. ICC-01/04-01/06 para 538. For the ICC, the requirements set out in Art. 8 (2)(d) and (f) ICC Statute are also jurisdictional requirements because

Regarding the necessary duration of armed violence, the *Tadić*-formula offers no specific criteria. However, jurisprudence of the International Criminal Tribunal for Rwanda (**ICTR**) considers armed violence that extends over a few months as 'protracted violence'.[417]

The IACHR, for example, held that even a military engagement lasting only for 30 hours amounts to a NIAC under Common Article 3.[418] Hence, armed violence is considered protracted if it reaches a magnitude which resembles the confrontation and armed clashes carried out by state armed forces.[419]

The second criterion in determining 'protracted armed violence' relates to the organization of the parties to an armed conflict. According to ICTY jurisprudence, an armed group must reach a certain level of organization as to enable it to carry out the obligations set out in Common Article 3.[420] Whilst it is presumed that state armed forces always reach that threshold, for NSAGs a 'minimum degree of organization and discipline' is required such as to permit them to 'respect international humanitarian law'[421].

In the *Tadić* case, the ICTY held that 'an organized armed group [...] normally has a structure, a chain of command and a set of rules as well as the outward symbols of authority'[422], and that a member to the group 'conforms to the standards prevailing in the group and is subject to the

in the necessary level of intensity is not fulfilled, the alleged crimes do not fall within the Court's jurisdictional scope, see, ICC, Prosecutor v Jean-Pierre Bemba Gombo, Decision Pursuant to Article 61(7)(a) and (b) of the Rome Statute on the Charges of the Prosecutor Against Jean-Pierre Bemba Gombo para 225.

417 ICTR, Prosecutor v Jean-Paul Akayesu, Trial Judgment paras 619 ff.

418 Inter-American Commission on Human Rights, Juan Carlos Abella v Argentina paras 1 and 156; Lindsay Moir, 'The Concept of Non-International Armed Conflict' in Andrew Clapham, Paola Gaeta and Marco Sassòli (eds), The 1949 Geneva Conventions - A Commentary 411; Jelena Pejić, 'Status of armed conflicts' in Elizabeth Wilmshurst and Susan Breau (eds), Perspectives on the ICRC Study on Customary International Humanitarian Law 86.

419 Eric David, 'Internal (Non-International) Armed Conflict' in Andrew Clapham and Paola Gaeta (eds), The Oxford Handbook of International Law in Armed Conflict 357.

420 Lindsay Moir, 'The Concept of Non-International Armed Conflict' in Andrew Clapham, Paola Gaeta and Marco Sassòli (eds), The 1949 Geneva Conventions - A Commentary 405.

421 ICRC, Armed Conflicts Linked to Disintegration of State Structures - Preparatory document drafted by the International Committee of the Red Cross for the first periodical meeting on international humanitarian law (International Committee Red Cross, 19-23 January 1998) para 6.

422 ICTY, Prosecutor v Dusko Tadić, Appeals Judgement para 120.

authority of the head of the group'[423]. ICTY jurisprudence has developed five groups of indicative factors for assessing the required organization of an armed group:[424]

The first group of factors relates to the presence of a command structure, such as the establishment of a general staff or high command[425] which appoints and gives directions to commanders[426], disseminates internal regulations[427], organizes the weapons supply[428], authorizes military action[429]. This group of factors also includes the existence of internal regulations setting out the organization and structure of the armed groups[430], the existence of headquarters[431], or the existence of an official spokesperson.[432]

The second group refers to the group's ability to determine a unified military strategy, to conduct large scale military operations[433], and the capacity to control territory.[434]

The third group's factors relate to the group's level of logistic capacities, such as the ability to recruit new members[435], the providing of military training[436], the organized supply of military weapons[437], or the supply and use of uniforms.[438]

---

423 Ibid.

424 For a depiction of the five groups and its indicative factors, see ICTY, Prosecutor v Ljube Boškoski and Johan Tarculovski, Trial Chamber Judgment paras 199-204.

425 ICTY, Prosecutor v Fatmir Limaj et al., Trial Judgement para 94; ICTY, Prosecutor v Ramush Haradinaj et al., Trial Judgement paras 60 and 65-68.

426 ICTY, Prosecutor v Fatmir Limaj et al., Trial Judgement paras 96 and 98 f.

427 Ibid para 98.

428 Ibid para 100; ICTY, Prosecutor v Ramush Haradinaj et al., Trial Judgement para 60.

429 ICTY, Prosecutor v Fatmir Limaj et al., Trial Judgement para 46.

430 Ibid para 98.

431 Ibid para 104; ICTY, Prosecutor v Ramush Haradinaj et al., Trial Judgement para 65.

432 ICTY, Prosecutor v Fatmir Limaj et al., Trial Judgement paras 99 and 102.

433 Ibid para 129; ICTY, Prosecutor v. Mrkšić et al., Trial Judgement, 27 September 2007, Case No. IT-95-13/1-T paras 410 and 417; ICTY, Prosecutor v Ramush Haradinaj et al., Trial Judgement para 87.

434 ICTY, Prosecutor v Fatmir Limaj et al., Trial Judgement para 158; ICTY, Prosecutor v Ramush Haradinaj et al., Trial Judgement paras 70-75.

435 ICTY, Prosecutor v Fatmir Limaj et al., Trial Judgement para 118; ICTY, Prosecutor v Ramush Haradinaj et al., Trial Judgement paras 83-85.

436 ICTY, Prosecutor v Fatmir Limaj et al., Trial Judgement para 119; ICTY, Prosecutor v Ramush Haradinaj et al., Trial Judgement para 86.

437 ICTY, Prosecutor v Fatmir Limaj et al., Trial Judgement paras 121 f.; ICTY, Prosecutor v Ramush Haradinaj et al., Trial Judgement paras 76-82; ICTY, Prosecutor v. Slobodan Milošević, Decision on Motion for Judgement of Acquittal, 16 June 2004, Case No. IT-02-54-T paras 23 f.

The fourth group includes factors, such as the establishment of disciplinary rules and mechanisms[439], the provision of proper training[440], and the existence of internal regulations and whether these are effectively disseminated to members.[441]

The fifth group includes factors regarding the group's ability to speak with one voice[442], hence, its capacity to act on behalf of its members in political negotiations with representatives of international organizations and foreign countries[443] and its ability to negotiate and conclude agreements such as cease fires[444].

As demonstrated above, the required degree of organization to engage in 'protracted violence' is lower than the degree of organization required to 'exercise responsible command and carry out sustained and concerted military operations' pursuant to Art. 1 (1) Additional Protocol II.[445]

The twofold test of 'intensity of hostilities' and 'organization of the parties', established by the ICTY in the *Tadić* jurisprudence, has been consistently applied in subsequent ICTY jurisprudence[446] as well as it has been adopted by subsequent ICTR jurisprudence[447] and ICC jurisprudence[448].

---

438 ICTY, Prosecutor v Fatmir Limaj et al., Trial Judgement para 123.

439 Ibid paras 113-117; ICTY, Prosecutor v Ramush Haradinaj et al., Trial Judgement para 69.

440 ICTY, Prosecutor v Fatmir Limaj et al., Trial Judgement para 119.

441 Ibid para 110.

442 ICTY, Prosecutor v Ramush Haradinaj et al., Trial Judgement para 88.

443 ICTY, Prosecutor v Fatmir Limaj et al., Trial Judgement paras 125-129.

444 ICTY, Prosecutor v. Enver Hadzihasanovic and Amir Kubura, Judgement, 15 March 2006, Case No. IT-01-47-T paras 20 and 23; ICTY, Prosecutor v Ramush Haradinaj et al., Trial Judgement para 88.

445 ICTY, Prosecutor v Ljube Boškoski and Johan Tarculovski, Trial Chamber Judgment para 197.

446 ICTY, Prosecutor v Dusko Tadić aka „Dule", Trial Judgment para 561 f.; ICTY, Prosecutor v Ragoljub Kunarac et al., Appeals Judgement, 12 June 2002, Case No. IT-96-23/1-A para 56; ICTY, Prosecutor v Dario Kordić and Mario Čerkez, Appeals Judgement para 336; ICTY, Prosecutor v Fatmir Limaj et al., Trial Judgement paras 83 f.; ICTY, Prosecutor v Ramush Haradinaj et al., Trial Judgement paras 37 f.; ICTY, Prosecutor v Mucić et al., Trial Judgement para 183.

447 ICTR, Prosecutor v Jean-Paul Akayesu, Trial Judgment paras 619-621; ICTR, Prosecutor v Georges Anderson Nderubumwe Rutaganda, Judgement and Sentence, 6 December 1999, Case No. ICTR-96-3-T para 92.

448 ICC, Prosecutor v. Thomas Lubanga Dyilo, Decision on the confirmation of charges, Case No. ICC-01/04-01/06 paras 232-234; ICC, Prosecutor v Thomas Lubanga Dyilo, Judgment pursuant to Article 74 of the Statute paras 533-536; ICC, Prosecutor v Jean-Pierre Bemba Gombo, Decision Pursuant to Article 61(7)(a) and (b) of the Rome Statute on the Charges of the Prosecutor Against Jean-Pierre Bemba

The ICTY jurisprudence played an invaluable role in specifying the legal prerequisites for classifying a situation of internal armed violence as a NIAC pursuant to Common Article 3 and, thereby, subjecting it to IHL.

4. Definition according to the Rome Statute of the ICC

The ICC has elaborated a definition of NIAC that follows a similar line of thinking. In Art. 8, the ICC Statute penalizes war crimes. Art. 8 (2) (c) ICC Statute penalize serious violations of Common Article 3 in the case of an armed conflict not of an international character. Art. 8 (2)(e) ICC Statute penalizes other violations of the laws and customs applicable in armed conflicts not of an international character. Hence, the ICC Statute refers to NIACs twice, borrowing the language of Common Article 3. The ICC Statute's drafters also included two paragraphs which stipulate that internal disturbances do not qualify as NIACs. Accordingly, Art. 8 (2) lit. (d) and (f) ICC Statute stipulate that paragraph (2) lit. (c) and (e) 'do not apply to situations of internal disturbances and tensions, such as riots, isolated and sporadic acts of violence and other acts of similar nature'. This is a literal adoption of the exclusion clause in Art. 1 (2) Additional Protocol II. However, paragraph (2) lit. (f) includes an additional sentence indicating that it applies to 'armed conflicts that take place in the territory of a State when there is protracted armed conflict between governmental authorities and organized armed groups or between such groups'. While this definition falls short of the Art. 1 (1) Additional Protocol II criteria, it includes elements of the *Tadić*-formula.

Hence, the definition set out in Art. 8 (2)(f) ICC Statute seems to fall in between the two thresholds of Common Article 3 and Art. 2 (1) Additional Protocol II.[449] The ICC Statute's separate enumeration of two sets of war crimes in NIACs followed by two separate thresholds leads to the question of whether Art. 8(2)(f) ICC Statute introduces a third definition of NIACs or whether it merely represents another codification of an existing threshold.[450]

Gombo para 234; ICC, Prosecutor v Ahmad Al Faqi Al Mahdi, Judgment and Sentence, 27 September 2016, Case No. ICC-01/12-01/15 para 49.

449 Éric David, Principes de droit des conflits armés (6th edn, Bruylant 2019) 129.

450 Anthony Cullen, The Concept of Non-International Armed Conflict in International Humanitarian Law 174; Lindsay Moir, 'The Concept of Non-International Armed Conflict' in Andrew Clapham, Paola Gaeta and Marco Sassòli (eds), The 1949

a. Textual interpretation of Art. 8 (2)(d) and (f) ICC Statute

The first sentence in Art. 8 (2)(f) ICC Statute indicating that paragraph (2)(e) 'does not apply to situations of internal disturbances and tension, such as riots, isolated and sporadic acts of violence or other acts of a similar nature' is an *in verbatim* copy of Art. 1 (2) Additional Protocol II. The second sentence of Art. 8 (2)(f) ICC Statute also reminds of the threshold of Common Article 3 by referring to 'armed conflicts that takes place in the territory of a State when there is protracted armed conflict between governmental authorities and organized armed groups or between such groups.' Some scholars argue that Art. 8 (2)(f) ICC Statute introduces another threshold for NIACs or acts as *lex posterior* to the definition in Additional Protocol II.[451] According to *Sassòli*, for example, Art. 8 (2)(f) ICC Statute introduces an intermediary threshold for the existence of a NIAC.[452] Similarly, *Schabas* argues that Art. 8 (2)(f) ICC Statute includes four categories of war crimes, two of them applicable in IACs, two of them in NIACs and within the subset of NIACs there are two distinct categories.[453]

Other scholars argue that the text of Art. 8 (2)(f) ICC Statute amounts to a positive formulation of the same threshold, thus, does not introduce a new threshold for the existence of a NIAC.[454] Rather is the text of Art. 8 (2)(f) ICC Statute a 'replica' of the *Tadić*-formula with regard to Common Article 3.[455] Accordingly, the ICC Statue adopts a single threshold for a situation to qualify as a NIAC and the only two distinctions within Art. 8 ICC Statute to be made are the distinction between a IAC and a

---

Geneva Conventions - A Commentary 395; Jelena Pejić, 'Status of armed conflicts' in Elizabeth Wilmshurst and Susan Breau (eds), Perspectives on the ICRC Study on Customary International Humanitarian Law 89; in this vein, see Éric David, Principes de droit des conflits armés 129.

451 Éric David, Principes de droit des conflits armés 119.

452 Marco Sassòli, Susan Carr and Antoine A. Bouvier, How does law protect in war? Vol. I (2nd edn, International Committee of the Red Cross 2006) 110.

453 William A. Schabas, An Introduction to the International Criminal Court (6th edn, Cambridge University Press 2020) 137.

454 Anthony Cullen, The Concept of Non-International Armed Conflict in International Humanitarian Law 178; Theodor Meron, 'The Humanization of Humanitarian Law' (2000) 94 The American Journal of International Law 239-278, 260.

455 Michael Bothe, 'War Crimes' in Antonio Cassese, Paola Gaeta and John R.W.D. Jones (eds), The Rome Statute of the International Criminal Court: A Commentary (1st edn, Oxford University Press 2002) 54.

NIAC and the distinction between a NIAC and internal disturbances and tensions that do not constitute an armed conflict at all.[456]

This interpretation is convincing for the following reasons: Both Art. 8 (2)(d) and (f) ICC Statute start with the term 'conflict not of an international character' which is a *verbatim* copy of the text of Common Article 3. This phrase represents the lower threshold for the existence of a NIAC and the corresponding application of IHL.[457] It would be odd to interpret the verbatim phrase of Common Article 3 differently in the context of the ICC Statute.[458] Also, neither Art. 8 (2)(d) nor Art. 8 (2)(f) ICC Statute include or refer to the requirements of 'territorial control' and 'responsible command' as stipulated in Art. 1 (1) Additional Protocol II. Thus, in logical conclusion, the ICC Statute stipulates one single threshold for the existence of a NIAC which is the one of Common Article 3, enriched through the ICTY in its *Tadić* jurisprudence.

b. Historical interpretation of Art. 8 (2)(d) and (f) ICC Statute

The interpretation of a uniform threshold in Art. 8(2)(d) and (f) ICC Statute finds support in the *travaux préparatoires* of the ICC Statute.[459]

During the Diplomatic Conference in Rome, the Preparatory Committee submitted a draft Statute for the consideration of the delegates.[460] In this draft Statute, sections C and D of Article 5*quarter* contained provisions relating to situations of NIACs.[461] Both sections were covered by a joint *chapeau*, stipulating that the provisions shall not apply to 'situations of internal disturbances and tensions, such as riots, isolated and sporadic acts of violence or other acts of similar nature.'[462] Although most delegates

456 Ibid 418; In this line see also Anthony Cullen, The Concept of Non-International Armed Conflict in International Humanitarian Law 179.

457 Anthony Cullen, The Concept of Non-International Armed Conflict in International Humanitarian Law 180.

458 Ibid 182; Lindsay Moir, 'The Concept of Non-International Armed Conflict' in Andrew Clapham, Paola Gaeta and Marco Sassòli (eds), The 1949 Geneva Conventions - A Commentary 395.

459 UN, Diplomatic Conference of Plenipotentiaries of an International Criminal Court (United Nations, 15 June - 17 July 1998), UN Doc. A/CONF.183, Vol. III, Reports and other documents 19 ff.

460 Ibid, Vol. III, Reports and other documents 13 ff.

461 Ibid, Vol. III, Reports and other documents 19 f.

462 Ibid, Vol. III, Reports and other documents 53.

were in support of including provisions relating to NIACs[463], a few delegates remained hesitant about the external intervention in internal affairs of sovereign states and questioned how the Court would determine situations not of an international character.[464] These delegates promoted a narrower threshold for NIACs, similar to the one stipulated in Art. 1 (1) Additional Protocol II.[465] Consequently, the Bureau of the Committee of the Whole formulated a proposal which amended the uniform threshold and introduced a separate, second threshold for section D on the basis of Art. 1 (1) Additional Protocol II.[466] However, various delegations criticized this proposal for not accurately mirroring the reality of armed conflicts where territorial control of the armed group is often absent.[467] Additionally, they criticized the introduction of a separate threshold for section D, as this resulted in two separate categories of war crimes within Article 5*quarter* which did not exist before.[468]

This led to a new proposal made by the delegation of Sierra Leone which suggested the inclusion of a threshold following the *Tadić*-formula.[469] The proposal introduced the phrase 'protracted armed conflict between govern-

463 US, Finnland, Sierra Leone, UK, Uganda, Switzerland, New Zealand, Isreal, Japan, Georgia, Trinidad and Tobago etc., see Anthony Cullen, The Concept of Non-International Armed Conflict in International Humanitarian Law 166 at fn 24.

464 See Delegate of Sudan (Mr. Fadl) who expressed concerns regarding the sovereignty of states: UN, Diplomatic Conference of Plenipotentiaries of an International Criminal Court (United Nations, 15 June - 17 July 1998), UN Doc. A/CONF.183, Vol. II, Summary Record of the plenary meetings and of the meetings of the Committee of the Whole, 5th meeting para 102; Anthony Cullen, The Concept of Non-International Armed Conflict in International Humanitarian Law 166.

465 See UN, Diplomatic Conference of Plenipotentiaries of an International Criminal Court (United Nations, 15 June - 17 July 1998), UN Doc. A/CONF.183, Vol. II, Summary Record of the plenary meetings and of the meetings of the Committee of the Whole, 4th meeting para 76 and 5th meeting para 107.

466 Ibid, Vol. III, Reports and other documents 215.

467 The delegate of Sierre Leone (Mr. Dabor), for example, highly criticized the newly presented narrow threshold for Section D and referred to the armed conflict which took place in his country at that time and where armed opposition groups did not control any territory, hence, not falling under the proposed higher threshold for Section D of Article 5 quarter. Ibid, Vol. II, Summary Records of the plenary meetings and of the meetings of the Committee of the Whole, 35th meeting para 8.

468 Ibid, Vol. II, Summary Records of the plenary meetings and of the meetings of the Committee of the Whole, 5th meeting para 101 and 33rd meeting paras 22-24. The Delegate of New Zealand (Mr. Don MacKay) stressed the same point, see ibid 34th meeting para 22.

469 ICTY, Prosecutor v Dusko Tadić aka „Dule", Decision on the Defence Motion for Interlocutory Appeal on Jurisdiction para 70.

mental authorities and organized armed groups or between such groups'[470] into the draft Statute's text. On July 17th, 1998, the Sierra Leonean proposal was formally concluded and became todays Art. 8 (2)(f) ICC Statue.[471]

Hence, Sierra Leone's proposal, was not meant to introduce a new, second threshold for situations of NIACs but to specify and provide further detail to the general threshold of the Court's jurisdiction for war crimes in NIACs.[472]

c. Customary status of Art. 8 (2)(c) and (e) ICC Statute

Additionally, the interpretation of a uniform threshold in Art. 8 (2)(d) and (f) ICC Statute is supported by the customary status of the underlying offences. The offences listed in Art. 8 (2)(d) and (e) ICC Statute amount to customary IHL.[473]

The ICRC Study on customary IHL does not apply different thresholds regarding war crimes in NIACs. Against this background, it appears evident that the offences listed in Art. 8 (2)(d) and (e) ICC Statute relate to one single threshold of NIAC. Any other interpretation would be contrary to customary international law.[474]

470 UN, Diplomatic Conference of Plenipotentiaries of an International Criminal Court (United Nations, 15 June - 17 July 1998), UN Doc. A/CONF.183, Vol. II, Summary Record of the plenary meetings and of the meetings of the Committee of the Whole, 35th meeting para 8.

471 Ibid, Vol. II, Summary Record of the plenary meetings and of the meetings of the Committee of the Whole, 37th meeting para 53.

472 In this vein Anthony Cullen, The Concept of Non-International Armed Conflict in International Humanitarian Law 177.

473 The offences listed in Art. 8 (2)(c) ICC Statute are covered in the following rules represented in Jean-Marie Henckaerts and Louise Doswald-Beck, Customary International Humanitarian Law Volume I: Rules (1st edn, Cambridge University Press 2005): Rules 87-90, 96 and 99-100. The offences listed in Art. 8 (2)(e) ICC Statute are covered in the following rules: Rules 1, 30, 33, 38-40, 52, 93-94, 146-137, 129, 65, 46, 92 and 50. See also Anthony Cullen, 'The Definition of Non-International Armed Conflict in the Rome Statute of the International Criminal Court: An Analysis of the Threshold of Application Contained in Article 8(2)(f)' (2008) 12 Journal of Conflict and Security Law 419-445, 444 at fn 105 f. who also lists the respective rules and corresponding state practice as provided for in the ICRC study.

474 See also Anthony Cullen, The Concept of Non-International Armed Conflict in International Humanitarian Law 184; Anthony Cullen, 'The Definition of Non-International Armed Conflict in the Rome Statute of the International Criminal Court: An Analysis of the Threshold of Application Contained in Article 8(2)(f)' 444.

Therefore, the thresholds of Art. 8 (2)(d) and (f) ICC Statute should be considered the same: Both are based on the threshold stipulated in Common Article 3, with the latter clarifying and developing the former.[475] Hence, the requirement of 'territorial control' is not part of the definition of a NIAC set out in Art. 8 (2)(f) ICC Statute, although it was initially proposed during the Rome Conference.[476] Likewise, Art. 8 (2)(f) ICC Statute does not include the Art. 1 (1) Additional Protocol II-requirement of 'responsible command'[477].

5. Conclusion

First and foremost, the term 'NIAC' describes a state of violence between two or more entities where at least one of them is not a state or not affiliated with a state. The term 'NIAC' is also a legal term which implies the applicability of a certain set of law. More precisely, it determines the scope of application of pertinent IHL rules and obligations. Surprisingly, neither treaty nor customary IHL explicitly define what a NIAC is, even though pertinent treaty provisions refer to the term, such as Common Article 3 or Art. 1 (1) Additional Protocol II. Given the lack of a statutory definition, international criminal tribunals, such as the ICTY, ICTR and ICC, have engaged in developing a detailed definition of NIAC.

As a result, two thresholds – or two categories – of NIACs have emerged. One based on Common Article 3 and further developed by, especially, ICTY jurisprudence, and one based on Art. 1 (1) Additional Protocol II.

The presence of violence forms the starting point for both thresholds. However, only violence which goes beyond internal disturbances and mere sporadic outbreaks opens the gateway for the application of pertinent IHL provisions. This holds true for both Common Article 3 and Art. 1 (1) Additional Protocol II. In other words, although Art. 1 (1) Additional Protocol II contains a different threshold of NIACs than Common Article 3, both pro-

---

475 Anthony Cullen, The Concept of Non-International Armed Conflict in International Humanitarian Law 180; Lindsay Moir, 'The Concept of Non-International Armed Conflict' in Andrew Clapham, Paola Gaeta and Marco Sassòli (eds), The 1949 Geneva Conventions - A Commentary 395.

476 UN, Diplomatic Conference of Plenipotentiaries of an International Criminal Court (United Nations, 15 June - 17 July 1998), UN Doc. A/CONF.183, Vol. III, Reports and other documents, 59 and 215.

477 ICC, Prosecutor v Thomas Lubanga Dyilo, Judgment pursuant to Article 74 of the Statute para 536.

visions equally demand violence which exceeds mere internal disturbances and tensions as stipulated in Art. 1 (2) Additional Protocol II.[478]

In addition to 'qualified violence' in the sense of Art. 1 (2) Additional Protocol II, both Common Article 3 and Art. 1 (1) Additional Protocol II postulate further prerequisites. Although not explicitly enshrined in the provision's text, the ICTY developed two conditions for assessing the existence of a NIAC pursuant to Common Article 3. Accordingly, the armed violence must qualify as 'protracted armed violence'[479]. The two criteria which have been established by the ICTY to determine the protracted nature of violence are (i) the intensity of the conflict, and (ii) the organization of the parties to the conflict.[480] This twofold test has been widely accepted and consistently applied by subsequent ICTY jurisprudence[481] as well as by subsequent ICTR jurisprudence[482] and ICC jurisprudence[483].

Hence, the first category of NIAC is based on Common Article 3 and requires protracted armed violence exerted by an organized armed group.[484]

The second category of NIAC is based on the threshold laid down in Art. 1 (1) Additional Protocol II. It is fulfilled once the respective organized armed group satisfies the requirements of 'territorial control', 'responsible command' and the ability to 'carry out sustained and concerted military operations' as to enable it (the group) to implement the Protocol. This

478 See also Yoram Dienstein, Non-International Armed Conflicts in International Law 55.

479 ICTY, Prosecutor v Dusko Tadić aka „Dule", Decision on the Defence Motion for Interlocutory Appeal on Jurisdiction para 70.

480 ICTY, Prosecutor v Dusko Tadić aka „Dule", Trial Judgment para 562.

481 ICTY, Prosecutor v Ragoljub Kunarac et al., Appeals Judgement para 56; ICTY, Prosecutor v Dario Kordić and Mario Čerkez, Appeals Judgement para 336; ICTY, Prosecutor v Fatmir Limaj et al., Trial Judgement paras 83 f.; ICTY, Prosecutor v Ramush Haradinaj et al., Trial Judgement paras 37 f.; ICTY, Prosecutor v Mucić et al., Trial Judgement para 184.

482 ICTR, Prosecutor v Jean-Paul Akayesu, Trial Judgment paras 619-621; ICTR, Prosecutor v Georges Anderson Nderubumwe Rutaganda, Judgement and Sentence para 92.

483 ICC, Prosecutor v. Thomas Lubanga Dyilo, Decision on the confirmation of charges paras 232-234; ICC, Prosecutor v Thomas Lubanga Dyilo, Judgment pursuant to Article 74 of the Statute paras 533-536; ICC, Prosecutor v Jean-Pierre Bemba Gombo, Decision Pursuant to Article 61(7)(a) and (b) of the Rome Statute on the Charges of the Prosecutor Against Jean-Pierre Bemba Gombo para 234; ICC, Prosecutor v Ahmad Al Faqi Al Mahdi, Judgment and Sentence para 49.

484 Dapo Akande, 'Classification of Armed Conflicts' in Ben Saul and Dapo Akande (eds), The Oxford Guide to International Humanitarian Law (1st edn, Oxford University Press 2020) 29-56, 40.

threshold is significantly higher than the one stipulated in Common Article 3.[485] Hence, a situation of internal armed violence which fulfills the high threshold of Art. 1 (1) Additional Protocol II automatically satisfies the threshold enshrined in Common Article 3.[486]

II. Applicable IHL to NIACs: Regulation by Analogy

Whereas the foregoing section elaborated on the definition(s) of the term 'NIAC', this section provides an overview of the applicable law to NIACs with a special focus on the historical development of humanitarian law applicable to NIACs. The humanitarian law of NIACs underwent a great development. Prior to the adoption of the four Geneva Conventions of 1949 and the adoption of Additional Protocol II to the four Geneva Conventions of 1977, NIACs have been regulated on an *ad hoc* basis only, rooted in the concepts of rebellion, insurgency, and belligerency. The subsequent systematic regulation of NIACs through conventional treaty and customary law has been modelled after the humanitarian law of IACs and has been considerably shaped through the jurisprudence of international criminal tribunals.

1. Legal regulation prior to 1949

During the 19th century, the prevailing view was that war can only be waged between two sovereign entities, namely, between states. There existed an omnipresent reluctance to acknowledge and regulate the scenario that also non-state entities such as insurgent groups could wage 'war' against a state government.[487] Situations of internal armed violence were considered to fall in the *domaine reservé* of states.[488] In other words, the laws of war were considered inapplicable to internal armed conflicts unless there was a

485 Lindsay Moir, 'The Concept of Non-International Armed Conflict' in Andrew Clapham, Paola Gaeta and Marco Sassòli (eds), The 1949 Geneva Conventions - A Commentary 411.
486 ICTR, Prosecutor v Georges Anderson Nderubumwe Rutaganda, Judgement and Sentence para 94.
487 ICRC, Commentary of 1987 Protocol Additional to the Geneva Conventions of 12 August 1949, and relating to the Protection of Victims of Non-International Armed Conflicts (Protocol II), 8 June 1977 para 4342.
488 Sandesh Sivakumaran, The Law of Non-International Armed Conflict 9.

recognition of belligerency.[489] This rooted in a strong sovereignty-oriented understanding of international law: states were fearful of any outside, third state intervention and considered internal uprisings as being under the sole merit of domestic law.[490] Nevertheless, internal armed violence did not remain completely unregulated. The concepts of rebellion, insurgency and belligerency amounted to an *ad hoc* regulation of civil strife and preceded the intensive efforts by the ICRC throughout the first half of the 19th century to regulate internal armed conflicts through IHL.

a. Ad hoc regulation trough the concepts of rebellion, insurgency and belligerency

Before the first codifications of the law applicable to internal armed conflict, international law categorized armed violence against the *de jure* government of a state by a NSAG into three different types with respectively different levels of intensity: rebellion, insurgency, and belligerency.[491]

Under traditional international law[492], a rebellion was any short-lived protest or threat to the incumbent government which could be so rapidly suppressed that it was not worthy of any acknowledgment at an external or international level.[493] Since situations of rebellion were outside the remit of international law, and considered to be solely an internal affair of the domestic state, rebels did not enjoy any rights nor protection under international law but were punished for their uprising according to domestic law.[494] The lack of regulation by international law ensured non-interference by external actors in internal affairs of sovereign states and strengthened the position of states.

489 Lindsay Moir, The law of internal armed conflict (1st edn, Cambridge University Press 2002) 11.

490 Ibid 11.

491 Ibid 4; Sandesh Sivakumaran, The Law of Non-International Armed Conflict 9; Heather Wilson, International law and the use of force by national liberation movements 23.

492 The term ‚traditional international law‘ was used by scholars to refer to the laws of war prior the 1949 codification. The ICTY Appeals Chamber in the *Tadić* jurisdiction decision used this term as well, see ICTY, Prosecutor v Dusko Tadić aka „Dule“, Decision on the Defence Motion for Interlocutory Appeal on Jurisdiction para 96.

493 Anthony Cullen, The Concept of Non-International Armed Conflict in International Humanitarian Law 9.

494 Heather Wilson, International law and the use of force by national liberation movements 23-24.

When a government failed to suppress the rebellion of a group, the internal conflict would shift to the level of insurgency. Compared to a situation of rebellion, a situation of insurgency amounted to a credible threat to the incumbent government.[495] The recognition of insurgency amounted to the acknowledgment that there was a 'factual relation' between the insurgent group and the state which needed to be regulated.[496] *Lauterpacht* opined that the recognition of insurgency creates a factual relation between the state and the insurgent party in terms of conveying rights and duties on the side of both parties but only in so far as they are expressly agreed upon [...] on the grounds of convenience, humanity and economic interest.[497]

Hence, insurgency was a concept which emerged out of necessity to regulate the relation towards an insurgent group because the respective state failed to suppress the rebellion during the first stage. However, the requirements of an 'insurgency' were far from clear-cut. There was no reference as to the necessary degree of intensity of violence, the extent of control over territory, the organization of the group, or the establishment of state-like structures.[498] Recognizing an insurgency implied that the state government was granting the opposing non-state party some sort of status and seeing the insurgent group as 'legal contestants, and not as mere lawbreakers' as was the case with rebellion.[499] However, the recognition of insurgency did not automatically result in the full applicability of humanitarian norms.[500] On the contrary, humanitarian norms applied only to the extent to which the insurgent group and the state have explicitly agreed upon in the act of

495 Erik Castrén, Civil War (1st edn, Suomalainen Tiedeakatemia 1966) 207-223.

496 Heather Wilson, International law and the use of force by national liberation movements 24.

497 Hersch Lauterpacht, Recognition in international law (1st edn, Cambridge University Press 1947) 276 f.; Anthony Cullen, The Concept of Non-International Armed Conflict in International Humanitarian Law 11 f.; Lindsay Moir, The law of internal armed conflict 5; Sandesh Sivakumaran, The Law of Non-International Armed Conflict 10.

498 Heather Wilson, International law and the use of force by national liberation movements 24; Anthony Cullen, The Concept of Non-International Armed Conflict in International Humanitarian Law 11.

499 Hersch Lauterpacht, Recognition in international law 270.

500 Erik Castrén, Civil War 207-223; Anthony Cullen, The Concept of Non-International Armed Conflict in International Humanitarian Law 12 f.; Sandesh Sivakumaran, The Law of Non-International Armed Conflict 14.

recognition. Hence, humanitarian protection was still very little and, more importantly, solely at the discretion of the state.[501]

The third stage related to belligerency. Recognized belligerency rendered a civil war to be treated as an inter-state conflict and brought into effect the whole set of the laws of war. The preconditions for recognition of belligerency were the following: firstly, armed violence must have escalated from one of a purely local character to one of a general character, resembling a traditional international war, involving a large proportion of population. Secondly, insurgents must occupy and administer a substantial part of the state's territory. Thirdly, insurgents must conduct hostilities in an organized manner following a responsible command. Lastly, hostilities must have reached such a magnitude that third states find it necessary to define their relation towards the contesting parties by granting them belligerent status.[502]

Interestingly, these criteria closely resemble the criteria set out in Art. 1 (1) Additional Protocol II. However, whereas the recognition of belligerency triggered the applicability of the whole set of laws of war, Art. 1 Additional Protocol II only brings into play the (still) limited scope of Additional Protocol II rules.[503]

Recognition of belligerency was first and foremost a political act, granted by third states whose economic or political interests were affected by the armed violence.[504] It concerned cases where the violence has reached such a magnitude that both sides to the conflict were to be treated as equal belligerent parties. Recognition of belligerency could be either granted by the host state or by any other third state. Recognition of belligerency triggered the law of neutrality regarding the relationship between the granting third state(s) and the parties to the conflict. Hence, the granting third state was obliged to refrain from intervening into the conflict and from

501 Anthony Cullen, The Concept of Non-International Armed Conflict in International Humanitarian Law 13 f.

502 Hersch Lauterpacht, Recognition in international law 176; see also Andrew Clapham, War (1st edn, Oxford University Press 2021) 247; GIAD Draper, 'Humanitarian Law and Internal Armed Conflicts' (1983) 13 Georgia Journal of International and Comparative Law 253-278, 257; Thomas Joseph Lawrence, The principles of international law (1st edn, Littleton, CO: F.B. Rothman 1987) 329; Lindsay Moir, The law of internal armed conflict 14; Sandesh Sivakumaran, The Law of Non-International Armed Conflict 11.

503 See also Lindsay Moir, The law of internal armed conflict 14.

504 Anthony Cullen, The Concept of Non-International Armed Conflict in International Humanitarian Law 17.

offering support or assistance to either of the parties to the conflict.[505] This diminished the latent inequality between the parties to the conflict and amounted to some moral support of the insurgent group by the declaring third state.[506]

Besides the applicability of the law of neutrality, belligerency came with benefits for all parties involved. For the insurgent party, recognition of belligerency amounted to moral support and lent some sort of recognized status to the group. The latent inequality between the fighting parties was diminished since the declaring state was prohibited from supporting the *de jure* government.[507] Recognized belligerency also allowed the respective insurgent group to institute blockades, to stop and search vessels, to seize contraband, and to convene prize courts.[508] Additionally, the recognition of belligerency resulted in the applicability of the laws of war equally for both parties.[509] This meant that also members of the respective insurgent group were granted the status of combatants, enjoyed combatant immunity and POW status upon capture.[510] Additionally, insurgents were neither prosecuted nor executed upon capture by the recognizing third state.[511] For the parent state, recognized 'belligerency' usually led to improved humanitarian standards which meant that better treatment of the members of the state's armed forces could be expected.

The decision to recognize belligerency was primarily a political one, done out of self-interest and for practical reasons.[512] Since the recognition of belligerency was at the discretion of the parent state or any third state, it usually came late during the conflict because states were still hesitant in conferring any status and equal rights to the insurgent party.[513]

---

505 Erik Castrén, Civil War 168; Andrew Clapham, War 248; Anthony Cullen, The Concept of Non-International Armed Conflict in International Humanitarian Law 20; Lindsay Moir, The law of internal armed conflict 7; Sandesh Sivakumaran, The Law of Non-International Armed Conflict 15.

506 Lindsay Moir, The law of internal armed conflict 8.

507 Ibid 8.

508 Andrew Clapham, War 248; Lindsay Moir, The law of internal armed conflict 8; Sandesh Sivakumaran, The Law of Non-International Armed Conflict 16.

509 Anthony Cullen, The Concept of Non-International Armed Conflict in International Humanitarian Law 20.

510 Sandesh Sivakumaran, The Law of Non-International Armed Conflict 16.

511 Ibid 14; Erik Castrén, Civil War 171.

512 Norman J. Paddelford, International law and diplomacy in the Spanish civil strife (1st edn, Macmillan 1939) 23; Lindsay Moir, The law of internal armed conflict 17; Sandesh Sivakumaran, The Law of Non-International Armed Conflict 15.

513 Lindsay Moir, The law of internal armed conflict 10.

To conclude, prior to the codification of the Geneva Conventions in 1949 and their Additional Protocols in 1979, belligerency was the only concept requiring the unequivocal adherence to international humanitarian norms for both parties to the armed conflict. Whereas belligerency brought into effect the whole set of (international) laws of war, the rules applying in other situations of intrastate violence were scarce and offered few rights and little humanitarian protection.

b. Development of a systematic IHL applicable to NIACs prior to 1949

Despite the concept of recognized belligerency, states remained opposed to a systematic regulation of internal armed conflicts through international law.[514] However, continuous efforts by the ICRC paved the way for regulating internal armed conflicts in a systematic manner and at an international level. Between the second half of the 19th century and the beginning of the 20th century, the ICRC convened several international conferences, established various expert commissions, and submitted several reports and draft resolutions regarding the expansion of applicable humanitarian rules and obligations to internal armed conflicts. This period has been marked by vehement efforts on behalf of the ICRC despite a strong rejection on behalf of states.

The discussion about including internal armed conflicts into the scope of application of international law started with elaborating on the mandate of national Red Cross societies in times of armed conflict.

At the Ninth International Conference, which took place in Washington in 1912, the question was whether national Red Cross relief societies should extend their mandate to provide relief to civil wars. Two reports – one by the American and one by the Cuban Red Cross – suggested to provide equal humanitarian aid in cases of civil strife.[515] The American report, titled 'Functions of Red Cross when Civil War or State of Insurrections exists', even suggested to regulate civil strife through an international convention. Both proposals did not meet much support since the prevailing view at that

514 Ibid 21.

515 ARC, Neuvième Conférence Internationale de la Croix-Rouge Tenue à Washington du 7 au 17 Mai 1912, Compte-rendu (The American Red Cross, 1912) 45-47 and 49.

time was that insurgent groups were criminals and international law should regulate the relation between states only.[516]

Also at the Tenth International Conference, which took place in Geneva in 1921 and in the spirit of the Russian civil war (1917-1921) and the Hungarian Revolution (1919), civil wars and the provision of humanitarian aid were on the agenda. A report of the ICRC, submitted to the Tenth Conference, stated that civil wars, if prolonged, would steadily become regular wars and suggested that Red Cross institutions should have a role to play in civil wars.[517] The Tenth Conference adopted a resolution devoted to civil strife. This resolution was titled 'Guerre civil' and prescribed that humanitarian relief must also be provided in civil wars.[518] The resolution was applied in Ireland (1922) and the Spanish Civil war (1936-1939).[519] Its steady application to situations of intra-state violence rendered it an 'unofficial convention in a non-international war'.[520]

Another important step in recognizing internal armed conflicts at the international level has been made a few years later, at the Sixteenth International Red Cross Conference in London in 1938. At this conference, the ICRC submitted a revised draft resolution on the protection of civilians, the wounded and sick, and prisoners. The ICRC draft resolution was titled 'Role and Activity of the Red Cross in time of Civil War'[521] and stipulated, *inter alia*, the following principles:

---

516 Sandesh Sivakumaran, The Law of Non-International Armed Conflict 32; see, for example, the statement (in French) of the Russian delegate who considered it impossible for national Red Cross societies to have a duty to perform towards insurgent groups since they can only be considered as criminals: 'Je considère en outre que les sociétès de la Croix-Rouge ne sauraient avoir de devoir à remplir auprès des bandes insurgées ou de révolutionnaires lesquelles ne peuvent être considérées par les lois de mon pays que comme des criminels', ARC, Neuvième Conférence Internationale de la Croix-Rouge Tenue à Washington du 7 au 17 Mai 1912, Compte-rendu (The American Red Cross, 1912) 45.

517 CICR, Rapport Général du Comité International de la Croix-Rouge sur son activité de 1912 à 1920 (Comité International Croix Rouge, 30 March 1921) 208 ('La guerre civile devant, si elle se prolongeait, devenir peu à peu une guerre régulière').

518 CICR, Dixième Conférence Internationale de la Croix-Rouge Tenue à Gèneve du 30 au 7 Avril 1921, Compte-rendu (Comité International Croix Rouge, 26 March 1921), XIV - Guerre Civile 217.

519 Sandesh Sivakumaran, The Law of Non-International Armed Conflict 34.

520 Ibid 34.

521 See ICRC, Role and Activities of the Red Cross in time of Civil War (International Committee Red Cross, June 1938).

(a) 'The sick and wounded, whether civilian or military shall be cared for and safeguarded in all circumstances'
(b) 'Civilians and military arrested or detained for any reason whatsoever, shall bet treated with humanity, protected against violence and insult and shall not be needlessly exposed to danger or unnecessary suffering'
(c) 'Persons captured during military operations or armed combats shall be treated like prisoners of war, according to the principles underlying the Hague Convention of 1907 and the Convention of July, 27, 1929, on the treatment of prisoners of war'.[522]

With only slight changes, the International Conference adopted the proposed resolution by the ICRC.[523] Accordingly, 'the XVIth International Red Cross Conference [...] requests the International Committee and the national Red Cross societies to endeavor to obtain:

(a) the application of the humanitarian principles which were formulated in the Geneva Convention of 1929 and the Xth Hague Convention of 1907, especially as regards the treatment of the wounded, the sick, and prisoners of war, and the safety of medical personnel and medical stores;
(b) humane treatment for all political prisoners, their exchange and, so far as possible, their release;
(c) respect of the life and liberty of non-combatants;
(d) facilities for the transmission of news of a personal nature and for the re-union of families;
(e) effective measures for the protection of children.'[524]

These enshrined principles closely resemble the provisions of Additional Protocol II of 1977.[525]

In 1946, the systematic regulation of internal armed conflicts through international law took serious upswing. In preparation of the Diplomatic Conference in 1949, the Commission at the Preliminary Conference recommended the introduction of a separate article at the head of the Convention on the Amelioration of the Conditions of the Wounded and Sick in Armies

522 Ibid 12 f.
523 ICRC, Report of the XVIth International Red Cross Conference (International Committee Red Cross, June 1938) 104.
524 Ibid 104.
525 Sandesh Sivakumaran, The Law of Non-International Armed Conflict 36.

in the Field of 1929[526], which would expressly cover civil wars. The proposal read as follows:

> 'In the case of armed conflict within the borders of a State, the Convention shall also be applied by each of the adverse parties, unless one of them announces expressly its intention to the contrary.'[527]

This draft provision was assessed by a group of government experts at a Conference held in 1947.[528] The group of government experts agreed on the Preliminary Conference's proposal to extend the scope of application of the two Geneva Conventions of 1929. Regarding the 1929 Convention on the Amelioration of the Condition of the Wounded and Sick in Armies in the Field, the pertinent draft provision read as follows:

> 'In case of civil war, in any part of the home or colonial territory of a Contracting Party, the principles of the Convention shall be equally applied by the said Party, subject to the adverse Party also conforming thereto.'[529]

Regarding the 1929 Convention Relative to the Treatment of Prisoners of War[530], the respective provision read as follows:

> 'In case of civil war, in any part of the home or colonial territory of a Contracting Party, the principles of the Convention shall also be applied by the said Party, subject to the adverse party also complying therewith.'[531]

---

526 Convention for the Amelioration of the Condition of the Wounded and Sick in Armies in the Field, 27 July 1929.

527 ICRC, Report on the Work of the Preliminary Conference of National Red Cross Societies for the study of the Conventions and of various Problems relative to the Red Cross (International Committee Red Cross, 26 July - 3 August 1946) 15.

528 ICRC, Report on the Work of the Conference of Government Experts for the Study of the Conventions for the Protection of War Victims (International Committee Red Cross, 14-26 April 1947).

529 Ibid 8; Sandesh Sivakumaran, The Law of Non-International Armed Conflict 37; Anton Schlögel, 'Civil War' (1970) 10 International Review of the Red Cross 123-134, 127.

530 Convention Relative to the Treatment of Prisoners of War, 27 July 1929.

531 ICRC, Report on the Work of the Conference of Government Experts for the Study of the Conventions for the Protection of War Victims (International Committee Red Cross, 14-26 April 1947) 103.

Hence, the group of government experts watered down the advanced proposal of the Preliminary Conference by referring to the Convention's principles only and introducing a reciprocity element.[532]

The ultimate step in promoting a systematic legal codification of internal armed conflicts took place at the Seventeenth International Red Cross Conference, held in Stockholm in 1948. There, the ICRC submitted draft Article 2 paragraph 4, the pioneer provision of Common Article 3, which foresaw the applicability of the respective Conventions to situations of internal armed conflicts.[533] It read as follows:

> 'In all cases of armed conflict which are not of an international character, especially in cases of civil war, colonial conflicts, or wars of religion, which may occur in the territory of one or more of the High Contracting Parties, the implementing of the principles of the present Convention shall be obligatory for each of the adversaries. The application of the Convention in these circumstances shall in nowise depend on the legal status of the parties to the conflict and shall have no effect on that status.'[534]

Besides the deletion of the phrase 'civil wars, colonial conflicts, or wars of religion', the Legal Commission sticked to the initially proposed language.[535] The relevant provision of the Draft Geneva Convention for the Relief of the Wounded and Sick of Armed Forces in the Field and the Draft Geneva Convention for the Relief of Wounded, Sick and Shipwrecked Members of Armed Forces on Sea, adopted at the end of the Stockholm

---

532 Jean S. Pictet, Commentary on the Geneva Convention (III) relative to the Treatment of Prisoners of War (International Committee of the Red Cross 1960) 31.

533 The Conventions which should be revised included the 1929 versions of Convention for the Amelioration of the Condition of the Wounded and Sick in Armies in the Field and the Convention Relative to the Treatment of Prisoners of War. The Hague Convention (X) for the Adaption to Maritime Warfare of the Principles of the Geneva Convention, 18 October 1907 was also revised and served as the foundation for a new Convention for the Relief of Wounded, Sick and Shipwrecked of Armed Forces on Sea and included the same Draft Article 2. Additionally, a new Convention on the protection of civilian persons in time of war as well as a new were on the agenda of the Conference in Stockholm.

534 See Draft Article 2 of ICRC, Draft Revised or New Conventions for the Protection of War Victims (International Committee Red Cross, May 1948) 5, 34 f., 52, 153 f., 222.

535 ICRC, The Geneva Conventions of August 12, 1949: Analysis for the use of National Red Cross Societies (ICRC 1950), Vol. II, 6; Sandesh Sivakumaran, The Law of Non-International Armed Conflict 39.

Conference – and later presented before the Diplomatic Conference in 1949 – read as follows:

> 'In all cases of armed conflict not of an international character which may occur in the territory of one or more of the High Contracting Parties, each of the adversaries shall be bound to implement the provisions of the present Convention. The Convention shall be applicable in these circumstances, whatever the legal status of the Parties to the conflict and without prejudice thereto.'[536]

The relevant provision of the Draft Convention on the Treatment of Prisoners of War and the new Draft Convention for the Protection of Civilian Persons in Time of War differed in the chosen terminology as it re-introduced a reciprocity clause. It read as follows:

> 'In all cases of armed conflict not of an international character which may occur in the territory of one or more of the High Contracting Parties, each of the Parties to the conflict shall be bound to implement the provisions of the present Convention, subject to the adverse party likewise acting in obedience thereto. The Convention shall be applicable in these circumstances, whatever the legal status of the Parties to the conflict and without prejudice thereto.'[537]

The ICRC then circulated the revised and new draft Conventions as adopted at the Stockholm Conference amongst the signatory states in preparation for the Diplomatic Conference, held in Geneva from April 21st to August 12th, 1949. This date marks a true breakthrough regarding the regulation of internal armed conflicts through IHL.

At the Diplomatic Conference, the agenda included the revision of the two 1929 Geneva Conventions, the revision of the Tenth Hague Convention of 1907 and the establishment of a new Convention on the protection of civilian persons in time of war.[538] The question about extending the scope of application of the respective Geneva Conventions to internal armed

---

536 ICRC, Revised and New Draft Conventions for the Protection of War Victims - Texts Approved and Amended by the XVIIth International Red Cross Conference (International Committee Red Cross, May 1948) 10 and 32.

537 Ibid 51 f. and 114.

538 See Federal Political Department Bern, Final Record of the Diplomatic Conference of Geneva of 1949 Vol. I, 24 October 1968, 47, 61, 73 and 113.

conflicts – as provided for in Draft Article 2 paragraph 4 – gave rise to long debates at the Diplomatic Conference.[539]

Overall, there were two main camps: One group of delegates was strongly opposed to including civil wars into the scope and another one supported and approved of the inclusion of civil wars, albeit under narrowing circumstances only. The delegates who were opposed to including internal armed conflicts into the scope of application of the four Geneva Conventions regarded it an encroachment on their sovereignty.[540] The UK delegate, for example, opined that it was impossible to oblige States to apply the Conventions to situations that were not war.[541] This statement is a vivid illustration of the still prevailing sentiment according to which international law is not apt to regulate internal armed conflicts. Even the delegations who were in support of extending the scope to NIACs wished to exclude internal uprising and disturbances from the scope of the Conventions as they wanted to retain their sovereign right to repress crimes jeopardizing their national security. Hence, many of them suggested narrowing features, such as 'territorial control', 'responsible authority', 'organized civil administration' or 'recognition of belligerency by the state government'.[542] The US delegate, for example, suggested that the Conventions should only include internal armed conflicts which would display the features of an insurgent party with (i) an 'organization, purporting to have the characteristics of a State', (ii) with an 'exercising de facto authority within a determinate territory', (iii) with 'armed forces acting under the direction of an organized civil authority', and (iv) 'the insurgent civil authorities must agree to be bound by the provisions of the Convention'.[543]

In a similar vein, the French delegate stipulated that the forces 'must be organized military forces belonging to a responsible authority capable of respecting, or enforcing respect for the Convention'[544].

At the end of the Diplomatic Conference of 1949 in Geneva and after lengthy debates, paragraph 4 of Draft Article 2 was replaced by Com-

539 See above I. 1.

540 For example the U.K. delegation, see Federal Political Department Bern, Final Record of the Diplomatic Conference of Geneva of 1949 Vol. II, Section B 10; likewise the Burmese delegate, see ibid 327.

541 Ibid, Vol. II, Section B 10.

542 See, for example, the suggestions made by the U.S. delegation, the Canadian delegation, the French delegation, the Australian delegation, ibid, Vol. II, Section B 12, 13, 10 and 15.

543 Ibid, Vol. II, Section B 12.

544 Ibid, Vol. II, Section B 10.

mon Article 3 as of today. This marked the hour of birth of a step-by-step systematic regulation of NIACs through both treaty and customary law.

It can be concluded that the years before the Diplomatic Conference in 1949 have been marked by intensive and continuous efforts on behalf of the ICRC to include NIACs into the respective Conventions' scopes of application. These years have also been marked by reluctant states in acknowledging the need to regulate NIACs through international law. This defensive stance rooted in a strongly sovereignty-oriented thinking. Nevertheless, this period has paved the way for regulating NIACs through a systematic body of IHL, starting with the inclusion of Common Article 3 into all four Geneva Conventions of 1949 and culminating in the adoption of Additional Protocol II of 1979.

2. Contemporary IHL applicable to NIACs

Although NIACs have become more numerous in the last decade, IACs still are considered the archetype of armed conflicts. Thus, it does not surprise that the law applicable to NIACs developed by drawing on the law applicable to IACs.[545] Nonetheless, IHL applicable to NIACs is not as extensively developed as IHL applicable to IACs. This is primarily owed to the fact that states have been and still are concerned about any possible implications for their sovereignty by comprehensively applying the law of armed conflict to situations of NIACs.[546]

The systematic regulation of NIACs emerged at two levels: at the level of treaty law and at the level of customary law. Both streams of law equally apply and supplement each other.

This sub-section provides an overview of the rules and obligations of both Common Article 3 and Additional Protocol II as the principal legal frameworks applicable to NIACs. It does not comprehensively elaborate on every single guarantee, right or prohibition enshrined in Common Article 3 and Additional Protocol II but touches upon the most pivotal provisions, respectively.

545 Sandesh Sivakumaran, The Law of Non-International Armed Conflict 64. Although, no 'mechanical transplant' of rules applicable in IACs to NIACs, see ICTY, Prosecutor v Dusko Tadić aka „Dule", Decision on the Defence Motion for Interlocutory Appeal on Jurisdiction paras 97-117.

546 Dieter Fleck, 'The Law of Non-International Armed Conflict' in Dieter Fleck (ed), The Handbook of International Humanitarian Law 643.

Whereas Common Article 3 is limited to rules on the protection of civilians and persons placed *hors de combat*, Additional Protocol II comprises both provisions relating to the protection as well as provisions relating to the conduct of hostilities.[547]

This sub-section continues with presenting an overview of additional treaty law applicable to NIACs albeit its non-exclusive humanitarian alignment as well as with assessing customary international law applicable to NIACs.

a. Common Article 3 to all four Geneva Conventions of 1949

With the adoption of the four Geneva Conventions in 1949 and the emergence of Common Article 3, situations of internal armed violence have finally been subject to regulation by an international treaty. Even though the drafters only adopted a single provision containing not more than an absolute minimum of protection for persons taking no part or no longer an active part in hostilities, it has been a groundbreaking first step in recognizing that NIACs warrant systematic regulation through conventional treaty law.

The rules contained in Common Article 3 amount to fundamental standards of protection for persons taking no active part in hostilities. Common Article 3 applies to 'each Party to the conflict', irrespective of reciprocity. The substance of Common Article 3 is limited to rules which reflect elementary considerations of humanity.[548]

In its paragraph (1), Common Article 3 starts with positing the general obligation of treating persons taking no active part in the hostilities, whether these are civilians or members of armed forces who have laid down

---

547 It has long been disputed whether international law regulates the conduct of hostilities in NIACs. Then there have been authors which claimed that Common Article 3 implicitly regulates the conduct of hostilities and other authors which advocated the view that Common Article 3 solely focuses on protective rules whereas Additional Protocol II and additional conventional instruments which extend their scope of application to NIACs regulate the conduct of hostilities. Others contend that not even Additional Protocol II contains rules on the conduct of hostilities. See, for example, Dieter Fleck (ed), The Handbook of International Humanitarian Law (4th edn, Oxford University Press 2021) 654. For a brief illustration of the different views, see Sandesh Sivakumaran, The Law of Non-International Armed Conflict 336.

548 ICJ, Military and Paramilitary Activities in and against Nicaragua (Nicaragua v United States of Amercia), Judgment para 218.

their arms or are placed *hors de combat*[549], humanely. The general rule of humane treatment operates 'without any adverse distinction founded on race, colour, religion or faith, sex, birth or wealth, or any other similar criteria'. Thus, the principle of humane treatment of persons taking no active part in hostilities can be considered the capstone of Common Article 3.[550]

The provision continues with stipulating specific rules of protection by prohibiting certain acts at any time during an ongoing NIAC. These prohibited acts are enlisted in Common Article 3 (1)(a)-(d) and refer, *inter alia*, to violence to life and person, murder of all kinds, mutilation, torture, cruel treatment, the taking of hostages, outrages upon personal dignity, and the passing of sentences and carrying out of executions without judgment previously pronounced by a regularly constituted court affording essential judicial guarantees. Common Article 3 is considered to be a 'convention in miniature'[551] laying down general principles only.[552] It is held in abstract generalities, lacking adequate detail and guidance for a comprehensive regulation.[553] For example, Common Article 3 does not define terms such as 'cruel treatment', 'regularly constituted court' or 'outrages upon personal dignity'. Common Article 3 also does not stipulate protection for active members of armed forces. Bearing in mind that, unlike in IACs, members of armed forces of an insurgent group are not considered combatants, hence, they do not enjoy combatant immunity in that they have a right to directly participate in hostilities pursuant to Art. 43 (2) Additional Protocol I nor do they enjoy POW status when captured pursuant to Art. 44 (1)

549 The term *hors de combat* is defined in Art. 41 (2) Additional Protocol I and refers to persons who are (a) in the power of the adverse party, who (b) express their intention to surrender, or who (c) have been rendered unconscious or otherwise incapacitated, leaving them incapable of defending themselves.

550 ICTY, Prosecutor v Kupreškić et al, Judgment, 14 January 2000, Case No. IT.95-16-T para 521.

551 Normally, this term is used in a positive way but during the Diplomatic Conference of Geneva of 1949, the delegate of USSR used it to criticize that Common Article 3 tried to squeeze the whole Convention into a few lines only, see Federal Political Department Bern, Final Record of the Diplomatic Conference of Geneva of 1949 Vol. II, Section B 98.

552 This term was used by Mr. Abi-Saab during the Diplomatic Conference of 1974-1977, see Federal Political Department Bern, Official Records of the Diplomatic Conference on the Reaffirmation and Development of International Humanitarian Law Applicable in Armed Conflicts 1974-1977, CCDH/I/SR.24 para 26.

553 Yoram Dienstein, Non-International Armed Conflicts in International Law 175.

Additional Protocol I, this lack of regulation is fatal.[554] Common Article 3 also does not relate to the conduct of hostilities as it does not contain provisions referring to targeting or lawful means and methods of combat during NIACs.[555] As such, Common Article 3 provides only an absolute minimum of regulation of NICAs.

b. Additional Protocol II

To date, Additional Protocol II to the four Geneva Conventions of 1977 is the sole conventional treaty which exclusively regulates NIACs. The text of Additional Protocol II is modelled after the text of the four Geneva Conventions of 1949 and Additional Protocol I, even though the aim was to adapt the existing law to the conditions special to situations of internal armed conflicts.[556]

Additional Protocol II was adopted with the purpose of developing and supplementing Common Article 3.[557] However, the Protocol limits its scope of application to those NIACs which satisfy the considerably high threshold set out in Art. 1(1) Additional Protocol II.[558] Thus, the involved NSAGs must be under responsible command and exercise territorial control which enables them to carry out sustained and concerted military operations. In contrast to Common Article 3, Additional Protocol II comprises both provisions on the protection of the civilian population and persons taking

554 Dieter Fleck, 'The Law of Non-International Armed Conflict' in Dieter Fleck (ed), The Handbook of International Humanitarian Law; Jean-Marie Henckaerts and Louise Doswald-Beck, Customary International Humanitarian Law Volume I: Rules, Rule 3 and Rule 106.

555 This is not an uncontested issue. Some authors argue that rules on the conduct of hostilities can be inferred/deduced from the protective character of Common Article 3. For example, Antonio Cassese, 'The Geneva Protocols of 1977 on the Humanitarian Law of Armed Conflict and Customary International Law' (1984) 3 UCLA Pacific Basin Law Journal 55-118, 107.

556 Michael Bothe, Karl Josef Partsch and Waldemar A. Solf, New Rules for Victims of Armed Conflict: Commentary on the Two 1977 Protocols Additional to the Geneva Conventions of 1949 (2nd edn, Martinus Nijhoff 2013) 641; Sandesh Sivakumaran, The Law of Non-International Armed Conflict 64.

557 See Art. 1(1) Additional Protocol II.

558 See above I. 2.

no or no longer a direct part in hostilities as well as provisions on conduct of hostilities.[559]

Additional Protocol II is divided into three main strands, comprising provisions relating to humane treatment[560], the wounded, sick and shipwrecked[561], and the civilian population[562]. Art. 4 Additional Protocol II carries the title 'Fundamental guarantees' and resembles the structure and content of Common Article 3. In its first paragraph, Art. 4 Additional Protocol II stipulates that all persons who do not or no longer take a direct part in hostilities shall be treated humanely without any adverse distinction. Art. 4 (2) Additional Protocol II enlists the prohibition of certain acts, similar to those prohibited in Common Article 3 (1). Art. 4 (3) Additional Protocol II provides special protection for children in NIACs. Notably, subparagraph (c) of Art. 4 (3) Additional Protocol II prohibits the recruitment of children under the age of fifteen in armed forces or in armed groups as well as it prohibits the direct participation in hostilities of children under the age of fifteen.

Art. 5 Additional Protocol II establishes minimum rules for the treatment of 'persons deprived of their liberty for reasons related to armed conflict whether they are interned or detained'. Art. 6 Additional Protocol II relates to the subject of prosecution and punishment of criminal offences related to NIACs. It corresponds to the prohibition of summary justice stipulated in Common Article 3 (1)(d) but entails more detailed requirements. Insofar, Art. 6 Additional Protocol II clarifies the content of Common Article 3 (1)(d), especially, regarding fair trial guarantees. In contrast to Common Article 3 (1)(d), the court need not be 'regularly constituted' but proceedings must be conducted 'independently and impartially'. In its second paragraph, Art. 6 Additional Protocol II enumerates fair trial guarantees in a non-exhaustive list, such as the presumption of innocence, the right to be informed without any delay of any charges and to defend oneself against them, freedom of self-incrimination, the principle of *nullum crimen, nulla poena sine lege*, etc. The catalogue of the enlisted fair trial guarantees has been inspired by Art. 14 and Art. 15 of the ICCPR.

---

559 Albeit not to the same extent as Additional Protocol I which dedicates a whole Part to rules on lawful means and methods of warfare, see Part III of Additional Protocol I titled 'Methods and Means of Warfare: Combatant and Prisoner-Of-War Status'.

560 Arts. 4-6 Additional Protocol II.

561 Arts. 7-12 Additional Protocol II.

562 Arts. 13-18 Additional Protocol II.

Art. 7 Additional Protocol II postulates comprehensive protection and medical care for wounded, sick and shipwrecked persons irrespective of whether they belong to the adverse party or not.

Art. 8 Additional Protocol II relates to the obligation of searching and collecting sick, wounded, and shipwrecked persons.

Arts. 9, 10, and 11 Additional Protocol II refer to the protection of medical and religious personnel, the protection of medical duties as well as the protection of medical units and transports. These articles ensure that medical personnel can exercise their duties adequately as to provide the wounded, sick and shipwrecked with the necessary care.

Art. 12 Additional Protocol II belongs to the strand of provisions which regulate the conduct of hostilities by stipulating lawful means and methods of warfare. The provision, *inter alia*, prohibits the improper use of distinctive emblems, such as the emblem of the red cross. Art. 13 (1) Additional Protocol II stipulates the general protection of the civilian population against dangers arising from armed violence. In its second paragraph, Art. 13 Additional Protocol II specifies that civilians shall not be object of attacks. Thereby, Art. 13 (1) and (2) Additional Protocol II reflect the general principle of distinction according to which all parties to the conflict shall distinguish between the civilian population and combatants and between civilian objects and military objectives.[563]

The catalogue continues with Art. 14 Additional Protocol II, another provision regulating the conduct of hostilities, rendering the starvation of the civilian population a prohibited method of combat. The provision also demands the protection of indispensable objects for civilian population, such as food-stuffs and areas for the production of food-stuffs, or drinking water installations.

Art. 16 Additional Protocol II posits the protection of cultural and spiritual heritage against acts of hostilities during armed conflict.

In sum, one can conclude that Additional Protocol II was drafted and adopted with the aim of supplementing Common Article 3 by providing more detailed rules and obligations applicable to NIACs. This aim has been accomplished, albeit with remaining constraints. The drafting process has been a balancing act of enhancing the regulation of NIACs through an exclusive international treaty and thereby *ipso facto* recognizing non-state parties equal to state parties to a conflict, while at the same time upholding

563 See Rule 1 in Jean-Marie Henckaerts and Louise Doswald-Beck, Customary International Humanitarian Law Volume I: Rules.

states' interest in sovereignty and supremacy. The prevalent sentiment was, still, that NIACs primarily pertain to the domestic sphere and, hence, do not warrant the same level of regulation through international law as IACs do. Thus, the text of Draft Protocol II has been greatly simplified. In its adopted version, Additional Protocol II contains 28 Articles whereas it contained 47 Articles in its proposed version. In contrast, Additional Protocol I comprises 102 Articles.[564]

c. Additional treaty law applicable to NIACs

The applicable IHL treaty law to NIACs - Common Article 3 and Additional Protocol II - is flanked by a variety of other international treaties which extend their scope of application to NIACs - both explicitly and implicitly - albeit focusing on the regulation of other subject matters distinct from conduct during NIACs. This section gives an exemplary illustration of additional international treaty law applicable to NIACs.

The first international treaty extending its scope of application to NIACs is the Hague Convention for the Protection of Cultural Property of 1954[565] **(CPCP)**. It supplements the protection of cultural property already provided for in Art. 16 Additional Protocol II. Art. 19 (1) CPCP stipulates that 'in the event of an armed conflict not of an international character occurring within the territory of one of the High Contracting Parties, each party shall be bound to apply, as a minimum, the provisions of the present Convention which relate to respect for cultural property'. The reference to 'provisions which relate to respect for cultural property' is unclear as this could mean to refer to Art. 4 CPCP solely, which is titled 'respect for cultural property', or to other provision of the convention which relate to respect for cultural property as well.[566] This provision is complemented by Arts. 3 (1) and 22 (1) of the Second Protocol to the CPCP of 1999[567] which stipulate that 'this Protocol shall apply in the event of an armed conflict not of an international character, occurring within the territory of one the Parties'.

564 Sandesh Sivakumaran, The Law of Non-International Armed Conflict 51.

565 Convention on the Protection of Cultural Property in the Event of Armed Conflict, UN Treaty Series Vol. 249 No. 3511, 14 May 1954.

566 Sandesh Sivakumaran, The Law of Non-International Armed Conflict 377.

567 Second Protocol to The Hague Convention of 1954 for the Protection of Cultural Property in the Event of Armed Conflict, UN Treaty Series Vol. 2253 No. 3511, 26 March 1999.

Further, the Convention on the Rights of the Child of 1989[568] **(CRC)** extends its scope of application to NIACs. Even though the convention itself addresses State Parties only, the convention's scope becomes applicable to NIACs through the Optional Protocol to the CRC on the Involvement of Children in Armed Conflict of 2000[569]. Art. 4 (1) of the Optional Protocol stipulates that 'Armed groups that are distinct from the armed forces of a State should not, under any circumstances, recruit or use in hostilities persons under the age of 18 years'. Hence, Art. 4 (1) of the Optional Protocols aligns with the prohibition on recruiting 'child soldiers' as stipulated in Art. 4 (3) Additional Protocol II, albeit applying a different age bar.

There also exists additional treaty law on lawful means and methods of warfare in NIACs.

The Convention on Certain Conventional Weapons of **(CCW)** applies to NIACs through Art. 1 (2) which extends the convention's as well as the five annexed Protocols' scope of application to 'situations referred to in Article 3 Common to the Geneva Conventions of 12 August 1949'. The object and purpose of the CCW is to ban and restrict the use of certain weapons which cause unnecessary or unjustifiable harm to members of armed forces or which affect the civilian population in an indiscriminate manner. The CCW is reflecting the general principle of IHL according to which it is prohibited to use means and methods of warfare which cause superfluous injury or unnecessary suffering[570] and to use weapons which are by nature indiscriminate[571].

Also pertaining to the domain of lawful means and methods of warfare, the Chemical Weapons Convention of 1997[572] **(CWC)** extends the convention's scope of application to NIACs, albeit implicitly only. Art. 1 CWC stipulates the obligation to 'never under any circumstance' 'develop, produce, otherwise acquire' or to 'transfer directly or indirectly' chemical weapons to anyone, to 'use chemical weapons' or to 'assist' or 'encourage' anyone to

568 Convention on the Rights of the Child, UN Treaty Series Vol. 1577 No. 27531, 20 November 1989.

569 Optional Protocol to the Convention on the Rights of the Child on the Involvement of Children in Armed Conflict, UN General Assemby Resolution A/RES/54/263, 25 May 2000.

570 See Jean-Marie Henckaerts and Louise Doswald-Beck, Customary International Humanitarian Law Volume I: Rules Rule 70.

571 See ibid Rule 71.

572 Convention on the Prohibition of the Development, Production, Stockpiling and Use of Chemical Weapons and on Their Destruction, UN Security Council Resolution A/RES/58/52, 29 April 1997.

engage in conduct prohibited by the CWC. Similarly, does the Biological Weapons Convention of 1975[573] **(BWC)** indirectly extends its scope to NIACs by requiring to 'never in any circumstances' to 'develop, produce, stockpile or otherwise acquire or retain' of biological and toxin weapons.

As outlined above, several international treaties extend their scope of application to NIACs, albeit their non-conflict related alignment. This remedies the partially insufficient regulatory density of NIACs through Common Article 3 and Additional Protocol II.

d. Customary IHL applicable in NIACs

NIACs are not solely regulated through humanitarian and non-humanitarian treaty law. NIACs are also subject to customary IHL. It would be beyond the scope of this section to give a comprehensive illustration of every customary law rule governing internal armed conflicts. Hence, this section presents an overview of customary IHL applicable to NIACs with a focus on customary IHL specifically regarding conduct of hostilities, hence, means and methods of warfare. Since NIAC-treaty law on lawful means and methods of warfare is rather scarce, customary IHL fills an important gap here.

Customary international law emerges from continual state practice (*usus* or *diuturnitas*) based on a sense of legal obligation (*opinio iuris* or *opinio necessitatis*).[574] For NIACs, the pertinent state practice and *opinio iuris* especially draws on the law of IACs.[575] Besides established state practice, international criminal tribunals have significantly contributed to the formation and recognition of customary international law relative to armed conflict. Additionally, the ICRC has played a vital role in the consolidation of

---

573 Convention on the Prohibition of the Development, Production and Stockpiling of Bacteriological (Biological) and Toxin Weapons and on Their Destruction, UN General Assembly Resolution A/RES/2826 (XXVI), 26 March 1975.

574 See Art. 38 (1)(b) of the Statute of the International Court of Justice, UN Treaty Series Vol. XV, 26 June 1945; Antonio Cassese, International law (2nd edn, Oxford University Press 2005) 156 f.; Mark Villiger, Commentary on the 1969 Vienna Convention on the Law of Treaties (1st edn, Martinus Nijhoff 2009) 4-10; Gerhard Werle and Florian Jeßberger, Principles of International Criminal Law (4th edn, Oxford University Press 2020) para 157.

575 Sandesh Sivakumaran, The Law of Non-International Armed Conflict 56 f.

customary international law applicable to NIACs as it published a study[576] on customary IHL in 2005, comprehensively listing every customary IHL rule.

The ICTY has been the first international criminal tribunal to suggest that there exists a body of customary law applicable to NIACs. In its well-known decision on jurisdiction in the *Tadić* case, the ICTY initially referred to three principal rules of IHL which are applicable to IACs and NIACs alike: the prohibition on attacking or bombing civilians, the prohibition on targeting non-military objectives, and the obligation of taking necessary precautions when attacking military objectives.[577] These principles culminate in the contemporary customary IHL principle of distinction. The principle of distinction is also applicable to NIACs and comprises several sub-principles such as, the principle to distinguish between civilians and combatants and between civilian objects and military objectives[578], the prohibition on indiscriminate attacks[579], to principle of proportionate attacks[580] and the principle of taking necessary precautions[581] to prevent incidental loss of civilian life, injury to civilians, damage to civilian objects or a combination thereof.[582] With Art. 13 (2) and (3) Additional Protocol II,

576 Jean-Marie Henckaerts and Louise Doswald-Beck, Customary International Humanitarian Law Volume I: Rules and Volume II: Practice. Hereafter, the ICRC Study on Customary IHL.

577 ICTY, Prosecutor v Dusko Tadić aka „Dule", Decision on the Defence Motion for Interlocutory Appeal on Jurisdiction para 100, referring to the Spanish Civil War (1936-1939) as bringing about the extension of some IHL rules to internal conflicts.

578 The distinction between civilian objects and military objectives was initially part of Draft Protocol II (Draft Article 24 (1)) but not adopted in the final text due to the aim of simplifying the convention's text. See Federal Political Department Bern, Official Records of the Diplomatic Conference on the Reaffirmation and Development of International Humanitarian Law Applicable in Armed Conflicts 1974-1977, Vol. IV, 71.

579 Rule 11 of the ICRC study on Customary IHL. The prohibition on indiscriminate attacks was initially part of Draft Protocol II (Draft Article 26 (3)) but not adopted in the final text due to the aim of simplifying the convention's text. See ibid, Vol. IV, 75.

580 Rule 14 of the ICRC Study on Customary IHL. Additional Protocol II does not contain an explicit provision on proportionate attacks.

581 Rule 15 of the ICRC Study on Customary IHL. Additional Protocol II does not contain an explicit provision on precautions in attack but it is implicitly enshrined in Art. 13 (1) Additional Protocol II which requires the general protection of the civilian population against the dangers arising from military operations.

582 See Rule 1 and Rule 7 of the ICRC Study on customary IHL by Jean-Marie Henckaerts and Louise Doswald-Beck, Customary International Humanitarian Law Volume I: Rules.

which prohibit any attack against the civilian population and demand the protection for as long as they do not take a direct part in hostilities, NIAC treaty law – at least partially – reflects the principle of distinction, and thus, reflects customary law.[583] The principle of proportionate attacks is not explicitly enshrined in Additional Protocol II but inherent to the obligation of humane treatment laid down in Art. 4 (1) Additional Protocol II.

The realization that many NIAC-treaty law provisions contained in either Common Article 3 or Additional Protocol II reflect customary IHL has been firmly promoted by the ICTY. In the *Tadić* case, the ICTY concurred with the authoritative ICJ ruling and reiterated that Common Article 3 as well as the core provisions of Additional Protocol II have gradually become customary international law.[584] As far as Additional Protocol II is repeating stipulated rules and guarantees enshrined in Common Article 3, those provisions have acquired customary law status as well.[585] This regards not only the principle of humane treatment[586] pursuant to Art. 4 (1) Additional Protocol II but also the fundamental guarantees enshrined in Art. 4 (2) Additional Protocol II, as well as the prohibition on summary justice enshrined in Art. 6 (2) Additional Protocol II. Customary law status can also be ascribed to the prohibition of rape enshrined in Art. 4 (2)(e) Additional Protocol II[587], the prohibition of slavery enshrined in Art. 4 (2)(f) Additional Protocol II[588], and the prohibition on the use and recruitment of 'child soldiers' as stipulated in Art. 4 (3)(c) Additional Protocol II.[589] Art. 17

583 See Rule 1 and Rule 6 of the ICRC Study on Customary IHL. Although, strictly speaking, it is terminologically incorrect to refer to 'combatants' in NIACs since combatant immunity (Art. 43 (2) Additional Protocol I) and POW-status (Art. 44 (1) Additional Protocol I) does not exist in NIACs. Hence, it would be more accurate to call members of the armed forces of a NSAGs 'fighters' or 'persons taking active part in hostilities'. Dieter Fleck (ed), The Handbook of International Humanitarian Law 644 also suggests this terminology.

584 ICTY, Prosecutor v Dusko Tadić aka „Dule", Decision on the Defence Motion for Interlocutory Appeal on Jurisdiction paras 98, 102 and 117.

585 Yoram Dienstein, Non-International Armed Conflicts in International Law 181; Dieter Fleck (ed), The Handbook of International Humanitarian Law 656.

586 See also Rule 87 of the ICRC Study on Customary IHL.

587 ICTY, Prosecutor v Anto Furundžija, Judgment, Case No. IT-95-17/1 para 168; see also Rule 93 of the ICRC Study on Customary IHL.

588 ICTY, Prosecutor v Milorad Krnojelac, Judgment, 15 March 2002, Case No. IT-97-25-T para 535; see also Rule 94 of the ICRC study on Customary IHL.

589 SCSL, Prosecutor v Sam Hinga Norman, Decision on Preliminary Motion Based on Lack of Jurisdiction (Child recruitment), 31 May 2004, Case No. SCSL-2004-14-AR72(E) para 17.

Additional Protocol II, which prohibits the displacement of the civilian population for reasons related to the armed conflict, also reflects customary international law.[590]

Beyond the customary law status of Common Article 3 and the core provisions of Additional Protocol II, both of which primarily relate to the protection of the civilian population and persons *hors de combat*, it is especially the customary law status of provisions relating to conduct of hostilities, hence, to lawful means and methods of warfare which is relevant for a cohesive illustration of the law regulating NIACs.

It begins with the general customary IHL rule on the prohibition of the use of means and methods of warfare which are of a nature to cause superfluous injury or unnecessary suffering.[591]

It continues with more specified customary law rules on prohibited *means* [emphasis added] of warfare applicable in NIACs, such as the prohibition on the use of indiscriminate weapons[592], the prohibition on the use of poison, poisoned weapons[593], or the prohibition on the use of biological and chemical weapons[594].

Customary law rules on prohibited *methods* [emphasis added] of warfare applicable in NIACs relate to, *inter alia*, the duty to provide quarter[595], which is also reflected in the prohibition of ordering that there shall be no survivors pursuant to Art. 4 (1) Additional Protocol II, the prohibition of attacks against persons *hors de combat*[596], which is also enshrined in Common Article 3 (1)(a), or to the prohibition of violence to life and person, in particular murder of all kinds of, *inter alia*, persons *hors de combat*.[597]

590 See ICTY, Prosecutor v Milorad Krnojelac, Judgment, 17 September 2003, Case No. IT-97-25-A para 220.

591 See Rule 70 in Jean-Marie Henckaerts and Louise Doswald-Beck, Customary International Humanitarian Law Volume I: Rules.

592 Rule 71 of the ICRC Study on Customary IHL.

593 Rule 72 of the ICRC Study on Customary IHL.

594 Rules 73 and 74 of the ICRC Study on Customary IHL.

595 Rule 46 of the ICRC Study on Customary IHL.

596 Rule 47 of the ICRC Study on Customary IHL.

597 Initially, Draft Protocol II contained an equivalent provision which was titled 'safeguard of an enemy hors de combat' (Draft Article 7). However, this provision did not make it into the final text of Additional Protocol II. Federal Political Department Bern, Official Records of the Diplomatic Conference on the Reaffirmation and Development of International Humanitarian Law Applicable in Armed Conflicts 1974-1977, Vol. IV, 22.

The destruction or seizure of property belonging to the adverse party unless required by imperative military reasons[598] is another customary IHL rule on prohibited methods of warfare which is applicable to NIACs. It is not included in Additional Protocol II but the ICC Statute, for example, considers it a war crime in NIACs to destroy or seize 'the property of an adversary unless such destruction or seizure be imperatively demanded by the necessities of the conflict'[599].

Further, the prohibition of pillage[600], also enshrined in Art. 4 (2)(g) Additional Protocol II, and the prohibition of starvation[601], also enshrined in Art. 14 Additional Protocol II, amount to customary IHL regarding prohibited methods of warfare applicable to NIACs.

The duty to allow and facilitate rapid and unimpeded passage of humanitarian relief for civilians in need also amounts to customary IHL applicable to NIACs.[602] Initially, it has been included in the text of Draft Protocol II but has been deleted later due to the aim of simplifying the Protocol's final text.[603] The same holds true regarding the prohibition of deception regarding the improper use of the White Flag of Truce or of other emblems, such as the distinctive emblems of the Geneva Conventions, the United Nations emblem, or other internationally recognized emblems.[604] Draft Protocol II used to encompass a prohibition regarding the misuse of recognized signs which has been deleted in the final text due to drafting cutbacks.[605] With Art. 12 Additional Protocol II, Additional Protocol II partly regulates the improper usage of distinctive emblems by referring to distinctive emblems of medical units and religious personnel.

One can conclude that customary international law governing NIACs began to form only after the periods of 1949 and 1977. Even during the

598 Rule 50 of the ICRC Study on Customary IHL.

599 See Art. 8 (2)(e)(xii) ICC Statute.

600 Rule 52 of the ICRC Study on Customary IHL.

601 Rule 53 of the ICRC Study on Customary IHL.

602 Rule 55 of the ICRC Study on Customary IHL.

603 See Draft Article 33 of Additional Protocol II in Federal Political Department Bern, Official Records of the Diplomatic Conference on the Reaffirmation and Development of International Humanitarian Law Applicable in Armed Conflicts 1974-1977, Vol. I and Vol. IV, 105 f.

604 See Rules 59-61 of the ICRC Study on Customary IHL.

605 Initially, Draft Article 23 (3) of Additional Protocol II encompassed the prohibition on recognized signs. See Federal Political Department Bern, Official Records of the Diplomatic Conference on the Reaffirmation and Development of International Humanitarian Law Applicable in Armed Conflicts 1974-1977 Vol. IV, 70 and Vol. VII, 129.

drafting process of Additional Protocol II, there was a prevalent hesitance among various state delegates in accepting that customary law also regulates internal armed conflicts. At that time, the prevailing view was that there was no consolidated state practice as regards the application of Common Article 3 and Additional Protocol II to internal armed conflicts which could be considered 'established custom'. This sentiment changed, especially, during the mid-1990s with the establishment of the UN *ad hoc* tribunals and an increasing focus on the human rights-orientation of IHL norms. Importantly, the expansion of applying customary law rules regarding conduct of hostilities to NIACs reflects an important trend of assimilating the law of both types of conflict and filling gaps which the partly rudimentary treaty law of NIACs leaves behind.

3. Conclusion

Prior to the adoption of the four Geneva Conventions of 1949 and its two Additional Protocols of 1977, the prevailing view was that international law only applies to 'wars' waged between two or more states. Armed violence exerted by insurgent groups vis-à-vis an incumbent state government was considered to fall within a state's sovereign legal order, and international law was considered unsuitable for regulating internal strife. Nevertheless, internal armed violence did not remain completely unregulated. During the first half of the 19th century, international law categorized internal armed violence as rebellion, insurgency or belligerency. However, IHL remained inapplicable to these categories of internal armed violence. Only a state of 'belligerency' has been considered grave enough to trigger the applicability of the laws of war.[606]

With the beginning of the 19th century, this sentiment changed – at least among the ICRC. Up until the adoption of the four Geneva Conventions of 1949, the ICRC has played an important role in initiating the regulation of internal strife through IHL. At numerous conferences and in continuous exchange with national Red Cross societies, the ICRC vigorously promoted the systematic regulation of NIACs through IHL. In contrast, states remained hesitant to regulate NIACs through a systematic body of law parallel to the regulation of IACs. This hesitance stemmed from an omnipresent fear of recognizing insurgent groups as equal parties to a

606 Anthony Cullen, The Concept of Non-International Armed Conflict in International Humanitarian Law 14.

conflict. Ultimately, the continuous efforts on behalf of the ICRC during the period before 1949 have paved the way for regulating NIACs through a systematic body of IHL, starting with the inclusion of Common Article 3 into all four Geneva Conventions of 1949, which ultimately expanded the Conventions' scope of application to NIACs, and culminating in the adoption of Additional Protocol II of 1979. Since then, NIACs have been subject to a step-by-step systematic regulation through both treaty and customary law.

The applicable humanitarian law of NIACs is modelled after the humanitarian law of IACs. Even though NIACs have gained the upper hand in the last decade, the applicable law to NIACs is less elaborated than the applicable law to IACs and often lacks necessary detail. Common Article 3, for example, omits any rules on conduct of hostilities, hence, on prohibited means and methods of warfare.

Likewise, the substance of Additional Protocol II is less extensive and less elaborated than the substance of Additional Protocol I, especially regarding rules on conduct of hostilities. This is the result of a firmly anchored sovereignty-oriented dichotomy between the legal regulation of interstate conflicts on the one hand and the legal regulation of internal armed conflicts on the other.

Ultimately, the fear of conferring a legal status to insurgent groups through the regulation of NIACs found expression in paragraph 4 of Common Article 3 which ensures that the provision's application 'shall not affect the legal status of the Parties to the conflict'. Nonetheless, the shortcomings of NIAC-treaty law have been remedied through expanding the scope of application of additional treaty law to NIACs as well as through applying customary IHL to NIACs alike. The trend of assimilating the law of both types of conflicts has been influenced by other branches of international law, such as IHRL, as well as it has been promoted by state practice and the jurisprudence of international criminal tribunals.[607]

607 Dieter Fleck (ed), The Handbook of International Humanitarian Law 646; Theodor Meron, 'The Humanization of Humanitarian Law' 261 ff.

Chapter 4: The Legality of Courts of NSAGs

> 'No state really accepts that armed groups are entitled to detain or try anyone.'[608]

This quote reflects the prevailing position of states towards the status of NSAGs as parties to NIACs and the legality of judicial mechanisms established by them.

The legality of courts of NSAGs can be based on three different legal frameworks: firstly, on the domestic law of a territorial state. Secondly, the own law of the respective NSAG could warrant the legality of establishing judicial institutions. And finally, insurgent courts could be legal according to IHL applicable to NIACs.

According to the law of the territorial state, the establishment of 'rebel courts' will always be illegal since the establishment of parallel, non-state governance structures is a serious encroachment on every state's sovereignty. It infringes upon the Westphalian system which is inherently linked to a state's claim to hold a monopoly over the administration of justice on its territory. By contrast, the establishment of 'rebel courts' will always be legal according to the insurgent group's own law – assuming the respective NSAG has adopted its own law.

Finally, the establishment of 'rebel courts' could be legal according to pertinent IHL provisions.

Even though the administration of justice is a governmental function par excellence, the applicable IHL framework in NICAs contains two provisions which explicitly address the administration of justice during NIACs: Common Article 3 (1)(d) and Art. 6 (2) Additional Protocol II. Both provisions regulate the establishment and operation of courts during armed conflict by imposing obligations and requirements as regards the constitution of the court as well as the execution of judicial proceedings.

According to Common Article 3 (1)(d), the respective adjudicating court must be 'regularly constituted' and must afford 'all judicial guarantees with are recognized as indispensable by all civilized people'.

---

608 Andrew Clapham, 'The Limits of Human Rights in Armed Conflicts and Other Situations of Armed Violence' in Bardo Fassbender and Knut Traisbach (eds), The Limits of Human Rights (1st edn, Oxford University Press 2019) 305-318, 315.

Art. 6 (2) Additional Protocol II demands that the adjudicating court must offer 'the essential guarantees of independence and impartiality'. Notably, it omits the requirement of being 'regularly constituted'.

This chapter seeks to demonstrate that IHL foresees the possibility for NSAGs to legally try individuals through their own courts during NIACs.

It focuses on the question to what extent courts of NSAGs can be considered legal in international law if they adhere to pertinent statutory requirements. It starts with determining the applicable scope of both Common Article 3 (1)(d) and Art. 6 Additional Protocol II in relation to courts of NSAGs (Section 1). Subsequently, the provisions' constituent elements of 'regularly constituted court', 'indispensable judicial guarantees' and 'independence and impartiality' will be assessed. This analysis will demonstrate normative as well as practical challenges when subjecting courts of NSAGs to the standards of Common Article 3 (1)(d) and Art. 6 (2) Additional Protocol II. Hence, the chapter continues by introducing corrective standards to strengthen the position of NSAGs and to remedy the inherent asymmetric nature of NIACs (Sections 2 and 3). Thereafter, the chapter elaborates on the norm character of both Common Article 3 (1)(d) and Art. 6 (2) Additional Protocol II and assesses whether these provisions indeed carry legality for courts of NSAGs (Section 4). Finally, the formulation of practical parameters shall indicate the type of NSAGs which will most likely be able to adhere to the standards of Common Article 3 (1)(d) and/or Art. 6 (2) Additional Protocol II (Section 5).

I. Scope of IHL Provisions Relating to the Administration of Justice by NSAGs

Before delving into an analysis of the constituent requirements of Common Article 3 (1)(d) and Art. 6 (2) Additional Protocol II, it should be noted that both provisions limit their scope of application to criminal law matters. Both norm texts explicitly refer to 'the passing of sentences' and the 'carrying out of executions'. This leaves out other areas frequently covered by 'rebel' administered justice, such as civil- and family law matters.

Additionally, Art. 6 (1) Additional Protocol II confines the provision's scope to the 'prosecution and punishment of criminal offences related to the armed conflict'. This narrowing requirement can also be found in Art. 5 (1) Additional Protocol II which relates to fundamental guarantees for persons whose liberty has been restricted 'for reasons related to the armed conflict'. Hence, whereas both provisions focus on the administration of justice in criminal law matters, Art. 6 Additional Protocol II solely applies to criminal offences which have a nexus to an armed conflict. The nexus requirement to an armed conflict is also a prerequisite in establishing war crimes pursuant to Art. 8 ICC Statute. According to the authoritative ICTY jurisprudence, a nexus to armed conflict requires that 'the existence of an armed conflict must, at a minimum, have played a substantial part in the perpetrator's ability to commit it, his decision to commit it, the manner in which it was committed or the purpose for which it was committed'[609]. A nexus element can be said to be established where the perpetrator acted 'in furtherance of or under the guise of the armed conflict'[610]. It is reasonable to interpret the nexus element in Art. 6 (1) Additional Protocol II in accordance with the well-known ICTY approach. Hence, the point of departure to determine the nexus would be the individual perpetrator and the specific offence.

In this regard, some authors define the nexus element in Art. 6 (1) Additional Protocol II to encompass crimes which have been committed by an individual utilizing the special situation during an armed conflict.[611] Others, however, argue that every prosecution and punishment conducted by an armed group is 'related to the armed conflict' since the armed conflict accommodates the parallel justice system in rebel held territory.

Hence, any recourse to administering justice during armed conflict by a NSAG is rooted in the existence of armed conflict and happens in furtherance of its overall conflict agenda.[612]

The interpretation of the nexus element in Art. 6 (1) Additional Protocol II very much depends upon whether one reads the suffix 'related to armed conflict' in reference to 'criminal offences' or in reference to 'the prosecution and punishment'. Since Art. 6 Additional Protocol II is an IHL provision, it is reasonable to determine the nexus element in an IHL-specific manner. Art. 6 Additional Protocol II is a provision applicable to NIACs, addressing the scope of penal prosecutions conducted by either party to

609 ICTY, Prosecutor v Ragoljub Kunarac et al., Appeals Judgement para 58.

610 Ibid.

611 Michael Bothe, Karl Josef Partsch and Waldemar A. Solf, New Rules for Victims of Armed Conflict: Commentary on the Two 1977 Protocols Additional to the Geneva Conventions of 1949, 740.

612 Such a view is adopted by René Provost, Rebel Courts: The Administration of Justice by Armed Insurgents 174 f. and 178. This approach does not necessarily hold true for the state parties to NIACs since the administration of justice by states is not wholly and systematically rooted in the existence of armed conflict.

the conflict. What is put into question is the extent of the applicability of IHL to 'rebel' administered justice. Bearing this in mind, the nexus in Art. 6 (1) Additional Protocol II seeks to limit the provision's applicability to times of armed conflict without postulating a subject matter limitation of the prosecuted crimes itself. Hence, the administration of criminal matters without a specific link to the existence of armed conflict is covered as well. This conclusion is consistent with the provision's aim to provide protection to persons who have been deprived of their liberty for reasons related to armed conflict. It is also systematically coherent as it corresponds to Common Article 3's implied nexus element 'in the case of armed conflict', included in the provision's *chapeau*.[613]

Accordingly, one can conclude that both provisions cover the administration of justice during NIACs related to criminal matters only. Having clarified the relevant scope of Common Article 3 and Art. 6 Additional Protocol II, Sections 2 and 3 will assess the provision's constituent elements and put them into the context of 'rebel courts'.

II. Common Article 3 (1)(d) to all four Geneva Conventions and Courts of NSAGs

Common Article 3 amounts to a treaty in miniature applicable to NIACs. The provision stipulates fundamental guarantees for persons taking no active part in hostilities, including members of the armed forces who have laid down their arms and those placed *hors de combat* by sickness, wounds, detention, or any other cause. One of those fundamental guarantees relates to criminal proceedings which must be conducted by a regularly constituted court affording fundamental judicial guarantees. The pertinent provision, Common Article 3 (1)(d), prohibits 'the passing of sentences and the carrying out of executions without previous judgement pronounced by a regularly constituted court, affording all the judicial guarantees which are recognized as indispensable by civilized people'.

613 In this line also ibid 179.

1. Common Article 3 (1)(d) to all four Geneva Conventions: analysis of its pertinent terms

The following analysis assesses the different interpretative approaches to the term 'regularly constituted court'. 'Regularly constituted court' is a term which has IHRL as well as ICL implications. Its interpretation ranges from referring to courts which have been established according to domestic law to courts fulfilling the requirements of independence and impartiality. The following interpretative analysis establishes an IHL specific interpretation of the relevant phrase 'regularly constituted court'. Such an IHL specific definition takes account of the context the provision operates in, namely, NIACs where at least one party to the conflict is not a state. Hence, an IHL specific definition of 'regularly constituted court' equally enables both state and non-state parties to establish regularly constituted courts. Such a wide, 'rebel'-friendly interpretation of Common Article 3 (1)(d) is consistent with the generic meaning to be given to the term in its context and in light of its object and purpose.

a. 'regularly constituted'

The term 'regularly constituted court' can be found in Common Article 3 (1)(d), in its equivalent ICL provision Art. 8 (2)(c)(iv) ICC Statute as well as in Art. 75 (4) Additional Protocol I – the latter containing fair trial guarantees applicable to IACs. It is not a commonly used terminology in other international legal instruments stipulating criteria for the administration of justice.[614] Common Article 3 (1)(d) closely resembles one component right of the right to a fair trial in IHRL, namely, the right to be tried by an 'independent and impartial', 'competent' tribunal 'established by law'. The IHRL-requirement of 'established by law' corresponds to the 'regularly constituted'-criterion set out in Common Article 3 (1)(d). Hence, the term 'regularly constituted' in Common Article 3 (1)(d) has human rights implications which must be considered in the term's interpretation. For this reason, the following analysis of the term 'regularly constituted' will concentrate on the impact of the fair trial requirement of 'established by

614 With the exception of Art. 66 Geneva Convention (IV) Relative to the Protection of Civilian Persons in Times of War which speaks of 'properly constituted, non-political military courts'.

law' in IHRL[615] while also highlighting other interpretative approaches to the term adopted by, for example, the ICRC or the ICC.

The right to a fair trial is stipulated in various human rights instruments, *inter alia*, in Art. 14 (1) ICCPR, Art. 6 (1) European Convention on Human Rights[616] (**ECHR**), Art. 47 EU Charter of Fundamental Rights[617] (**EUCFR**), Art. 7 (1) African Charter on Human and Peoples' Rights[618] (**ACHPR**) or Art. 8 (1) American Convention on Human Rights[619] (**ACHR**). With only minor differences in terminology, the aforementioned human rights provisions specify that for a trial to be fair it must be conducted by an independent and impartial tribunal. In addition to that, Art. 14 (1) ICCPR and Art. 8 (1) ACHR demand that the tribunal is competent as well as established by law – notably, Art. 8 (1) ACHR requires the tribunal to be 'previously established by law'. Similarly, Art. 6 (1) ECHR requires that the tribunal must be established by law. Art. 47 (2) EUCFR also requires an 'independent and impartial tribunal previously established by law'. Hence, the 'established by law'-criterion is the common requirement which IHRL stipulates for the establishment of courts.

The 'established by law'-criterion resembles the requirement that the respective tribunal must be 'competent'. Both criteria relate to the existence and the work of the court, respectively. The European Court of Human Rights (**ECtHR**), for example, interprets these criteria by demanding that the judicial organization, including the establishment of a tribunal as well as its work and personnel composition, must be regulated by law emanating from parliament.[620] The word 'law' has been interpreted by the ECtHR as meaning 'domestic law', implying that 'domestic law' emanates from

615 However, those criteria will be assessed in detail when discussing Art. 6 (2) Additional Protocol II as a legal basis for courts of NSAGs.

616 European Convention on Human Rights, Council of Europe Treaty Series No. 5, 3 September 1953.

617 Charter of Fundamental Rights of the European Union, Official Journal of the European Union 2012/C 326/02, 1 December 2009.

618 African Charter on Human and Peoples' Rights, Organization of African Unity Doc. CAB/LEG/67/3 rev.5, 21 I.L.M 58 (1982) 21 October 1986.

619 American Convention on Human Rights, UN Treaty Series Vol. 1144 No. 17955, 22 November 1969.

620 See, e.g., ECtHR, Leo Zand v Austria, Decision, Application No. 7360/76 para 69; ECtHR, Savino and Others v Italy, Chamber Judgment, 28 April 2009, Application Nos. 17214/05, 20329/05 and 42113/04 para 94; ECtHR, Pandjikidzé and Others v Georgia, Judgment, 27 October 2009, Application No. 30323/02 para 105.

states[621]. According to the definition of the ECtHR, courts of NSAGs would never be considered 'established by law'.

The differentiation between 'established by law' and 'previously established by law' occurring in, *inter alia*, Art. 8 (1) ACHR and Art. 47 (2) EU-CFR, relates to the controversy whether *ad hoc* established courts or special tribunals can be considered lawful. The Inter-American Court of Human Rights (**IACtHR**), for example, held that the right to a fair trial shall protect persons from being tried by 'special tribunals set up for the case, or *ad hoc*'[622]. The right to a fair trial requires states 'not to create tribunals that do not use the duly established procedures to displace the jurisdiction normally belonging to the ordinary courts'.

By contrast, the ICCPR, the ECHR as well as the ACHPR omit the word 'previously' which implies that special or *ad hoc* tribunals are lawful if their establishment is based on law emanating from parliament.

In line with the state-centric interpretation of the 'established by law'-criterion followed in many IHRL instruments, the ICRC study on customary IHL stipulates that a 'a court is regularly constituted if it has been established and organised in accordance with the laws and procedures already in force in a country.'[623] The ICRC study on customary IHL stipulates that the right to a fair trial amounts to customary international law, applicable to both IACs and NIACs. In its Rule 100, the study states that 'No one may be convicted or sentenced, except pursuant to a fair trial affording all essential judicial guarantees.'[624] The study reaffirms that a fair trial must be provided for by an 'independent, impartial and regularly constituted court'[625], hence, by a court that has been established in accordance with the law already in existence before the outburst of armed violence. Accordingly, this definition renders a legal establishment of courts of NSAGs in times of armed conflict almost impossible. Since the pertinent phrase stipulated by the ICRC study on customary IHL must be understood as solely referring to the law of the respective state, only such courts established by NSAGs which would

621 ECtHR, Gudmundur Andri Ástrádsson v Iceland, Judgment, 1 December 2020, Application No. 26374/18 para 229.

622 IACtHR, Apitz Barbara et al. ("First Court of Administrative Disputes") v Venezuela, Judgment, 5 August 2008, Case No. Series C No. 182 para 50; IACtHR, Case of Castillo Petruzzi et al. v Peru, Judgment, 30 May 1999, Case No. Series C No. 52 para 129 referring to 'regular courts'.

623 Jean-Marie Henckaerts and Louise Doswald-Beck, Customary International Humanitarian Law Volume I: Rules Rule 100, 355.

624 Ibid Rule 100, 352.

625 Ibid Rule 100, 354.

continue to apply the law of the government, and which would make use of the judicial institutions of the government – the respective group is usually fighting against – were to be considered lawful according to this definition.

Interestingly, the ICRC commentary does not mention the 'regularly constituted court'-criterion but instead focuses on the criteria of impartiality and independence. The ICRC commentary stresses the different formulation in Art. 6 (2) Additional Protocol II which speaks of a court 'offering the essential guarantees of independence and impartiality' omitting the requirement of a regularly constituted court. According to the ICRC commentary on Common Article 3 (1)(d), the requirements of independence and impartiality of the judiciary are the touchstones for interpreting whether a court is 'regularly constituted'. Hence, an alternative approach of interpreting the 'regularly constituted court'-criterion is to focus on the way the respective court operates rather than on how it is established.[626]

This shift of focus in defining a 'regularly constituted court' has also been followed by the ICC. Art. 8 (2)(c)(iv) ICC Statute criminalizes the conduct laid down in Common Article 3 (1)(d) and, thereby, translates a fundamental guarantee of the humanitarian law framework applicable to NIACs into the field of ICL. Art. 8 (2)(c)(iv) ICC Statute is an *in verbatim* copy of Common Article 3 (1)(d), except for the change in words as regards 'civilized people' and 'generally'. The ICC Elements of Crimes (**ICC EoC**) specify that a 'regularly constituted court' is a court which affords the 'essential guarantees of independence and impartiality'.

Hence, similar to the ICRC commentary, the ICC mingles the 'established by law'-criterion with the 'independence and impartiality'-criteria. The ICC EoC's definition reads as follows:

> 'the court that rendered judgement was not "regularly constituted", that is, it did not afford the essential guarantees of independence and impartiality, or the court that rendered judgement did not afford all other judicial guarantees generally recognized as indispensable under international law'.[627]

Hence, the ICC EoC mingle the *de jure*-requirement of Common Article 3 (1)(d) with the conduct-requirement of Art. 6 (2) Additional Proto-

626 For the sake of coherency, these criteria will be discussed in the section on Art. 6 (2) Additional Protocol II.

627 'that is' in the English text and 'en ce sens qu'il' in the French text.

col II[628] in a manner which suggests that the establishment of a court is 'regular', hence, 'according to law' and 'lawful' if it adheres to the requirements of 'independence and impartiality'.[629] This assumption has recently been confirmed by the Court in the case against Mr. *Al Hassan* concerning the situation in the Republic of Mali. Mr. *Al Hassan* is charged with, *inter alia*, the NIAC war crime of 'the passing sentencing and the carrying out of without previous judgment pronounced by a regularly constituted court, affording all judicial guarantees which are generally recognized as indispensable' pursuant to Art. 8 (2)(c)(iv) ICC Statute. The Confirmation of Charges decision follows the definition set out in the ICC EoC. It highlights that for determining whether a court is regularly constituted, the focus rests on the question whether it (the court) is capable of providing independent and impartial proceedings and not on the question of how the court was initially established.[630] Pre-Trial Chamber II explicitly held that 'les caractéristiques d'indépendance et d'impartialité *sont* les caractéristiques requises pour qu'un tribunal soit considéré comme "régulièrement constitué" au sens du Statut.'[631] According to the ICC's understanding, the Drafters of the ICC Statute consciously departed from the definition set out in Common Article 3 (1)(d) and drafted the war crime of Art. 8 (2)(c)(iv) ICC Statute in a manner which disregards the formal act of establishment of a court to be a constitutive element of the crime's *actus reus*.

As will be discussed later in this chapter[632], departing from a *de jure*-centered approach to interpreting the term 'regularly constituted' is warranted by the ordinary meaning to be given to the provision's terms, its context as well as by its object and purpose.

---

628 This becomes also apparent in the confirmation of charges decision in the Al Hassan case, see, ICC, Prosecutor v Al Hassan Ag Abdoul Aziz Ag Mohamed Ag Mahmoud, Rectificatif à la Décision relative á la confiramtion des charges portées contre Al Hassan Ag Abdoul Aziz Ag Mohamed Ag Mahmoud para 358.

629 This observation has also been made by Jonathan Somer, 'Jungle justice: passing sentence on the equality of belligerents in non-international armed conflict' 674.

630 'Cette interprétation met donc l'accent sur la capacité du tribunal de conduire un procès équitable plûtot que sur la façon dont il est établi.' See ICC, Prosecutor v Al Hassan Ag Abdoul Aziz Ag Mohamed Ag Mahmoud, Rectificatif à la Décision relative á la confiramtion des charges portées contre Al Hassan Ag Abdoul Aziz Ag Mohamed Ag Mahmoud para 376.

631 Ibid para 376.

632 See under II. 2. B.

b. 'judicial guarantees which are recognized as indispensable'

In its second half-sentence, Common Article 3 (1)(d) demands that the respective court must provide for 'judicial guarantees which are recognized as indispensable'. Common Article 3 (1)(d) does not include a list with specific judicial guarantees which must be adhered to. However, Art. 6 (2) Additional Protocol II does contain such a list. The judicial rights enumerated in Art 6 (2)-(4) Additional Protocol II are considered customary international law and, for the most part, are based on Art. 14 and Art. 15 ICCPR.[633] Additionally, Art. 75 (4) Additional Protocol I also provides for a list with specific judicial guarantees, again influenced by Art. 14 and Art. 15 ICCPR. The ICRC commentary suggests interpreting the phrase in Common Article 3 (1)(d) in accordance with the judicial guarantees explicitly listed in Art. 6 (2) Additional Protocol II and Art. 75 (4) Additional Protocol I, respectively. This is reasonable against the backdrop of enhancing 'systemic integrity'[634] in international law. Likewise, the ICC suggests drawing on the judicial guarantees contained in Art. 6 (2) Additional Protocol II, Art. 75 (4) Additional Protocol I as well as in other human rights treaties such as the ICCPR, ECHR, ACHR, or ACHPR.[635]

Accordingly, 'judicial guarantees which are recognized as indispensable' contain, *inter alia*, the right to be informed without delay about the particulars of the offence, the right to have the necessary means of defence, the right to be presumed innocent until proven guilty, the right to be tried in one's presence, the right to be tried without undue delay[636], the right not to be compelled to testify against oneself, the principle of individual criminal liability, the principle of *nullum crimen, nulla poena sine lege*, as well as the right to be advised of one's judicial and other remedies and of the time limits within which they may be exercised.[637] The list of judicial guarantees in Art. 75 (4) Additional Protocol I contains three additional guarantees:

633 See Rule 100 in Jean-Marie Henckaerts and Louise Doswald-Beck, Customary International Humanitarian Law Volume I: Rules 357-370.

634 Katharine Fortin, 'The Procedural Right to a Remedy When the State has Left the Building? A Reflection on Armed Groups, Courts and Domestic Law' 405.

635 ICC, Prosecutor v Al Hassan Ag Abdoul Aziz Ag Mohamed Ag Mahmoud, Rectificatif à la Décision relative á la confiramtion des charges portées contre Al Hassan Ag Abdoul Aziz Ag Mohamed Ag Mahmoud para 383.

636 See, e.g., in Art. 14 (3)(c) ICCPR, Art. 7 (1) ACHPR.

637 ICRC, Commentary of 2016 on Convention (I) for the Amelioration of the Condition of the Wounded and Sick in Armed Forces in the Field (International Committee of the Red Cross 2016) para 685; ICC, Prosecutor v Al Hassan Ag Abdoul Aziz Ag Mohamed Ag Mahmoud, Rectificatif à la Décision relative á la confiramtion des

the right to present and examine witnesses, the right to have the judgment pronounced publicly, and the right not to be prosecuted or punished twice for the same offence under the same law and judicial procedure (*ne bis in idem*).

Interestingly, the right not to be punished twice was not included into the list of Art. 6 (2) Additional Protocol II as the drafters considered it difficult to apply this principle in the context of a NIAC where at least one party to the conflict is not a state.[638]

c. A fit for purpose definition of 'regularly constituted court'

The foregoing analysis of the 'regularly constituted court'-criterion stipulated in Common Article 3 (1)(d) revealed that its interpretation carries implications from other realms of international law.

Firstly, it carries ICL implications due to the criminal transposition of Common Article 3 (1)(d) into the war crime stipulated in Art. 8 (2)(c)(iv) ICC Statute. The ICC interprets the term 'regularly constituted court' as a court which adheres to the requirements of 'independence and impartiality'.

Secondly, the pertinent term 'regularly constituted court' has an IHRL connotation because of the provision's strong resemblance with the IHRL component right of being tried by an 'independent' and 'impartial' tribunal, 'established by law'. A synopsis of Common Article 3 (1)(d) and the right to a fair trial component in IHRL reveals that the IHL-term 'regularly constituted court' in Common Article 3 (1)(d) corresponds to the IHRL-term 'established by law'. International and regional human rights bodies have interpreted the latter term by requiring a tribunal that has been established by state law emanating from parliament. This interpretation is particularly sensitive given the fact that Common Article 3 (1)(d) is an IHL provision applicable to NIACs, where at least one party is not a state.

---

charges portées contre Al Hassan Ag Abdoul Aziz Ag Mohamed Ag Mahmoud para 384.

638 ICRC, Commentary of 2016 on Convention (I) for the Amelioration of the Condition of the Wounded and Sick in Armed Forces in the Field para 687; Michael Bothe, Karl Josef Partsch and Waldemar A. Solf, New Rules for Victims of Armed Conflict: Commentary on the Two 1977 Protocols Additional to the Geneva Conventions of 1949, 745.

The 'regularly constituted court'-requirement is, in its core, a requirement stipulated by IHL applicable to NIACs. Hence, Common Article 3 (1) (d) operates in a different context than Art. 6 (1) ECHR, Art. 14 (1) ICCPR or Art. 8 (1) ACHR do, and this context matters. The latter provisions are part of either international or regional human rights instruments, and as such, they address states in the first place.[639] Common Article 3 (1)(d) operates in the context of NIACs and addresses the parties thereto. Importantly, Common Article 3 (1)(d) also addresses non-state actors. Therefore, a fit for purpose interpretation of Common Article 3 (1)(d) should take account of the context the provision operates in. It should be tailored to the special context of NIACs where at least one party to it is not a state. It should be based in IHL and it should depart from the state-centricity of international law.

For this reason, the requirement of a 'regularly constituted court' in Common Article 3 (1)(d), specified through its IHRL connotation of 'established by law', must be defined in a manner which renders an inclusion of a non-state party to the conflict equally possible. This, ultimately, leads one to ask whether 'established by law' should be defined to include law of NSAGs as well.

2. Enabling NSAGs to convene courts 'established by law': a departure from state centricity in international law

Common Article 3 (1)(d) demands that the respective court must be 'regularly constituted' which means that it must be 'established by law'. In the context of courts established by NSAGs during armed conflict, the pondering question is whose law is meant by that formulation: the law of the respective domestic state or the law of the respective NSAG. Since Common Article 3 (1)(d) applies to NIACs where at least one party to it is not a state, it is inevitable to raise the question whether the word 'law' is confined to state law or whether the context Common Article 3 (1)(d) operates in, namely NIACs, demands an interpretation of the word 'law'

639 Although many scholars have discussed and promoted the human rights obligations of NSAGs too, see e.g. Andrew Clapham, Human Rights Obligations of Non-State Actors; Katharine Fortin, The Accountability of Armed Gorups under Human Rights; Tilman Rodenhäuser, Organizing Rebellion: Non-State Armed Groups under International Humanitarian Law, Human Rights Law, and International Criminal Law.

which includes non-state law. This ultimately is a question of whether one applies a state centric or a non-state centric approach in defining the terms 'regularly constituted' and 'established by law', respectively.

a. 'Established by (state) law': traditional state-centricity in international law

A state-centric interpretation of the word 'law' would encompass domestic law of states only. Consequently, the establishment of courts by NSAGs during NIACs would never be in accordance with Common Article 3 (1) (d). In other words, NSAGs would not be equally entitled to install their own judicial mechanisms during armed conflict – only states would be entitled to do so. Judicial mechanisms of NSAGs would only correspond to this narrow interpretation if the respective NSAG operated in already existing (state) courts and applying already existing (state) law.[640] Such a state-centric view, for example, is adopted by the ICRC study on customary IHL which states that a court is regularly constituted if it 'has been established and organised in accordance with the laws and procedures already in force in a country'.[641] This view was also adopted by the US Supreme Court in the *Hamdan v Rumsfeld* decision concerning the legality of the Guantanamo Military Commission, a military court, at Guantanamo Bay.[642] In his dissenting opinion, Justice *Alito* reasoned that a regularly constituted court is 'a court that has been appointed, set up, or established in accordance with the domestic law of the appointing country'[643].

Such a view, however, denies the reality of archetypical NIAC-dynamics where usually the involved NSAG is fighting the incumbent state government to either seek a reform or to replace it. Hence, the respective NSAG will most likely never apply already existing state law when administering justice but, on the contrary, apply its own law.

---

640 See Mark Klamberg, 'The Legality of Rebel Courts during Non-International Armed Conflicts' (2018) 16 Journal of International Criminal Justice 235-263, 243 and Sandesh Sivakumaran, 'Courts of Armed Opposition Groups: Fair Trials or Summary Justice?' 499 f.

641 See Jean-Marie Henckaerts and Louise Doswald-Beck, Customary International Humanitarian Law Volume I: Rules Rule 100, 355.

642 Supreme Court of the United States, Hamdan v Rumsfeld, Secretary of Defense et al., Judgment, 29 June 2006, Case No. 05-184. In this decision, the US Supreme Court ruled that the military court at Guantanamo Bay was illegal under the Geneva Conventions because it was not 'regularly constituted'.

643 Ibid, Dissenting opinion (Alito).

Moreover, a state-centric approach renders the provision's *chapeau*, according to which the guarantees enlisted in Common Article 3 should equally apply to both parties to the conflict, effectless. It diminishes the principle of equality of belligerents.

Ultimately, it does not take account of the context the provision operates in, namely, NIACs where at least one party is always non-state. Notably, this approach also renders the judicial guarantees enshrined in Common Article 3 (1)(d) and Art. 6 (2) Additional Protocol II effectless in NIACs which are fought solely between NSAGs with no state party involved.[644]

b. 'Established by (non-) state law'?

By contrast, a non-state centric interpretation of the terms 'regularly constituted' and 'established by law' would equally include the law of the respective NSAG. In this case, 'rebel courts' would be 'regularly constituted' and 'established by law' if they were established according to the law of the respective group. Such an interpretation is promoted by the provision's plain text, the context it operates in as well as by its object and purpose as a fundamental guarantee applicable to both parties in a NIAC. Hence, an interpretation of Common Article 3 (1)(d) according to which a court is 'regularly constituted' if it is either established according to the law of the respective state or according to the law of the respective NSAG is warranted by Art. 31 (1) VCLT, the general rule on interpretation of treaties.

Firstly, the plain meaning of the word 'law' does not imply the nature of the entity creating and adjudicating it. Law as such refers to norms and doctrines which are perceived as binding by a certain community.[645] The Oxford Dictionary of Law defines 'law' as an 'enforceable body of rules that govern any society'[646]. As such, law can be created by states but also by non-state entities.

---

644 Also noted by Ezequiel Heffes, 'Generating Respect for International Humanitarian Law: The Establishment of Courts by Organized Non-State Armed Groups in Light of the Principle of Equality of Belligerents' 190 f. He also draws attention to the scenario where a third state is involved in a NIAC, which raises the question of whose domestic law would apply.

645 I do not intend to delve into other meanings of law such as the laws of nature or the laws of logic.

646 Jonathan Law (ed), A Dictionary of Law (10th edn, Oxford University Press 2022) 316.

Secondly, a contextual interpretation of Common Article 3 (1)(d) demands the inclusion of law created by NSAGs. The prohibition on summary justice enshrined in Common Article 3 (1)(d) is part of the IHL body applicable to NIACs. In the context of NIACs one party to it will always be non-state. Hence, the context of NIACs demands a broad interpretation of the terms 'regularly constituted' and 'established by law', including 'law' of the non-state party. Additionally, the combined context of Common Article 3 (1)(d) and Art. 6 (2) Additional Protocol II warrants a non-state friendly interpretation of the pertinent term. Art. 6 (2) Additional Protocol II also addresses the installment of judicial mechanisms in times of NIACs. Art. 6 (2)(c) Additional Protocol II refers to 'the law' when stipulating the principle of *nullum crimen, sine lege praevia* according to which 'no one shall be held guilty of any criminal offence on account of any act or omission which did not constitute a criminal offence, under the law, at the time when it was committed'.[647] Similarly, does Art. 6 (2) (d) Additional Protocol II refer to 'law' when stipulating the presumption of innocence. Hence, both Common Article 3 (1)(d) and Art. 6 (2) Additional Protocol II refer to the word 'law' in their material scope and both provisions apply to NIACs where at least one party to the conflict is not a state. Interestingly, Art. 6 (2)(c) Additional Protocol II uses the term 'under the law', not indicating which or whose law is meant. By contrast, Art. 75 (4)(c) Additional Protocol I which stipulates the same guarantee but for IACs, speaks of 'national or international law'.[648] Hence, the wording in Art. 6 (2)(c) Additional Protocol II, plainly referring to 'the law', is a conscious omission of the words 'national' or 'international'.[649]

The *travaux préperatoires* of the Diplomatic Conference on the Reaffirmation and Development of International Humanitarian Law Applicable in Armed Conflicts 1974-1977 reveal that the delegates intended to broaden the

647 It reads as follows: 'no one shall be held guilty of any criminal offence on account of any act or omission which did not constitute a criminal offence, under the law, at the time it was committed'.

648 So does Art. 15 (1) ICCPR.

649 The French text of Art. 6 (2)(c) Additional Protocol II, however, speaks of 'le droit national ou international'. See ICRC, Commentary of 1987 Protocol Additional to the Geneva Conventions of 12 August 1949, and relating to the Protection of Victims of Non-International Armed Conflicts (Protocol II), 8 June 1977 para 4606.

scope of 'the law' in Art. 6 (2)(c) Additional Protocol II to also cover law enacted by an insurgent group.[650]

One delegate has wisely put it: 'Draft Protocol II must be drawn up in realistic fashion, taking careful account of the special nature of non-international armed conflicts. In such conflicts there was often a lack of symmetry between the two parties, with one tending to be considerably stronger than the other.'[651]

The delegates have recognized the possibility of insurgent groups to establish courts according to their own set of law and intended to enable courts of NSAGs to equally be covered by the provision's material scope.[652] The delegate of Nigeria, for example, pointed out that that 'it was only logical that if rebels could organize themselves sufficiently to observe the Protocols, and thereby enjoy their protection, they could also organize a recognizable body of law.'[653] This view is also supported by the Commentary on Additional Protocol II which speaks of the 'possible co-existence of two sorts of national legislations, namely that of the state and that of the insurgents'[654]. In a similar vein, the UK Manual of the Law of Armed Conflict, for example, adopts a broad definition of 'law' according to which 'the law' in Art. 6 (2)(c) Additional Protocol II 'could also be wide enough to cover "laws" passed by an insurgent authority'[655].

650 Michael Bothe, Karl Josef Partsch and Waldemar A. Solf, New Rules for Victims of Armed Conflict: Commentary on the Two 1977 Protocols Additional to the Geneva Conventions of 1949, 746.

651 Delegate of Spain (Mr. Murillo Rubiera), Federal Political Department Bern, Official Records of the Diplomatic Conference on the Reaffirmation and Development of International Humanitarian Law Applicable in Armed Conflicts 1974-1977, Vol. VIII, CDDH/I./SR.34, para 26.

652 Ibid, Vol. IX, CDDH/I/SR. 63, paras 59-64, and CDDH/I/SR. 64, paras 54 and 79.

653 See Delegat of Nigeria (Mr. Abdul-Malik), ibid, Vol. VIII, CDDH/I/SR.34, para 20.

654 Yves Sandoz, Christophe Swinarski and Bruno Zimmermann (eds), Commentary on the Additional Protocols of 8 June 1977 to the Geneva Conventions of 12 August 1949 (1st edn, International Committee of the Red Cross and Martinus Nijhoff 1987) 1339; ICRC, Commentary of 1987 Protocol Additional to the Geneva Conventions of 12 August 1949, and relating to the Protection of Victims of Non-International Armed Conflicts (Protocol II), 8 June 1977 para 4605; Ezequiel Heffes, 'Generating Respect for International Humanitarian Law: The Establishment of Courts by Organized Non-State Armed Groups in Light of the Principle of Equality of Belligerents' 192.

655 UK Ministry of Defence (2004) The Joint Service Manual of the Law of Armed Conflict 404 at fn 94; Ezequiel Heffes, 'Generating Respect for International Humanitarian Law: The Establishment of Courts by Organized Non-State Armed Groups in Light of the Principle of Equality of Belligerents' 192.

Hence, a contextual interpretation of Common Article 3 (1)(d) which takes special account of the provision's link to Art. 6 (2) Additional Protocol II, suggests a broad and non-state-friendly interpretation of the pertinent terms, enabling NSAGs to equally fulfill *de jure* requirements such as 'regularly constituted'. Consequently, applying Common Article 3 (1)(d) to a non-state party involved in a NIAC leads to the conclusion that a court is 'regularly constituted' and established by law' if the respective NSAGs has installed its judicial mechanisms in accordance with its own set of law.

The conclusion resulting from a contextual analysis is also bolstered by real life examples. In Afghanistan, the Taliban produced its own Code of Conduct, the 'Layha for the Mujahideen', which also provides for a *jus in bello* section, albeit based on Islamic Law and not on international humanitarian treaty law.[656] The Sudan People's Liberation Army (**SPLA**) adopted its own law, titled 'Laws of the New Sudan, SPLA Act 2003', which regulated the establishment of so-called courts-martial and even provided for the principle of *ne bis in idem*. During the armed conflict in El Salvador between 1980-1992, the FMLN have relied on their own set of law which was codified in a document titled 'Principles, Norms and Measures Ordered by FMLN in the Course of the War'[657]. In this document, the FMLN codified provisions and fundamental guarantees related to the group's own penal system. In its third report, ONUSAL assessed the group's codified guarantees in relation to criminal proceedings and found that those guarantees fell short of the requirements stipulated in both Common Article 3 (1)(d) and Art. 6 (2) Additional Protocol II.[658] Albeit criticizing the shortcomings of the FMLN's codified judicial guarantees, ONUSAL considered non-state law in its assessment of Art. 6 Additional Protocol II.[659] This implies that ONUSAL accepted the general competence of NSAGs to issue their own laws.[660] It also suggests that the term 'law' in Art. 6 (2)(c) and (d) Additional Protocol II refers not only to state law but also to law that might have been adopted by NSAGs.

---

656 Muhammad Munir, 'The Layha for the Mujahideen: an analysis of the code of conduct for the Taliban fighters under Islamic Law' (2011) 93 International Review of the Red Cross 81-102, 85.

657 See Liesbeth Zegveld, The Accountability of Armed Opposition Groups in International Law 70 at fn 33.

658 ONUSAL, Third report of the United Nations Observer Mission in El Salvador (United Nations Observer Mission in El Salvador 19 February 1991) para 113.

659 See also Liesbeth Zegveld, The Accountability of Armed Opposition Groups in International Law 70 f.

660 Ibid 70.

Thirdly, the inclusion of non-state law into the scope of Common Article 3 (1)(d) also corresponds to the telos of Common Article 3. Common Article 3 stipulates fundamental guarantees applicable to NIACs which, according to the provision's *chapeau*, 'each Party to the conflict shall be bound to apply'. This phrase mirrors the so-called 'equality of belligerents'-principle which is central to *jus in bello*. The 'equality of belligerents'-principle ensures that all parties to the conflict have the same scope of rights and obligations regardless of their cause. The underlying idea that the warring parties to the conflict must adhere to certain rules of warfare irrespective of the justness of the cause to resort to armed conflict can be traced back already to Grotius' time.[661] This principle is central to the distinction between *jus in bello* and *jus ad bellum*. Whereas *jus ad bellum* refers to the legality of the use of force[662], *jus in bello* relates to the lawfulness of conduct during ongoing armed conflict. Notably, *jus in bello* applies equally to all parties to the armed conflict regardless of whether the initial use of force was in breach of *jus ad bellum* or not. At the same time, the applicability of IHL to conduct in armed conflict (*jus in bello*) does not legitimize the initial use of force (*jus ad bellum*).[663] Hence, *jus ad bellum* and *jus in bello* operate autonomously. For IACs, paragraph 5 of the Preamble to Additional Protocol I explicitly refers to the 'equality of belligerents'-principle by stating that 'the provisions of the Geneva Conventions of 12 August 1949 and of this Protocol must be fully applied in all circumstance to all persons who are protected by those instruments, without any adverse distinction based on the nature or origin of the armed conflict or on the causes espoused by or attributed to the Parties to the conflict'. For NIACs, the principle's applicability is implied in Common Article 1 to all four Geneva Conventions which stipulates that the Conventions shall be respected in 'all circumstances', and in Common Article 2 which stipulates that the Convention applies 'to all cases of declared war or [of] any other armed conflict'. It is also implied in the *chapeau* of Common Article 3 which refers to 'each Party to the conflict'.

---

661 See Stephen C. Neff, Hugo Grotius - On the Law of War and Peace (1st edn, Cambdrige University Press 2012).

662 See Art. 2 (4) UN Charta prohibiting any threat or use of force not justified under Art. 51 UN Charta.

663 See Preamble Additional Protocol I, 'Expressing their conviction that nothing in this Protocol or in the Geneva Conventions of 12 August 1949 can be construed as legitimizing or authorizing any act of aggression or any other use of force inconsistent with the Charter of the United Nations'.

Hence, the 'equality of belligerents'-principle stresses that the obligations and rights stipulated by *jus in bello* apply equally to both parties to the conflict.

Translated to NIACs, an effective 'equality of belligerents'- principle ensures the same rights for a NSAG as it does for the opposing – often state – party. Additionally, it ensures that NSAGs are equally able to fulfil the obligations stipulated by IHL.

Translated to the prohibition of 'summary justice' stipulated in Common Article 3 (1)(d), the principle warrants that NSAGs are equally able to install judicial mechanisms as their opposing party. Therefore, the 'regularly constituted court'-criterion must be interpreted to cover non-state law as well.[664]

This view is also endorsed by the ICRC. In its commentary on the Geneva Convention (I), the relevant passage reads as follows:

> 'Common Article 3 requires "a regularly constituted court". If this would refer exclusively to state courts constituted according to domestic law, non-State armed groups would not be able to comply with this requirement. The application of this rule in common Article 3 to "each Party to the conflict" would then be without effect. Therefore, to give effect to this provision, it may be argued that courts are regularly constituted as long as they are constituted according to the "laws" of the armed group'[665].

---

664 Ezequiel Heffes has been one of the first legal scholars to advance the opinion that the law of NSAGs should find equal recognition in the installment of judicial mechanisms during armed conflict pursuant to Common Article 3 (1)(d) and Art. 6 (2) Additional Protocol II. See Ezequiel Heffes, 'Generating Respect for International Humanitarian Law: The Establishment of Courts by Organized Non-State Armed Groups in Light of the Principle of Equality of Belligerents' 192; Ezequiel Heffes, 'The establishment of courts by armed groups: what is the legal basis?' (Humanitarian Law&Policy Blog accessed 27 May 2021; Ezequiel Heffes, 'Administration of justice by armed groups: Some legal and practical concerns' (Humanitarian Law&Policy Blog, 22 November 2018) accessed 27 May 2021 This view is endorsed by Jonathan Somer, 'Jungle justice: passing sentence on the equality of belligerents in non-international armed conflict' 687.

665 ICRC, Commentary of 2016 on Convention (I) for the Amelioration of the Condition of the Wounded and Sick in Armed Forces in the Field, Common Article 3 para 692; Ezequiel Heffes, 'Generating Respect for International Humanitarian Law: The Establishment of Courts by Organized Non-State Armed Groups in Light of the Principle of Equality of Belligerents' 191.

Finally, such a 'rebel'- friendly approach in interpreting Common Article 3 (1)(d) has also been promoted by other scholars in the academic debate on the legality of 'rebel courts'.[666]

Some of them advance policy considerations and claim that the acknowledgment of law by NSAGs would generate respect for IHL. They continue to reason that courts of NSAGs could be an immediate forum to enforce IHL during armed conflict to reduce the climate of impunity and, therefore, that courts of NSAGs may enhance overall compliance with relevant IHL norms.[667]

In conclusion, it is logical, consistent and, most importantly, it is doctrinally coherent to interpret the pertinent phrase of Common Article 3 (1)(d) in a manner which equally enables NSAGs to establish 'regularly constituted courts'. Otherwise IHL would stipulate an obligation which, in a NIAC, cannot possibly be fulfilled by one party to the conflict, which is the non-state party. This would run counter to the fundamental idea of IHL applicable to NIACs which is to postulate rules and obligations each party to the conflict shall be bound to apply.[668]

3. Conclusion

The analysis of the pertinent phrase 'regularly constituted court' in Common Article 3 (1)(d) leaves one to conclude that a court is regularly constituted if it is established according to the law of the party concerned, be it a state or a non-state party.[669] Otherwise, the provision's *chapeau*

666 Mark Klamberg, 'The Legality of Rebel Courts during Non-International Armed Conflicts' 242 f. and 262 f.; Sandesh Sivakumaran, The Law of Non-International Armed Conflict 306; Jonathan Somer, 'Jungle justice: passing sentence on the equality of belligerents in non-international armed conflict' 687-689.

667 Ezequiel Heffes, 'Generating Respect for International Humanitarian Law: The Establishment of Courts by Organized Non-State Armed Groups in Light of the Principle of Equality of Belligerents' 184; Sandesh Sivakumaran, The Law of Non-International Armed Conflict 549; Jan Willms, 'Courts of armed groups - a tool for inducing higher compliance with international humanitarian law?' in Heike Krieger (ed), Inducing Compliance with International Humanitarian Law - Lessons fron the African Great Lakes Region (1st edn, 2015) 149-180, 172 f.

668 See *chapeau* of Common Article 3.

669 This view is supported by Jan Willms, 'Courts of armed groups - a tool for inducing higher compliance with international humanitarian law?' in Heike Krieger (ed), Inducing Compliance with International Humanitarian Law - Lessons fron the African Great Lakes Region 152 as well as by Ezequiel Heffes, 'Generating Respect

would be obsolete. Despite the strong contextual arguments which suggest a wide, 'rebel'-friendly interpretation of the term 'regularly constituted', it is especially the 'equality of belligerents'- principle which provides the basis for affirming that 'regularly constituted' in Common Article 3 (1)(d) must be understood and applied as encompassing courts established by NSAGs according to their own law. Being mindful of the fact that both Common Article 3 and Art. 6 Additional Protocol II stipulate equal rights for states and NSAGs, it is logical and consistent to argue that if states can rely on their domestic law for the establishment of courts, NSAGs must be able to do the same. Within the scope of Common Article 3 (1)(d) this means that a court of a NSAG is 'regularly constituted' if it is 'established by its law'. Hence, a fit for purpose definition of Common Article 3 (1)(d) is found in the IHL framework applicable to NIACs and departs from the state-centricity of international law.

III. Article 6 (2) Additional Protocol II and Courts of NSAGs

Since Additional Protocol II is supplementing and developing Common Article 3[670], it also provides for fair trial guarantees, albeit in more detail. Especially, it clarifies the notion of 'essential judicial guarantees' in Art. 6 (2)(a)-(f) Additional Protocol II which is also expressed in the second half-sentence of Common Article 3 (1)(d). Art. 6 (2) Additional Protocol II stipulates that 'No sentence shall be passed and no penalty shall be executed on a person found guilty of an offence except pursuant to a conviction pronounced by a court offering the essential guarantees of independence and impartiality'.

1. Art. 6 (2) Additional Protocol II: analysis of its pertinent terms

The following analysis assesses the requirements of 'independence and impartiality' stipulated in Art. 6 (2) Additional Protocol II as well as the provision's enlisted judicial guarantees. It continues by demonstrating the

for International Humanitarian Law: The Establishment of Courts by Organized Non-State Armed Groups in Light of the Principle of Equality of Belligerents' 191.

670 ICRC, Commentary of 1987 Protocol Additional to the Geneva Conventions of 12 August 1949, and relating to the Protection of Victims of Non-International Armed Conflicts (Protocol II), 8 June 1977 para 4597.

capacity problem many NSAGs will likely face when being subjected to the relatively high standards of Art. 6 (2) Additional Protocol II. A uniform application of Art. 6 (2) Additional Protocol II to all parties of NIACs will always result in substantive inequality due to the inherent asymmetry in power relations and resources in traditional NIACs which are fought between state- and non-state parties. Therefore, the section concludes by seeking to formulate a differential standard which shall be adopted when applying Art. 6 (2) Additional Protocol II to NIACs and which shall remedy the disparities in power and resources of the warring parties to ultimately reach substantive equality.

a. 'Independence and impartiality'

The text of Art. 6 (2) Additional Protocol II almost *verbatim* repeats the text of Common Article 3 (1)(d), however, with one significant modification. In contrast to Common Article 3 (1)(d), which requires a 'regularly constituted court' providing 'all the judicial guarantees which are recognized as indispensable by civilized people', Art. 6 (2) Additional Protocol II requires a court 'offering the essential guarantees of independence and impartiality' while at the same time explicitly enumerating some of these fundamental guarantees in Art. 6 (2)(a)-(f) Additional Protocol II.

As mentioned above, this presents a shift from applying a *de jure*-based approach towards applying a conduct-based approach in assessing the legality of administering justice in times of armed conflict.[671] Since the provision's requirements of 'independence and impartiality' are not inextricably linked to a *de jure* status as opposed to the 'regularly constituted'-criterion set out in Common Article 3 (1)(d), Art. 6 (2) Additional Protocol II loosens the requirements for NSAGs to lawfully conduct criminal proceedings in times of armed conflict.

671 Mark Klamberg, 'The Legality of Rebel Courts during Non-International Armed Conflicts' 244; Jonathan Somer, 'Jungle justice: passing sentence on the equality of belligerents in non-international armed conflict' 670; see also ICRC, Commentary of 2016 on Convention (I) for the Amelioration of the Condition of the Wounded and Sick in Armed Forces in the Field para 678; see also ICC, Prosecutor v Al Hassan Ag Abdoul Aziz Ag Mohamed Ag Mahmoud, Rectificatif à la Décision relative á la confiramtion des charges portées contre Al Hassan Ag Abdoul Aziz Ag Mohamed Ag Mahmoud para 376 where Pre-Trial Chamber I held the following: 'Cette interprétation met donc l'accent sur la capacité du tribunal de conduir und procès équitable plutôt que sur la façon dont il est établi.'

Interestingly, the ICRC commentary notices that this shift of focus aimed at taking account of the special situation of NIACs, which is, having two or more parties fighting each other with often different resources and capacities and the unlikeliness for NSAGs to establish 'regularly constituted' courts according to national law.[672] Like Common Article 3 (1)(d), the requirements of 'independence and impartiality' laid down in Art. 6 (2) Additional Protocol II have IHRL implications too. Albeit both criteria are related to each other and do overlap, they still have a legal content of their own.[673]

According to the UN Human Rights Committee (**UNHRC**), 'independence' requires an 'actual independence of the judiciary from political interference by the executive branch and legislature'[674]. The functions and competencies of the executive and judiciary should be clearly distinguishable and the executive should not be able to control the judiciary.[675] The independence-requirement also refers to the procedure and qualifications for the appointment of judges as well as to the criteria and procedures regarding their tenure, promotion, suspension and dismissal.[676] The ICTR follows a similar line by requiring that a tribunal must be free from external, especially, political authority and pressure.[677] The ICRC commentary on customary IHL defines the independence of a court as being able to perform its functions independently from any other branch of the government, especially the executive.[678]

672 Yves Sandoz, Christophe Swinarski and Bruno Zimmermann (eds), Commentary on the Additional Protocols of 8 June 1977 to the Geneva Conventions of 12 August 1949 para 4600.

673 IACtHR, Apitz Barbara et al. ("First Court of Administrative Disputes") v Venezuela, Judgment para 55.

674 Human Rights Committee United Nations, General Comment No. 32 on Art. 14: Right to equality before courts and tribunals and to a fair trial, CCPR/C/GC/32, 23 August 2007 para 19.

675 Ibid para 19; Amal Clooney and Philippa Webb, The Right to a Fair Trial in International Law (1st edn, Oxford University Press 2021) 83.

676 Human Rights Committee United Nations, General Comment No. 32 on Art. 14: Right to equality before courts and tribunals and to a fair trial, CCPR/C/GC/32, 23 August 2007 para 19. This approach is also followed by the IACtHR, see IACtHR, Case of Reverón Trujillo v Venezuela, Judgment, 30 June 2009, Case No. Series C No. 179 paras 71, 75 and 80.

677 ICTR, The Prosecutor v Nahimana et al., Appeals Judgment, 28 November 2007, Case No. ICTR-99-52-A para 19.

678 Jean-Marie Henckaerts and Louise Doswald-Beck, Customary International Humanitarian Law Volume I: Rules Rule 100, 355.

The second criterion, the impartiality of courts, comprises two elements: a subjective and an objective one.[679] For instance, the UNHRC held that impartiality requires that 'judges must not be influenced by personal bias or prejudice, nor harbour preconceptions about the particular case before them, nor act in ways that improperly promotes the interests of one of the parties to the detriment of the other.'[680] Additionally, the objective side to the impartiality-test demands that the judicial body must appear impartial to a reasonable observer.[681] In a similar vein, the ICTR stresses that not only the judicial personnel must be subjectively impartial, hence, free from personal bias or predispositions, but also there must not be any circumstances which objectively would give rise to doubt the appearance of impartiality.[682] Likewise, the ICRC study on customary IHL requires that the judges 'must not harbour preconceptions about the matter before them, nor act in a way that promotes the interest of one side.'[683] Other international bodies, including the ECtHR[684], the IACtHR[685], as well as the ICC[686] have defined the impartiality requirement in a similar manner.

b. Judicial guarantees of Art. 6 (2)(a)-(f) Additional Protocol II

The judicial guarantees enlisted in Art. 6 (2)(a)-(f) Additional Protocol II closely resemble those which are enumerated in Art. 75 Additional Protocol I, and are based on Art. 14 and Art. 15 ICCPR. The list in Art. 6 (2)

679 See Amal Clooney and Philippa Webb, The Right to a Fair Trial in International Law 107-111.

680 Human Rights Committee United Nations, General Comment No. 32 on Art. 14: Right to equality before courts and tribunals and to a fair trial, CCPR/C/GC/32, 23 August 2007. para 21.

681 Ibid para 21.

682 ICTR, The Prosecutor v Nahimana et al., Appeals Judgment paras 48 f.

683 Jean-Marie Henckaerts and Louise Doswald-Beck, Customary International Humanitarian Law Volume I: Rules, Rule 100, 356.

684 ECtHR, Case of Aviso Zeta AG v Austria, Judgment, 21 June 2018, Application No. 5734/14 paras 42-45; ECtHR, Case of Morice v France, Judgment, 23 April 2015, Application No. 29369/10 paras 73-78.

685 IACtHR, Apitz Barbara et al. ("First Court of Administrative Disputes") v Venezuela, Judgment para 56; IACtHR, Case of Barreto Leiva v Venezuela, Judgment, 17 November 2009, Case No. Series C No. 206 para 98.

686 The ICC considers the objective impartiality-test to be the relevant standard of assessment, see ICC, The Prosecutor v Abdallah Banda Abakaer Norain et al., Decision of the plenary of the judges on the „Defence Request for the Disqualification of a Judge" of 2 April 2012, 5 June 2012, Case No. ICC-02/05-03/09-344-Anx para 11.

Additional Protocol II is not exhaustive as the insertion of 'in particular' suggests. Interestingly, the right not to be punished twice for the same offence (*ne bis in idem*) was not included into the list of Art. 6 (2) Additional Protocol II.

The drafters considered it difficult to apply this principle in the context of a NIAC where at least one party to the conflict is not a state.[687] They were aware of the fact that *ne bis in idem* in NIACs would need to apply inter-party, hence, between the jurisdiction of the respective state government and the (*de facto*) jurisdiction of the respective NSAG involved in the conflict. Such an application of *ne bis in idem* would have conferred – at least for the limited purpose of determining the scope of *ne bis in idem* in NIACs – a formal status to the respective NSAG while at the same time it would have diminished the state's monopoly over the use of justice – a consequence the delegates cautiously sought to prevent.

However, instead of not applying the principle of *ne bis in idem* at all in NIACs, the principle should apply also in times of NIACs, namely in the way it is stipulated in Art. 75 (4)(h) Additional Protocol I, hence, within the jurisdiction of the same party.

Concerning the other judicial guarantees, Art. 6 (2)(a) Additional Protocol II ensures that one is informed about the particulars of an alleged offence without undue delay and provides for the right to have all necessary means of defence.

Art. 6 (2)(b) Additional Protocol II stipulates the principle of individual criminal responsibility.

Art. 6 (2)(c) Additional Protocol II enshrines the principle of *nulla poena lege praeiva* as well as the rule of non-reciprocity according to which 'no one shall be held guilty of any criminal offence on account of any act or omission which did not constitute a criminal offence, under the law, at the time when it was committed'. The provision almost *verbatim* copies the text of Art. 15 (1) ICCPR with, however, an important modification. Whereas Art. 15 (1) ICCPR speaks of 'national or international law', Art. 6 (2)(c) Additional Protocol II refers to 'the law' plainly. The drafters intentionally deviated from the wording of the ICCPR-stipulated principle to take

687 ICRC, Commentary of 2016 on Convention (I) for the Amelioration of the Condition of the Wounded and Sick in Armed Forces in the Field para 687; Michael Bothe, Karl Josef Partsch and Waldemar A. Solf, New Rules for Victims of Armed Conflict: Commentary on the Two 1977 Protocols Additional to the Geneva Conventions of 1949 745; Yoram Dienstein, Non-International Armed Conflicts in International Law 191.

account of the special situation of NIACs where at least one party to it is not a state.[688] They were aware of the fact that the term 'national or international law' would create difficulties and confusion because no state would recognize 'the ideas of rebels' as domestic law and they intended to also include the law of the respective NSAG.[689] This broadly held language enables NSAGs to equally apply Art. 6 (2)(c) Additional Protocol II in reference to their own law.

The list in paragraph (2) continues with the presumption of innocence pursuant to Art. 6 (2)(d) Additional Protocol II, the right to be tried in presence pursuant to Art. 6 (2)(e) Additional Protocol II and the right not to be compelled to testify against oneself pursuant to Art. 6 (2)(f) Additional Protocol II.

2. The capacity of NSAGs to conduct 'independent and impartial' proceedings and to adhere to fundamental judicial guarantees

As with Common Article 3 (1)(d), the question which arises when analyzing Art. 6 (2) Additional Protocol II in the context of 'rebel courts' is whether NSAGs can establish tribunals which provide the essential guarantees of independence and impartiality. The crux lies in assessing whether courts of the respective NSAG operate independently from other branches of the group's overall governance system, especially, whether a judicial body operates independently from the group's executive branch which includes its armed forces and relates to its overall belligerent agenda. Additionally, the appointed judges need to be impartial. In particular, judges must not be part of or affiliated with the fighting forces of the respective NSAG.

Further, the judicial institution(s) of the respective NSAG need to adhere to the judicial guarantees enumerated in Art. 6 (2)(a)-(f) Additional Protocol II when conducting criminal proceedings.

---

688 Michael Bothe, Karl Josef Partsch and Waldemar A. Solf, New Rules for Victims of Armed Conflict: Commentary on the Two 1977 Protocols Additional to the Geneva Conventions of 1949, 746 f.

689 Federal Political Department Bern, Official Records of the Diplomatic Conference on the Reaffirmation and Development of International Humanitarian Law Applicable in Armed Conflicts 1974-1977, Vol. IX, CDDH/I/SR. 63, paras 59-64, and CDDH/I/SR. 64 paras 54 and 79.

a. Courts of NSAGs during armed conflict: a capacity problem

Art. 6 (2) Additional Protocol II requires that criminal proceedings are carried out by a court 'offering the essential guarantees of independence and impartiality', including the judicial guarantees enlisted thereafter.

In the context of courts established by NSAGs, the requirement of independence entails that the group's judiciary must be clearly separable from other branches of the group's overall governance system, such as the legislative and executive branch of the group. Especially, the group's judiciary must be free from any outside, often political pressure and interference. Most crucially, the group's judiciary must operate independently from the group's political and military wing and must not be influenced by corresponding political strategies and military objectives related to the conflict. This appears particularly challenging considering the usually tight entanglement between a group's overall conflict strategies and its deployment of governance tools – a NSAG's judiciary being one of them. In contrast to the opposing state party, insurgent groups often deploy judicial mechanisms as part of their overall governance system which, in turn, contributes to achieving the overall military objective of winning the conflict.[690] Hence, whereas states are operating their judiciary alongside the conflict and, importantly, do so in continuance before the outbreak of it, NSAGs engage in the administration of justice only due to the outbreak of the conflict and may do so in promotion of winning the conflict. Consequently, the operation of a NSAG's judiciary may be closely intertwined with the group's military agenda of winning the conflict and its accompanying political agenda of either replacing the incumbent state government or pursuing separation and the creation of a new state.

The situation is similar regarding the impartiality-requirement set out in Art. 6 (2) Additional Protocol II. NSAGs need to secure that those persons who administer justice do so impartially. This requires judges and other legal personnel to act freely from personal and, especially, from conflict-related bias and prejudice. Judges must not harbour preconceptions about a certain matter before them nor act in ways that improperly promote the interests of one of the parties to the detriment of the other, for example, by applying the law differently according to whether the accused person is a civilian, belongs to the group's own fighting forces or to the fighting

690 Winning the armed conflict will always be the primary and necessary goal to achieve subsequent goals, such as the replacement of the incumbent state government or the separation of the territorial state.

forces of the opposing (often state) party. Crucially, trials must not be instrumentalized for conflict-related aims and objectives. Again, this is especially challenging considering the close intertwining of a group's overall military agenda of winning the conflict and the deployment of governance structures.

Compliance with the 'independence and impartiality'-requirement of Art. 6 (2) Additional Protocol II is especially delicate considering the often loose and *ad hoc* structures of many NSAGs. It requires a high level of organization and a command structure to be able to secure that a judiciary operates both independently and impartially. Most NSAGs will lack the necessary capacities and resources to establish advanced structures which are elemental in guaranteeing independently and impartially operating judicial institutions.[691]

In the same vein, most NSAGs will have difficulties providing the enlisted judicial guarantees in Art. 6 (2)(a)-(f) Additional Protocol II as it equally requires a considerable amount of resources to establish and maintain a judiciary's adherence to fair trial guarantees.

b. Towards substantive equality: seeking a differentiated solution

The above considerations touch upon the dilemma resulting from an undifferentiated application of the 'equality of belligerents'-principle in IHL applicable to NIACs: substantive inequality.

State parties will always have more resources and more capacities to fulfill the requirements of Art. 6 (2) Additional Protocol II compared to non-state parties. States can rely on their preexisting governance apparatus which non-state parties cannot, since NSAGs often only emerge during and due to armed conflict and, therefore, at best only establish *ad hoc* governance structures.

Hence, whereas in the context of Common Article 3 (1)(d) the 'equality of belligerents'-principle secured substantive equality of its warring parties by enabling a broad interpretation of 'regularly constituted', it hampers substantive equality in the context of Art. 6 (2) Additional Protocol II. A uniform application of Art. 6 (2) Additional Protocol II to state and non-state parties alike echoes preexisting power structures with the likelihood to

691 This observation was also made by Peter Rowe, 'War Crimes' in Dominic McGoldrick, Peter Rowe and Eric Donnelly (eds), The Permanent International Criminal Court - Legal and Political Issues (1st edn, Hart Publishing 2004) 203-230, 227.

further perpetuating them. Thus, to ultimately achieve substantive equality, one must apply a corrective standard which remedies these disparities in power and resources.

Such a corrective standard has been formulated in IHL to incentivize better compliance with IHL by NSAGs: the so-called 'sliding scale of obligations'-standard.[692]

This 'sliding scale of obligations'-standard stipulates that the better organized a NSAG is and the more stable control over territory it exercises, the more IHL rules it must adhere to. At the same time, it stresses that an indispensable humanitarian minimum of guarantees and protection must be preserved. The basic concept of a 'sliding scale of obligations'- standard lies in limiting the applicable IHL obligations to NIACs in accordance with a group's capability to comply with them. This shall enhance overall compliance with IHL and the protection of victims.

Such a 'sliding scale of obligations'-standards is also applicable to Art. 6 (2) Additional Protocol II in NIACs. It even is implicitly rooted in the different thresholds of Common Article 3 on the one hand, and Art. 1 (1) Additional Protocol II on the other.

Applying the 'sliding scale of obligations'-standard to Art. 6 (2) Additional Protocol II shall enable NSAGs to equally participate in the administration of justice during NIACs. It shall enforce substantive equality. Promoting the 'equality of belligerents'-principle in the context of Common Article 3 (1)(d) led to the conclusion that the provision's core requirement of a 'regularly constituted court' must be interpreted as encompassing courts established by NSAGs according to their own law.

Hence, in the context of Common Article 3 (1)(d), the 'equality of belligerents'-principle leads to substantive equality. By contrast, in the context of Art. 6 (2) Additional Protocol II, a uniform application of the 'equality of belligerents'-principle leads to substantive inequality.

This is owed to the fact that most NIACs are fought between a state and a non-state party with often substantially different powers, capacities, and resources. Applying the 'equality of belligerents'-principle to differently situated parties results in substantive inequality, favoring the more powerful. In NIACs, this will likely be the involved state party. Hence, establishing substantive equality requires one to treat differently equipped subjects in

692 See Marco Sassòli and Yuval Shany, 'Should the obligations of states and armed groups under international humanitarian law really be eqaul?' (2011) 93 International Review of the Red Cross 425-442, 428 f.

a different manner.[693] The 'sliding scale of obligations'-standard is a useful tool to overcome this inequality.

Applied to Art. 6 (2) Additional Protocol II, this standard follows the premise that the better organized a group is and the more territorial control it exercises, the more obligations stipulated in Art. 6 (2)(a)-(f) Additional Protocol II become applicable. At the same time, an indispensable core of independence and impartiality as well as an indispensable minimum of judicial guarantees must be always adhered to, irrespective of any group's organization and territorial control.

Translated to the scenario of a NSAG which is fighting a stronger state or a stronger other non-state party, a 'sliding-scale of obligations'- standard leads to the following formula:

1. Every NSAG must always ensure a clear institutional separation of its judiciary from its political and military wing. This means that any group's judiciary must be free from political interference, especially, free from military pressure relating to the overall aim of winning the conflict.
2. For example, judges who adjudicate cases must not be a member of or affiliated with the armed forces or the political wing of that group. They must enjoy ultimate decision-making power without being subject to the discretion of either military commanders or political party members.
3. Judges must not adjudicate justice in favour of the group's own military strategies. Especially, they must apply the law indifferently irrespective of whether the accused person is a civilian, belongs to the group's own fighting forces or to the fighting forces of the opposing (often state) party.
4. The more power and the more resources a NSAG may gain in the course of a conflict, the sharper the standard to comply with the provision's requirements of 'independence and impartiality' shall become.
5. Concerning the enlisted judicial guarantees in Art. 6 (2)(a)-(f) Additional Protocol II, every NSAG shall provide for the principle of legality enshrined in Art. 6 (2)(c) Additional Protocol II, the presumption of innocence in Art. 6 (2)(d) Additional Protocol II as well as the right to have all the necessary means of defence pursuant to Art. 6 (2)(a) Additional Protocol II. These rights shall be regarded as an indispensable minimum which must be adhered to irrespective of a group's organization and degree of territorial control.

693 The same thought was formulated by Yuval Shany in responding to Marco Sassòli's proposal to abandon the 'equality of belligerents'-principle for the sake of enhancing compliance with IHL in NIACs. See ibid 435.

6. The more power and the more resources a NSAG may gain during the conflict, the more judicial guarantees included in the list of Art. 6 (2) (a)-(f) Additional Protocol II shall become applicable.

In summary, a 'sliding scale of obligations'-standard is warranted to overcome capacity disparities and to ultimately reach substantive equality between the addressees of Art. 6 (2) Additional Protocol II. Such a standard complements the promotion of the 'equality of belligerents'-principle in the context of Common Article 3 (1)(d). It allows for a flexible assessment throughout the course of conflict, being able to respond to changing power dynamics while at the same time preserving an indispensable minimum of protection relative to the victims of NIACs. It also means that a one-size-fits-all definition for the legality of courts of NSAGs during armed conflict cannot be formulated nor applied.

3. Conclusion

The foregoing normative analysis of both Common Article 3 (1)(d) and Art. 6 (2) Additional Protocol II assessed the provisions' pertinent requirements for the establishment of judicial mechanisms during NIACs. A court must be 'regularly constituted', in other words, 'established by law' and it must operate 'independently and impartially' while adhering to essential fair trial guarantees.

Applying these two provisions to NSAGs entails normative as well as practical challenges.

The normative challenge primarily relates to the interpretation of a *de jure* criterion which is determined by a predominant Westphalian understanding of international law, in favor of state sovereignty. Transposed to the scenario of non-state judicial mechanisms established in NIACs, this normative challenge arises when interpretating the phrase 'regularly constituted' pursuant to Common Article 3 (1)(d): can courts of NSAGs be regularly constituted if they have been established according to the group's own law?

The practical challenge primarily relates to a lack of capacity on behalf of NSAGs to live up to certain IHL stipulated rules and obligations. Transposed to the scenario of non-state judicial mechanisms established in NIACs, this capacity problem arises when applying Art. 6 (2) Additional Protocol II in an undifferentiated manner to NSAGs: do NSAGs have the resources to conduct independent and impartial criminal proceedings and offering essential fair trial guarantees?

The foregoing sections not only identified the normative and practical challenges of putting courts of NSAGs into the context of Common Article 3 (1)(d) and Art 6 (2) Additional Protocol II, they also sought to formulate corrective standards to remedy those challenges.

A complementary application of the 'equality of belligerents'-principle and the 'sliding scale of obligations'-standard ensures that courts of NSAGs have an equally realistic chance to legally install judicial mechanisms in armed conflict as their – usually state – opponents. Promoting the 'equality of belligerents'-principle in the context of Common Article 3 (1)(d) results in the conclusion that a NSAG's court is 'regularly constituted' if it has been established according to the law of the respective group. Promoting a 'sliding-scale of obligations'-standard in the context of Art. 6 (2) Additional Protocol II ensures that a NSAG must only comply with those obligations it is practically capable of complying with while upholding an indispensable minimum of protection.

In its combined effect, the 'equality of belligerents'-principle and the 'sliding scale of obligations'-standard facilitate that NSAGs truly have the same right and the same capability to install judicial mechanisms and to comply with the respective statutory requirements.[694]

IV. Legality or Lawfulness? – The Normative Reach of Common Article 3 (1)(d) and Art. 6 (2) Additional Protocol II

The present section assesses whether conformity with Common Article 3 (1)(d) and Art. 6 (2) Additional Protocol II and its stipulated requirements leads to the legality of courts of NSAGs established during NIACs. In doing so, the present section draws on a contemporary debate about the role and status of NSAGs in IHL which revolves around the thesis that IHL does not regulate the legality of conduct by NSAGs because IHL provisions do not entail legal bases or rights. This assumption will be challenged by analyzing the nature of IHL, and the nature of Common Article 3 (1)(d) and Art. 6 (2) Additional Protocol II in particular. This analysis will detect

694 This idea has been advanced by Ezequiel Heffes. See Ezequiel Heffes, 'Generating Respect for International Humanitarian Law: The Establishment of Courts by Organized Non-State Armed Groups in Light of the Principle of Equality of Belligerents' 196 f.

a misconception regarding the legality of conduct in IHL and demonstrate that IHL provisions can carry legality, albeit relative legality.

1. The debate and its origin: regulation vs. authorization

There are authors which assert that IHL as *jus in bello* does not provide for rights or legal bases. They argue that IHL does not comprise provisions which regulate the legality of conduct but rather provisions which regulate the lawfulness of conduct in times of armed conflict by weighing concerns of military necessity against concerns of humanitarian harm.[695] This view implicitly claims that for conduct to be legal it must be attributable to a legal basis or must flow from holding a right to perform the resepective conduct. In other words, one cannot infer a right from the fact that IHL regulates certain conduct in armed conflict. This assertion forms the focus of the scholarly debate about the right or power of NSAGs to detain in NIACs which has emerged in the last few years and has been subject of extensive scholarly works[696] as well as jurisprudence[697]. In this regard, while

695 Frédéric Mégret, 'Detention by Non-State Armed Groups in NIACs: IHL, International Human Rights Law and the Question of the Right Authority' in Ezequiel Heffes, Marcos D. Kotlik and Manuel J. Ventura (eds), International Humanitarian Law and Non-State Actors: Debates, Law and Practice (1st edn, Asser Press 2020) 170-191.

696 Andrew Clapham, 'Detention by Armed Groups under International Law' (2017) 93 International Law Studies 1-43; Ryan Goodman, 'Authorization versus Regulation of Detention in Non-International Armed Conflicts' (2015) 91 International Law Studies 155-170; Ezequiel Heffes, Detention by Non-State Armed Groups under International Law (1st edn, Cambridge University Press 2022); Ezequiel Heffes, 'Detentions by Armed Opposition Groups in Non-International Armed Conflicts: Towards a New Characterization of International Humanitarian Law' (2015) 20 Journal of Conflict and Security Law 229-250; Frédéric Mégret, 'Detention by Non-State Armed Groups in NIACs: IHL, International Human Rights Law and the Question of the Right Authority' in Ezequiel Heffes, Marcos D. Kotlik and Manuel J. Ventura (eds), International Humanitarian Law and Non-State Actors: Debates, Law and Practice; Joshua Joseph Niyo, 'Non-State Armed Groups and the Power to Detain in Non-International Armed Conflict' (2020) 53 Israel Law Review 3-33.

697 The High Court of Justice Queen's Bench Division, Serdar Mohammed v Ministry of Defence, Judgment, 2 May 2014, Case No. 2014 EWHC 1369 (QB) paras 241 ff. The ECtHR has extensively ruled on the arbitrariness of detention by NSAGs, especially by unrecognized de facto entities in NIACs, by subjecting the conduct to Art. 5 ECHR, see, e.g., ECtHR, Case of Cyprus v Turkey, Judgment, 10 May 2001, Application No. 25781/94 para 96; ECtHR, Case of Ilaşcu and others v Moldocia and Russia, 8 July 2004, Application No. 48787/99 para 436.

Common Article 3 (1) and Arts. 5 and 6 Additional Protocol II regulate detention in NIACs, they do not confer a right or authorization to detain, hence, they do not regulate the legality of detention in NIACs.

The present debate about the legality of 'rebel courts' in NIACs resembles the scholarly debate about the right of NSAGs to detain in NIACs. Therefore, one is confronted with the same assertion regarding the legality of conduct pursuant to pertinent IHL provisions. Accordingly, the fact that Common Article 3 (1)(d) and Art. 6 (2) Additional Protocol II regulate the way in which sentences shall be passed and penalties shall be executed does not automatically mean that those provisions entail a right to administer justice during armed conflict. Hence, neither Common Article 3 (1)(d) nor Art. 6 (2) Additional Protocol II would constitute a legal basis for the installment of judicial mechanisms in times of armed conflict.[698]

This leads one to ask what Common Article 3 (1)(d) and Art. 6 (2) Additional Protocol II address if not the legality of the circumscribed conduct. What is the nature of those two provisions?

Undoubtedly, Common Article 3 (1)(d) and Art. 6 (2) Additional Protocol II regulate the conduct of administering justice during NICAs by imposing certain requirements and safeguards. A court must be regularly constituted, it must afford all the judicial guarantees which are recognized as indispensable by civilized peoples, and it must operate independently and impartially. The crux lies in assessing whether a regulating norm or an obligation-norm also entails a permission to perform the conduct besides restricting it and, if yes, whether such an implied permission equals a legal basis. Only if the latter can be answered in the affirmative would Common Article 3 (1)(d) and Art. 6 (2) Additional Protocol II be considered legal bases for the installment of judicial mechanisms during NIACs. Only then would such a conduct be legal according to the above-outlined assertion.

The answers to these questions may be found in legal theory as well as in an analysis of the nature of IHL and an analysis of the nature of Common Article 3 (1)(d) and Art. 6 (2) Additional Protocol II in particular.

698 Ezequiel Heffes, 'The establishment of courts by armed groups: what is the legal basis?' is indicating that in seeking a legal basis for courts of NSAGs, one should look at the law of the respective group instead of looking at Common Article 3 (1)(d) and Art. 6 (2) Additional Protocol II. René Provost has also written on the nature of Common Article 3 (1)(d) and Art. 6 (2) Additional Protocol II as rights for the administration of justice in NIACs, see René Provost, Rebel Courts: The Administration of Justice by Armed Insurgents 101-217.

a. The nature of norms

In legal theory, the nature or character of norms can be categorized into primarily three deontic modes. Deontic modes relate to the concept of the 'obligatory', the 'permitted', and the 'forbidden'. Accordingly, norms can prescribe a certain conduct in the form of an obligation, they can proscribe a certain conduct in the form of a prohibition, and they can allow for a certain conduct in the form of a permission.[699] Concerning the latter, one can distinguish between strong and weak permissions: A strong permission is based on the existence of a norm which enables the exercise of an action (existence of an enabling norm) whereas a weak permission is a permission which results from the absence of a norm prohibiting the exercise of an action (absence of a prohibiting norm).[700] Conduct which is not forbidden or not subject to a prohibiting norm could be said to be permitted, however, weakly permitted only. Hence, acts which are strongly permitted are always also weakly permitted but not vice versa.

One may reason that strong permissions have greater normative force because the legal system has taken an active position on the deontic character or nature of the norm.[701]

A permission transforms into a right or a legal basis if it correlates with a simultaneous prohibition of others to hinder the holder of the right from exercising the permitted conduct. Hence, a right limits the freedom of action of others.[702] In other words, the holder of a right has a claim to be able to exercise the permitted action whereas any third person must refrain from obstructing the holder of the right to do the permitted action. By contrast, a simple – be it a strong or a weak – permission, is just a permission. Additionally, a right or a legal basis is linked to the principle of legality which ensures that the exercise of a certain right ought not be restricted or limited except by law, and that any restriction of the enjoyment of a certain right must follow a legitimate purpose.

---

699 Georg Henrik von Wright, Norm and Action: a logical enquiry (1st edn, Routledge 1963) 71. He distinguishes between the 'ought'-character and the 'may'-character of norms, the former being obligation-norms and the latter being permissive norms. He also refers to them as O-norms and P-norms.

700 Ibid 86.

701 Ibid 86.

702 Ibid 89. See also Christopher Greenwood, 'The Relationship between ius ad bellum and ius in bello' (1983) 9 Review of International Studies 221-234, 228.

b. The nature of Common Article 3 and Art. 6 (2) Additional Protocol II

Turning back to the initial question whether Common Article 3 (1)(d) and Art. 6 (2) Additional Protocol II restrict, permit or even confer a right, we must assess their nature as IHL norms applicable to NIACs. For this purpose, it is useful, first, to assess the nature of IHL in general, and second, to assess the nature of Common Article 3 (1)(d) and Art. 6 (2) Additional Protocol II in particular.

IHL is a legal framework designed to regulate warfare conduct by striking a balance between military necessity and humanitarian considerations. It aims at providing fundamental guarantees relating to the protection of persons affected by armed conflict. For this reason, IHL is imposing obligations upon the warring parties to minimize humanitarian harm.

An attentive study of the texts of the four Geneva Conventions of 1949 and its two Additional Protocols of 1977 reveals that IHL-obligations restrict more than they permit. Therefore, some authors have argued that IHL cannot possibly entail permissive rules as this would contradict *jus ad bellum*.[703] Given the fact that most conflicts are in breach of Art. 2 (4) UN Charta – if not justified by individual or collective self-defence according to Art. 51, authorization by the UN Security Council pursuant to Art. 42, or invitation by the territorial government – they argue that IHL can only regulate conduct during armed conflict but not permit it. In other words, where the initial use of force is in breach of *jus ad bellum*, hence illegal, any subsequent use of force such as the attack on members of the opposing armed forces, cannot be legal under *jus in bello*.[704]

This position can be traced back to the theory of discriminatory application of IHL and the distinction between humanitarian rules on the one hand and belligerent rights on the other.[705] The theory of discriminatory

703 Pointed out by Anne Quintin, The Nature of International Humanitarian Law - A Permissive or Restrictive Regime? (1st edn, Edward Elgar 2020) 11-19.

704 Ibid 12.

705 Lassa Oppenheim and Hersch Lauterpacht (eds), International Law: A Treatise (7th edn, Longmans, Green and Co 1952) Vol. 2, Disputes, War and Neutrality 217-223 distinguishing between the 'guilty belligerent' waging an illegal war and, therefore, not being entitled to all the rights and of the necessity of mutual 'observance of rules of warfare as generally recognised' *durante bello* irrespective of the illegality of the war; Hans Wehberg, The Outlawry of War (1st edn, Carnegie Endowment for International Peace 1931) 84; Quincy Wright, 'The Outlawry of War and the Law of War' (1953) 47 The American Journal of International Law 365-376, 370 ff., having developed the theory of discriminatory application of IHL as first.

application of IHL emerged following the adoption of the Kellog-Briand Pact in 1928[706] and pre-dated the adoption of the UN Charta as well as the adoption of the two Additional Protocols of 1977. Supporters of this theory advocated a discriminatory application of *jus in bello* depending on the 'lawfulness' of the initial use of force, whereas others opined for an equal application of *jus in bello* to all warring parties irrespective of the (il-)legality of the initial use of force.[707]

With the adoption of the two Additional Protocols in 1977, the theory of discriminatory application of IHL was abandoned.[708] The 'equality of belligerents'-principle, also known as the principle of separation, replaced the theory of discriminatory application and stipulates that *jus in bello* applies autonomously from *jus ad bellum*.[709]

Hence, the existence of permissive rules within IHL does not contradict *jus ad bellum*. The principle of separation or the principle of equality of belligerents implies that IHL can permit conduct in armed conflict without legitimizing the initial use of force and vice versa. To conclude, the nature of IHL provisions may be both restrictive and permissive.

However, most IHL provisions are formulated in a binding and compulsory manner, using terms like 'prohibited', 'shall not' or 'must'. In cases where IHL permits a certain conduct it does so on the condition of adherence to certain requirements and guarantees postulated by the respective provision. IHL does not permit conduct with a corresponding obligation of others to respect that right and to not hinder the right holder from exercising the permitted action. Such an interpretation would contradict

706 The Kellogg-Briand Pact, 27 August 1928.

707 Advocates of the principle of equality of belligerents include, for example, François Bugnion, 'Guerre juste, guerre d'agression et droit international humanitaire' (2002) 84 International Review of the Red Cross 523-546; Josef L. Kunz, 'The Laws of War' (1956) 50 American Journal of International Law 313-337, 319 and 322. Kunz is also giving a detailed overview on the different positions concerning the discriminatory vs. equal application of IHL; Henri Meyrowitz, Le Prinicipe de L'égalité des belligérants devant le droit de la guerre (1st edn, Éditions A. Pédone 1970) 106-140 also assessing and criticizing the theory of discriminatory application. Also Hersch Lauterpacht stressed the consistent humanitarian character of IHL, rejecting any differentiation between the aggressor party and the party not having initially violated *jus ad bellum* and thereby deviating from his earlier opinion (see supra fn 705), see Hersch Lauterpacht, 'The Limits of the Operation of the Law of War' (1953) 30 British Yearbook of International Law 206-243, 213 f.

708 See Preambular (4) and (5) Additional Protocol I. Anne Quintin, The Nature of International Humanitarian Law - A Permissive or Restrictive Regime? 14 and 17.

709 See above II. 2. b.

the 'equality of belligerents'-principle according to which all parties to the conflict have the same rights. Hence, IHL entails weak permissions but not strong permissions.

Thus, speaking of legal bases or rights in IHL is terminologically incorrect.

This conclusion implies that Common Article 3 (1)(d) and Art. 6 (2) Additional Protocol II do not constitute legal bases. Common Article 3 (1)(d) and Art. 6 (2) Additional Protocol II stipulate requirements and safeguards which must be adhered to when administering justice in NIACs. To this extent, they obligate and prescribe the way the warring parties should administer justice during armed conflict. They neither entail an obligation to administer justice nor a prohibition to administer justice. Logically, a norm which prescribes how a certain conduct must be performed implicitly permits that very conduct if it is consistent with the stipulated requirements. However, it is not the same to say that any permission, be it implicit or explicit, equals a legal basis or a right.

The nature of Common Article 3 reveals itself by looking at the provision's language and its object and purpose. Common Article 3 is formulated in a restrictive manner. The provision entails fundamental guarantees which must be *adhered* to at all times during NIACs [emphasis added]. Common Article 3 is worded in a binding and obligatory manner. It is not worded in an enabling or even entitling manner. Already the *chapeau* of Common Article 3 speaks of 'bound to apply'. The provision's text continues by stipulating that 'the following acts are and shall remain prohibited at any time and in any place whatsoever with respect to the above-mentioned persons'. Bearing this prefix in mind, Common Article 3 (1)(d) is also clearly worded in a compulsory manner as it prohibits 'the passing of sentences and carrying out of executions without previous judgement pronounced by a regularly constituted court, affording all the judicial guarantees which are recognized as indispensable by civilized peoples.' The compulsory and restrictive wording of Common Article 3 reflects the provision's telos. Common Article 3 is considered a 'minimum yardstick' for NIACs and a reflection of 'elementary considerations of humanity'[710]. Its drafters intended to stipulate an indispensable minimum of humanitarian protection applicable to NIACs. The focus rested on enhancing protection

710 ICRC, Commentary of 2016 on Convention (I) for the Amelioration of the Condition of the Wounded and Sick in Armed Forces in the Field para 9; see also ICJ, Military and Paramilitary Activities in and against Nicaragua (Nicaragua v United States of Amercia), Judgment paras 218 f.

for the victims of armed conflict by stipulating fundamental guarantees. One can conclude that Common Article 3 (1)(d) regulates the performance of administering justice during NIACs by imposing obligations. It thereby, permits the administration of justice during NIACs on the condition that the conduct fulfills the provision's requirements. This permission is a weak permission. Thus, Common Article 3 (1)(d) does not confer a right to install judicial mechanisms during NIACs.

The analysis of the nature of Additional Protocol II leads to the same conclusion. Additional Protocol II is formulated in a restrictive and compulsory manner. Most of the Protocol's provisions are phrased in a way according to which certain conduct ought to fulfill certain requirements or according to which certain conduct must not be done.[711] The 'ought'-character and the 'must not'-character are interdefinable: conduct which ought to be done must not be left undone while conduct which must not be done ought to be left undone. The provisions entailed in Additional Protocol II are all formulated in this manner: for instance, Art. 4 Additional Protocol II – the equivalent provision to Common Article 3 – stipulates fundamental guarantees by enlisting certain acts which 'shall remain prohibited at any time and in any place whatsoever'. Art. 13 (2) Additional Protocol II, for example, reads as follows:

> 'The civilian population as such, as well as individual civilians, shall not be the object of attacks. Acts or threats of violence the primary purpose of which is to spread terror among the civilian population are prohibited.'

Art. 14 Additional Protocol II, for example, stipulates that the 'Starvation of civilians as a method of combat is prohibited.' Art. 6 (2) Additional Protocol II stipulates that 'No sentence shall be passed and no penalty shall be executed on a person found guilty for an offence except pursuant to a conviction pronounced by a court offering the essential guarantees of independence and impartiality'. The restrictive and compulsory wording of Additional Protocol II also reflects the telos of Additional Protocol II. The dafters' intent was to develop a more enhanced legal instrument for better protection of victims of NIACs by supplementing the brief set of

711 According to von Wright's analysis of norms, such provisions are called obligation-norms and prohibition-norms. Georg Henrik von Wright, Norm and Action: a logical enquiry 71.

rules laid out in Common Article 3.[712] Additional Protocol II primarily entails provisions regarding the protection of the civilian population as well as of the wounded, sick and shipwrecked. This was a deliberate choice of the drafters, so combatants in NIACs would not be given too many rights which would have made them appear to be on the same level as their state opponent.[713] Hence, like Common Article 3 (1)(d), Art. 6 (2) Additional Protocol II permits the administration of justice during NIACs on the condition that the conduct fulfills the provision's requirements. This permission is a weak permission. Thus, Art. 6 (2) Additional Protocol II does not confer a right to install judicial mechanisms during NIACs.

This leads to the conclusion that the above claim according to which IHL does not entail rights is correct, although only partially: Common Article 3 (1)(d) and Art. 6 (2) Additional Protocol II do not confer a right to administer justice during NIACs. However, it is incorrect to conclude that therefore the establishment of courts by NSAGs cannot be legal according to these provisions. The following section demonstrates that Common Article 3 (1)(d) and Art. 6 (2) Additional Protocol II stipulate relative legality for the administration of justice during NIACs.

2. Resolving a misconception: relative legality

The previous section concluded that a permission flowing from the adherence to an ought-norm, hence a weak permission, does not constitute a right or legal basis. Common Article 3 (1)(d) and Art. 6 (2) Additional Protocol II are weak permission-norms as they render the conduct of administering justice in NIACs 'permitted' or 'not prohibited' on the condition that the conduct fulfills the provisions' requirements. This section demonstrates that even though Common Article 3 (1)(d) and Art. 6 (2) Additional Proto-

712 Yves Sandoz, Christophe Swinarski and Bruno Zimmermann (eds), Commentary on the Additional Protocols of 8 June 1977 to the Geneva Conventions of 12 August 1949 para 4337.

713 See proposal of Mr. Hussain (delegate of Pakistan) who suggested to delete Part IV on means and methods of combat of the Draft Protocol to not risk encroaching on the sovereignty of any State Party, Federal Political Department Bern, Official Records of the Diplomatic Conference on the Reaffirmation and Development of International Humanitarian Law Applicable in Armed Conflicts 1974-1977, Vol. VII, CDDH/SR.49 para 11, referring to the Pakistani proposal CDDH/427 of 31 May 1977. See also Michael Bothe, Karl Josef Partsch and Waldemar A. Solf, New Rules for Victims of Armed Conflict: Commentary on the Two 1977 Protocols Additional to the Geneva Conventions of 1949, 606 f.

col II are weak permission-norms, they render the administration of justice in NIACs legal if the conduct fulfills the provisions' requirements, respectively. By stipulating obligations for conduct during armed conflict, IHL carries relative legality: relative to an ongoing armed conflict and relative to the conformity with the respective obligation-norm. Therefore, the above assertion according to which courts of NSAGs cannot be legal pursuant to IHL because CA 3 (1)(d) and Art. 6 (2) Additional Protocol II do not confer a right is flawed and unconvincing for the following three reasons:

Firstly, such an assertion exacerbates the asymmetric nature of NIACs as it is linked to a dominant Westphalian interpretation of IHL, securing the sovereignty of states. It is an assertion which will likely be made by state parties to a NIAC. If neither Common Article 3 (1)(d) nor Art. 6 (2) Additional Protocol II provide a legal basis or right to install judicial mechanisms during NIACs, then courts established during armed conflict would never be considered legal according to IHL but – at best – considered as lawful or legitimate means of warfare if the requirements of Common Article 3 (1)(d) and/or Art. 6 (2) Additional Protocol II are fulfilled. This would hold true for both warring parties, state and non-state. Notably, the state party will argue that the installment of judicial mechanisms in armed conflict is legal according to domestic law. The non-state party could promote the same argument, presumed it has its own set of law. Nevertheless, the involved state party will consider the installment of judicial mechanisms of NSAGs according to the group's own law illegal and in breach of domestic law. This strikes at the central tenet of the ubiquitous equality problem in NIACs: states will always resort to their own domestic law, arguing that any conduct which is not regulated through IHL is legal according to domestic law while at the same time disregarding this line of argumentation on behalf of the involved non-state party. What follows is an insuperable inequality of the parties to a NIAC perpetuated by the application of IHL in a state-centric fashion.

Including 'rebel courts' into the scope of both Common Article 3 (1)(d) and Art. 6 (2) Additional Protocol II renders state courts and non-state courts on equal footing. Considering 'rebel courts' legal according to Common Article 3 (1)(d) and Art. 6 (2) Additional Protocol II on the condition that their establishment and functioning is consistent with the provisions' requirements, diminishes the supremacy of state parties to a NIAC and their monopoly over the administration of justice on national territory relative to armed conflict.

Secondly, the above-outlined assertion disregards the autonomy of *jus in bello* with regard to *jus ad bellum*. *Jus ad bellum* rules on the legality of the resort to armed force. By contrast, *jus in bello* regulates conduct in times of armed conflict which often is in breach with *jus ad bellum*, hence, illegal. Thus, *jus in bello* regulates conduct in times of an illegal state. At first glance, it appears logical and reasonable to argue that *jus in bello* cannot possibly render conduct during armed conflict legal, considering that the overall state in which the respective conduct occurs is illegal. Such an argumentation, however, misses the mark: *jus in bello* operates independently from *jus ad bellum*.

In NIACs, matters are made complicated by the fact that *jus ad bellum* is replaced by the domestic law of the respective state.[714] The use of internal force by an insurgent group against the territorial state does not violate 'international' *jus ad bellum*[715] but it does violate the domestic law of the respective state. Thus, states will consider any recourse to armed violence illegal as well as any subsequent conduct occurring during armed conflict. This reveals the overarching dilemma of *jus in bello* applicable to NIACs: it suffers from the Westphalian system in international law. The initial breach of domestic law latently prevails in the application of *jus in bello* and thereby hinders a genuinely autonomous application of it. Hence, in NIACs, the continuity of domestic law interferes with the autonomy of IHL. It collides with the nature of *jus in bello*, which is, ruling on the (relative) legality of conduct in armed conflict. In IACs, on the other hand, the applicable *jus ad bellum* remains silent on subsequent conduct occurring during armed conflict. Therefore, it is widely accepted that during armed conflict, IHL addresses the legality of conduct. In IACs, the involved parties are more willing to fully surrender to IHL as the sole applicable legal framework whereas in NIACs, the asymmetry of the involved parties results in an insurmountable conviction that the domestic law of the respective state prevails.

Finally, the above assumption that IHL provisions do not regulate the legality of conduct during armed conflict since they do not confer rights confuses two different matters and plays with linguistic subtleties dominated by the aim to secure states' interests. It confuses the legality of conduct

714 Yoram Dienstein, Non-International Armed Conflicts in International Law 5; GIAD Draper, 'Humanitarian Law and Internal Armed Conflicts' 254 f.

715 The prohibition formulated in Art. 2 (4) UN Charta does not address the threat or use of force by NSAGs vis-à-vis states.

due to holding a right to perform the respective conduct with the legality of conduct due to its conformity with legal requirements stipulated in a provision. As shown above[716], it is dogmatically correct and undisputed that IHL provisions do not confer rights or legal bases. One might also argue that legality resulting from holding a right has a greater normative force than legality resulting from the adherence to an obligation-norm. However, it is dogmatically incorrect to conclude that legality necessitates the existence of a right. It is – again – a conclusion drawn by a state-centered interpretation of IHL norms.

In summary, the reason why many scholars remain hesitant in accepting that *jus in bello* of NIACs can rule on the legality of conduct occurring during armed conflict is engrained in the recurring concern not to encroach on states' sovereignty. It inevitably perpetuates the asymmetry of the warring parties to NIACs, disregards the separation between *jus ad bellum* and *jus in bello* and, thereby, renders the 'equality of belligerents'-principle effectless.

This section reasoned that although Common Article 3 (1)(d) and Art. 6 (2) Additional Protocol II are first and foremost obligation-norms and only conditional permission-norms, they carry relative legality for the respective conduct within the framework of IHL. Thus, the passing of sentences and the execution of punishments is not prohibited, hence, permitted and legal during armed conflict if it follows a judgment pronounced by a regularly constituted court which adheres to the essential guarantees of independence and impartiality and to those fundamental judicial guarantees which are recognized as indispensable by all civilized peoples.

V. Factual Parameters for the Legality of Courts of NSAGs

Whereas Sections 2 and 3 have focused on a dogmatic analysis of the pertinent provisions' requirements, this section formulates two parameters indicating the type of NSAG which most likely is able to fulfill the requirements of Common Article 3 (1)(d) and Art. 6 (2) Additional Protocol II.

A few years ago and for the first time, a national court ruled on the legality of courts of NSAGs according to international law and formulated respective parameters. The case was adjudicated before the Swedish District Court in 2017 and concerned a defendant who joined one of the many

716 See above IV. 1. b.

armed opposition groups in Syria called 'The Sulemain Company'.[717] The defendant, Mr. *Sakhanh* stood trial before a Swedish court. At that time, he was residing in Sweden and held Swedish refugee status. Mr. *Sakhanh* was charged with the aggravated crime against international law according to chapter 22, paragraph 6, section 1 and 2 of the Swedish Penal Code as well as according to Common Article 3 for the execution of several death sentences which were imposed on enemy detainees by the judicial body of the Sulemain group and based on existing Syrian law. In his defence, Mr. *Sakhanh* argued that the execution of the death sentences was lawful because the death sentences were based a pronouncement of a verdict following a fair trial. In elaborating on Mr. *Sakhanh*'s defence, the District Court ruled on the legality of 'rebel courts' in international law. The Swedish District Court held that in order for a court of a NSAG to be lawful according to thc applicable IHL in NIACs, firstly, the court's mandate must be limited to upholding discipline among the group's own armed forces and, secondly, limited to upholding law and order on a given territory in relation to the civilian population, under, thirdly, the condition that the court is staffed with personnel who were appointed as judges or officials in the judiciary prior to the outbreak of the conflict. As a fourth condition, the Swedish District Court held that the court must apply law which was in effect before the outburst of the conflict, or at least the law must not differ from the law that existed before the conflict in a way that would be to the detriment of the individual.[718]

The Swedish District Court's ruling on the legality of courts established by NSAGs during armed conflict is a policy decision in favor of upholding the state's integrity and sovereignty with regard to the monopoly over the use of justice. Albeit ruling that, in principle, NSAGs can lawfully convene and operate courts during armed conflict, the Swedish judges were considerate in keeping the scope limited enough to not infringe upon states' sovereignty.[719] Until up to date, the Swedish District Court is the only

717 Stockholms Tingsrätt (Swedish Discrict Court), Prosecutor v Omar Sakhanh Haisam Sakhanh, Judgment, 16 February 2017, Case No. B 3786-16.

718 Mark Klamberg, 'The Legality of Rebel Courts during Non-International Armed Conflicts' 257. See also Jonathan Somer, 'Opening the Floodgates, Controlling the Flow: Swedish Court Rules on the Legal Capacity of Armed Groups to Establish Courts' (Ejil: Talk!, 10 March 2017) accessed 27 May 2021.

719 Jonathan Somer, 'Opening the Floodgates, Controlling the Flow: Swedish Court Rules on the Legal Capacity of Armed Groups to Establish Courts'.

national court which assessed the legality of courts of NSAGs according to international law in a domestic setting.[720]

In a similar manner, this section formulates two practical parameters which shall supplement the normative parameters stipulated in Common Article 3 (1)(d) and Art. 6 (2) Additional Protocol II.

As demonstrated above[721], the overarching problem of assessing the standards of Common Article 3 (1)(d) and Art. 6 (2) Additional Protocol II in the context of courts of NSAGs is a problem of capacity.[722] Most NSAGs will likely lack the necessary capacity to adhere to the relatively high standards of Art. 6 (2) Additional Protocol II in particular.

According to the previous doctrinal assessment, NSAGs must have adopted their own law which the installment of their judicial mechanisms must be based on, and, NSAGs must provide for the essential guarantees of independence and impartiality when conducting criminal proceedings. Even with the combined approach of enhancing the 'equality of belligerents'-principle on the one hand and applying the 'sliding scale of obligations'-standard on the other, it still requires a fairly high degree of organization and adequate personnel as well as financial resources to be able to fulfill the provision's requirements. The following two parameters are elemental in indicating those types of NSAGs which are likely able to fulfill the requirements of both Common Article 3 (1)(d) and Art. 6 (2) Additional Protocol II:

(1) a high level of organization including stable structures and clear divisions of, especially, the political, the military, and the judicial wing of the group's governance system, combined with
(2) stable and long-term control over territory.

720 The District Court's decision was confirmed in Svea hovrätt (Swedish Appeal Court), Prosecutor v Omar Sakhanh Haisam Sakhanh, Judgment, 31 May 2017, Case No. B 2259-17 and in Högsta domstolen (Swedish Supreme Court), Prosecutor v Omar Sakhanh Haisam Sakhanh, Judgment, 20 July 2017, Case No. B 3157-17.

721 See above III. 2.

722 Ezequiel Heffes, 'Administration of justice by armed groups: Some legal and practical concerns'; Ezequiel Heffes, 'Generating Respect for International Humanitarian Law: The Establishment of Courts by Organized Non-State Armed Groups in Light of the Principle of Equality of Belligerents' 194; Jan Willms, 'Courts of armed groups - a tool for inducing higher compliance with international humanitarian law?' in Heike Krieger (ed), Inducing Compliance with International Humanitarian Law - Lessons fron the African Great Lakes Region 175; Liesbeth Zegveld, The Accountability of Armed Opposition Groups in International Law 72 ff.

These two features are key for any NSAG to generate the necessary resources for complying with the requirements of Common Article 3 (1) (d) and, especially, the judicial guarantees enshrined in Art. 6 (2) Additional Protocol II.[723] Hence, the practical parameters of 'organization' and 'stable control over territory' supplement the theoretical corrective standards in interpreting the pertinent provisions for the establishment of judicial institutions by NSAGs during armed conflict. Realistically, most NSAGs in contemporary NICAs will still lack the necessary degree of organization and territorial control to fulfill the requirements of both Common Article 3 (1)(d) and Art. 6 (2) Additional Protocol II, albeit applying the corrective standards of equality of belligerents and of a sliding-scale of obligations. The reality of NIACs is one where the average NSAG does not possess large capacities nor exhibits advanced structures. It is more probable that courts of so-called *de facto* authorities, which usually have established stable control over territory and civilians for a reasonable amount of time, will fall under the outlined scope.

VI. Conclusion

On the example of assessing the legality of administering justice during NIACs pursuant to Common Article 3 (1)(d) and Art. 6 (2) Additional Protocol II, this chapter outlined the overall equality problem in NIACs due to their asymmetric nature which is perpetuated by an undifferentiated, state-centric interpretation of pertinent IHL norms. It sought to interpret the two relevant provisions of IHL applicable to NIACs in a 'non-state'-friendly way, by strengthening the 'equality of belligerents'-principle and by recalling the autonomy of *jus ad bellum* and *jus in bello*.

Courts of NSAGs are legal pursuant to Common Article 3 (1)(d) and Art. 6 (2) Additional Protocol II if their constitution and operation fulfills the provisions' requirements. Where necessary, the law of the respective NSAG is equally included as the law of the respective state party to a NIAC. A combined approach of the 'equality of belligerents'- principle and the 'sliding scale of obligations'-standard ensures that NSAG are equally able to fulfill the provisions' requirements. Most importantly, this chapter demonstrated that conformity with Common Article 3 (1)(d) and Art. 6 (2) Additional Protocol II, being the two IHL provisions addressing and regu-

723 Yoram Dienstein, Non-International Armed Conflicts in International Law 178.

lating the administration of justice during NIACs, results in the relative legality of courts of NSAGs during NIACs.

Chapter 5: The Rule of Ne Bis In Idem and Courts of NSAGs

Whereas Chapter 4 assessed the recognition of courts of NSAGs as legal institutions according to pertinent IHL provisions, the present chapter elaborates on the recognition of judgments rendered by courts of NSAGs according to pertinent ICL provisions.

It analyzes whether judgments rendered by courts of NSAGs can be recognized in the context of *ne bis in idem* in ICL according to the ICC Statute. It does so by assessing the question whether courts of NSAGs can be subsumed under the Statute's upward *ne bis in idem* principle enshrined in Art. 20 (3) ICC Statute. The resulting findings carry implications and consequences for the recognition of non-state administered justice in the wider admissibility-regime before the ICC.

The present research endeavor of linking courts of NSAGs, a widely spread phenomenon in times of armed conflict, to the *ne bis in idem* principle in ICL, a fundamental criminal law principle, faces one challenge in particular: applying a state-centric law maxim to conduct of a non-state actor.

This chapter will first delineate different dimensions of the *ne bis in idem* principle according to the level it operates at, be it at the international, European, or national level (Section 1). It will then illustrate the *ne bis in idem* prinicple in ICL as part of the admissibility-test before the ICC on the example of Art. 20 ICC Statute (Section 2). Section 2 aims at presenting an overview of the *ne bis in idem*'s operability before the ICC. This includes an illustration of the admissibility-procedure before the ICC. Subsequently, the chapter ties the principle of *ne bis in idem* in ICL to the phenomenon of courts of NSAGs on the example of Art. 20 (3) ICC Statute and assesses whether courts of NSAGs can be considered as 'another court' (Section 3). This legal analysis addresses the core dilemma of the principle's bifurcated protective purpose: balancing the interests of states with the interests of the individual. Finally, the chapter develops guiding parameters for the inclusion of judgments rendered by courts of NSAGs into the *ne bis in idem* principle pursuant to Art. 20 (3) ICC Statute by examining how the ICC has previously dealt with the administration of justice by non-state entities (Section 4).

I. Ne Bis In Idem: An Overview of its Different Dimensions

The rule of *ne bis in idem* derives from the Roman Law principle *nemo debet bis vexari pro una et eadem causa* and means that no one shall be tried twice for the same cause.[724] Today, known in short as *ne bis in idem*, the principle ensures that no one shall be tried twice for the same matter.[725] *Ne bis in idem* is neither a customary rule[726] of international law nor a *ius cogens* norm.[727] However, the principle forms part of almost all national legal orders as well as international, European and other regional human rights instruments. Hence, it enjoys universal validity and is so widely accepted that it can be considered a general principle of criminal law.[728]

There exists considerable variation amongst national and international bodies regarding the interpretation and application of the *ne bis in idem*

---

724 Gerard Conway, '*Ne Bis in Idem* in International Law' (2003) 3 International Criminal Law Review 217-244, 221; Carl-Friedrich Stuckenberg, 'Double Jeopardy and Ne Bis in Idem in Common Law and Civil Law Jurisdictions' in Darryl K. Brown, Jenia I. Turner and Bettina Weisser (eds), The Oxford Handbook of Criminal Process (1st edn, Oxford University Press 2019) 457-475, 458.

725 Whether the term '*idem*' refers to the same conduct or same crime depends on the respective legal framework which enshrines the *ne bis in idem* principle. Art. 14 (7) ICCPR, for example, speaks of the prohibition to be tried or punish again for the 'same offence' whereas Art. 8 (4) ACHR prohibits a new trial for the 'same cause' which is interpreted as meaning 'same conduct'.

726 Dissenting Antonio Cassese, International Criminal Law (3rd edn, Oxford University Press 2013) 319.

727 Bas van Bockel, 'The ,European' *Ne Bis in Idem* Prinicple, Substances, Sources, and Scope' in Bas van Bockel (ed), Ne Bis in Idem in EU Law (1st edn, Cambridge University Press 2016) 13-52, 14.

728 For an overview of constitutions providing for *ne bis in idem* see Mahmoud C. Bassiouni, 'Human rights in the context of criminal justice: identifying international procedural protections and equivalent protections in national constitutions' (1992) 3 Duke Journal of Comparative & International Law 235-297, 288 ff.; see also Keilin Anderson and Adaena Sinclair-Blakemore, 'Ne bis in idem, nulla poena sine lege and Domestic Prosecutions of International Crimes in the Aftermath of a Trial at the International Criminal Court' (2021) 21 International Criminal Law Review 35-66, 40; Bas van Bockel, 'The ,European' *Ne Bis in Idem* Prinicple, Substances, Sources, and Scope' in Bas van Bockel (ed), Ne Bis in Idem in EU Law 13; Amal Clooney and Philippa Webb, The Right to a Fair Trial in International Law 778; Carl-Friedrich Stuckenberg, 'Double Jeopardy and Ne Bis in Idem in Common Law and Civil Law Jurisdictions' in Darryl K. Brown, Jenia I. Turner and Bettina Weisser (eds), The Oxford Handbook of Criminal Process 457; ACtHPR, Sebastien Germain Ajavon v Republic of Benin, Judgment (Merits), 29 March 2019, Application No. 013/2017 para 178.

principle. The principle can apply in an intra-state or inter-state context. It can protect both states' interests and individuals' rights.

States' interest in the sense that it ensures the integrity and authority of the judiciary as well as its operability by consolidating the efficient use of investigative, prosecutorial and judicial resources.[729] And individual rights in the sense that it ensures legal certainty and prevents unnecessary stress and anxiety for the individual by protecting them from being subject to double prosecution or double punishment for the same act.[730]

Most controversial among courts and human rights bodies is the interpretation of the term '*idem*', in other words, whether the rule of *ne bis in idem* protects from double prosecution and punishment for the same offence or the same crime (*idem crimen*) or for the same conduct, the same set of facts, the same historical event (*idem factum*). There also exist differences regarding the principle's geographical scope, namely, whether it applies in an intra-state context only or in an inter-state context as well.

The principle's heterogeneous alignment in national, regional and international instruments hinders a uniform interpretation and application. The following sub-sections (Sub-Sections 1 to 4) present an overview of the principle's different dimensions depending on the body of law it is embedded in.

1. Ne bis in idem in human rights law

Ne bis in idem found its way into IHRL after World War II. It is explicitly enshrined in only a few human rights frameworks, such as in the International Covenant for Civil and Political Rights or the American Convention on Human Rights.

Art. 14 (7) ICCPR reads as follows:

> 'No one shall be liable to be tried or punished again for an offence for which he has already been finally convicted or acquitted in accordance with the law and penal procedure of each country.'

Art. 8 (4) ACHR grants the individual protection from a possible re-trial only if the previous trial resulted in an acquittal. It reads as follows:

729 Amal Clooney and Philippa Webb, The Right to a Fair Trial in International Law 779.

730 Ibid.

> 'An accused person acquitted by a nonappealable judgment shall not be subjected to a new trial for the same cause'.

The ACHPR, for example, does not explicitly provide for a provision that enshrines the principle of *ne bis in idem*. However, the ACtHPR held that it is implicitly enshrined in the Charter's right to a fair trial pursuant to Art. 7 ACHPR. The ACtHPR applies Arts. 3 (1) and 7 of the Protocol to the African Charter on Human and Peoples' Rights on the Establishment of African Court on Human and Peoples' Rights[731] to extend its jurisdiction and apply human rights which are not explicitly enshrined in the ACHPR itself but in other human rights instruments by means of a comparative interpretation.[732] Regarding the rule of *ne bis in idem*, this comparative interpretation is based on Art. 14 (7) ICCPR. Additionally, the ACtHPR has recognized the *ne bis in idem* principle as a 'general principle of (criminal) law'[733].

Ne bis in idem in IHRL is not an absolute guarantee. For instance, both the ICCPR as well as ACHR foresee exceptions to the rule of *ne bis in idem*: A second trial does not violate *ne bis in idem*, if the initial prosecution suffered fundamental defects in due process, if the initial prosecution lacked a real intent to bring the person concerned to justice or if new facts are discovered after the initial prosecution has been concluded.

These exceptions are not explicitly mentioned in Art. 14 (7) ICCPR but they are implied in General Comment No. 32 which states that 'the prohibition of article 14, paragraph 7, is not at issue if a higher court quashes a conviction and orders a retrial', and Art. 14 (7) ICCPR 'does not prohibit the resumption of a criminal trial justified by exceptional circumstances, such as the discovery of evidence which was not available or known at

731 Protocol to the African Charter on Human And Peoples' Rights on the Establishment of an African Court on Human and Peoples' Rights, Organization of African Unity (OAU), 10 June 1998.

732 See ACtHPR, Armand Guehi v United Republic of Tanzania, 7 December 2018, Application No. 001/2015 para 38; ACtHPR, Wilfred Onyango Nganyi & 9 others v United Republic of Tanzania, Judgment, 18 March 2016, Application No. 006/2013 paras 164-167; IACtHR, Joint Law Report 2019: African Court on Human and Peoples' Rights, European Court of Human Rights and Inter-American Court of Human Rights) 25.

733 ACtHPR, Sebastien Germain Ajavon v Republic of Benin, Judgment (Merits) para 178.

the time of acquittal'[734]. According to the UNHRC, the court must disclose with sufficient detail what the new evidence or new facts entail.[735] The IACtHR recognizes exceptions for so-called 'fraudulent' *res iudicata* cases. Similar to the categories of 'unwillingness' in the admissibility test pursuant to Art. 17 (2)(a)-(c) ICC Statute, the IACtHR held that Art. 8 (4) ACHR does not apply where (i) the court which rendered the first verdict had the intent to 'shield the accused party from criminal responsibility', (ii) 'the proceedings were not conducted independently or impartially in accordance with due procedural guarantees', and (iii) 'there was no real intent to bring those responsible to justice'.[736] It also held that *ne bis in idem* is not triggered if investigations are re-opened due to new facts or evidence after a final acquittal.[737]

Even though *ne bis in idem* is enshrined in various IHRL instruments, the following three requirements form a common core:

Firstly, *ne bis in idem* as an international human right applies to criminal offences only, hence, not to disciplinary or administrative measures.[738]

Secondly, there exists disunity as to whether *ne bis in idem* as an international human right refers to the prohibition from being tried and punished twice for the same offence or for the same conduct (*idem crimen* vs. *idem factum*-approach). There prevails consensus regarding the fact that the rule of *ne bis in idem* is not applicable where an individual is tried twice but for different facts. The UNHRC, for example, takes a narrow approach and

734 Human Rights Committee United Nations, General Comment No. 32 on Art. 14: Right to equality before courts and tribunals and to a fair trial, CCPR/C/GC/32, 23 August 2007. para 56.

735 Amal Clooney and Philippa Webb, The Right to a Fair Trial in International Law 817; UNHRC, Juan Almirati Nieto v Uruguay, Decision, 25 July 1983, Comm. No. 92/1981 para 10.5

736 IACtHR, Almonacid-Arellano et al. v Chile, Judgment, Case No. 154, 26 September 2006, para 154; IACtHR, Case of Castillo Petruzzi et al. v Peru, Judgment para 153; IACtHR, The Rochela Massacre v Colombia, Judgment, 11 May 2007, Case No. Series C No. 163 para 197; IACtHR, Case of Nadege Dorzema et al. v Dominican Republic, Judgment, 24 October 2012, Case No. Series C No. 251 para 195.

737 IACtHR, Case of Almonacid-Arellano et al. v Chile, Judgment, 26 September 2006, Case No. Series C No. 154 para 154.

738 Human Rights Committee United Nations, General Comment No. 32 on Art. 14: Right to equality before courts and tribunals and to a fair trial, CCPR/C/GC/32, 23 August 2007. para 57; UNHRC, Andrés Felipe Arias Leiva v Colombia, Decision, 27 July 2018, Comm. No. 2537/2015 para 10.8; Sarah Joseph and Melissa Castan, The International Covenant on Civil and Political Rights: Cases, Materials, and Commentary (3rd edn, Oxford University Press 2013) 518.

follows the 'same offence'-approach.[739] By contrast, the UN Working Group on Arbitrary Detention follows a clear 'same conduct'-approach. In a case concerning the prosecution for treason following a previous prosecution for terrorism which related to the same set of facts, the Working Group established that a 'same offence'-approach would undermine the protection of *ne bis in idem*.[740] Likewise, the IACtHR follows a 'same offence'-approach based on the terminology of 'same cause' in Art. 8 (4) ACHR. The IACtHR held that the 'principle is intended to protect the rights of individuals who have been tried for specific facts from being subjected to a new trial for the same cause [...] the American Convention uses the expression "*the same cause*", which is a much broader term in the victim's favour'[741].

Also the ACtHPR's latest jurisprudence on *ne bis in idem* reveals that the court defines the '*idem*' element in a factual way, assessing whether the respective second prosecution relates to essentially the same facts compared to the first one.[742]

Thirdly, the rule of *ne bis in idem* is only triggered by a final decision on the merits. The '*bis*' element refers to irrevocable decisions which have reached the stage of *res iudicata*.[743]

As far as the geographical scope of *ne bis in idem* as an international human right is concerned, it protects from double prosecutions within the jurisdiction of one state only. Hence, it applies intra-state only. This holds true for Art. 14 (7) ICCPR, Art. 8 (4) ACHR as well as for Art. 7 ACHPR which *ne bis in idem* is an integral part of.[744] Nevertheless, the UNHRC

739 Human Rights Committee United Nations, General Comment No. 32 on Art. 14: Right to equality before courts and tribunals and to a fair trial, CCPR/C/GC/32, 23 August 2007. para 54.

740 United Nations Working Group on Arbitrary Detention, Communication addressed to the Government of Peru, Opinion No. 27/2000, 14 September 2000 paras 14 f.

741 IACtHR, Case of Loayza-Tamayo v Peru, Judgment, 27 November 1998, Case No. Series C No. 33 para 66.

742 See ACtHPR, Sebastien Germain Ajavon v Republic of Benin, Judgment (Merits) paras 180 and 182.

743 Amal Clooney and Philippa Webb, The Right to a Fair Trial in International Law 803.

744 Human Rights Committee United Nations, General Comment No. 32 on Art. 14: Right to equality before courts and tribunals and to a fair trial, CCPR/C/GC/32, 23 August 2007. para 57; ACtHPR, Sebastien Germain Ajavon v Republic of Benin, Judgment (Merits) para 179; Amal Clooney and Philippa Webb, The Right to a Fair Trial in International Law 799.

emphasized that states should still engage in ensuring the prevention of re-trials through international conventions.[745]

2. Ne bis in idem as a national (criminal law) guarantee

The rule of *ne bis in idem* is part of more than fifty national legal orders. It usually forms part of statutory law[746] and is included in either the substantive or procedural penal code of the respective state .[747] Sometimes the principle of ne *bis in idem* amounts to a constitutional right.[748] For instance, the fifth Amendment to the US Constitution was the first constitutional documentation of the rule of *ne bis in idem* at a national level.[749]

Even though most states recognize the *ne bis in idem* guarantee, varying conditions and restrictions dominate its application at the national level. The underlying rationale, however, is the same: *ne bis in idem* at the national level aims at the protection of the individual from any misuse of a state's *ius puninendi.* In many countries, *ne bis in idem* forms part of the rule of law and is considered an expression of the principle of proportionality. It also relates to the establishment of legal certainty, to upholding the integrity and authority of judgment and to ensure the operability of the judiciary.

When determining the scope of *ne bis in idem* at a national level, one must differentiate between common law and civil law countries. This relates to the chosen terminology of the guarantee as well as to its substantive scope. Common law countries speak of two different pleas: *autrefois acquit*

745 Human Rights Committee United Nations, General Comment No. 32 on Art. 14: Right to equality before courts and tribunals and to a fair trial, CCPR/C/GC/32, 23 August 2007. para 57 referring to Art. 20 (3) ICC Statute in fn 117.

746 Mahmoud C. Bassiouni, 'Human rights in the context of criminal justice: identifying international procedural protections and equivalent protections in national constitutions' 289.

747 See, for example, Art. 68 (1) of the Dutch Penal Code, Art. 360 of the Belgian Code of Criminal Procedure, Art. 17 (1) No. 7 of the Polish Code of Criminal Procedure or Art. 6 of the French Code of Criminal Procedure. It is also implicitly regulated in Sec. 352 of the Austrian Code of Criminal Procedure which regulates the re-opening of criminal proceedings.

748 Astrid Reisinger Coracini and Immi Tallgren, 'Art. 20 - *Ne bis in idem*' in Kai Ambos (ed), Rome Statute of the International Criminal Court - Article-by-Article Commentary (4th edn, C.H. Beck, Hart, Nomos 2022) 1091-1129, 1097; see, for example, Art. 103 (3) of the German Constitution (Grundgesetz) or Art. 23 (3) of the Estonian Constitution.

749 Gerard Conway, '*Ne Bis in Idem* in International Law' 222.

(former acquittal) and *autrefois convict* (former conviction). They also refer to 'double jeopardy'. In civil law countries, the rule is mostly named '*ne bis in idem*', '*non bis in idem*' or 'prohibition on double punishment'. A substantial difference between common law and civil law tradition in determining and applying the rule of *ne bis in idem* concerns the determination of the same matter. Most countries of common law tradition apply *ne bis in idem in abstracto*, focusing on the same offence in determining the '*idem*' element. Most civil law countries, in contrast, apply the rule *in concreto*, hence, focusing on the same set of facts or the same historical event for defining the '*idem*' element. For example, Austria[750], Germany[751], Italy[752], Spain[753], France[754], Belgium[755] or Poland[756] determine '*idem*' by assessing whether a second prosecution would relate to the same set of facts. The Netherlands, for instance, follows a combined approach according to which '*idem*' relates to the same set of facts as well as to a similar reproach of guilt which is determined by the legally protected interests of the offence and its legal classification.[757]

Another fundamental difference relates to the scope of the '*bis*' element. In common law tradition, for example, there is a prohibition on the appeal

750 Irene Gartner, 'Austria - Concurrent National and International Criminal Jurisdiction and the Prinicple ,ne bis in idem'' (2002) 73 Revue Internationale de Droit Pénal 787-809, 788.

751 Wolfgang Schomburg, 'Germany, concurrent national and international criminal jurisdiction and the principle ,ne bis in idem'' (2003) 73 Revue Internationale de Droit Pénal 941-964, 942.

752 Mario Pisani, 'Italie - Le prinicple ne bis in indem au niveau internationa et le procédure pénale italienn' (2002) 73 Revue Internationale de Droit Pénal 1017-1029, 1017.

753 María Del Mar Díaz Pita, 'España, Informe sobre el principio non bis in idem y la concurrenciade jurisdicciones entre los tribunals penales españoles y los tribunales penales internacionales' (2002) 73 Revue Internationale de Droit Pénal 873-899, 879.

754 Laurent Desessard, 'France - Les compétences criminelles concurrentes nationales et internationales et le principle ne bis in idem' (2002) 73 Revue Internationale de Droit Pénal 913-940, 915.

755 Tom Vander Beken, Gert Vermeulen and Thérèse Ongena, 'Belgium - Concurrent National and International Criminal Jurisdiction and the Prinicple ,ne bis in idem'' (2002) 73 Revue Internationale de Droit Pénal 811-848, 812.

756 Leszek Kubicki, 'Pologne - Les compétences criminelles concurrentes nationales et internationales et le principle ne bis in idem ' (2002) 73 Revue Internationale de Droit Pénal 1037-1050, 1039.

757 André Klip and Harmen Van der Wilt, 'The Netherlands and *non bis in idem*' (2002) 73 Revue Internationale de Droit Pénal 1091-1137, 1095.

of an acquittal by the prosecution.[758] This is closely linked to the jury system and the idea that an appellate court, comprised of professional judges only shall not be able to squash the verdict rendered by a jury which is considered as a representative group from society reaching a fair and reasonable decision.[759] In civil law countries, in turn, an appeal of an acquittal is not regarded as a breach of *ne bis in idem* but rather as a continuation of the original case. Within civil law countries, *ne bis in idem*, in principle, is triggered only by final decisions on the merits of the case rendered by criminal courts.[760] However, it need not always be a final *judgment* [emphasis added] on the merits of the case. Germany, for example, also considers a fixed penal order for summary punishment a bar to the re-opening of a case.[761]

In some countries a final so-called *non-lieu* decision of the prosecutor, in other words, a decision of the prosecutor not to open criminal proceedings or to discontinue criminal proceedings, triggers the applicability of *ne bis in idem* as well.[762] In France, for example, only a case dismissal based on legal grounds equals a final judgment and, hence, triggers the *ne bis in idem* guarantee.[763]

The geographical scope of *ne bis in idem* is uniformly regulated, regardless of common law or civil law peculiarities. *Ne bis in idem* is limited to the national jurisdiction of the respective state, hence, it applies in an intra-state context only.

---

758 Alexander Poels, 'A Need for Transnational Non Bis In Idem Protection in International Human Rights Law' (2005) 23 Netherlands Quarterly of Human Rights 329-348, 332.

759 Gerard Conway, '*Ne Bis in Idem* in International Law' 228.

760 Laurent Desessard, 'France - Les compétences criminelles concurrentes nationales et internationales et le principle ne bis in idem' 916; Irene Gartner, 'Austria - Concurrent National and International Criminal Jurisdiction and the Prinicple ‚ne bis in idem'' 788 f.; André Klip and Harmen Van der Wilt, 'The Netherlands and *non bis in idem*' 1092 and 1094; Tom Vander Beken, Gert Vermeulen and Thérèse Ongena, 'Belgium - Concurrent National and International Criminal Jurisdiction and the Prinicple ‚ne bis in idem'' 813.

761 See Sec. 410 (3) of the German Code of Criminal Procedure (StPO).

762 See, e.g., Art. 327 (1) of the Polish Code of Criminal Procedure in Leszek Kubicki, 'Pologne - Les compétences criminelles concurrentes nationales et internationales et le principle ne bis in idem ' 1040; see also Sec. 109 of the Austrian Code of Criminal Procedure in Irene Gartner, 'Austria - Concurrent National and International Criminal Jurisdiction and the Prinicple ‚ne bis in idem'' 790 f.

763 Laurent Desessard, 'France - Les compétences criminelles concurrentes nationales et internationales et le principle ne bis in idem' 916.

As far as exceptions to *ne bis in idem* are concerned, many countries foresee the possibility of re-opening a case under certain circumstances regulated through statutory law. Only a few countries foresee this possibility also to the detriment of the individual, for example, in the case of new or newly discovered evidence.[764]

3. Ne bis in idem in European criminal law

European law incorporates the *ne bis in idem* guarantee through various provisions and instruments which primarily serve EU law interests. The *ne bis in idem* guarantee is enshrined in three different EU regulatory frameworks, namely, in Art. 4 of Protocol 7 additional to the European Convention on Human Rights[765] (**Protocol 7 additional to ECHR**), in Art. 50 EUCFR and in Arts. 54-58 of the Convention Implementing the Schengen Agreement of 14 June 1985[766] (**CISA**). These three legal frameworks differ in their aims and objectives which is also reflected in the respective stipulation of the *ne bis in idem* guarantee in these frameworks. The *ne bis in idem* guarantee in EU law must be interpreted through the lens of the inherent objectives of the EU *acquis*, such as integration, harmonization, mutual trust and recognition.

764 See, e.g., Sec. 362 (5) of the German Code of Criminal Procedure (StPO), Chapter 58 Sec. 3 of the Swedish Code of Procedure, Sec. 976 (1) of the Danish Administrative Justice Act or Sec. 8 of the Irish Criminal Procedure Act of 2010 ;The re-opening of a case to the detriment of the individual is not possible in, for example, Belgium, France, Italy, Spain, Estonia or Slovenia, see Deutscher Bundestag Wissenschaftliche Dienste, Die Wiederaufnahme eines durch rechtskräftiges Urteil abgeschlossenen Strafverfahrens zuungunsten des Angeklagten aufgrund neuer Erkenntnisse - Überblick über die Rechtslage im Ausland, 31 January 2019), WD - 3000 - 262/18, 5-11 and Deutscher Bundestag Wissenschaftliche Dienste, Die Wiederaufnahmen von Strafverfahren zuungusten des Beschuldigten aufgrund nachträglich veränderter Beweislage - Überblick über die Rechtslagen in ausgewählten Ländern, 3 March 2022), WD 7 - 3000 - 007/22, 5-7.

765 See Art. 4 (1) of the Council of Europe, Protocol No. 7 to the Convention for the Protection of Human Rights and Fundamental Freedoms, European Treaty Series No. 117, 22 November 1984 according to which 'No one shall be liable to be tried or punished again in criminal proceedings under the jurisdiction of the same State for an offence for which he has already been finally acquitted or convicted in accordance with law and penal procedure of that State'.

766 Convention Implementing the Schengen Agreement of 14 June 1985 between the Governments of the States of the Benelux Economic Union, the Federal Republic of Germany and the French Republic, on the Gradual Abolition of Checks at their Common Borders, EUR-Lex Doc. No. 42000A0922(01), 19 June 1990.

a. Art. 4 Protocol 7 additional to ECHR

The *ne bis in idem* guarantee enshrined in Art. 4 Protocol 7 additional to ECHR constitutes an absolute human right, which Member States cannot derogate from, not even in times of war or other situations of public emergency.[767] It reads as follows:

> '1. No one shall be liable to be tried or punished again in criminal proceedings under the jurisdiction of the same State for an offence for which he has already been finally acquitted or convicted in accordance with the law and penal procedure of that State.
> 2. The provisions of the preceding paragraph shall not prevent the reopening of the case in accordance with the law and penal procedure of the State concerned, if there is evidence of new or newly discovered facts, or if there has been a fundamental defect in the previous proceedings, which could affect the outcome of the case.'

The provision speaks of 'criminal proceedings' but not explicitly of a criminal offence. However, the ECtHR held that the nature of the 'same offence' must be criminal. In *Engel and Others v the Netherlands*[768], the ECtHR developed the so-called 'Engel'-criteria to determine whether an offence is criminal in nature. According to this test, not only the legal classification of the offence but also the nature of the offence together with the repressing and deterrent character of the penalty, and the type and degree of severity of penalty are determinative for the criminal nature of the respective offence.[769]

Concerning the '*bis*' element, Art. 4 Protocol 7 additional to ECHR contains at least two distinct guarantees: the guarantee of not being tried twice (no second prosecution[770]) and the guarantee of not being punished twice (no accumulation of punishment with respect to the same offence). In *Zolutkhin v Russia*, the ECtHR identified a third, distinct guarantee which

767 See Art. 4 (3) Protocol 7 additional to ECHR in conjunction with Art. 15 ECHR.

768 ECtHR, Case of Engel and Others v The Netherlands, Judgment, 8 June 1976, Application Nos. 5100/71, 5101/71, 5102/71, 5354/72, 5370/72.

769 Ibid para 82; see also ECtHR, Guide on Article 4 of Protocol No. 7 to the European Convention on Human Rights: Right not to be tried or punished twice (Council of Europe 2022) para 9; Christoph Safferling, Towards an International Criminal Procedure (1st edn, Oxford University Press 2001) 58.

770 ECtHR, Case of Franz Fischer v Austria, Judgment, 29 May 2001, Application No. 37950/97 para 29; see also ECtHR, Case of Sergey Zolotukhin v Russia, Judgment, 10 February 2009, Application No. 14939/03 para 98.

is the guarantee of not being liable to be tried twice.[771] This refers to the protection from also pretrial stages of prosecution.[772] Concerning the '*idem*' element, Art. 4 Protocol 7 additional to ECHR speaks of the 'same offence'. Contrary to a first intuition, the ECtHR has interpreted the element of 'same offence' in a broad manner which prohibits a second prosecution based on the 'same conduct'[773]. By stipulating that the 'same conduct' can also comprise several offences, the ECtHR follows the conduct-approach (*idem factum*) which focuses on the identity of a set of facts or the identity of one historical event.[774] According to the ECtHR's jurisprudence regarding the material scope of Art. 4 Protocol 7 additional to ECHR, it famously held that the provision 'prohibits the prosecution or trial of a second offence in so far as it arises from identical facts or facts which are substantially the same'[775] – 'an approach which emphasizes the legal characterization of the two offences would be too restrictive'[776]. Otherwise, the principle's application would be impractical and ineffective.[777] Concerning the principle's geographical scope, Art. 4 Protocol 7 additional toECHR is applicable only with the jurisdiction of one state.

Finally, Art. 4 Protocol 7 additional to ECHR requires that the individual has been finally acquitted or convicted but the provision does not require that – in case of a conviction – the penalty has already been enforced or is about to be enforced. The protected interest of Art. 4 Protocol 7 additional to ECHR is the individual who shall have a procedural right to protect themselves from any misuse of the state's *ius puniendi*.

---

771 ECtHR, Case of Sergey Zolotukhin v Russia, Judgment para 110.

772 Bas van Bockel, 'The 'European' Ne Bis in Idem Principle: Substances, Sources, and Scope' in Bas van Bockel (ed), Ne Bis in Idem in EU Law (1st edn, Cambridge University Press 2016) 13-52, 18.

773 ECtHR, Case of Gradinger v Austria, Judgment, 23 October 1995, Application No. 15963/90 para 55.

774 ECtHR, Case of Oliveira v Switzerland, Judgment, 30 July 1998, Application No. 25711/94 paras 25-29; see also ECtHR, Case of Franz Fischer v Austria, Judgment para 25.

775 ECtHR, Case of Sergey Zolotukhin v Russia, Judgment paras 73 and 79-82.

776 Ibid paras 78 and 82 f.

777 Xavier Groussot and Angelica Ericsson, 'Ne Bis In Idem in the EU and ECHR Legal Orders - A Matter of Uniform Interpretation?' in Bas van Bockel (ed), Ne Bis in Idem in EU Law (1st edn, Cambridge University Press 2016) 53-102, 71.

b. Art. 50 EUCFR

The *ne bis in idem* guarantee is also provided for in Art. 50 EUCFR. Contrary to Art. 4 Protocol 7 additional to ECHR, Art. 50 EUCFR amounts to EU primary law. The provisions' texts are almost identical.[778] Art. 50 EUCFR reads as follows:

> 'No one shall be liable to be tried or punished again in criminal proceedings for an offence for which he has already been finally acquitted or convicted within the Union in accordance with the law.'

The significant difference of the provision's scope compared to the one of Art. 4 Protocol 7 additional to ECHR, is its geographical reach. Art. 50 EUCFR is not confined to one jurisdiction only. Instead, the provision speaks of anyone who has been acquitted or convicted 'within the Union'. Hence, the provision applies transnationally between the jurisdictions of several Members States. However, it equally applies to internal situations. Thus, compared to Art. 4 Protocol 7 additional to ECHR, Art. 50 EUCFR provides more protection which is in accordance with the so-called homogeneity clause in Art. 52 (3) EUCFR.

Art. 50 EUCFR only applies to situations where the respective Member State is implementing Union Law.[779] In other words, the *ne bis in idem* guarantee in Art. 50 EUCFR is only triggered and will only unfold its protection if the situation at hand arises from having a Member State implementing Union Law. Whether a Member State is implementing Union Law at a national level and, thereby, triggers the applicability of the Charter has been established in the *Åkerberg Fransson* case before the European Court of Justice (**ECJ**).[780] Accordingly, the respective Member State is implementing Union Law when it applies national legislation which falls within the scope of Union Law.[781] It remains unclear how strong the link between

---

778 Martin Böse, 'The Transnational Dimension of the *ne bis in idem* Principle and the Notion of *res iudicata* in the European Union' in Martin Böse et al. (eds), Justice Without Borders - Essays in Honour of Wolfgang Schomburg (1st edn, Brill Nijhoff 2018) 49-72, 60.

779 See Art. 51 (1) EUCFR.

780 See ECJ, Åklagaren v Hans Åkerberg Fransson, Judgment (Grand Chamber), 26 February 2016, Case No. C-617/10 paras 16, 19, 21 and 27; Further elaboration on the ECJ's jurisprudence regarding the scope of the Charter would go beyond the present work's research endeavor.

781 Ibid para 21; In this case the Grand Chamber held that the tax penalties and the criminal proceedings to which Mr. *Åkerberg Fransson* has been subjected are related

national law and EU law must be in order for the Charter to apply.[782] The ECJ's jurisprudence suggests a conclusion whereby the Charter applies to national law falling within the scope of EU law irrespective of the degree the national law is determined by Union Law.[783]

Concerning the '*idem*' element, the ECJ's jurisprudence developed a 'threefold identity' requirement for '*idem*': the 'identity of facts, unity of offender and unity of the legal interest protected'[784].

c. Art. 54 CISA

Finally, the *ne bis in idem* guarantee is also enshrined in Arts. 54-58 CISA. Art. 54 CISA enshrines the principle itself whereas Art. 55 CISA provides for exemption clauses. Arts. 56-58 CISA stipulate further specifications. Art. 54 CISA constitutes secondary EU law. It reads as follows:

> 'A person whose trial has been finally disposed of in one Contracting Party may not be prosecuted in another Contracting Party for the same acts provided that, if a penalty has been imposed, it has been enforced, is actually in the process of being enforced or can no longer be enforced under the laws of the sentencing Contracting Party.'

Against the backdrop of creating a unified Area of Freedom, Security and Justice (**AFSJ**), the Schengen Agreement of 1985[785] and the CISA are functionally linked to the objective of free movement of persons. Another fundamental aspect in establishing an AFSJ is the cross-border enforcement of

---

to breaches of his obligation to declare VAT. These obligations, in turn, constitute implementations of Union Law for the purpose of Art. 51 (1) EUCFR. See ibid para 27.

782 See also Bas van Bockel, 'The ‚European' *Ne Bis in Idem* Prinicple, Substances, Sources, and Scope' in Bas van Bockel (ed), Ne Bis in Idem in EU Law 34.

783 ECJ, Stefano Melloni v Ministerio Fiscal, Judgment (Grand Chamber), 26 February 2013, Case No. C-399/11 para 28; see also Bas van Bockel, 'The ‚European' *Ne Bis in Idem* Prinicple, Substances, Sources, and Scope' in Bas van Bockel (ed), Ne Bis in Idem in EU Law 39.

784 See ECJ, Aalborg Portland A/S and Others v Commission of the European Communities, Judgment, 7 January 2004, Case Nos. C-204/00 P, C-205/00 P, C-211/00 P, C-213/00 P, C-217/00 P, C-218/00 P para 338.

785 Agreement between the Governments of the States of the Benelux Economic Union, the Federal Republic of Germany and the French Republic on the gradual abolition of checks at their common borders (Schengen Agreement), Official Journal L 239, 22/09/2000 P. 0013-0018, 14 June 1985.

criminal law through mutual assistance and mutual recognition in criminal matters, extradition[786] and transfer and enforcement of judgments. Hence, the CISA was drawn up in the spirit of intergovernmental cooperation and is closely linked to extradition issues.[787] Thus, the principle of *ne bis in idem* as stipulated in Art. 54 CISA must be interpreted in the light of mutual assistance in criminal matters. It primarily serves as an instrument to promote and enhance the effective transnational enforcement of criminal law. The human right of protecting the individual from double prosecution within the Union also plays a role.[788] This prioritization is reflected in the enforcement-requirement of Art. 54 CISA which shall ensure that in the AFSJ the impunity of persons which have been definitely convicted and sentenced in an EU Member State is prevented.[789]

Concerning the '*idem*' element, Art. 54 CISA speaks of the 'same acts' instead of the 'same offence'. A literal reading of 'same acts' suggests that the legal classification of the offence covering the respective set of facts is irrelevant. Accordingly, the ECJ holds that the formulation of 'same acts' in Art. 54 CISA refers to a situation where there is a 'set of concrete circumstances which are inextricably linked together' in time, in space, and by their subject- matter, 'irrespective of the legal classification given to them or the legal interest protected'.[790] 'The same acts' mean 'one single timeframe, one single space but also one single intent'.[791]

Concerning the geographical scope, Art. 54 CISA raises *ne bis in idem* to a transnational level as it applies interjurisdictional between its Member

786 See Council Framework Decision of 13 June 2002 on the European arrest warrant and the surrender procedures between Member States, Doc. No. 2002/584/JHA, 13 June 2002.

787 Bas van Bockel, 'The ‚European' *Ne Bis in Idem* Prinicple, Substances, Sources, and Scope' in Bas van Bockel (ed), Ne Bis in Idem in EU Law 23.

788 Martin Böse, 'The Transnational Dimension of the *ne bis in idem* Principle and the Notion of *res iudicata* in the European Union' in Martin Böse et al. (eds), Justice Without Borders - Essays in Honour of Wolfgang Schomburg 59.

789 ECJ, Criminal proceedings against Zoran Spasic, Judgment, 27 May 2014, Case No. C-129/14 PPU paras 62 f.

790 ECJ, Criminal proceedings against Leopold Henri Van Esbroeck, Judgment, 9 March 2006, Case No. C-436/04 paras 36-38 and para 42; ECJ, Jean Leon Van Straaten v Staat der Nederlanden and Republiek Italië, Judgment, 28 September 2006, Case No. C-150/05 para 62; ECJ, Criminal proceedings against Norma Kraaijenbrink, Judgment, 18 July 2007, Case. No C-367/05 para 36.

791 Bas van Bockel, 'The ‚European' *Ne Bis in Idem* Prinicple, Substances, Sources, and Scope' in Bas van Bockel (ed), Ne Bis in Idem in EU Law 50.

States.[792] The provision renders the applicability of *ne bis in idem* dependent on the enforcement of a penalty (so-called 'enforcement condition'). The ECJ held that the 'execution condition laid down in Article 54 CISA does not call into question the *ne bis in idem* principle as such'[793] and, therefore, amounts to a limitation compatible with the horizonal clause in Art. 52 (1) EUCFR. Additionally, Art. 54 CISA requires that a trial has been 'finally disposed of'. This refers to a final judgment on the merits of a case resulting from a fully conducted trial.[794] The finality element refers to the respective national procedural law of the sentencing state according to which a judgment has been concluded which triggers the effect of *res iudicata*. However, in later judgments, the ECJ adopted a broader understanding of *res iudicata* which also included final decisions subject to revision in case of new evidence.[795] It also included decisions to discontinue criminal proceedings (*ordonnance de non-lieu*).[796]

Art. 55 CISA provides for exemption clauses referring to categories of offences which relate to the sovereignty and territorial integrity of the respective Contracting Party. These are offences, for example, where the acts took place in the territory of that Contracting Party, the acts to which the foreign judgment relates constitute an offence against national security or other equally essential interest of that Contracting Party or where the acts to which the foreign judgment relates were committed by officials of that Contracting Party.[797] Theses intergovernmental exception clauses in Art. 55 CISA mitigate the protection of Art. 54 CISA.

792 Martin Böse, 'The Transnational Dimension of the *ne bis in idem* Principle and the Notion of *res iudicata* in the European Union' in Martin Böse et al. (eds), Justice Without Borders - Essays in Honour of Wolfgang Schomburg 50.

793 ECJ, Criminal proceedings against Zoran Spasic, Judgment para 58.

794 ECJ, Criminal proceedings against Filomeno Mario Miraglia, Judgment, 10 March 2005, Case No. C-469/03 paras 30 and 35; Martin Böse, 'The Transnational Dimension of the *ne bis in idem* Principle and the Notion of *res iudicata* in the European Union' in Martin Böse et al. (eds), Justice Without Borders - Essays in Honour of Wolfgang Schomburg 53.

795 Martin Böse, 'The Transnational Dimension of the *ne bis in idem* Principle and the Notion of *res iudicata* in the European Union' in Martin Böse et al. (eds), Justice Without Borders - Essays in Honour of Wolfgang Schomburg 57; see also ECJ, Criminal proceedings against Hüseyin Gözütok and Klaus Brügge, Judgment, 11 February 2003, Case Nos. C-187/01, C-385/01 para 48.

796 ECJ, Criminal proceedings against M, Judgment, 5 June 2014, Case No. C-398/12 para 41.

797 See Art. 55 (1)(b) and (c) CISA.

4. Ne bis in idem in IHL

Ne bis in idem is also a guarantee in times of armed conflict. It is enshrined in Art. 75 (4)(h) Additional Protocol I, hence, it applies in IACs only. The provision reads as follows:

> 'No one shall be prosecuted or punished by the same Party for an offence in respect of which a final judgement acquitting or convicting that person has been previously pronounced under the same law and judicial procedure'.

Art. 75 (1) Additional Protocol I renders the provision's applicability dependent on three criteria: (i) the person in question must be affected by a situation referred to in Art. 1 Additional Protocol I, (ii) the person must be in the power of a party to the conflict and (iii) the person does not benefit from a more favourable treatment under the Conventions or the Protocol.[798]

A person is 'affected by a situation declared as war or any other armed conflict according to Art. 1 (3) Additional Protocol I in conjunction with Common Article 2 if they are exposed to the dangers resulting from the armed conflict whether or not they participated in the hostilities or because they are taking part in hostilities and therefore must abide by certain rules of conduct with respect to the adverse party and to the civilian population.[799]

A person is 'in the power of a party to the conflict' if they are in enemy hands or have fallen into the hands or power of the enemy.[800] *Ne bis in idem* in Art. 75 (4)(h) Additional Protocol I is only applicable within the same Party and the same law and judicial procedure. Hence, it does not protect from a second prosecution or second trial initiated by the adverse Party to the conflict.

---

798 See Art. 75 (1) Additional Protocol I; see also Michael Bothe, Karl Josef Partsch and Waldemar A. Solf, New Rules for Victims of Armed Conflict: Commentary on the Two 1977 Protocols Additional to the Geneva Conventions of 1949, 515.

799 ICRC, Commentary of 1987 Protocol Additional to the Geneva Conventions of 12 August 1949, and relating to the Protection of Victims of Non-International Armed Conflicts (Protocol II), 8 June 1977 para 4485.

800 ICRC, Commentary of 1987 Protocol Additional to the Geneva Convention of 12 August 1949, and relation to the Protection of Victims of International Armed Conflicts (Protocol I), 8 June 1977 (International Committee of the Red Cross 1987) para 2910.

Interestingly, Additional Protocol II which relates to the protection of victims of NIACs does not contain an equivalent provision providing for a *ne bis in idem* guarantee. During the drafting process, Draft Article 9 (3) of the ICRC, the predecessor norm of Art. 6 Additional Protocol II, did contain a *ne bis in idem* rule. It read as follows:

> 'No one shall be liable to be prosecuted or punished for an offence for which he has already been finally acquitted or convicted'.

However, *ne bis in idem* was not incorporated into the final text of Art. 6 Additional Protocol II since the Drafters of Additional Protocol II considered it unrealistic that it would apply between an insurgent court and state courts.[801] To do so would have amounted to a 'serious encroachment on national law'[802].

5. Conclusion

This section presented an overview of the different levels the rule of *ne bis in idem* can operate at. *Ne bis in idem* is a fundamental human right which shall protect the individual from double prosecution and, thereby, provide them with legal certainty regarding their conviction or acquittal. It is linked to the principle of proportionality as the initiation of new criminal proceedings – if not legally regulated as exemption clauses – amounts to a disproportionate use of a state's *ius puniendi.*[803] Historically, *ne bis in idem* was applicable within the same jurisdiction of one state. Gradually, *ne bis in idem* was introduced into other legal frameworks, many of them operating inter-state, hence, inter-jurisdictional, be it at a regional, European, or international level. Hence, international law- and, especially, European law-influences have changed the scope of *ne bis in idem* from

801 See ICRC, Commentary of 2016 on Convention (I) for the Amelioration of the Condition of the Wounded and Sick in Armed Forces in the Field para 587; Michael Bothe, Karl Josef Partsch and Waldemar A. Solf, New Rules for Victims of Armed Conflict: Commentary on the Two 1977 Protocols Additional to the Geneva Conventions of 1949, 745.

802 See Mr. Hussain's (delegate of Pakistan) opinion on a possible application of *ne bis in idem* in relation to 'rebel courts': Federal Political Department Bern, Official Records of the Diplomatic Conference on the Reaffirmation and Development of International Humanitarian Law Applicable in Armed Conflicts 1974-1977, Vol. VIII, CDDH/I/SR.33 para 67.

803 Bas van Bockel, 'The ,European' *Ne Bis in Idem* Prinicple, Substances, Sources, and Scope' in Bas van Bockel (ed), Ne Bis in Idem in EU Law 13.

a pure human right confined to the jurisdiction of one state towards an instrument which navigates two or more concurrent competent jurisdictions and resolves jurisdictional conflicts. This development resulted in a twofold protective scope of *ne bis in idem*: on the one hand it is a core procedural safeguard of the individual to challenge the misuse of a state's *ius puniendi* and to prevent a second trial or a second punishment for the same crime or conduct. On the other hand, the principle serves states' interests and their jurisdictional claims. Lifting *ne bis in idem* to the international plane transformed the principle's scope into allocating concurrent jurisdictions to enhance the efficient enforcement of criminal law.

II. Ne Bis In Idem before the ICC

Ne bis in idem is part of many international criminal law instruments, such as, the Draft Code of Crimes against Peace and Security of Mankind[804], the ICTY[805] and ICTR[806] Statutes and the ICC Statute[807].

This section focuses on the *ne bis in idem* principle enshrined in the ICC Statute. Since *ne bis in idem* forms an integral part of the admissibility regime before the ICC, the section starts with illustrating the procedure of the ICC's admissibility-test before it demonstrates the relevance and function of the *ne bis in idem* principle within the former.

1. The admissibility assessment before the ICC

The ICC is an arbiter of its own jurisdiction. According to the ICC Statute's Preamble paragraph 10, Art. 1 and Art. 17, the ICC shall exercise its jurisdiction complementary to national jurisdictions only. With two or more concurrent jurisdictions, each empowered to exercise its competence, it

804 See Art. 12 of Draft Code of Crimes Against the Peace and Security of Mankind, Yearbook of International Law Commission 1996, Vol. II, December 1996 according to which 'No one shall be tried for a crime against the peace and security of mankind of which he has already been finally convicted or acquitted by an international criminal court'.

805 Art. 10 of the Statute of the International Criminal Tribunal for the Former Yugoslavia, UN Doc. S/25704, 3 May 1993.

806 Art. 9 of the Statute of the International Criminal Tribunal for Rwanda, UN Doc. S/RES/955, 8 November 1994.

807 Art. 20 ICC Statute.

requires a mechanism to regulate which jurisdiction proceeds under which circumstances.[808] The admissibility test allocates the concurrent criminal jurisdictions between the ICC and its State Parties to prosecute genocide, war crimes, crimes against humanity and the crime of aggression. It is anchored in Art. 17 ICC Statute and led by the raison d'être of the ICC to only complement national jurisdictions but not supplanting them. This is reflected in the famous principle of complementarity according to which the ICC shall only be competent to exercise its power to prosecute the crimes of most serious concern to the international community where states are unable or unwilling to do so genuinely. Hence, the ICC functions as a court reservée to ensure that – where national jurisdictions fail to take 'appropriate'[809] action – those crimes do not go unpunished.

a. Structure of Art. 17 ICC Statute

The admissibility-test comprises three prongs – although some subsume the second prong under the first: the principle of complementarity, the rule of *ne bis in idem*, and the element of sufficient gravity.

Art. 17 ICC Statute comprises three paragraphs. Art. 17 (1) consists of four subparagraphs and describes three different scenarios in which the Court must assess the admissibility of a case. These three scenarios differ from one another with regard to how far the investigations or prosecutions at the national level have reached.

Art. 17 (1)(a) ICC Statute relates to the situation where a case is being investigated or prosecuted at the national level by a state which has jurisdiction over it. Art. 17 (1)(b) ICC Statute relates to the situation where a case has been investigated by a state and the state decided to not prosecute the person in question. Finally, Art. 17 (1)(c) ICC Statute relates to the situation where a person has already been tried by another court for conduct which is subject of the complaint.

808 Horizontal level, concurrent jurisdictions between two or more states, principle of 'subsidiarity' applies according to which the territorial state or the state of nationality enjoys jurisdictional 'priority', see William A. Schabas and Mohamed M. El Zeidy, 'Art. 17 - Issues of admissibility' in Kai Ambos (ed), Rome Statute of the International Criminal Court - Article-by-Article Commentary (4th edn, C.H. Beck, Hart, Nomos 2022) 945-1009, 947.

809 See Art. 17 (1)(a) ICC Statute which speaks of 'unwilling or unable genuinely to carry out the investigation or prosecution' and Art. 17 (1)(c) ICC Statute which speaks of 'the unwillingness or inability of the State genuinely to prosecute'.

In the first two scenarios, a case before the ICC is considered inadmissible where the respective state is or was unwilling or unable to prosecute the person genuinely. In the third scenario, namely, in the scenario where a person has already been tried, Art. 17 (1)(c) ICC Statute contains a cross-reference to Art. 20 (3) ICC Statute which stipulates the *ne bis in idem* principle between national jurisdictions and the ICC's jurisdiction. According to Art. 20 (3) ICC Statute, a case before the Court is considered admissible where the proceedings in the other court 'were for the purpose of shielding the person concerned from criminal responsibility for crimes within the jurisdiction of the Court; or Otherwise were not conducted independently or impartially in accordance with the norms of due process, recognized by international law and were conducted in a manner which, in the circumstances, was inconsistent with an intent to bring the person concerned to justice.'[810] These two criteria closely resemble the unwillingness-criteria set out in Art. 17 (2)(a) and (c). The provision continues with the fourth subparagraph, subparagraph (d) which refers to the gravity of a situation which must be 'sufficient to justify further action by the court'.

Finally, Art. 17 (1) and (2) define the terms of unwillingness and inability.

b. The pertinent steps of an admissibility-test according to Art. 17 ICC Statute

Bearing in mind the structure of Art. 17 ICC Statute, this part provides an overview of the individual steps of the admissibility test. The admissibility procedure follows a two-step order: the assessment of complementarity according to Art. 17 (1)(a)-(b) and Art. 17 (2)-(3) ICC Statute and the assessment of sufficient gravity pursuant to Art. 17 (1)(d) ICC Statute.

The complementarity assessment, in turn, also consists of two limbs: firstly, there must be some legal activity on a national level. Secondly, the proceedings at a national level must be or must have been conducted genuinely, in other words, the state which has jurisdiction over the case must be or must have been able and willing to prosecute the person in question in a genuine manner.

810 See Art. 20 (3)(a) and (b) ICC Statute.

aa. Inactivity

In considering whether a case is admissible under Art. 17(1)(a)-(b) ICC Statute, the initial questions to ask are whether there are ongoing investigations or prosecutions, or whether there have been investigations in the past, and the state having jurisdiction has decided not to prosecute the person concerned. 'It is only when the answers to these questions are in the affirmative that one must look to the second halves of sub-paragraphs (a) and (b) [...] To do otherwise would be to put the cart before the horse.'[811] Presuming the admissibility of a case before the ICC where there is or has been a state of inactivity at national level is convincing for the following reasons:

Firstly, such a presumption is supported by *argumentem a contrario* of a plain reading of Art. 17 (1)(a)-(c) ICC Statute. Art. 17 (1)(a)-(c) ICC Statute speak of 'a case is being investigated or prosecuted', a 'case has been investigated' and 'the person concerned has already been tried'. This implies that the admissibility-test before the ICC is triggered in cases of national jurisdictional activity only. In cases of inaction, the Court would not have to assess the unwillingness and inability of a state.[812]

Secondly, a presumption of admissibility in cases of inactivity finds support in the jurisprudence of the ICC itself. In the early years of the Court, several Pre-Trial Chambers have reasoned on the question of inactivity.[813]

---

811 ICC, Prosecutor v Germain Katanga and Mathieu Ngudjolo Chui, Judgment on the Appeal of Mr. Germain Katanga against the Oral Decision of Trial Chamber II of 12 June 2009 on the Admissibility of the Case, 25 September 2009, Case No. ICC-01/04-01/07 OA 8 para 78; see also ICC, Prosecutor v Saif Al-Islam Gaddafi and Abdullah Al-Senussi, Judgment on the Appeal of Libya against the decision of Pre-Trial Chamber I of 31 May 2013 entitled „Decision on the admissibiltiy of the case against Saif Al-Islam Gaddafi", 21 May 2014, Case No. ICC-01/11-01/11-547-Red para 213; ICC, Prosescutor v Alfred Yekatom and Patrice-Edouard Ngaissona, Decision on the Yeaktom Defence's Admissibility Challenge, 28 April 2020, Case No. ICC-01/14-01/18 para 17.

812 This scenario is also known as the concept of 'uncontested admissibility' see William A. Schabas and Mohamed M. El Zeidy, 'Art. 17 - Issues of admissibility' in Kai Ambos (ed), Rome Statute of the International Criminal Court - Article-by-Article Commentary 960.

813 ICC, Prosescutor v Alfred Yekatom and Patrice-Edouard Ngaissona, Decision on the Yeaktom Defence's Admissibility Challenge para 17; ICC, Prosecutor v Simone Gbagbo, Public redacted Decision on Côte d'Ivoire's challenge to the admissibility of the case against Simone Gbagbo, 11 December 2014, Case No. ICC-02/11-01/12 paras 27 ff.

Pre-Trial Chamber I in the *Lubanga* case held that 'The first part of the test relates to national investigations, prosecutions and trials concerning the case at hand insofar as such case would be admissible only if those States with jurisdiction over it have *remained inactive in relation to that case* [emphasis added] or are unwilling or unable, within the meaning of article 17(1)(a) to (c), 2 and 3 of the Statute'[814]. It also held that '[...] in the absence of any acting State, the Chamber need not make any analysis of unwillingness or inability'[815]. Very recently, the ICC took a stand on the question of inactivity within the admissibility-test and reasoned that firstly, inactivity on behalf of national authorities leads to the admissibility of a situation before the Court and secondly, the ICC does not need to adopt a 'step-by-step'-approach and providing the state with more time to start an investigation.[816]

Thirdly, a teleological interpretation of Art. 17 ICC Statute also supports the assumption that inactivity leads to admissibility. The object and purpose of Art. 17 ICC Statute is to ensure that the ICC operates as a court of last resort only, retaining the primary jurisdictions over the most serious crimes of concern to the international community with states at the

814 See ICC, Prosecutor v Thomas Lubanga Dyilo, Decision on the Prosecutor's Application for a warrant of arrest, Article 58, 10 February 2006, Case No. ICC-01/04-01/06 para 29; see also fn 19 in that decision which speaks of an 'interpretation a contrario of article 17, paras 1(a) to (c) of the Statute'; William A. Schabas and Mohamed M. El Zeidy, 'Art. 17 - Issues of admissibility' in Kai Ambos (ed), Rome Statute of the International Criminal Court - Article-by-Article Commentary 962; see also William A. Schabas, The International Criminal Court: A Commentary on the Rome Statute (2nd edn, Oxford University Press 2016) 455.

815 ICC, Prosecutor v Thomas Lubanga Dyilo, Decision on the Prosecutor's Application for a Warrant of Arrest, 10 February 2006, Case No. ICC-01/04-01/06-8 para 40; see also ICC, Prosecutor v Germain Katanga and Mathieu Ngudjolo Chui, Judgment on the Appeal of Mr. Germain Katanga against the Oral Decision of Trial Chamber II of 12 June 2009 on the Admissibility of the Case para 78. In a similar vein, see also ICC, Prosecutor v William Samoei Ruto et al., Judgment on the appeal of the Republic of Kenya against the decision of Pre-Trial Chamber II of 30 May 2011 entitled „Decision on the Application by the Government of Kenya Challenging the Admissibility of the Case Pursuant to Article 19(2)(b) of the Statute", 30 August 2011, Case No. ICC-01/09-01/11 OA para 41.

816 See ICC, Prosescutor v Alfred Yekatom and Patrice-Edouard Ngaissona, Decision on the Yeaktom Defence's Admissibility Challenge para 5 where the Defence challenged the admissibility and suggested the adoption of a so-called sequential approach offering national authorities with more time. Trial Chamber V rejected this approach and stressed that 'increasing or encouraging State capacity for the investigation and prosecution of the most serious international crimes is not within the Chamber's purview' see ibid para 22.

national level while at the same time ensuring the effective prosecutions of those crimes and fighting impunity. With a focus on the aim of fighting impunity and ensuring the effective prosecutions of international crimes, the provision of Art. 17 ICC Statute must be read in a way which stipulates a presumption of admissibility of cases before the Court where a state has remained inactive at national level. Art. 17 ICC Statute is formulated in a negative way where cases are inadmissible if certain requirements are met. Inadmissibility, in turn can be rebutted where the state is 'unable or unwilling to genuinely prosecute'[817]. This indicates that cases are generally regarded admissible before the Court. In other words, Art. 17 ICC Statute stipulates the exceptions to the rule. Such an interpretation is supported by paragraph 4 of the ICC Statute's Preamble which stresses that 'the most serious crimes of concern to the international community must not go unpunished' and 'their effective prosecution must be ensured by taking measures at the national level and by enhancing international cooperation'. The object and purpose of ensuring effective prosecution and ending impunity would be undermined if cases where national courts remain inactive would be considered inadmissible merely because Art. 17 ICC Statute does not explicitly regulate this scenario.[818]

Finally, this interpretation is supported by a systemic comparison to Arts. 18 and 19 ICC Statute. According to Art. 19 (2)(b) ICC Statute a state may only challenge the admissibility of a case before the ICC 'on the ground that it is investigating or prosecuting the case or has investigated or prosecuted'. According to Art. 18 (1) and (2) ICC Statute, a state can only request a deferral on grounds of (in)admissibility if the state 'is investigating or has investigated its nationals or others within its jurisdiction with respect to criminal acts which may constitute crimes referred to in article 5'.[819]

Thus, the first limb of the admissibility-assessment, thus, is the verification of whether national proceedings are or have been taking place.

bb. 'Unwilling or unable genuinely to investigate and prosecute'

The assessment of 'unwillingness' or 'inability' to 'genuinely prosecute' constitutes the second limb of the complementarity-test within the admissibili-

817 Jann K. Kleffner, Complementarity in the Rome Statute and National Criminal Jurisdictions (1st edn, Oxford University Press 2008) 104 f.

818 See also ibid 105.

819 Ibid 105.

ty procedure and is further defined in Art. 17 (2) and (3) ICC Statute. The burden of proof rests with the state which is challenging the admissibility before the Court.[820] The high level of detail in proving that a state is indeed carrying out 'genuine' proceedings makes it often difficult to discern the difference between 'inactivity' on the one hand and 'unwillingness' and 'inability' on the other.[821] Especially the line between 'unwillingness' and 'inactivity' is blurred because the Court often assesses the quality of national proceedings in order to determine whether a state is indeed investigating and prosecuting or not.[822] Since the ICC has been mostly concerned with situations where national authorities remained inactive, jurisprudence on the interpretation of the terms 'unwilling' or 'unable' – especially on the former – is rather scarce.[823]

Art. 17 (2) ICC Statute defines the 'unwillingness' of a state to genuinely investigate and prosecute by referring to three separate criteria: (a) when national proceedings were or are being conducted with a purpose to shield the person concerned from criminal responsibility[824], (b) when there is or has been any unjustified delay in the national proceedings[825], or (c) when national proceedings are or were not conducted independently or

820 ICC, Prosecutor v Saif-Al Islam Gaddafi and Abdullah Al-Senussi, Decision on the admissibility of the case against Saif Al-Islam Gaddafi, 31 May 2013, Case No. ICC-01/11-01/11-344-Red paras 46 and 52; ICC, Prosecutor v William Samoei Ruto et al., Judgment on the appeal of the Republic of Kenya against the decision of Pre-Trial Chamber II of 30 May 2011 entitled „Decision on the Application by the Government of Kenya Challenging the Admissibility of the Case Pursuant to Article 19(2)(b) of the Statute" para 62.

821 William A. Schabas and Mohamed M. El Zeidy, 'Art. 17 - Issues of admissibility' in Kai Ambos (ed), Rome Statute of the International Criminal Court - Article-by-Article Commentary 970.

822 Ibid 970; see, e.g. ICC, Prosecutor v Saif Al-Islam Gaddafi and Abdullah Al-Senussi, Decision on the admissibility of the case against Abdullah Al-Senussi, 11 October 2013, Case No. ICC-01/11-01/11-466-Red para 210 where the Chamber noticed that 'the two limbs of the admissibility test, while distinct, are nonetheless intimately and inextricably linked. [...] evidence put forward to substantiate the assertion of ongoing proceedings covering the same case before the Court may also be relevant to demonstrate their genuineness.'

823 See also William A. Schabas and Mohamed M. El Zeidy, 'Art. 17 - Issues of admissibility' in Kai Ambos (ed), Rome Statute of the International Criminal Court - Article-by-Article Commentary 971.

824 See Art. 17 (2)(a) ICC Statute.

825 See Art. 17 (2)(b) ICC Statute.

impartially and were not conducted in a manner consistent with an intent to bring the person to justice[826].

The element of 'unwillingness' becomes exclusively relevant in cases which first are declared inadmissible before the Court but later exhibit one of the 'flaws' enumerated in Art. 17 (2)(a)-(c) ICC Statute. For example, where national proceedings are experiencing a deliberate prolongation, this would amount to 'unwillingness' according to Art. 17 (2)(b) ICC Statute and may appear only after the Court initially declared a case inadmissible because the national proceedings were considered genuine.[827]

The situation in Libya recently gave cause to elaborate on suitable criteria to determine the 'inability' of a state to genuinely investigate and prosecute. Art. 17 (3) ICC Statute defines 'inability' as 'a total or substantial collapse or unavailability of its national judicial system', the inability to 'obtain the accused or the necessary evidence and testimony' or otherwise the inability of the state to 'carry out its proceedings'. Criteria which found consideration in determining a state's ability to genuinely investigate and prosecute were 'the existence of a political situation that makes holding trials impossible, a debilitating lack of judges, prosecutors and other court personnel, obstruction by uncontrolled elements that render the system unavailable, public disorder, natural disaster or chaos resulting from a civil war'[828].

Whereas the 'inability-assessment' according to Art. 17 (3) ICC Statute is more fact-driven and objective in nature, the 'unwillingness'-test pursuant to Art. 17 (2 ICC Statute includes an assessment of the quality of national proceedings by the Court.

Turning to the second half of the quality assessment of national proceedings, Art. 17 (1)(a)-(b) ICC Statute links the words 'unwilling or unable' to the adjective 'genuinely'.

A plain reading of genuinely could mean 'authentic or real – something that has the quality of what it is purported to be or to have'[829]. The ILC

826 See Art. 17 (2)(c) ICC Statute.

827 William A. Schabas and Mohamed M. El Zeidy, 'Art. 17 - Issues of admissibility' in Kai Ambos (ed), Rome Statute of the International Criminal Court - Article-by-Article Commentary 971.

828 ICC, Prosecutor v Saif-Al Islam Gaddafi and Abdullah Al-Senussi, Decision on the admissibility of the case against Saif Al-Islam Gaddafi para 143.

829 William A. Schabas and Mohamed M. El Zeidy, 'Art. 17 - Issues of admissibility' in Kai Ambos (ed), Rome Statute of the International Criminal Court - Article-by-Article Commentary 972; see also Jann K. Kleffner, Complementarity in the Rome Statute and National Criminal Jurisdictions 115.

Draft Statute of 1994 used the term 'ineffective' in its Draft Preamble.[830] However, many delegations criticized the term as being too subjective, placing the Court in a position of passing judgment on the penal system of a state which would constitute an encroachment on states' sovereignty.[831] In preparation of the Rome Conference, the Preparatory Committee discussed terms such as 'good-faith effort' and 'duly tried'[832]. At the Rome Conference, many delegations were of the view that subjective criteria should be omitted and that the Court should be cautious in judging the quality of national proceedings. The word 'genuine' was considered 'the least objectionable word'[833]. While some authors[834] argue that 'genuinely' refers to the last part of the phrase, hence, to 'investigate and prosecute' other authors[835] and, importantly, the ICC[836] seems to adopt an interpretation according to which 'genuinely' refers to 'unwilling' and 'unable'.

cc. 'Sufficient gravity'

Art. 17 (1)(d) ICC Statute stipulates a last requirement of the admissibility-test, the element of 'sufficient gravity'. While any violation of international criminal law should be considered grave, the criterion of 'gravity' set out

---

830 See UN, Yearbook of the International Law Commission (1st edn, 1994), Vol. II Part 2, 27.

831 See UN, Diplomatic Conference of Plenipotentiaries of an International Criminal Court (United Nations, 13 September 1996), UN Doc. A/51/22, Vol. I, Proceedings of the Preparatory Committee during March-April and August 1996 para 161.

832 See ibid para 154.

833 See John T. Holmes, 'Complementarity: National Courts versus the ICC' in Antonio Cassese, Paola Gaeta and John R.W.D. Jones (eds), The Rome Statute of the International Criminal Court: A Commentary (1st edn, Oxford University Press 2002) 667-686, 674; William A. Schabas and Mohamed M. El Zeidy, 'Art. 17 - Issues of admissibility' in Kai Ambos (ed), Rome Statute of the International Criminal Court - Article-by-Article Commentary 971.

834 Jann K. Kleffner, Complementarity in the Rome Statute and National Criminal Jurisdictions 115. Following this interpretation, see also William A. Schabas and Mohamed M. El Zeidy, 'Art. 17 - Issues of admissibility' in Kai Ambos (ed), Rome Statute of the International Criminal Court - Article-by-Article Commentary 972.

835 John T. Holmes, 'Complementarity: National Courts versus the ICC' in Antonio Cassese, Paola Gaeta and John R.W.D. Jones (eds), The Rome Statute of the International Criminal Court: A Commentary 674; Frank Meyer, 'Complementing Complementarity' (2006) 6 International Criminal Law Review 549-583, 566.

836 ICC, Prosecutor v Saif-Al Islam Gaddafi and Abdullah Al-Senussi, Decision on the admissibility of the case against Saif Al-Islam Gaddafi para 139.

in Art. 17 (1)(d) ICC Statute must be understood as an additional threshold to ensure that the Court's jurisdiction only comprises cases which genuinely warrant the intervention by the ICC.[837] It secures the operability and efficiency of the ICC. This criterion reflects the inherent limitation of the Court's mandate, namely, that the primary burden of investigating and prosecuting international crimes rests with national courts. In the course of the last years, various Pre-Trial Chambers have attempted to summarize the gravity-assessment which, accordingly, should include: (i) 'a generic assessment [...] of whether the groups of persons that are likely to form the object of the investigation capture those who may bear the greatest responsibility for the alleged crimes committed; and (ii) gravity must be assessed from both a "quantitative" and "qualitative" viewpoint and factors such as nature, scale and manner of commission of the alleged crimes, as well as their impact on victims are indicators for the gravity of a given case'[838].

2. The admissibility-regime and its relation to the ne bis in idem principle

This sub-section highlights the role of the *ne bis in idem* principle within the admissibility-regime before the ICC and is limited to Art. 20 (3) ICC Statute.

Art. 20 ICC Statute comprises three different scopes of application of the rule of *ne bis in idem* regarding criminal proceedings before the ICC. Art. 20 (1) ICC Statute provides for the *ne bis in idem* rule regarding former proceedings before the Court itself. Art. 20 (2) ICC Statute stipulates the *ne bis in idem* rule regarding subsequent criminal proceedings at the national level and is also referred to as the so-called downward *ne bis in idem*. Art. 20 (3) ICC Statute covers situations where an individual has been tried by 'another court' at the national level and subsequently faces criminal

837 William A. Schabas, The International Criminal Court: A Commentary on the Rome Statute 463.

838 ICC, Situation on the Registered Vessels of the Union of the Comoros, the Hellenic Republic and the Kingdom of Combodia, Decision on the request of the Union of the Comoros to review the Prosecutor's decision not to initiate an investigation, 16 July 2015, Case No. ICC-01/13 para 21; see also ICC, Situation in the Republic of Kenya, Decision Pursuant to Article 15 of the Rome Statute on the Authorization of an Investigation into the Situation in the Republic of Kenya, 31 March 2010, Case No. ICC-01/09-19-Corr paras 60-62; William A. Schabas, The International Criminal Court: A Commentary on the Rome Statute 465.

proceedings before the ICC. Art. 20 (3) ICC Statute is also referred to as the so-called upward *ne bis in idem* and reads as follows:

> 'No person who has been tried by another court for conduct also proscribed under article 6,7, 8 or 8bis shall be tried by the Court with respect to the same conduct [...]'

unless the proceedings in the other court were not conducted genuinely pursuant to subparagraphs (a) and (b).

The rule of *ne bis in idem* becomes relevant within the admissibility process twice, although in slightly different manners:

The first time the Court touches upon the rule of *ne bis in idem* is within the merits of Art. 53 (1)(b) and Art. 17 (1)(a) and (b) ICC Statute, hence, at the stage of the initiation of an investigation of a potential case before the ICC. In this course, the ICC examines whether there are either ongoing proceedings or whether there has been a discharge of proceedings at national level. As described above, this assessment is reflecting the principle of complementarity within the admissibility-test. Since this concerns the early stage of initiating an investigation before the ICC, prior to the commencement of an investigation, the ICC must construe a potential case because the suspect and crimes have not been identified yet.[839] The ICC examines whether 'the groups of persons involved that are likely to be the object of an investigation for the purpose of shaping the future case(s)' and the conduct fulfilling 'the crimes within the jurisdiction of the Court allegedly committed during the incidents that are likely to be the focus of an investigation'[840] are the 'same' for the sake of determining the scope and contours of a case which will then be the object of the subsequent admissibility-test. Hence, at this initial stage, the Court borrows the '*idem*' element of the rule of *ne bis in idem* to determine the parameters of a potential case before the Court and to assess whether it is congruent with the respective case before a national court. Hence, at this stage, the rule

839 ICC, Situation in the Republic of Kenya, Decision Pursuant to Article 15 of the Rome Statute on the Authorization of an Investigation into the Situation in the Republic of Kenya para 48; see also Rod Rastan, 'What is a 'case' for the purpose of the rome statute?' (2008) 19 Criminal Law Forum 435-448, 441 f.

840 See ICC, Situation in the Republic of Kenya, Decision Pursuant to Article 15 of the Rome Statute on the Authorization of an Investigation into the Situation in the Republic of Kenya para 182; ICC, Situation in the Islamic Republic of Afghanistan, Decision Pursuant to Article 15 of the Rome Statute on the Authorisation of an Investigation into the Situation in the Islamic Republic of Afghanistan, 12 April 2019, Case No. ICC-02/17-33 para 72.

of *ne bis in idem* is used as a tool to establish potential reference cases(s) before the Court. A substantive assessment of the principle's constitutive elements does not take place.

The second time the Court is confronted with the rule of *ne bis in idem* is within the merits of Art. 53 (1)(b) and Art. 17 (1)(c) in conjunction with Art. 20 (3) ICC Statute. *Ne bis in idem* as stipulated in Art. 20 (3) ICC Statute forms part of the admissibility through the cross reference made in Art. 17 (1)(c) ICC Statute. According to Art. 17 (1)(c) ICC Statute, a case before the Court is inadmissible where 'The person concerned has already been tried for conduct which is the subject of the complaint, and a trial by the Court is not permitted under article 20, paragraph 3;'. Pursuant to Art. 20 (3) ICC Statute, this requires the ICC to assess whether the national criminal proceedings have been conducted in a 'genuine manner'. *In concreto*, the ICC verifies if the national proceedings:

(a) 'were for the purpose of shielding the person concerned from criminal responsibility for crimes within the jurisdiction of the Court; or
(b) Otherwise were not conducted independently or impartially in accordance with the norms of due process recognized by international law and were conducted in a manner which, in the circumstances, was inconsistent with the intent to bring the person concerned to justice.'

In contrast to Art. 17 (1)(a)-(b) ICC Statute, proceedings at the national level have been terminated and resulted in a final decision on the merits. At this stage, the Court carries out a substantive assessment of *ne bis in idem* and examines each of its constitutive elements as well as the exemption requirements set out in Art. 20 (3)(a)-(b) ICC Statute. The exemption-clauses of Art. 20 (3)(a)-(b) ICC Statute are an *in verbatim* copy of two of the unwillingness-criteria stipulated in Art. 17 (2)(a) and (c) ICC Statute. This bears additional testimony to the interrelation between the rule of *ne bis in idem* and the overall admissibility-regime.

It appears difficult do establish and prove that national proceedings were conducted with a purpose of shielding the person concerned from justice. Historically, the Court reasoned that, for example, charging an alleged genocide as an evidently disproportionate ordinary crime at national level amounts to a 'sham' trial and, hence, fulfills the exemption clause of Art. 20 (3)(a) ICC Statute. The second exemption clause, Art. 20 (3)(b) ICC Statute, closely resembles the first one, especially, concerning the subjective element according to which national proceedings must have been conducted in a manner consistent 'with an intent to bring the person concerned to justice'. In so far, it is hard to decipher a difference between subparagraph (a) and subparagraph (b). The reference to independent and impartial proceedings relates to international human rights standards regarding a fair trial.[841]

In conclusion, one can reason that *ne bis in idem* in ICL as stipulated in Art. 20 (2) and (3) ICC Statute applies inter-jurisdictional - except for Art. 20 (1) ICC Statute which applies intra-jurisdictional. The upward *ne bis in idem* in Art. 20 (3) ICC Statute is structurally embedded in the admissibility-regime of the ICC through the cross-reference made in Art. 17 (1)(c) ICC Statute. The admissibility-regime is a mechanism *sui generis* to allocate concurrent jurisdictions between the ICC and its State Parties. Hence, the protective function of *ne bis in idem* in the ICC Statute is not merely human rights oriented. *Ne bis in idem* within the ICC Statute is also a tool to regulate jurisdictional claims. Ultimately, this becomes evident through the principle's systematical placement within Part 2 of the Statute, titled 'Jurisdiction, Admissibility and Applicable Law'.

3. Conclusion

The admissibility-regime before the ICC sees states as the privileged agents to administer justice.[842] The ICC was built with the mission to complement national jurisdictions of states in the fight against impunity for perpetrators of the most serious crimes of international concern. This mission is reflected in the principle of complementarity, the guiding prong of the Court's admissibility-test. The principle of complementarity is embedded in states sovereignty. It amounts to the 'core' of the ICC Statute and is anchored in the Statute's Preamble as well as in Art. 1 and Art. 17 ICC Statute.[843] It dictates the presumption that states enjoy primacy over the investigation and prosecution of the core crimes of genocide, war crimes, crimes against humanity and the crime of aggression. Accordingly, *non*-state administered justice [emphasis added] through courts of NSAGs, although operating also

841 See above Chapter 4: The Legality of Courts of NSAGs, III. 1. a.

842 René Provost, Rebel Courts: The Administration of Justice by Armed Insurgents 410.

843 William A. Schabas, The International Criminal Court: A Commentary on the Rome Statute 447 referring to the principle of complementarity as the Court's 'DNA'; see also William A. Schabas and Mohamed M. El Zeidy, 'Art. 17 - Issues of admissibility' in Kai Ambos (ed), Rome Statute of the International Criminal Court - Article-by-Article Commentary 949.

at a national level, does not fit into the admissibility-regime dominated by a state-centered view on law enforcement. However, historically, the ICC has been confronted with non-state administered justice through courts of NSAGs when assessing the admissibility of a case. Until now, the Court limited its elaboration on the recognition of non-state administered justice within the regime of Art. 17 ICC Statute to conclude that such entities are not states and, hence, cannot find consideration. This conclusion, however, is too simplistic as it neglects the potential of courts of NSAGs to contribute to the fight against impunity for the most serious crimes of international concern – most of them taking place in the wake of armed conflicts. It also fails to account for an existing reality of proliferating 'rebel' justice along with a change of paradigm in the enforcement of law during armed conflict. Further, it ignores the pertinent terminology of Art. 17 (1)(c) and Art. 20 (3) ICC Statute which opens the gateway for including courts of NSAGs into the admissibility-test before the ICC through recognizing their judgments in the upward *ne bis in idem* rule. This will be elaborated on in the following section.

III. Art. 20 (3) ICC Statute and Courts of NSAGs: Opening the Gateway

This section assesses whether the admissibility-regime before the ICC as laid out in Section 2 can be broadened to also include non-state administered justice through courts of NSAGs. It does so by analyzing the text of Art. 17 (1)(c) ICC Statute in conjunction with Art. 20 (3) ICC Statute and linking the provisions to the phenomenon of courts of NSAGs and their judgements. This analysis will predominantly revolve around the interpretation of the term 'tried by another court' in Art. 20 (3) ICC Statute and its potential to open the door for including courts of NSAGs.
This analysis is warranted for the following reasons:

Firstly, the texts of both Art. 17 (1)(c) and Art. 20 (3) ICC Statute omit any explicit reference to state jurisdiction(s) or state courts only. Art. 20 (3) ICC Statute speaks of 'another court' instead of, for example, 'another court of a state'. Art. 17 (1)(c) ICC Statute refers to 'the person concerned has already been tried'. Compared to the narrower terminology at other parts in the Statute[844] it is worth analyzing whether the broad term in Art. 20 (3)

844 See, e.g., Art. 17 (1)(a)-(b) and Art. 19 (2)(b) ICC Statute speaking of 'a State which has jurisdiction', Preamble (1) and Art. 1 ICC Statute speaking of 'national crimi-

ICC Statute facilitates the inclusion of courts of NSAGs. This legal endeavor is not as illusive or far-fetched as it might seem in the context of *ne bis in idem* operating at a national, hence, intra-state level. The *ne bis in idem* rule in the ICC Statute applies across multiple jurisdictions and, therefore, must be considered in a *sui generis* context.[845]

Secondly, the ICC's subject matter jurisdiction relates to conduct which primarily takes place during armed conflict, a field which courts of NSAGs usually operate in. Hence, the ICC's jurisdiction is normatively tied to situations of armed conflict which makes the ICC Statute a pivotal forum to elaborate on the recognition of 'rebel' administered justice.[846] IHL, the applicable legal framework during armed conflicts, acknowledges the possibility for NSAGs to legally engage in the administration of justice according to Common Article 3 (1)(d) and Art. 6 (2) Additional Protocol II. Hence, against the backdrop of aiming at 'systemic integrity of international law', it is worthwhile to elaborate whether ICL takes up on the IHL postulated possibility for NSAGs to legally administer justice during armed conflict.

Thirdly, it is an existing reality that during armed conflict many NSAGs engage in the administration of justice through their own courts. The provision of justice mechanisms in 'rebel'-held territory is a popular tool to exercise control and to maintain law and order within the group's own ranks as well as within the civilian population the group seeks to govern. 'Rebel' administered justice may also be provided with the aim of repressing and punishing violations of IHL. In the context of prosecuting penal matters through courts of NSAGs, the rule of *ne bis in idem* becomes relevant when bearing in mind the possibility of re-trials before other law enforcement bodies which are different from the respective 'rebel court', namely, before national courts or international courts such as the ICC.

From an accused's point of view, the potential applicability of *ne bis in idem* to courts of NSAGs is fundamental. Imagine an admissibility challenge pursuant to Art. 19 (2)(a) ICC Statute based on Art. 17 (1)(c), Art. 20 (3) ICC Statute where a defendant rises an alleged infringement on the principle of *ne bis in idem* because they already stood trial for the

---

nal jurisdictions' compared to, for example, Art. 28 (a)(i) and (b)(iii) ICC Statute speaking of 'competent authorities for investigation and prosecution' leaving out an explicit state component.

845 Keilin Anderson and Adaena Sinclair-Blakemore, 'Ne bis in idem, nulla poena sine lege and Domestic Prosecutions of International Crimes in the Aftermath of a Trial at the International Criminal Court' 42.

846 René Provost, Rebel Courts: The Administration of Justice by Armed Insurgents 409 refers to this as an 'organic link'.

same conduct before a court of a NSAG. The wording of Art. 17 (1)(c) and Art. 20 (3) ICC Statute is substantially different from Art. 17 (1)(a)-(b) ICC Statute. Instead of referring to 'a State which has jurisdiction' they speak of 'the person concerned has already been tried' and 'no person who has been tried by another court', respectively. Both provisions leave out an explicit state component which may allow opening the door for non-state administered justice.

1. Courts of NSAGs as 'another court'?: testing the term's elasticity

The following part assesses whether the term 'another court' in Art. 20 (3) ICC Statute can be interpreted to also include courts established by NSAGs during armed conflict ('rebel court'-friendly interpretation). In doing so, the term 'another court' will be interpreted from a textual perspective, taking into account the context of *ne bis in idem* in the ICC Statute, namely, its structural embedment into the overall admissibility and complementary regime as well as in light of the object and purpose of *ne bis in idem* in ICL.

Thereby, the analysis follows the traditional rules on interpretation of treaties pursuant to Art. 31 (1) VCLT according to which a treaty shall be interpreted in 'good faith in accordance with the ordinary meaning to be given to the terms of the treaty in their context and in light of its object and purpose'. Additionally, supporting arguments will be formulated to expand the application of the term 'another court' to courts of NSAGs. This analysis is pondering against the backdrop of 'rebel'-adjudicated justice as an increasingly applied tool during armed conflict. Hence, the law must adapt to changing realities on the ground.

a. Textual interpretation

According to the text of Art. 20 (3) ICC Statute, the reference point for the upward *ne bis in idem* principle is 'another court' or 'proceedings in the other court'. The term 'court' is not legally defined in international law. This is owed to the circumstance that the word 'court' derives its meaning and content from the normative setting it is put in. This normative setting can range from a domestic legal norm, an international treaty norm, a soft law guideline, etc.

A first access to interpreting the word 'court' is looking at the generic sense of the word. In its generic sense, the word 'court' refers to any judicial body which applies legal rules to a set of facts and reaching a binding conclusion for the parties involved.

Adding a legal layer to the generic meaning of the term, the word 'court' refers to 'a body established by law for the administration of justice'.[847]

As has been argued above[848], 'established by law' is not a criterion which is per se limited to state law. An insurgent group may as well have its own law according to which it establishes courts and administers justice.

A textual interpretation of the word 'court', be it in its generic or in its legal sense, does not necessarily refer to state courts only. This assumption is supported in a ruling of the ECtHR which held that a tribunal is not characterized by its name but by 'its judicial function, that is to say determining matters within its competence on the basis of rules of law and after proceedings conducted in a prescribed manner'. The ECtHR also held that a court or judicial body does not 'necessarily need to be understood as signifying a court of law of the classic kind, integrated within the standard judicial machinery of the country'[849].

The term 'other' means different from or distinct to something. Hence, in the context of Art. 20 (3) ICC Statute 'another court' in its general sense means any other court than the ICC.

Bearing in mind that Art. 20 (3) ICC Statute participates in the overall admissibility scheme, it is evident that the word 'another' relates to the ICC. Hence, in its ordinary meaning the phrase 'another court' in Art. 20 (3) ICC Statute means any court *other* than the ICC [emphasis added]. A court of an insurgent group party to a NIAC is a judicial body which administers justice by applying legal rules to a set of facts. It is also different to the ICC.[850] Therefore, a purely textual interpretation of the term 'another

847 Jonathan Law (ed), A Dictionary of Law; interestingly, the ICC also distinguishes between the plain word 'court' and the legal term 'regularly constituted court', hence, a court which has been established according to (state) law, see ICC, Prosecutor v Al Hassan Ag Abdoul Aziz Ag Mohamed Ag Mahmoud, Rectificatif à la Décision relative á la confiramtion des charges portées contre Al Hassan Ag Abdoul Aziz Ag Mohamed Ag Mahmoud paras 374 f.

848 See above Chapter 4: The Legality of Courts of NSAGs, II. 2.

849 ECtHR, Case of Campbell and Fell v The United Kingdom, Judgment, 28 June 1984, App. Nos. 7819/77, 7878/77 para 76.

850 In this line, see Ahmed Samir Hassanein, 'Physical and Legal Inability under Article 17(3) of the Rome Statute' (2015) 15 International Criminal Law Review 101-123, 107; Jan Willms, 'Courts of armed groups - a tool for inducing higher compliance with international humanitarian law?' in Heike Krieger (ed), Inducing Compliance with International Humanitarian Law - Lessons fron the African Great Lakes Region 165.

court' accommodates the inclusion of courts of NSAGs into the scope of Art. 20 (3) ICC Statute.

Such a 'rebel court'-friendly interpretation is also supported when looking at the generic meaning of the term 'another court' in its contextual embedment in the ICC Statute. Art. 17 (1)(a)-(b) ICC Statute speak of 'a State which has jurisdiction' whereas Art. 17 (1)(c) ICC Statute speaks of 'tried by another court', leaving out an explicit state component.[851] The different wording suggests a different meaning and gives reason to believe that the abandonment of any explicit state reference has been deliberate. Hence, according to a textual interpretation of Art. 20 (3) ICC Statute, the principle of *ne bis in idem* pertains to any 'other court' regardless of its nature, hence, regardless of whether it is state- or non-state administered.[852] Thus, courts of NSAGs can qualify as 'another court' within Art. 20 (3) ICC Statute.

b. Contextual interpretation

Including 'rebel courts' into the scope of Art. 20 (3) ICC Statute could be barred if the term 'another court' is to be understood as inherently state-owned, in other words, if the term 'court' equals 'state institutions' only. One might reach such a conclusion when interpreting the word 'another court' solely from the perspective of its contextual embedment into the overall admissibility regime set out in Art. 17 ICC Statute, especially, when interpreting it in light of the principle of complementarity set out in Art. 17 (1)(a)-(c) ICC Statute.

851 The same holds true for the French version of the provision, speaking of 'un Ètat ayant compétence' in Art. 17 (1)(a) and (b) ICC Statute and 'a déjà été jugée' in paragraph (c).

852 In this line, see also Jann K. Kleffner, Complementarity in the Rome Statute and National Criminal Jurisdictions 125; Jann K. Kleffner, 'The law and policy of complementarity in relation to 'criminal proceedings' carried out by non-state organized armed groups' in Carsten Stahn and Mohamed M. El-Zeidy (eds), The International Criminal Court and Complementarity - From Theory to Practice (1st edn, Cambridge Universtiy Press 2011) 707-720, 718. Contrary to this conclusion, see William A. Schabas and Mohamed M. El Zeidy, 'Art. 17 - Issues of admissibility' in Kai Ambos (ed), Rome Statute of the International Criminal Court - Article-by-Article Commentary 980 f.

As outlined above[853], Art. 17 ICC Statute regulates the admissibility of a case before the ICC. In its *chapeau*, Art. 17 ICC Statute refers to the Preamble and Art. 1 ICC Statute, both of which stipulate that the Court's jurisdiction is complementary to national criminal jurisdictions only.

The *ne bis in idem* principle is part of the admissibility-test through the cross-reference made in Art. 17 (1)(c) ICC Statute. Even though the formulations in Art. 17 (1)(c) ICC Statute, speaking of a person that 'has already been tried', and in Art. 20 (3) ICC Statute, speaking of 'another court', do not reveal any explicit state reference, these terms are situated in a specific normative context, namely, the context of Art. 17 ICC Statute. Art. 17 ICC Statute ensures the distribution of jurisdiction between the ICC and national courts. The term 'national criminal jurisdictions', containing the word 'nation', implies a state-centric interpretation of jurisdiction. Thus, the focus clearly rests on state administered justice only.[854]

Consequently, a contextual interpretation of the term 'another court' which focuses on the normative setting of Art. 20 (3) ICC Statute within Art. 17 ICC Statute encompasses courts of 'national criminal jurisdictions', in other words, courts of nations or courts of states only.[855] Hence, a contextual interpretation excludes any non-state administered courts from the provision's scope and considers a textual interpretation which allows to detach the word 'court' in Art. 20 (3) ICC Statute from its normative setting an artificial splitting of one coherent system.

Notwithstanding the fact that a contextual interpretation of 'another court' is plausible, it remains puzzling that the Drafters of the Rome Statute chose a different, wider terminology in Art. 17 (1)(c) and Art. 20 (3) ICC Statute than in other provisions surrounding the admissibility regime. If the scope of Art. 20 (3) ICC Statute is meant to be limited to state jurisdictions only, the Drafters could have easily added the prefix 'national' or the suffix 'of a State' to the term 'another court'. Even if the different terminology in Art. 20 (3) ICC Statute, leaving out an explicit state component, is to be treated as nothing more than a so-called 'editorial mistake'

853 See above II. 1.

854 Gaiane Nuridzhanian, 'Ne Bis In Idem in Article 20(3) of the Rome Statute and Non-State Courts' (2019) 18 The Law & Practice of International Courts and Tribunals 219-239, 224.

855 Astrid Reisinger Coracini and Immi Tallgren, 'Art. 20 - *Ne bis in idem*' in Kai Ambos (ed), Rome Statute of the International Criminal Court - Article-by-Article Commentary 1118.

or 'drafting artifact'[856], there is a greater potential in the apparently insignificant difference of words. The broadly held terminology in Art. 20 (3) ICC Statute, referring to 'another court' and leaving out any state reference, opens a gateway for a necessary adaption of the existing law to a changing reality, that is, treating the establishment and operation of courts of NSAGs not only as a potential war crime conduct but considering it a potential additional tool in the enforcement of law during armed conflict.

c. Teleological interpretation

Limiting the term 'another court' in Art. 20 (3) ICC Statute to national criminal jurisdictions jeopardizes the object and purpose of *ne bis in idem*. By contrast, including courts of NSAGs into the scope of Art. 20 (3) ICC Statute enhances the accused's protection against being put twice in judicial jeopardy.

Assessing the telos of Art. 20 (3) ICC Statute warrants assessing the object and purpose of Art. 17 ICC Statute as well.

Within Art. 17 ICC Statute, the protected interests at stake are bifurcated.[857] The provision provides for a system that allocates the concurring jurisdictional competences between the ICC and its State Parties to investigate and prosecute international crimes. Art. 17 (1)(a)-(b) and (d) ICC Statute reflect this allocation of jurisdictional competences. Thus, Art. 17 (1)(a)-(b) and (d) ICC Statute aim at safeguarding the sovereignty of states. The provision also aims at the Statute's general objectives of ensuring accountability for the most serious crimes of concern to the international community and ending impunity for the perpetrators of these crimes.[858] Art. 17 (1)(c) in conjunction with Art. 20 (3) ICC Statute, on the contrary, aims at protecting the accused from being tried twice in the same matter.[859] In this regard, Art. 17 ICC Statute combines bifurcated interests.

856 Kevin Jon Heller, 'Could a Non-State Actor Challenge Admissibility?' (OpinioJuris, 19 August 2012) <http://opiniojuris.org/2012/08/19/could-a-non-state-actor-challenge-admissibility/> accessed 12 October 2022.

857 ICC, Prosecutor v Germain Katanga and Mathieu Ngudjolo Chui, Reasons for the Oral Decision on the Motion Challenging the Admissibility of the Case (Article 19 of the Statute), 16 June 2009, Case No. ICC-01/04-01/07-1213-tENG para 48.

858 See ICC Preamble (4) and (5).

859 ICC, Prosecutor v Germain Katanga and Mathieu Ngudjolo Chui, Reasons for the Oral Decision on the Motion Challenging the Admissibility of the Case (Article 19 of the Statute) para 48.

The same holds true for the *ne bis in idem* guarantee in general. The *ne bis in idem* guarantee serves different interests depending on whether it operates at an intra-or inter-jurisdictional level. At an intra-jurisdictional level, *ne bis in idem* shall ensure respect for the authority and integrity of a legal system by acknowledging the finality of judgments (*res iudicata* effect). Thereby it aims at preserving legal certainty and restoring peace under the law[860]. It also aims at protecting the individual from the possibility of being prosecuted twice for the same conduct or crime.[861] Additionally, it promotes the efficient use of investigative, prosecutorial and judicial resources and thereby serving the judicial economy.[862]

Ne bis in idem as enshrined in the ICC Statute applies at an inter-jurisdictional, hence, at an international level. Parallel to the protected interests in Art. 17 ICC Statute, this results in a two-pronged tree of protected interests: on the one hand the principle aims at safeguarding the accused's rights but on the other hand it aims at securing the jurisdictional competences of different State Parties to the Rome Statute to prosecute the four core crimes.[863] Art. 20 (3) ICC Statute forms part of the admissibility regime and the notion of complementarity.[864] Hence, when assessing the telos of the upward *ne bis in idem* principle, one needs to consider the provision's structural and functional position within the admissibility and complementarity regime.

Due to the provision's structural position within Part 2 of the Rome Statute which carries the title 'Jurisdiction, Admissibility and Applicable Law' – instead of, for example, being put in Part 3 'General principles of criminal law' or Part 6 'The trial' containing the rights of the accused – some authors argue that Art. 20 (3) ICC Statute primarily serves as an 'engine' or 'catalyst' of the Statute's complementary jurisdiction.[865] *Bernard*,

860 Carl-Friedrich Stuckenberg, 'Double Jeopardy and Ne Bis in Idem in Common Law and Civil Law Jurisdictions' in Darryl K. Brown, Jenia I. Turner and Bettina Weisser (eds), The Oxford Handbook of Criminal Process 460.

861 Amal Clooney and Philippa Webb, The Right to a Fair Trial in International Law 779.

862 Ibid 779.

863 Diane Bernard, '*Ne bis in idem* - Protector of Defendants' Rights or Jurisdiction Pointsman?' (2011) 9 Journal of International Criminal Justice 863-880, 866 and 871.

864 See Art. 17 (1)(c) ICC Statute.

865 Antonio Cassese classifies the *ne bis in idem* principle as an obstacle to the exercise of national power, see Antonio Cassese, International Criminal Law 319; Gerard Conway argues that *ne bis in idem* plays a role in the mandate of ICL, see Gerard Conway, '*Ne Bis in Idem* in International Law' 223.

for example, argues that the *ne bis in idem* principle in the Rome Statute serves as a 'pointsman' in the concurrence of competences.[866] This function would supersede the protection of the accused's rights when applying the principle of *ne bis in idem* in an inter-jurisdictional context, which is the case with Art. 20 (3) ICC Statute. Similarly, *Reisinger Coracini* and *Tallgren* opine that the upward *ne bis in idem* guarantee in the Rome Statute amounts to 'the ultimate checkpoint in allocating the tasks of national and international criminal justice according to the notion of complementarity' and thereby rendering the individual a 'side-figure' only.[867]

It is true that these assumptions find support in the structural embedment of Art. 20 (3) ICC Statute into the admissibility regime of Art. 17 ICC Statute. They are also bolstered by the fact that Art. 20 (3) ICC Statute does not provide for an absolute protection of the individual from double prosecution and punishment but instead allows for exceptions in its subsections (a) and (b) which, again, facilitate the admissibility of a case and, therefore, the possibility of the Court to exercise its jurisdiction over a case.

However, it is not convincing to argue that the structural embedment of the ICC's upward *ne bis in idem* principle suppresses the original rationale behind the *ne bis in idem* precept, which is to protect the individual from being prosecuted or punished twice for the same conduct or crime and thereby avoiding repetitive stress and anxiety upon the accused person. On the contrary, the 'stronger' rationale of Art. 20 (3) ICC Statute is the protection of the individual from being put twice in judicial jeopardy. Thus, including courts of NSAGs into the scope of Art. 20 (3) ICC Statute enhances the accused's protection from being put twice in judicial jeopardy. This approach is more convincing for the following reasons:

Firstly, the structural embedment of the upward *ne bis in idem* principle into Part 2 of the Statute is not a substantive decision regarding the object and purpose of that provision. The *ne bis in idem* principle does not lose its nature as a core procedural safeguard of the accused 'merely' due to its structural position in a legal text. If the principle of *ne bis in idem* was to be understood as primarily regulating the allocation of jurisdictional competences, it could have been merged within Art. 17 ICC Statute. Instead, it is articulated in a separate provision. The structural position of Art. 20

866 Diane Bernard, '*Ne bis in idem* - Protector of Defendants' Rights or Jurisdiction Pointsman?' 871.

867 Astrid Reisinger Coracini and Immi Tallgren, 'Art. 20 - *Ne bis in idem*' in Kai Ambos (ed), Rome Statute of the International Criminal Court - Article-by-Article Commentary 1096.

ICC Statute is nothing more than a functional decision following the logics of drafting a coherent legal system. The principle of *ne bis in idem* thematically fits into the admissibility regime and principle of complementarity because by addressing the ICC and 'another court' it directly relates to the exercise of concurrently competent jurisdictions. Not linking Art. 20 (3) ICC Statute to the admissibility regime in Art. 17 ICC Statute would have amounted to a systematic error by the Drafters of the Statute.

Secondly, the fact that the nature of the ICC Statute added a second rationale to the *ne bis in idem* principle does not deprive the principle of its nature as a core procedural safeguard of the accused. Hence, Art. 20 (3) ICC Statute contributes to the complementarity principle, but it is not defined by it. *Ne bis in idem's* original subject of protection is the accused and not the state. Translated to the scenario of a previously held trial by a court of a NSAG, the *ne bis in idem* guarantee is equally important for an individual who is facing a possible (re-) trial before the ICC than for an individual who previously stood trial before a state court. In other words: for an accused the nature of the entity which tries or tried them is irrelevant for the importance of the *ne bis in idem* guarantee. Irrespective of whether an accused has faced trial conducted by a state administered court or by a non-state administered court, a re-trial in the same matter would always infringe on their right of *ne bis in idem* as enshrined in Art. 20 (3) ICC Statute.

Hence, the broader one interprets the scope of Art. 20 (3) ICC Statute, the greater the protection of the accused is. Therefore, including courts of NSAGs into the ambit of 'another court' enhances the accused's protection from being put twice in judicial jeopardy. This conclusion is consistent with the telos of *ne bis in idem*.

d. Historical interpretation

The foregoing interpretation of the term 'another court' in Art. 20 (3) ICC Statute considering its generic meaning, its context as well as the provision's object and purpose led to an inconclusive result regarding the inclusion of courts of NSAGs into the provision's scope. A textual interpretation of the term 'another court' facilitates the inclusion of courts of NSAGs whereas a contextual interpretation, giving effect to the structural embedment of Art. 20 (3) ICC Statute in the overall admissibility regime and the notion of complementarity, bars such an inclusion. Assessing the object and purpose of Art. 20 (3) ICC Statute did also not lead to a clear result: interpreting the telos of Art. 20 (3) ICC Statute in a way of emphasizing the provision's link to the principle of complementarity excludes courts of NSAGs from the scope of Art. 20 (3) ICC Statute, whereas emphasizing the provision's purpose of protecting the accused from being put twice in judicial jeopardy accommodates their inclusion into the provision's scope.

According to Art. 32(a) VCLT, one shall hold recourse to the *travaux préparatoires* of a treaty and the circumstances of its conclusion when the interpretation of a treaty norm in light of its ordinary meaning, its context and its object and purpose leaves the meaning of the respective term 'ambiguous'.

The *travaux préparatoires* on the rule of *ne bis in idem* do not provide any explicit information about the Drafters' view on courts of NSAGs. As *Kleffner* pointed out, there is not 'any document of the Court and its organs in the public domain that would suggest that any thought has been given to the possibility of such proceedings', and by 'such' proceedings carried out by NSAGs are referred to.[868]

However, the preparatory works give a useful insight regarding the principle's function and object and purpose as part of the ICC Statute from which, in turn, one can deduce the Drafters' view on courts of NSAGs. The preparatory works reveal that by translating the rule of *ne bis in idem* to the level of ICL, the principle experienced a transformation in its object and purpose from primarily being a procedural right of the accused towards primarily becoming a tool for allocating concurrent competent jurisdictions of states.

The focus during the negotiations in Rome rested on regulating the Court's jurisdictional competence in relation to that of states. The principle of complementarity has been the fundament of the ICC Statute's drafting process. One delegate put it succinctly when stating that upholding 'primacy of national criminal jurisdictions should be the bedrock of the entire Statute'.[869] Hence, the drafting negotiations were led by the mission

868 Jann K. Kleffner, 'The law and policy of complementarity in relation to 'criminal proceedings' carried out by non-state organized armed groups' in Carsten Stahn and Mohamed M. El-Zeidy (eds), The International Criminal Court and Complementarity - From Theory to Practice 708.

869 UN, Diplomatic Conference of Plenipotentiaries of an International Criminal Court (United Nations, 15 June - 17 July 1998), UN Doc. A/CONF.183, Vol. II, Summary Records of the plenary meetings and of the meetings of the Committe of the Whole, 12th meeting para 10, Delegate of India (Mr. S. R. Rao).

to articulate 'mutual respect and trust'[870] between the ICC and national jurisdictions, to 'preserve national sovereignty'[871] and to regulate that 'the Court's jurisdiction should be complementary to that of national courts'[872]. These have been the main objectives in the drafting process and, as such, they framed the drafting process of other provisions as well. Many delegations stressed the close link of the principle of *ne bis in idem* to the notion of admissibility.[873] As a result, the principle of *ne bis in idem* was drafted and discussed under the auspices of the notion of complementarity.

The negotiations of Art. 20 ICC Statute were guided by the same goal as the ones of Art. 17 ICC Statute, namely, the goal to preserve and secure state sovereignty. Consequently, the Drafters were discussing *ne bis in idem* in relation to 'national courts' and 'national criminal jurisdictions' solely and the question whether the term would also refer to non-state courts was absent of any recognition or debate. Against the backdrop of trying to maneuver the ICC's jurisdiction around states' jurisdiction, it would have been illogical to consider courts of insurgent groups, a subject which is not a state but encroaches on state sovereignty, within the scope of Art. 20 (3) ICC Statute.

e. Equality of belligerents

A consistent application of the 'equality of belligerents'-principle warrants expanding the term 'another court' in Art. 20 (3) ICC to courts of NSAGs. The principle would be jeopardized if criminal proceedings carried out by NSAGs which fulfill the requirements set out in Common Article 3 (1) (d) and Art. 6 (2) Additional Protocol II did not enjoy recognition by the ICC while state conducted proceedings did – and notably irrespective of whether the respective state adheres to the relevant statutory requirements.[874]

---

870 Ibid 12th meeting para 1, Delegate of Iraq (Mr. Mahmoud).
871 Ibid 12th meeting para 7, Delegate of Pakistan (Mr. Mahmood).
872 Ibid 12th meeting para 5, Delegate of Indonesia (Mr. Effendi).
873 See ibid 11th meeting para 22, Delegate of Canada (Mr. Holmes).
874 Jann K. Kleffner, 'The law and policy of complementarity in relation to 'criminal proceedings' carried out by non-state organized armed groups' in Carsten Stahn and Mohamed M. El-Zeidy (eds), The International Criminal Court and Complementarity - From Theory to Practice 719.

The principle of equality of belligerents is rooted in IHL and elementary to the distinction between *jus ad bellum* and *jus in bello.*[875] Whereas *jus ad bellum* differentiates between legal and illegal recourse to the use of force[876], *jus in bello* applies equally to both parties regardless of whether the initial use of force violated *jus ad bellum* or not. Hence, the 'equality of belligerents'-principle in IHL stipulates that all parties to an armed conflict have the same rights and obligations, regardless of the origin or cause of the armed violence[877] – thereby rejecting the doctrine of just war.[878] It is a principle which is central to the law of armed conflict, even though its applicability to NIACs has been highly contested during the drafting process of the four Geneva Conventions of 1949. This is rooted in the fact that the 'equality of belligerents'-principle strikes at the central tenet of states as being sovereign subjects of international law while insurgent groups are not.

As discussed above[879], the asymmetry of the parties involved in NIACs renders an equal application of the rights and duties of IHL also practically difficult, since the non-state party will always have less capacity and resources than the involved state party. Hence, one might think that the 'equality of belligerents'-principle[880] has no room in the law of NIACs. Nevertheless, scholars have repeatedly discussed the principle also in the

875 See above Chapter 4: The Legality of Courts of NSAGs, II. 2. a.; Henri Meyrowitz, Le Prinicipe de L'égalité des belligérants devant le droit de la guerre 400; Christopher Greenwood, 'The Relationship between ius ad bellum and ius in bello' 225; Jonathan Somer, 'Jungle justice: passing sentence on the equality of belligerents in non-international armed conflict' 659; Marco Sassòli and Yuval Shany, 'Should the obligations of states and armed groups under international humanitarian law really be eqaul?' 427.

876 See Art. 2 (4) in conjunction with Art. 51 UN Charta.

877 Christopher Greenwood, 'The Relationship between ius ad bellum and ius in bello' 225; Hersch Lauterpacht, 'The Limits of the Operation of the Law of War' 210.

878 The doctrine of just war can be traced back to early history, in ancient Greece (Plato) and ancient Rome (Camillus and Cicero). It also relates to Grotius' work (On the Law of War and Peace, 1625) on the so-called 'regular war' and the distinction between 'public war' and 'private war', the former being waged with lawful authority whereas the latter is not. For a quick overview on early and just war law see Andrew Clapham, War 10-19.

879 See Chapter 3: Non-International Armed Conflicts and International Humanitarian Law, III. 2.

880 Also known as the principle of symmetry or principle of duality. See Michael Mandel, 'Aggressors' Rights: The Doctrine of ,Equality between Belligerents' and the Legacy of Nuremberg' (2011) 24 Leiden Journal of International Law 627-650.

realm of NIACs since there do exist a few *jus ad bellum* provisions which apply to NIACs as well.[881]

One might ask why the 'equality of belligerents'-principle, belonging to the realm of IHL, should find consideration in the realm of ICL. In other words, one could question why the inclusion of 'rebel courts' into the scope of pertinent ICL provisions, namely, Art. 20 (3) ICC Statue, should also be based on the 'equality of belligerents'-principle. The answer to this question lies in the interactive relationship between these two bodies of international law and the aim of achieving 'systemic integrity of international law'[882]. IHL regulates conduct in times of armed conflict to minimize humanitarian harm and casualties. ICL, in turn, stipulates individual criminal responsibility for, *inter alia*, breaches of IHL. Therefore, ICL operates as an extension of IHL. ICL is the pertinent realm of international law designed to regulate the adjudication of international crimes through judicial institutions, be it at the national, regional or international level. Hence, ICL is the competent forum in international law to address the issue of legal recognition of judgments regarding the adjudication of international crimes. This renders ICL a particular fruitful forum to assess the recognition of insurgent administered justice. Aiming at 'systemic integrity of international law', the 'equality of belligerents'-principle of IHL, which enables NSAGs to administer justice in times of armed conflict, should be reflected in ICL. Hence, a consistent application of the 'equality of belligerents'-principle demands that judgments concluded by legally established courts of NSAGs according to the requirements set out in both Common Article 3 (1)(d) and/or Art. 6 (2) Additional Protocol II find equal recognition in the principle of *ne bis in idem* as judgments adjudicated by courts of states.

881 See, e.g., Jonathan Somer, 'Jungle justice: passing sentence on the equality of belligerents in non-international armed conflict' 663 interpreting the 'equality of belligerents'-principle in NIACs as a narrow concept providing for equal rights and obligations but not meaning equal status; François Bugnion, '*Jus ad bellum, jus in bello* and non-international armed conflicts' (2003) 6 Yearbook of International Humanitarian Law 167-198, 181 f. referring to the construct of 'recognition of belligerency'.

882 For an explanation of the term see Katharine Fortin, 'The Procedural Right to a Remedy When the State has Left the Building? A Reflection on Armed Groups, Courts and Domestic Law' 405.

f. Thinking command responsibility pursuant to Art. 28 ICC Statute further

The concept of command responsibility enshrined in Art. 28 ICC Statute gives additional cause to recognize 'rebel' administered justice within the legal framework of the ICC Statute.[883]

Art. 28 ICC Statute enshrines the principle of command responsibility according to which a military commander, a person effectively acting as a military commander, or any other superior can be held criminally responsible for crimes which are being or have been committed by their subordinates. This mode of criminal liability links the individual culpability of a superior to their failure of properly exercising control over their subordinates. This failure lies in not having taken all necessary and reasonable measures within their power to prevent or repress the commission of crimes or to submit the matter to the competent authorities for investigation and prosecution. Art. 28 ICC Statute stipulates a *sui generis* mode of liability and can be considered an 'original creation' of the field of ICL.[884] It is framed as an omission liability, hence, it depends on a legal obligation to act.[885] This responsibility flows from the superior-subordinate relationship and the effective control and authority a commander holds over their subordinates. The duty has its origins in the law of armed conflict and the concept of 'responsible command'[886].

---

883 There exist other provisions in the Rome Statute which also give cause for discussing the possibility of recognizing NSAG-administered justice within the realm of ICL, see, e.g., Art. 78(2) ICC Statute which allows for the deduction of 'any time spent otherwise in detention in connection with conduct underlying the crime' in determining the sentence of imprisonment before the ICC. The formulation is sufficiently broadly held to also consider including detention orders by NSAGs. See, Jan Willms, 'Courts of armed groups - a tool for inducing higher compliance with international humanitarian law?' in Heike Krieger (ed), Inducing Compliance with International Humanitarian Law - Lessons fron the African Great Lakes Region 149-180, 165. An analysis of other pertinent provisions and their relation to non-state administered justice would go beyond the scope of this work which is why the author focuses on Art. 28 ICC Statute solely.

884 Gerhard Werle and Florian Jeßberger, Principles of International Criminal Law para 579.

885 Guénaël Mettraux, The Law of Command Responsibility (1st edn, Oxford University Press 2009) 38.

886 Ibid 53; ICTY, Prosecutor v Sefer Halilović, Judgment, 16 November 2005, Case No. IT-01-48-T para 40.

A comparison of the texts of Art. 28 ICC Statute and Art. 20 (3) ICC Statute reveals a parallel between the term 'another court' on the one hand and the term 'competent authorities' on the other, since both provisions abstain from explicitly referring to a state component – and, notably, they do so while participating in a legal framework which evolves around state administered justice. This begs the question whether the term 'competent authority' in Art. 28 (a)(ii)-(b)(iii) ICC Statute includes non-state authorities such as courts of NSAGs. If this can be answered in the affirmative, it would support an equally broad interpretation of the term 'another court' in Art. 20 (3) ICC Statute given the similar language of the two provisions.[887] Even more so, the aim of promoting 'systemic integrity'[888] in ICL would demand such a conclusion: if the exercise of criminal justice by NSAGs through their own judicial institutions was recognized under the doctrine of command responsibility pursuant to Art. 28 ICC Statute, it would be systemically inconsistent if another provision of the same legal framework, namely Art. 20 (3) ICC Statute, would deny recognition of the very same act.

Thus, it is pertinent to assess whether the term 'competent authorities' stipulated in Art. 28 ICC Statute includes courts of NSAGs.

In the *Bemba* case, the ICC assessed whether the availability of judicial institutions of a NSAG suffices for a superior to discharge their duty to prevent or to repress the commission of crimes by their subordinates or to submit the matter to the competent authorities according to Art. 28 (a)(ii) and (b)(iii) ICC Statute. In reasoning whether Mr. *Bemba* took all necessary and reasonable measures to prevent or to repress the crimes committed by members of the Mouvement de Libération du Congo troops (**MLC**), the ICC referred to his material ability to prevent and repress the commission of crimes by members of the MLC troops due to the 'the availability of a functioning military system through which he could have punished crimes committed and prevented their future repetition'.[889]

---

887 Jann K. Kleffner seems to be in support of considering proceedings conducted by non-state armed groups as a possibility within Art. 17 (1)(c) and Art. 20 (3) ICC Statute.

888 See Katharine Fortin, 'The Procedural Right to a Remedy When the State has Left the Building? A Reflection on Armed Groups, Courts and Domestic Law', 405 who sheds light on the problem of 'systemic integrity of international law'.

889 ICC, Prosecutor v Jean-Pierre Bemba Gombo, Decision Pursuant to Article 61(7)(a) and (b) of the Rome Statute on the Charges of the Prosecutor Against Jean-Pierre Bemba Gombo para 501.

The ICC repeatedly mentioned the existence of 'a military judicial system to which Mr. *Bemba* was able to submit matters for investigation and prosecution'[890]. Even though the Court assessed the judicial institutions of the MLC in the context of the second duty within Art. 28 ICC Statute, namely, the duty 'to repress' the commission of crimes by subordinates, and not within the context of the duty to submit the matter to the 'competent authorities', the Court – at least implicitly – acknowledged the possibility of NSAGs to administer justice through their own institutions without automatically committing the war crime of Art. 8 (2)(c)(iv) ICC Statute. A nuanced assessment of the Court's legal reasoning in this case reveals a tendency regarding the question whether judicial institutions of NSAGs could be qualified as 'competent authorities' within the scope of Art. 28 ICC Statute.

Pre-Trial Chamber II stated that the duty to 'repress' contains two distinct duties: on the one hand, the duty to stop an ongoing crime from continuing to be committed. On the other hand, the duty to sanction or punish the subordinates for their commission of the crime(s). It considered 'punishing' an alternative duty within the obligation to 'repress' compared to the third duty stipulated in Art. 28 ICC Statute, namely, the duty to 'submit the matter to competent authorities for investigation and prosecution'[891]. The Chamber went on by stating that the duty to punish can be discharged in two different ways: either by the superior himself taking the necessary and reasonable measures to punish the respective subordinate(s) or by referring the matter to 'competent authorities'.[892]

This alternative comparison implies that the ICC interprets the term 'competent authorities' as meaning '*other* competent authorities' [emphasis added], thus, acknowledging that also authorities of NSAGs can be 'competent' to investigate and prosecute. This hypothesis is bolstered by the Court's remarks on the duty to 'submit the matter to the competent authorities for investigation and prosecution' where it states that this duty

890 Ibid paras 461 and 493.

891 Ibid para 439; this viewpoint was upheld by the Trial Chamber in its judgment, see ICC, Prosecutor v Jean-Pierre Bemba Gombo, Judgment pursuant to Article 74 of the Statute, 21 March 2016, Case No. ICC-01/05-01/08-3343 para 206.

892 ICC, Prosecutor v Jean-Pierre Bemba Gombo, Decision Pursuant to Article 61(7)(a) and (b) of the Rome Statute on the Charges of the Prosecutor Against Jean-Pierre Bemba Gombo para 440.

'*remedies* a situation where commanders do not have the ability to sanction their forces' [emphasis added].[893]

Hence, the ICC puts the commander's own ability to investigate and punish in alternation to the submission of the matter to an external authority competent to investigate and prosecute. The Court held that 'if the commander has no power to sanction those who committed the crimes, he has an obligation to submit the matter to the competent authorities'.[894] 'This obligation to submit the matter also arises where the commander has the ability to take certain measures, but such measures would be inadequate'.[895] The alternated relation of the commander's own ability to investigate and to prosecute the matter on the one hand, and the duty to submit the matter to competent authorities in case the commander is unable to adequately execute their own investigations and prosecutions on the other, implies that the Court focuses on a conduct-based approach in interpreting the term 'competent' instead of on a *de jure*-based approach as has been advocated by Amnesty International in that case.

In the ICC's view, 'Mr. Bemba was the competent authority to investigate and prosecute the crimes'.[896] He was so because, according to the Trial Chamber, he had a functioning military judicial system at hand equipping him with an 'extensive material ability' to 'initiate genuine and full investigations into the commission of crimes' and to properly try and punish any soldiers alleged of having committed crimes.[897] Trial Chamber III referred to the groups own 'court-martial' as well as to the pre-existing court system in the Democratic Republic of Congo (**DRC**) which was controlled by MLC members.[898] It went on by holding that in those circumstances where Mr. *Bemba* 'failed to empower other MLC officials to fully and adequately investigate and prosecute allegations of crimes, he cannot be said to have submitted the matter to the competent authorities for investigation and prosecution'.[899]

Even though the Appeals Chamber reversed the Trial Judgment, it did not contest the Trial Chamber's reasoning regarding the availability of a

893 Ibid 442.
894 ICC, Prosecutor v Jean-Pierre Bemba Gombo, Judgment pursuant to Article 74 of the Statute para 208.
895 Ibid para 208.
896 Ibid para 733.
897 Ibid para 729.
898 Ibid para 402.
899 Ibid para 733.

functioning judicial system which Mr. *Bemba* should have referred the respective matters to. Quite the opposite, the Appeals Chamber recognized that judicial processes established by NSAGs should be considered as a measure to prevent or to repress the commission of crimes by subordinates or to submit the matter to competent authorities, irrespective of its execution.[900]

Thus, one can conclude that the ICC interprets the term 'competent authority' in Art. 28 ICC Statute in a way which includes non-state judicial authorities such as courts established by NSAGs. Accordingly, 'systemic integrity of international law' demands that the term 'another court' in Art. 20 (3) ICC Statute must equally include non-state judicial institutions.

g. Return to ne bis in idem as a human right

Finally, the human right character of *ne bis in idem* demands that the guarantee includes judgments rendered by courts of NSAGs. The human right of not being tried and not being punished twice for the same conduct or the same crime is the animating rationale of the *ne bis in idem* principle. Under this condition, it would be unreasonable not to grant a defendant the protection from being put twice in judicial jeopardy merely because of the status (state vs. non-state) of the domestic prosecutorial entity (or lack thereof).

Whether one interprets the phrase 'tried by another court' in Art. 20 (3) ICC Statute in a way to encompass state courts only or to extend it to courts of insurgent groups, is a decision between formalism vs. functionalism.[901] In other words, it is a decision whether one interprets the role of *ne bis in idem* formally or functionally.

A formalist approach to the interpretation of international law in general and the Rome Statute in particular, considers states the sole legitimate and

900 ICC, Prosecutor v Jean-Pierre Bemba Gombo, Judgment on the appeal of Mr Jean-Pierre Bemba Gombo against Trial Chamber III's „Judgment pursuant to Article 74 of the Statute", 8 June 2018, Case No. ICC-01/05-01/08 A para 180; see also Alessandro Mario Amoroso, 'Should the ICC Assess Complementarity with Respect to Non-state Armed Groups?' (2018) 16 Journal of International Criminal Justice 1063-1091, 1071 and Sandesh Sivakumaran, The Law of Non-International Armed Conflict 557.

901 Jens David Ohlin is using these two terms regarding the protective alignment of *ne bis in idem* in ICL in commenting on Kevin John Heller's blog post: Kevin Jon Heller, 'Could a Non-State Actor Challenge Admissibility?'.

recognized subjects of international law. Since the ICC Statute is a treaty which was signed and ratified by states only, it applies to states only. A formalist approach to the interpretation of Art. 20 (3) ICC Statute and the phrase 'tried by another court' focuses on the status of the domestic prosecutorial entity which must be a state administered entity. A formalist approach to the role of *ne bis in idem* in ICL gives prominence to the principle's catalyzing role in securing states' interests regarding the allocation of concurrent competent jurisdictions. Consequently, a formalist approach applies Art. 20 (3) ICC Statute solely with regard to national criminal jurisdictions of *states* [emphasis added]. Since NSAGs are unequal to states, a formalist approach renders the application of Art. 20 (3) ICC Statute to courts different from those of states impossible.

By contrast, a functionalist approach to interpreting and applying the ICC Statute's *ne bis in idem* principle not only accommodates but warrants the inclusion of courts of NSAGs. The primary function of the *ne bis in idem* principle is to provide a defendant with the procedural right to challenge any possible re-trial stemming from a second prosecution for the same matter. This protection is of fundamental importance to the individual irrespective of whether the prosecutorial entity is state or non-state administered. It would be to the detriment of the principle's protective function if one rendered its application dependent on the formal status of the prosecutorial entity.

The question whether the ICC Statute's upward *ne bis in idem* covers judgments of insurgent courts creates a tension between the principle's dichotomous protected interests: not considering the jurisprudence of courts of NSAGs relevant in the application of Art. 20 (3) ICC Statute corresponds to the principle's aim to secure states' interests and their jurisdictional claims while at the same time it diminishes the protection of the individual from being put twice in judicial jeopardy. Including courts of NSAGs into the scope of Art. 20 (3) ICC Statute enhances the principle's aim to protect the individual from a possible re-trail for the same conduct or the same crime while at the same time encroaching on state's sovereignty.

What lies at the core of this interpretative debate is the question whether there is a so-called rank ratio or hierarchy regarding the principle's underlying protected interests which would allow to resolve the tension. In other words, the question is which underlying rationale should prevail: the human right not to be punished twice for the same matter or the catalyst tool to promote national (state) jurisdictions and to secure state sovereignty.

The answer must be to the individual's advantage. The words *ne bis in idem* describe the principle's ultimate purpose: no one must be punished twice for the same matter. *Ne bis in idem*, in its original existing, is supposed to protect the individual from being tried or punished twice for the same matter. The principle's translation into the ICC Statute, a treaty which applies across multiple State Parties, added the additional layer of also securing the sovereignty of multiple states and their jurisdictional competences. However, the protection of the individual is even more important in the context of an inter-jurisdictional application of the *ne bis in idem* rule as it is the case within the context of the Rome Statute. The risk to be tried and punished twice for the same conduct or the same crime rises exponentially with the number of potentially involved states. It does so even more with the reality of insurgent groups operating their own courts as an additional actor in the exercise of criminal jurisdiction.

This suggests that in the event of a collision of these bifurcated interests, the former suppresses the latter.

h. Interim conclusion

The foregoing doctrinal analysis tried to advocate an interpretation of Art. 20 (3) ICC Statute and its relevant term 'another court' which accommodates the inclusion of courts convened by NSAGs. It tried to exhaust the potential of a broadly held terminology to illustrate how the existing law could be interpreted and applied to a changing reality regarding the administration of justice by other entities than states.

The gateway in the ICC Statute which facilitates a debate about the recognition of alternative justice mechanisms, is Art. 17 ICC Statute and, through the cross-reference made in Art. 17 (1)(c) ICC Statute, Art. 20 (3) ICC Statute.

Art. 20 (3) ICC Statute has been formulated in a language which – giving effect to its ordinary meaning – does not per se exclude courts of NSAGs from its scope. Art. 20 (3) ICC Statute stipulates that 'no person who has been tried by another court for conduct also proscribed under article 6, 7, 8 or 8*bis* shall be tired by the Court with respect to the same conduct'. Art. 20 (3) ICC Statute leaves out any explicit state-component, unlike Art. 17 ICC Statute which Art. 20 (3) ICC Statute is systemically linked to through Art. 17 (1)(c) ICC Statute. With the omission of any explicit state component, the term 'another court', first and foremost, means any court other than the ICC. A court of a NSAG is 'another court' than the ICC. A textual interpretation, therefore, accommodates a 'rebel court'-friendly interpretation of Art. 20 (3) ICC Statute.

However, a textual interpretation of 'another court' which includes courts of NSAGs into its scope faces the critique of leaving aside the provision's structural embedment into the admissibility regime. Art. 17 ICC Statute has been drafted in a manner which only encompasses 'national criminal jurisdictions', hence, facilitating a state-aligned adjudication of justice only.[902] The formulation leaves no room for including also non-state administered forms of justice, such as courts of NSAGs.[903] One could argue, as might be evident from the viewpoint of a contextual interpretation, that the state-centric conception of Art. 17 ICC Statute concerning the administration of justice also holds true for Art. 20 (3) ICC Statute which Art. 17 (1)(c) ICC Statute refers to. Accordingly, 'another court' in Art. 20 (3) ICC Statute would be read as meaning 'another court of a state'.

The same conclusion is reached when analyzing the *travaux préparatoires* of the ICC Statute. The predominant sentiment during the drafting of the ICC Statute was that rebel groups would either not convene their own courts and adjudicate (criminal) justice or even if they would it is irrelevant in relation to the ICC and its jurisdiction. Although the Drafters of Additional Protocol II, at a much earlier stage in the history of international law, paid attention to the reality that in a NIAC both parties to the conflict will likely make use of judicial governance structures which, in turn, becomes relevant in the doctrine of *ne bis in idem* and especially from the viewpoint of the individual, the Drafters of the Rome Statute decided to not shed any light on this matter.

Hence, a historical interpretation of the term 'another court' in Art. 20 (3) ICC Statute leads to the realization that courts of NSAGs have not been foreseen by the Drafters of the Rome Statute. However, the result of a historical interpretation is not authoritative in international law since, pursuant to Art. 32 VCLT, an analysis of the drafters' intent in formulating international conventions merely serves as a supplementary mean of interpretation. This is indeed vital since the interpretation of an international convention should allow for reacting to a shift in paradigm which the drafters could not have foreseen when drafting the convention but which

902 See above III. 1. b.

903 This also concerns other, alternative forms of justice, such as truth commissions, commissions of inquiry or reparation programs, irrespective of whether they are state-conducted or initiated by NSAGs.

urges to adapt the initially foreseen scope of that convention. Justice administered by NSAGs through their own institutions is a steadily growing phenomenon which demands a corresponding change in the application of the existing body of law.

Additionally, the telos of Art. 20 (3) ICC Statute which, *inter alia*, refers to the protection of the accused from a possible re-trial as well as the objectives of fighting impunity and ensuring accountability demand an interpretation which enables the legal practitioner to subsume courts of NSAGs under the term 'another court' in Art. 20 (3) ICC Statute.[904]

Most importantly, a 'rebel court'-friendly interpretation of Art. 20 (3) ICC Statute finds support in the ICC's own jurisprudence. In the *Bemba* case, the ICC adjudicated that courts of armed groups should be recognized as a measure in assessing whether the superior discharged their duty to prevent or repress the commission of crimes by their subordinates or to submit the matter to competent authorities. More importantly, the ICC implicitly held that courts of NSAGs can be the 'competent authority' to investigate and prosecute the respective crimes without automatically fulfilling the war crime of Art. 8 (2)(c)(iv) ICC Statute. A systemically coherent interpretation and application of the ICC Statute demands that if the ICC recognizes courts of NSAGs under the scope of individual criminal liability pursuant to Art. 28 ICC Statute, it must also recognize the verdicts issued by these institutions in the Statute's own *ne bis in idem* principle according to Art. 20 (3) ICC Statute. Such a finding is also consistent with the 'equality of belligerents'-principle central to the *jus in bello*.

Further, a 'rebel court'-friendly interpretation of Art. 20 (3) ICC Statute enhances the ICC's basic philosophy of fighting impunity for those perpetrators of crimes which are of concern to the international community as a whole.[905]

And, last but not least, a 'rebel court'-friendly interpretation of Art. 20 (3) ICC Statute is an important first step in not staying oblivious to a changing reality when adjudicating conflict-related justice.

904 See also William A. Schabas and Mohamed M. El Zeidy, 'Art. 17 - Issues of admissibility' in Kai Ambos (ed), Rome Statute of the International Criminal Court - Article-by-Article Commentary 980 f. who consider it 'likely' that trials conducted by courts of NSAGs will be included in the scope of Art. 20 (3) ICC Statute.

905 See Preamble (5) of the ICC Statute.

2. Final conviction or acquittal

When referring to the previously conducted trial at a national level, the text of Art. 20 (3) ICC Statute uses the phrase 'the person concerned has already been tried'. The generic meaning of the phrase 'has already been tried' suggests that the court at the national level has instigated a trial. Since Art. 20 (3) ICC Statute forms part of the admissibility-test, it is useful to look at the other scenarios captured in Art. 17 ICC Statute to determine the precise procedural stage which the previously held trial at a national level must have reached. Art. 17 (1)(a) ICC Statute, speaking of 'the case is being investigated or prosecuted', refers to ongoing investigations whereas Art. 17 (1)(b) ICC Statute, speaking of 'the case has been investigated', refers to a situation where investigations have come to an end due to a decision not to prosecute the respective person. Hence, a systematic overview suggests that Art. 17 (1)(c) ICC Statute, speaking of 'has already been tried', in turn, refers to the completion of a trial which results in a verdict convicting or acquitting the respective person.

Undisputedly, Art. 17 (1)(c) ICC Statute in conjunction with Art. 20 (3) ICC Statute require a concluded trial with a decision on the merits.[906] Notwithstanding the fact that the wording of the text in Art. 17 (1)(c) and Art. 20 (3) does not explicitly mention an element of finality, the ICC has adopted a narrow approach by also requiring a *final* [emphasis added] verdict which 'acquired a *res judicata* effect'.[907] This line of interpretation is consistent with the jurisprudence of the UN *ad hoc* tribunals[908] as well as with corresponding international human rights standards.[909]

Hence, when applying Art. 20 (3) ICC Statute to judgments rendered by courts of NSAGs, the ICC's upward *ne bis in idem* guarantee would be triggered by a final judgment only or a decision on the merits of the case. This presupposes that the respective NSAGs has installed a judicial system

906 ICC, Prosecutor v Jean-Pierre Bemba Gombo, Decision on the Admissibility and Abuse of Process Challenges, 24 June 2010, Case No. ICC-01/05-01/08-802 para 248.

907 ICC, Prosecutor v Saif Al-Islam Gaddafi, Decision on the ‚Admissibility Challenge by Dr. Saif Al-Islam Gaddafi pursuant to Articles 17(1)(c), 19 and 20(3) of the Rome Statute', 5 April 2019, Case No. ICC-01/11-01/11-662 paras 36 ff. and para 47; see also UN, Diplomatic Conference of Plenipotentiaries of an International Criminal Court (United Nations, 13 September 1996), UN Doc. A/51/22, Vol. I, Proceedings of the Preparatory Committee during March-April and August 1996, 39.

908 See ICTR, Prosecutor v Laurent Semanza, Decision, 31 May 2000, Case No. ICTR-97-20-A paras 74 f.; ICTR, Prosecutor v Joseph Nzabirinda, Judgment, 23 February 2007, Case No. ICTR-2001-77-T para 46.

909 See Art. 14 ICCPR which speaks of 'finally convicted or acquitted'.

with various instances which requires resources and capacities not every NSAG will possess.

Hence, dependent on the group's structure, organization and access to resources, a NSAG's judicial system can be elaborated enough to include different judicial instances to fulfill the finality criterion.

3. 'shall be tried by the Court with respect to the same conduct'

Art. 20 (3) ICC Statute bars a re-trial before the ICC following a previous trial before a domestic court for 'conduct also proscribed under article 6, 7, 8 or 8*bis*', presumed the potential re-trial before the ICC concerns the 'same conduct'. During the drafting process of the *ne bis in idem* principle there has been a significant change in words regarding the respective phrase 'for conduct also proscribed under article 6, 7, 8 or 8*bis*' of Art. 20 (3) ICC Statute.

In 1996, the Preparatory Committee proposed a language which, for the '*idem*' part, focused on the same crime. Draft Article 42 (1) stipulated that 'No person shall be tried before any other court for acts constituting a crime of the kind referred to in article 20'[910]. Draft Art. 42 (2) which enshrined the upward *ne bis in idem* principle also used to include an 'ordinary crime'-clause in its sub-paragraph (a), parallel to the Statutes of the UN *ad hoc* tribunals.[911] It read as follows:

> 'A person who has been tried by another court for acts constituting a crime of the kind referred to in article 20 may be tried under this Statute only if: (a) The acts in question were characterized by that court as an ordinary crime and not as a crime which is within the jurisdiction of the Court.'[912]

910 UN, Diplomatic Conference of Plenipotentiaries of an International Criminal Court (United Nations, 13 September 1996), UN Doc. A/51/22, 1996, Vol. II, Compilations of proposals 86.

911 See Art. 10 (2)(a) ICTY Statute and Art. 9 (2)(a) ICTR Statute.

912 UN, Yearbook of the International Law Commission, 1994, Vol. II Part 2, Report of the Commission to the General Assembly on the work of its forty-sixth session 57.

The successor Draft Article on *ne bis in idem*, Draft Article 12 of the ILC's report in 1996 also foresaw an 'ordinary crime'-clause within the upward *ne bis in idem*.[913]

Similarly, in 1998, the Drafting Committee proposed a formulation according to which 'A person shall not be criminally responsible under this Statute unless the conduct in question constitutes [...] a crime within the jurisdiction of the Court.'[914] However, the final draft of the (upward) *ne bis in idem* rule shifted the language towards focusing on the same conduct for the '*idem*' element as it read that 'no person who has been tried by another court for conduct also proscribed under article 5'[915].

The systematics within today's Art. 20 ICC Statute reveal a different terminology in Art. 20 (1)-(3) ICC Statute regarding the '*idem*' element. Whereas Art. 20 (1) and (3) IC Statute follow a conduct-based approach in determining the '*idem*' element, Art. 20 (2) ICC Statute, which stipulates the downward *ne bis in idem*, follows a crime-based approach.

This differentiation has its roots in the principle of complementarity. By adopting the narrow crime-based approach within the downward *ne bis in idem*, the Statute corresponds to its primary aim of complementing national criminal jurisdictions only. The ICC does not enjoy primacy jurisdiction as did the UN *ad hoc* tribunals.[916] Thus, domestic courts shall still be able to try the respective individual for other crimes than the ones which fall under the Court's subject matter jurisdiction.

By adopting the wider, conduct-based approach in Art. 20 (1) and Art. 20 (3) ICC Statute, in turn, the Statute upholds the principle's original aim of protecting the individual from being tried twice for the same matter. However, the conduct-based approach in in the upward *ne bis in idem* of Art. 20 (3) ICC Statute also, once again, reflects the Court's fundamental mission to grant national courts a prerogative in exercising criminal

913 UN, Yearbook of the International Law Commission (1st edn, 1996), Vol. II Part 2, Report of the Commission to the General Assembly on the work of its forty-eight session 36.

914 UN, Diplomatic Conference of Plenipotentiaries of an International Criminal Court (United Nations, 15 June - 17 July 1998), UN Doc. A/CONF.183, 1998, Vol. III, Reports and other documents 150.

915 See ibid Vol. III, Reports and other documents 29.

916 Linda E. Carter, 'The Principle of Complementarity and the International Cirminal Court: The Role of Ne Bis in Idem ' (2010) 8 Santa Clara Journal of International Law 165-198, 189.

jurisdiction. The ICC shall be barred from exercising its jurisdiction if a national court has made use of it.[917]

Again, the flexible conception of the '*idem*' throughout the provision of Art. 20 ICC Statute is owed to the fact that the principle of *ne bis in idem*, specifically in the context of the ICC Statute which applies to multiple states, has to strike a balance between two competing rationales: the rationale of serving state interests and preserving their sovereign right to exercise criminal jurisdiction as well as the rationale of protecting the individual from becoming subject of any misuse of states' *ius puninendi*, on the other.

Against the backdrop of the provision's clear language, its systematics as well as its drafting history, it is clear that within today's Art. 20 (3) ICC Statute, the legal characterization of the respective conduct before domestic courts is irrelevant.[918] Art. 20 (3) ICC Statute allows for a successful *ne bis in idem* challenge whenever a person has already been tried for the same 'conduct also proscribed under article 6, 7, 8 or 8*bis*' before a domestic court. 'The question of whether domestic investigations are carried out with a view to prosecuting "international crimes" is not determinative'[919]. Hereby, the ICC Statute considers a weighing and value ratio of crimes depending on their legal definition or legal categorization immaterial for the applicability of the upward *ne bis in idem*.[920]

Thus, whereas under the Statutes of the UN *ad hoc* tribunals an individual could be tried for murder at a national level and then face trial before one of the tribunals for the crime of genocide based on the same act, this scenario is impossible before the ICC.

Translated to former judgments and decisions rendered by courts of NSAGs, Art. 20 (3) ICC Statute would apply regardless of the legal qualification the court of the respective NSAG attributes to the conduct. The conduct in question need not live up to the definition of an international

917 Noting the exemption clauses in Art. 20 (3)(a)-(b) ICC Statute.

918 Astrid Reisinger Coracini and Immi Tallgren, 'Art. 20 - *Ne bis in idem*' in Kai Ambos (ed), Rome Statute of the International Criminal Court - Article-by-Article Commentary 692.

919 ICC, Prosecutor v Saif-Al Islam Gaddafi and Abdullah Al-Senussi, Decision on the admissibility of the case against Saif Al-Islam Gaddafi para 85.

920 Whereas the sentiment during the ILC-drafting process was that any crime which was not tried under the category of an international crime was considered a 'lesser crime' which did not encompass the full extent of the criminal conduct, see UN, Yearbook of the International Law Commission, 1996, Vol. II Part 2, Report of the Commission to the General Assembly on the work of its forty-eighth session 38.

crime. Given the reality that most NSAGs convene courts during ongoing military operations and the fact that the establishment of a judicial system is deployed as a tool of general governance objectives, such as remaining law and order within the civil population or demonstrating power and authority, it appears highly unlikely that a NSAG is applying ICL as enshrined in the ICC Statute. In other words, it is highly unlikely that a NSAG will prosecute and punish conduct which is in breach with IHL under the legal classification of, *inter alia*, war crimes as enshrined in the ICC Statute.

Most NSAGs will likely apply their own law and their own codes of conduct. This is to be distinguished from the prosecution and punishment of ordinary crimes not related to the armed conflict, which are crimes where the perpetrator is not utilizing the special situation of armed conflict. The prosecution of such crimes would never live up to 'conduct also proscribed under article 6, 7, 8 or 8*bis*'.

4. Conclusion

Analyzing the relation of 'rebel courts' to the principle of *ne bis in idem* as stipulated in Art. 20 (3) ICC Statute is not new to the scholarly debate about 'rebel governance' and international law.[921] Already a decade ago, scholars have discussed whether courts of NSAGs and their judgments should find recognition in applying the rule of *ne bis in idem*. Recently, the question of the role of non-state actors in international law, and ICL in particular, has gained topicality with the *Al Hassan* case before the ICC, the Court's first case which, *inter alia*, revolves around the question whether the establishment and operation of a court by a NSAG fulfills the war crime of Art. 8 (2)(c)(iv) ICC Statute.

The foregoing section assessed whether courts of NSAGs can be included into the upward *ne bis in idem* principle pursuant to Art. 20 (3) ICC Statute.

The explicitly wide terminology which refers to proceedings carried out by 'another court' is the impetus for assessing whether courts of NSAGs can qualify as 'another court'. The interpretative analysis resulted in the observation that, especially, a historical approach which emphasizes the

921 René Provost has recently published a book on 'rebel justice' where he, *inter alia*, assesses the issue of 'insurgent complementarity', see René Provost, Rebel Courts: The Administration of Justice by Armed Insurgents.

Drafters' intent, as well as a contextual approach which highlights the principle's structural embedment into the admissibility regime pursuant to Art. 17 ICC Statute, hinder the inclusion of courts of NSAGs into the provision's scope. However, a recollection of the original telos of *ne bis in idem* not only facilitates but also calls for including judgments rendered by courts of NSAGs. *Ne bis in idem* shall protect the individual from being tried and punished twice for the same matter. This protection is even more important in the context of an inter-jurisdictional application of *ne bis in idem* as it is the case within the context of the ICC Statute. The risk of being tried and punished twice for the same conduct or the same crime rises exponentially with the number of potentially involved states. Denying judgments of courts by NSAGs any recognition under the principle of *ne bis in idem* in Art. 20 (3) ICC Statute would create a fair trial *lacuna* for the accused person who faces a possible re-trial before the ICC.[922] It would also mean that the existing law in its unaltered interpretation and application stays ignorant to a changing reality on the ground.

IV. Parameters for Recognizing Judgments of Courts of NSAGs within Art. 20 (3) ICC Statute

The foregoing normative analysis revolving around the interpretation of pertinent norms within the ICC Statute, namely Art. 17 (1)(c), Art. 20 (3) and Art. 28 ICC Statute, aimed at highlighting the statutory gateways for a possible recognition of courts of NSAGs in ICL. Due to their specific language, Art. 17 (1)(c), Art. 20 (3) and Art. 28 ICC Statute enable a debate about recognizing non-state administered justice within ICL, a framework which, until up to date, relates to state jurisdictions only.

This analysis has been theoretical and abstract. Thus, this final section seeks to add a practical component by, firstly, illustrating pertinent cases before the ICC where the Court had to elaborate on the administration of justice by non-state entities (Sub-section 1) and secondly, by formulating parameters for an inclusion of courts of NSAGs and their judgments into the scope of Art. 20 (3) ICC Statute (Sub-section 2).

922 See ECtHR, Case of Cyprus v Turkey, Judgment para 98 in which the ECtHR held that to not recognize the remedies provided by the *de facto* organs in the Turkish Republic of Norther Cyprus for deprivation of property would risk a human rights vacuum for the local population. See also Katharine Fortin, 'The Procedural Right to a Remedy When the State has Left the Building? A Reflection on Armed Groups, Courts and Domestic Law' 406.

1. The ICC and the administration of justice by non-state entities: an extract

To date, the ICC has been confronted with the administration of justice by non-state entities during armed conflict on especially two occasions. In both cases, the Court had to elaborate on the relevance of non-state administered justice when examining the admissibility of the respective case, more precisely, when assessing the Court's complementary jurisdiction according to Art. 17 ICC Statute.

The first case concerns the situation in Georgia. In 2015, the Prosecution requested the authorization from Pre-Trial Chamber I pursuant to Art. 15 (3) ICC Statute to proceed with an investigation into the situation of Georgia. In January 2016, Pre-Trial Chamber I granted the Prosecutor's request to proceed with the investigation *proprio motu*. The investigation addresses the alleged war crimes and crimes against humanity committed in and around South Ossetia in the course of an international armed conflict from July 1st until October 10th, 2008 involving armed forces from Georgia, South Ossetia and Russia.[923]

South Ossetia is a region within Georgia, governed by a *de facto* regime exercising control over the territory. In its request to authorize an investigation, the former ICC Chef Prosecutor, Mrs. *Bensouda*, preliminarily assessed the admissibility of a case before the ICC. In her assessment, the Prosecutor concluded, firstly, that Georgian national authorities remained inactive at the time of the request and that no further concrete and progressive investigative steps were to be expected, secondly, that Russian national authorities were engaged in ongoing investigations albeit facing obstacles as regards the access to evidence, and thirdly, that any investigative steps taken by authorities of South Ossetia were not relevant in the admissibility test pursuant to Art. 17 (1)(a) ICC Statute due to the fact that 'it considers South Ossetia to be part of the territory of Georgia and not a State within the meaning of article 17.'[924]

The Prosecutor concluded that Art. 17 ICC Statute applies to national authorities of states only. Hence, investigations taken up by *de facto* authorities do not fall under the provision's scope and, consequently, do not

---

923 ICC, Situation in Georgia, Decision on the Prosecutor's Request for authorization of an investigation, Case No. ICC-01/15-12, 27 January 2016.

924 ICC, Situation in Georgia, Corrected Version of „Request for authorisation of an investigation pursuant to article 15", 16 October 2015, ICC-01/15-4-Corr, 17 November 2015, Case No. ICC-01/15-4-Corr2 para 322.

bar the admissibility of a case. For the sake of completeness, however, the Prosecutor stated that proceedings conducted by the *de facto* authorities of South Ossetia were not criminal in nature, and hence, would also for this reason not bar the admissibility. In its decision on the authorization of an investigation, Pre-Trial Chamber I confirmed that 'any proceedings undertaken by the *de facto* authorities of South Ossetia are not capable of meeting the requirements of article 17 of the Statute, due to South Ossetia not being a recognized State.'[925]

Thus, the Court's finding suggests that it only considers criminal proceedings carried out by state authorities relevant when deciding upon the admissibility of a situation pursuant to Art. 17 ICC Statute.

Notably, Judge *Kovács* delivered a Dissenting Opinion on the decision authorizing the investigation in the situation in Georgia. In his Dissenting Opinion, Judge *Kovács* pinpoints the elemental problem of trying to include non-state entities into the admissibility regime pursuant to Art. 17 ICC Statute: The interpretation and application of the Rome Statute would need to be adapted according to changing realities to remain legitimate and functional.

The relevant passage of Judge *Kovács*' remarks reads as follows:

> 'I belief that the Majority oversimplifies the issue at stake. The question of recognition of certain acts of entities under general international law is much more complex. Within the context of the Rome Statute, I find that automatically following a too rigid approach might result in some absurd conclusions. For instance, there may be some entities whose status is contested, yet they still enjoy undisputed control over the territory and have the capacity to exercise criminal jurisdiction. [...] Perhaps depriving all of these entities from having a *locus standi* for the limited purpose of exercising criminal jurisdiction and thereafter lodging admissibility challenges before the Court might result in an increase in the impunity gap. A too categorial standpoint could run against the basic philosophy of the ICC, namely to put an end to impunity because it could suggest *nolens-volens* that, even if you punish, it will not be taken into consideration.'[926]

---

925 ICC, Situation in Georgia, Decision on the Prosecutor's request for authorization of an investigation, 27 January 2016, Case No. ICC-01/15-12 para 40.

926 ICC, Situation in Georgia, Seperate Opinion of Judge Péter Kovács, 27 January 2016, Case No. ICC-01/15-12-Anx-Corr para 65.

He continued in reasoning that:

> 'The issue becomes more problematic when entities as such carry out genuine investigations, prosecutions and trial proceedings against a particular person and those proceedings are disregarded or the person may be barred from lodging a ne bis in idem challenged under Art. 19 (2)(a) because domestic proceedings have not been conducted by a "State". I cannot exclude, therefore, that if a de facto regime passed a proper sentence following the principles of due process in law for one or more of the crimes falling within the jurisdiction of the Court, this could furnish a sufficient basis for an admissibility challenge under Art. 19 (2) (a) together with articles 17 (1)(c) and 20 (3) of the Statute. I consider that this matter requires a *case-by-case* assessment without having an automatic effect on the legal status of the non-recognized entity.'[927]

Judge *Kovác*'s deliberations demonstrate that a change in paradigm regarding the recognition of non-state administered justice is indicated and that non-state courts are not per se irrelevant in the ICC's admissibility assessment.

The second occasion concerns the situation in Libya. The situation in Libya initially concerned three distinct cases with only one of them still pending before the ICC. The latter concerns the case against Mr. *Al-Islam Gaddafi*. The former two cases which have already been closed concerned Mr. *Al-Senussi* and Mr. *Al-Werfalli*. The case against Mr. *Al-Werfalli* is of particular interest and relevance when considering the administration of justice by NSAGs during armed conflict in the context of the ICC's admissibility- and complementarity-regime.

In the case against Mr. *Al-Werfalli*, a commander within the Libyan National Army (**LNA**), the ICC was confronted with non-state adjudicated justice in the context of assessing the case's admissibility before the Court. On February 26th, 2011, the UNSC referred the situation in Libya since February 15th, 2011 to the Prosecutor of the Court pursuant to UNSC Resolution 1970.[928] During the pre-trial stage, after the issuance of the first warrant of arrest and before the issuance of the second warrant of arrest, it was reported that Mr. *Al-Werfalli* was facing criminal proceedings conducted by a military prosecutor in Libya upon the orders of the commander

927 Ibid para 66.

928 UN Security Council Resolution 1970 (2011), UN Doc. S/RES/1970 (2011), 26 February 2011.

of the LNA, General *Haftar*.[929] In this non-public report, it was claimed that any criminal proceedings initiated by the Court would be inadmissible pursuant to Art. 17 (1)(a) ICC Statute since Mr. *Al-Werfalli* was already facing investigations in Libya upon the initiative taken by the commander of the LNA.

The LNA constitutes a NSAG to the ongoing NIAC in Libya, consisting of army units, ex-revolutionary groups and tribal militias.[930] Importantly, the LNA is not a state. Even though the criminal investigations were claimed to be executed by a military prosecutor, they were ordered and initiated by General *Haftar*, a military commander of a NSAG. This suggest that the proceedings were closely linked to the NSAG and its overall military aims. Consequently, the Court had to elaborate on the issue whether criminal proceedings conducted by a NSAG could bar further proceedings by the Court. In the second warrant of arrest-decision, Pre-Trial Chamber I declared that the national proceedings were insufficient with regard to the positive complementarity test.[931] Pre-Trial Chamber I held that 'irrespective of whether the entity exercising authority in the territory controlled by the LNA can be considered a State for the purposes of article 17 of the Statute, there remains a situation of inactivity.'[932] It further stated that the proceedings allegedly initiated by the LNA authorities against Mr. *Al-Werfalli* do not render the case inadmissible pursuant to Art. 17 (1)(a) ICC Statute, since they fail the test of 'tangible, concrete and progressive investigative steps'.[933]

It appears that Pre-Trial Chamber I deliberately avoided to answer the question whether the entity exercising authority in the territory controlled by the LNA can be considered a state for the purpose of Art. 17 (1) (a)-(c) ICC Statute or whether the military prosecution by the LNA can be

929 ICC, Prosecutor v Mahmoud Mustafa Busayf Al-Werfalli, Second Warrent of Arrest, 4 July 2018, Case No. ICC-01/11-01/17 para 22.

930 ICC, Prosecutor v Mahmoud Mustafa Busayf Al-Werfalli, Warrant of Arrest, Case No. ICC-01/11-01/17, 15 August 2017 para 6 ('Al-Werfalli Arrest Warrant'); Alessandro Mario Amoroso, 'Should the ICC Assess Complementarity with Respect to Non-state Armed Groups' (2018) 16 JICJ 1063, 1066.

931 ICC, Al-Werfalli Second Arrest Warrant para 29.

932 ICC, Prosecutor v Mahmoud Mustafa Busayf Al-Werfalli, Second Warrent of Arrest para 27.

933 Ibid para 27; see also ICC, Prosecutor v Simone Gbagbo, Decision on Cote d'Ivoire's challenge to the admissibility of the case against Simone Gbagbo, Case No. ICC-02/11-01/12, 11 December 2014 para 65.

attributed to the Libyan government.[934] The Court did not delve into the doctrinal assessment whether courts of NSAG could be included into the overall admissibility regime according to Art. 17 ICC Statute or whether the provision addresses state authorities only.

On June 15th, 2022, Pre-Trial Chamber I terminated proceedings against Mr. *Al-Werfalli* following the Prosecution's notification of his passing and request to withdraw the warrants of arrest.[935]

Interestingly, the case against Mr. *Al-Werfalli* was the first case before the ICC which could have given cause for the ICC to elaborate on the validity and relevance of non-state administered justice within the admissibility-test before the Court in more detail. The decision on the second warrant of arrest shows that the ICC recognized the – still rare – circumstance that the admissibility objections – surprisingly brought forward by the state of Libya – related to ongoing national proceedings conducted by non-state authorities. Unfortunately, the Court jumped to the conclusion that irrespective of the nature of the adjudicating body at the national level, the lack of concrete and tangible investigative steps rendered the case admissible.

A possible third future scenario relates to the ongoing investigation in the situation of Ukraine, which gained new prominence with the Russian armed attack on February 24th, 2022.

It appears reasonable that there will be a similar admissibility-scenario as with the situation in Georgia and proceedings carried out by the *de facto* authorities of South Ossetia. In case the self-proclaimed People's Republics of Donetsk and Luhansk also initiate investigations into allegedly committed war crimes, crimes against humanity and genocide committed on Ukrainian territory from November 21st, 2013 onwards[936], the ICC would – again – need to elaborate on the validity and relevance of non-state administered justice in relation to the Court's complementary jurisdiction. It remains to be seen if the ICC uses the situation in the Ukraine to delve into a detailed doctrinal analysis of Art. 17 and Art. 20 ICC Statute, respectively and to assess under which circumstances non-state entities should find recognition in the admissibility regime.

---

934 Ibid para 27; Alessandro Mario Amoroso, 'Should the ICC Assess Complementarity with Respect to Non-state Armed Groups?' 1067.

935 ICC, Prosecutor v Mahmoud Mustafa Busayf Al-Werfalli, Decision terminating proceedings against Mr Mahmoud Mustafa Busayf Al-Werfalli, Case No. ICC-01/11-01/17-24, 15 June 2022.

936 This marks the day the government of Ukraine lodged its declaration to accept the ICC's jurisdiction pursuant to Art. 12 (3) ICC Statute.

So far, the ICC justified its exclusion of non-state administered justice from the admissibility-scope by referring to the plain text of Art. 17 (1)(a)-(b) ICC Statute which speak of 'a State which has jurisdiction' and the 'case has been investigated by a State which has jurisdiction'. Undoubtedly, this is a reasonable first conclusion. However, it is also a simplified conclusion, ignoring the need of adapting the law to a changing reality of proliferating non-state administered justice.

Finally, the most recent scenario where the ICC has been confronted with non-state administered justice relates to the *Al Hassan* case in the situation in the Republic of Mali. Mr. *Al Hassan* has been charged with, *inter alia*, the war crime of 'the passing of sentences and the carrying out executions without previous judgement pronounced by a regularly constituted court, affording all judicial guarantees which are generally recognized as indispensable' pursuant to Art. 8 (2)(c)(iv) ICC Statute. On June 26th, 2024, the ICC Trial Chamber X convicted Mr. *Al Hassan* for, *inter alia*, the war crime of passing sentences without due process in relation to the same facts pursuant to Art. 8 (2)(c)(iv) ICC Statute.[937] The pivot point relates to the ICC's interpretation of the term 'regularly constituted court' and the question whether a NSAG can establish a court regularly, hence, according to law. Trial Chamber X noted that for a court to be 'regularly constituted', it must be independent and impartial.[938] Remarkably, in reasoning whether a court of a NSAG can be 'regularly constituted', Trial Chamber X considered the potential limitations of armed groups' capabilities and capacities to identify fair trial guarantees that are realistic. For example, it reasoned that a court by a NSAG may not be able to successfully comply with the same level of independence required by a state court.[939] It further argued that 'the independence requirement does not necessarily preclude a court from having executive branch members on the bench'.[940] Hence, in assessing whether a court established by a NSAG can be 'regularly constituted', hence legal in the context of Art. 8 (2)(c)(iv) ICC Statute, Trial Chamber X adopted a fluid approach, taking account of the limited capacities of many NSAGs. This reasoning resembles the 'sliding scale of obligations'-standard

937 ICC, Prosecutor v Al Hassan Ag Abdoul Aziz Ag Mohamed Ag Mahmoud, Trial Judgment, Case No. ICC-01/12-01/18, 26 June 2024.

938 ICC, Prosecutor v Al Hassan Ag Abdoul Aziz Ag Mohamed Ag Mahmoud, Trial Judgment, Case No. ICC-01/12-01/18, 26 June 2024 para 1175.

939 ICC, Prosecutor v Al Hassan Ag Abdoul Aziz Ag Mohamed Ag Mahmoud, Trial Judgment, Case No. ICC-01/12-01/18, 26 June 2024 para 1173.

940 Ibid.

suggested by *Sassòli* and *Shany.*[941] In doing so, Trial Chamber X applied pertinent ICL and IHL provisions in accordance with its addresses, being mindful of the inherent asymmetry of NIACs. It thereby enhances the 'equality of belligerents'-principle.

The Chamber's deliberations on that matter carry pivotal implications for the issue of recognizing non-state administered justice before the ICC. It can be regarded as a crucial first step in recognizing that NSAGs should be equally able to establish 'regularly constituted' courts. Hence, it is a crucial first step for the ICC in adapting the existing law to a changing reality regarding the adjudication of conflict related justice.

2. Parameters for including courts of NSAGs into the scope of Art. 20 (3) ICC Statute

'Rebel' judicial governance relates to the prosecution and punishment of offences occurring during armed conflict. Those offences are not necessarily criminal in nature, nor are they necessarily linked to the actual armed conflict or military operations. Often rebel judicial governance covers a wide range of human behavior, corresponding to private law, family law or criminal matters. This is owed to the fact that the installment of judicial mechanisms primarily follows the purpose of maintaining law and order in the territory under insurgent control. Hence, 'rebel' judicial activity is often more a tool of an overall governance system than it specifically aims at penalizing crimes related to the armed conflict. However, recognition of insurgent administered justice in the context of the upward *ne bis in idem* in ICL shall be established, if at all, only for conduct which falls under the subject matter jurisdiction of the ICC. Hence, only for criminal conduct which could be qualified as one of the core crimes enlisted in Art. 5 ICC Statute.

The following criteria for recognizing judgments rendered by courts of NSAGs in the upward *ne bis in idem* principle pursuant to Art. 20 (3) ICC Statute are divided into normative requirements and factual parameters. These suggested criteria stem from the conclusions drawn from the foregoing analyses about the legality of courts of NSAGs on the one hand and the recognition of courts of NSAGs in Art. 20 (3) ICC Statute on the other.

941 See above Chapter 4: The Legality of Courts of NSAGs, III. 2. b.

Thus, this final sub-section is bridging the gap between the legality of courts of NSAGs according to IHL and the recognition of courts of NSAGs according to ICL.

a. Normative requirements

The normative requirements for recognizing judgments rendered by courts of NSAGs in the context of *ne bis in idem* pursuant to Art. 20 (3) ICC Statute stem from the assessment of the legality of courts of non-state armed groups as well as from the foregoing doctrinal analysis of Art. 20 (3) ICC Statute.

This means that, firstly, only those judgments which have been adjudicated by courts of NSAGs which adhere to the standards stipulated in Common Article 3 (1)(d) and Art. 6 (2) Additional Protocol II should be considered in the Statute's upward *ne bis in idem* principle. This shall only include courts of NSAGs which have been 'regularly constituted', hence, which have been established by the law of the respective group and only such courts of NSAGs which operate 'independently and impartially' and which adhere to the essential judicial guarantees relative to a group's capacity.

Secondly, only such judgments rendered by courts of NSAGs which adhere to the requirements of Art. 20 (3)(a) and (b) ICC Statute shall be recognized in the ICC's upward *ne bis in idem*. Hence, the proceedings before courts of NSAGs must not have been for the purpose of shielding the person concerned from justice as well as they must have been conducted independently and impartially in accordance with the norms of due process recognized by international law and in a manner that is consistent with an intent to bring the person concerned to justice. The requirement stipulated in Art. 20 (3)(b) ICC Statute corresponds to the 'independence and impartiality'-requirement of Art. 6 (2) Additional Protocol II. The subjective criteria of not shielding a person from justice and the intent to bring the person concerned to justice are more difficult to assess. In essence, it requires the ICC to conduct a case-by-case assessment of the respective insurgent group's conducted proceedings. Thus, it provides the ICC a wide margin of discretion and can function as a key point for controlling the inclusion of 'rebel' administered justice into the scope of Art. 20 (3) ICC Statute.

b. Factual parameters

In accordance with the above-formulated parameters[942] indicating the likeliness of a NSAG's adherence to the requirements of Common Article 3 (1) (d) and Art. 6 (2) Additional Protocol II, the same factual parameters also indicate the likeliness that judgments rendered by courts of NSAGs adhere to the standards of Art. 20 (3)(a) and (b) ICC Statute.

Hence, the factual parameters of

(1) a high level of organization including stable structures and clear divisions of, especially, the political, the military, and the judicial wing of the group's governance system, combined with
(2) stable and long-term control over territory

are strong indicators for a group's ability to conduct independent and impartial proceedings in accordance with the norms of due process recognized by international law pursuant to Art. 20 (3)(b) ICC Statute.

Current ICC jurisprudence which has been confronted with non-state administered justice – mainly by so-called *de facto* authorities – has implicitly formulated a requirement of 'state likeness' by reiterating that non-state judicial activity cannot be considered due to the entity not being a state. In a similar vein, a German court has recently held that time served in the Kurdish led camp 'Al Hol', located in North-East Syria and under the control of the AANES administration, cannot find recognition when imposing a subsequent penalty for the crime of participating in a terrorist organization such as the ISIS, since such an internment has not been ordered and conducted by state authorities.[943]

The above-formulated parameters of organized structures and stable territorial control translate to such a 'state-likeness'-standard.

Formulating general parameters which shall indicate the conformity of a group's administration of criminal justice with the purpose-driven requirements set out in Art. 20 (3)(a) and the second half-sentence of subparagraph (b) ICC Statute, namely the intent or purpose of bringing the person concerned to justice, is difficult. It is difficult to elaborate on general objective parameters which shall indicate the existence of a subjective criterion. However, the focus of a group's judicial system may indicate whether criminal proceedings are conducted with a genuine intent to deliver justice.

---

942 See above Chapter 4: The Legality of Courts of NSAGs, V.

943 Kammergericht Berlin, Anrechnung von Freiheitsentziehung im Ausland, Judgment, 23 April 2021, Case No. (6) 2 StE 6/20-3 (2/20) = NStZ-RR 2022, 62.

Hence, those NSAGs which engage in the administration of justice for the purpose of penalizing and remedying the wrongdoing instead of instrumentalizing the provision of justice mechanisms in support of their military strategies, such as demonstrating power or keeping the local population in check, are most likely to fulfill the subjective criteria of Art. 20(3)(a)-(b) ICC Statute. This relates, especially, to cases where the administration of justice is not only a cog in the machine of the group's overall governance system.

c. Examination process: a proposal

This section suggests a three-step assessment for the recognition of non-state administered justice before the ICC, based on the foregoing analyses on the legality of courts of NSAGs and their recognition within the *ne bis in idem* guarantee:

(1) If the respective NSAG exhibits so-called 'state-like structures', hence, if the respective group operates according to organized structures and exercises stable and long-term territorial control, the ICC need not assess whether the respective court of a NSAG is legal pursuant to Common Article 3 1(d) and Art. 6 (2) Additional Protocol II. In other words, the ICC need not assess whether the respective insurgent judiciary adheres to fair trial guarantees or conducts independent and impartial proceedings. This is owed to the circumstance that the ICC is not a supranational human rights court. It is also in line with the 'equality of belligerents'-principle, since the ICC does not assess the legality of a respective state court when examining the admissibility of a potential case.
Thus, a NSAGs which exhibits state-like features shall enjoy the presumption of legality. However, an assessment of a NSAGs adherence to Art. 20 (3)(a) and (b) ICC Statute remains valid.

(2) If the respective NSAG fails to exhibit state-like structures, the ICC shall assess the group's adherence to Common Article 3 (1)(d) and Art. 6 (2) Additional Protocol II and, in a second step, shall verify whether the respective group's judiciary adheres to the standards stipulated in Art. 20 (3)(a) and (b) ICC Statute.

(3) If the respective NSAGs neither exhibits state-like structures nor do the group's courts adhere to the requirements of Common Article 3 (1) (d) and Art. 6 (2) Additional Protocol II, the ICC need not consider

judicial decisions rendered by such NSAGs within the Statute's admissibility-test, comprising, *inter alia*, the upward *ne bis in idem* principle.

In sum, this proposed case-by-case assessment seeks to take up on Judge *Kovác*'s liberal stance towards a possible recognition of non-state administered justice before the ICC. It provides the ICC a wide margin of appreciation and can function as an important set screw for controlling the inclusion of non-state administered justice into the ICC's admissibility regime.

3. Conclusion

There is a Westphalian conception of how justice should be delivered, namely, through institutions emanating from the state.

The ICC follows this line in exercising its complementary jurisdiction in relation to state jurisdictions only and considering states as privileged agents of administering justice (justice from 'above'). This renders the ICC an 'agent-dependent'[944] enterprise, since it does not solely matter how well justice is done but primarily by whom it is done. This inevitably marginalizes alternative criminal justice mechanisms within the framework of the ICC, namely, justice mechanisms coming from 'below', such as courts of NSAGs.

Looking at the wording of Art. 17 ICC Statute as well as at the Preamble and Art. 1 ICC Statute, the state-centered approach of the ICC Statute towards its admissibility- and complementarity-regime becomes evident.

One may reasonably draw the conclusion that the drafters of the ICC Statute intentionally excluded any form of non-national, in other words, non-state administered justice. Yet, it is also conceivable that they may not have envisaged the possibility that the ICC could eventually be confronted with genuine criminal prosecutions carried out by non-state entities. However, present situations before the ICC show that it is reasonable to believe that non-state administered justice will be a recurring scenario which the ICC will be confronted with in the context of assessing the admissibility of a case. Of course, the ICC could always rely on the plain language of Art. 17 ICC Statute which refers to states' jurisdictions and excludes any investigations carried out by non-state entities from the provision's scope.

944 This term was used by René Provost, Rebel Courts: The Administration of Justice by Armed Insurgents 409.

However, this work sought to prove that a nuanced doctrinal analysis of the provisions of Art. 17 (1)(c) and Art. 20 (3) ICC Statute allows for the inclusion of non-state administered justice. Especially in combination with a doctrinal analysis of Common Article 3 (1)(d) and Art. 6 (2) Additional Protocol II under the light of the 'equality of belligerents'-principle it becomes clear that such an inclusion is even indicated.

Thereby, this work took up on the contemporary debate about the role and status of NSAGs in international law.

Characteristic for this debate is a so-called 'fear of legitimization'. This 'legitimization fear' is particularly delicate in the present debate about the recognition of non-state administered justice. Since the parallel administration of justice by NSAGs encroaches on every state's sovereignty, there is a strong resistance to granting decisions issued by courts of NSAGs any legal recognition or legal effect.

In this vein, the ICRC commentary of 2016 on Common Article 3 indicates that 'nothing in the article implies that a State must recognize or give legal effect to the results of a trial or other judicial proceedings conducted by a non-State Party to the conflict.'[945] This comment relates to Common Article 3's last paragraph according to which 'The application of the preceding provisions shall not affect the legal status of the Parties to the conflict'.

However, analyzing the legality of 'rebel courts' according to IHL[946] and their possible recognition in the ICL *ne bis in idem* precept pursuant to Art. 20 (3) ICC Statute does not automatically transfer a status to NSGAs nor does it amount to condoning or legitimizing these entities' goals and purposes.

It 'simply' amounts to a legal analysis of a factual scenario. There exists an organic link between 'rebel' administered justice during NIACs and the field of operation of the ICC and other international criminal law tribunals. In other words, the administration of justice by NSAGs during armed conflict has repercussions at the level of ICL. These repercussions warrant a careful doctrinal analysis and assessment.

In this line, the present work assessed whether courts of NSAGs can be legal according to IHL and whether their judgments can be recognized in *ne bis in idem* according to ICL.

---

945 ICRC, Commentary of 2016 on Convention (I) for the Amelioration of the Condition of the Wounded and Sick in Armed Forces in the Field para 695.

946 See above Chapter 4: The Legality of Courts of NSAGs.

This work's deliberations lead to the conclusion that, firstly, Common Article 3 (1)(d) and Art. 6 (2) Additional Protocol II establish the legality of courts of NSAGs during NIACs if the statutory standards are met, and secondly, that judgments rendered by legally established courts should be recognized in the ICC's upward *ne bis in idem* principle which forms part of the Court's admissibility regime. This conclusion promotes systemic integrity in international law.

Chapter 6: Summary and Conclusions

This chapter comprises the final theses and conclusions stemming from the foregoing chapters.

1. Even though IACs are considered the archetype of armed conflicts, NIACs have gained the upper hand throughout the last decades.
2. A widespread, socio-political phenomenon during NIACs is the establishment of parallel governance structures by NSAGs. Political science literature refers to this as 'rebel governance'.[947] 'Rebel governance' relates to the organization of a civilian population within 'rebel' held territory for a public purpose and, especially, occurs in situations where the respective NSAG has established a certain degree of control over territory and/or population and possesses a certain degree of organization.
3. The provision of parallel judicial mechanisms forms an important part of 'rebel governance' during armed conflict.
4. Insurgent administration of justice has many facets.[948] It can range from loose and *ad hoc* processes to elaborate and advanced mechanisms, including the establishment and operating of a group's own institutions such as courts. Insurgent administration of justice can be directed towards the civilian population, towards the group's own members or towards individuals belonging to the adversary party/parties. It can cover the adjudication of ordinary disputes as well as it may address conduct specifically linked to armed hostilities.
5. As much as there exists variation, insurgent administered justice usually aims at common effects. These include, *inter alia*, upholding law and order within the group's own ranks or within the local civilian population as well as generating civilian support and building legitimacy.[949]
6. Insurgent judicial governance encroaches on the Westphalian system of state sovereignty and the inherent claim of states to a monopoly over the use of force.

947 See above Chapter 2: Non-State Armed Groups and Judicial Governance, II.

948 See above Chapter 2: Non-State Armed Groups and Judicial Governance, III. 1. and 2.

949 See above Chapter 2: Non-State Armed Groups and Judicial Governance, III. 3.

7. However, IHL applicable to NIACs contains two provisions which explicitly foresee the possibility for NSAGs to administer justice during armed conflict. These are Common Article 3 (1)(d) and Art. 6 (2) Additional Protocol II.[950] Both provisions apply to criminal proceedings only. They stipulate requirements which must be adhered to when conducting criminal proceedings in times of armed conflict to prevent summary justice and to secure fair trial guarantees.
8. According to Common Article 3 (1)(d), a court must be 'regularly constituted' and must afford 'all the judicial guarantees which are recognized as indispensable by civilized peoples'.
9. A court is 'regularly constituted' if it is 'established by law'.[951]
10. The requirement of a 'regularly constituted court', hence, a court 'established by law' must be interpreted in light of the 'equality of belligerents'-principle of IHL. This principle requires that NSAGs must be equally able to meet statutory requirements as their – usual – state opponents. Consequently, an 'equality of belligerents'-approach to defining the requirement of 'established by law' results in a broad understanding of the term 'law' which includes the law of the respective NSAG.[952]
11. Similarly, Art. 6 (2) Additional Protocol II requires the respective court to offer 'the essential guarantees of independence and impartiality'. Notably, it omits the requirement of 'regularly constituted'.[953]
12. A court is 'independent' if it operates free from external interference by the executive or legislative branch. A court is 'impartial' if its judges are not influenced by personal bias or prejudice nor harbor preconceptions about the case before them nor act in ways which improperly promotes the interests of one of the parties to the detriment of the other.
13. Applying the requirements of Art. 6 (2) Additional Protocol II to courts established by NSAGs during armed conflict reveals a so-called capacity problem: most NSAGs will lack the necessary resources to adhere to the high standards of Art. 6 (2) Additional Protocol II. It also reveals an equality problem: state parties will always have more

950 See above Chapter 4: The Legality of Courts of NSAGs, I.
951 See above Chapter 4: The Legality of Courts of NSAGs, II. 1. a.
952 See above Chapter 4: The Legality of Courts of NSAGs, II. 2.
953 See above Chapter 4: The Legality of Courts of NSAGs, III. 1.

resources and more capacities to fulfill the requirements of Art. 6 (2) Additional Protocol II compared to non-state parties.[954]

14. Therefore, the requirements of Art. 6 (2) Additional Protocol II must be interpreted by applying a so-called 'sliding scale of obligations'-approach. This 'sliding scale of obligations'-standard stipulates that the better organized a NSAGs is and the more stable control over territory it exercises, the more IHL rules it must adhere to.
15. Translated to the scenario of administering justice during armed conflict, this standard ensures that NSAGs are equally able to fulfill the judicial guarantees stipulated by Art. 6 (2)(a)-(f) Additional Protocol II as their – usually stronger and better equipped – state opponent. It dictates that the better organized a NSAGs is and the more territorial control it exercises, the more obligations stipulated in Art. 6 (2)(a)-(f) Additional Protocol II become applicable.[955]
16. A combined application of the 'equality of belligerents'-principle and the 'sliding-scale of obligations'-standard ensures that NSAGs are equally able to fulfill the statutory requirements of Common Article 3 (1)(d) and/or Art. 6 (2) Additional Protocol II as their state opponents.[956]
17. If NSAGs meet the requirements set out in Common Article 3 (1)(d) and/or Art. 6 (2) Additional Protocol II, they are legally convening courts according to IHL.[957]
18. Although Common Article 3 (1)(d) and Art. 6 (2) Additional Protocol II are primarily obligation-norms and only conditional permission-norms, they carry relative legality for the installment of judicial mechanisms during NIACs.[958]
19. Those who argue that IHL does not regulate the legality of conduct during armed conflict because IHL provisions do not confer rights or legal bases perpetuate the asymmetry of the warring parties to NIACs, disregard the distinction between *jus ad bellum* and *jus in bello*, and deny IHL authority.[959]
20. Hence, courts of NSAGs which comply with the statutory requirements of Common Article 3 (1)(d) and/or Art. 6 (2) Additional Pro-

954 See above Chapter 4: The Legality of Courts of NSAGs, III. 2. a.
955 See above Chapter 4: The Legality of Courts of NSAGs, III. 2. b.
956 See above Chapter 4: The Legality of Courts of NSAGs, III. 3.
957 See above Chapter 4: The Legality of Courts of NSAGs, IV.
958 See above Chapter 4: The Legality of Courts of NSAGs, IV. 1. b.
959 See above Chapter 4: The Legality of Courts of NSAGs, IV. 2.

tocol II are legal according to IHL and may fill a legal void which threatens to erase in situations where the 'state has left the building' and governmental authorities are no longer in place.

21. A systematically consistent application of international law warrants that courts which have been legally convened according to pertinent IHL provisions find recognition in pertinent ICL provisions.[960]
22. The assessment of recognizing judgments rendered by insurgent courts in ICL focuses on pertinent provisions stipulated in the ICC Statute. These are Art. 17 ICC Statute which enshrines the ICC's admissibility regime and Art. 20 (3) ICC Statute which stipulates the *ne bis in idem* principle. *Ne bis in idem* pursuant to Art. 20 (3) ICC Statute forms part of the admissibility-test through the cross-reference made in Art. 17 (1) (c) ICC Statute.[961]
23. The admissibility regime reflects the ICC's jurisdictional mandate of complementing national jurisdictions of states. Accordingly, *non*-state administered justice through courts of NSAGs, although operating also at a national level, does not fit into the admissibility-regime.[962]
24. The structural embedment of *ne bis in idem* within the ICC's admissibility regime results in a bifurcated protective purpose of Art. 20 (3) ICC Statute: it serves as an instrument for allocating concurrent jurisdictions as well as it protects the individual from being tried or punished twice for the same matter.[963] Hence, the analysis of recognizing courts of NSAGs in the ICC Statute's *ne bis in idem* principle addresses the core dilemma of the principles bifurcated protection when applied in an inter-jurisdictional context: balancing the interests of states with the interests of individuals.
25. According to Art. 20 (3) ICC Statute, 'no person who has been tried by another court for conduct also proscribed under article 6, 7, 8 or 8*bis* shall be tried by the Court with respect to the same conduct'. The broadly held terminology in Art. 20 (3) ICC Statute, referring to 'tried by another court' and leaving out any state reference, facilitates the inclusions of courts of NSAGs.[964]
26. The absence of the word 'state' in Art. 20 (3) ICC Statute is more than a 'drafting artifact'. Albeit the provision's structural embedment into the

960 See above Chapter 1: An Introduction, II.
961 See above Chapter 5: The Rule of Ne Bis In Idem and Courts of NSAGs, II. 1. and 2.
962 See above Chapter 5: The Rule of Ne Bis In Idem and Courts of NSAGs, II. 3.
963 See above Chapter 5: The Rule of Ne Bis In Idem and Courts of NSAGs, II. 2.
964 See above Chapter 5: The Rule of Ne Bis In Idem and Courts of NSAGs, III. 1. a.

overall admissibility regime which revolves around 'national criminal jurisdictions', Art. 20 (3) ICC Statute opens a necessary gateway for the inclusion of courts of NSAGs into the ICC Statute's complementarity regime.[965]

27. Including courts of NSAGs into the scope of Art. 20 (3) ICC Statute enhances the accused's protection from being put twice in judicial jeopardy.[966]
28. The human right no to be tried and not to be punished twice for the same conduct or crime is the animating rationale of the *ne bis in idem* principle. Under this condition, it would be unreasonable not to grant a defendant the protection from being put twice in judicial jeopardy merely because of the status (state vs. non-state) of the domestic prosecutorial entity (or lack thereof).[967]
29. A 'rebel court'-friendly interpretation of Art. 20 (3) ICC Statute finds support in the Court's own jurisprudence. In the *Bemba* case, the ICC implicitly held that courts of NSAGs can be the 'competent authority' to investigate and prosecute the respective crimes without automatically fulfilling the war crime of Art. 8 (2)(c)(iv) ICC Statute.
30. A systematically consistent interpretation and application of the ICC Statute demands that if the ICC recognizes courts of NSAGs under the scope of individual criminal liability pursuant to Art. 28 ICC Statute, it must also recognize the judgments issued by these institutions in the Statute's own *ne bis in idem* principle pursuant to Art. 20 (3) ICC Statute.[968]
31. A 'rebel court'-friendly interpretation of Art. 20 (3) ICC Statute enhances the ICC's basic philosophy of fighting impunity for those perpetrators of crimes which are of concern to the international community as a whole.[969]
32. Finally, a 'rebel court'-friendly interpretation of Art. 20 (3) ICC Statute is an important first step in adapting the existing law to a changing reality when adjudicating conflict-related justice. This change in paradigm relates to considering the establishment and operation of

965 See above Chapter 5: The Rule of Ne Bis In Idem and Courts of NSAGs, III. 1. b.
966 See above Chapter 5: The Rule of Ne Bis In Idem and Courts of NSAGs, III. 1. c.
967 See above Chapter 5: The Rule of Ne Bis In Idem and Courts of NSAGs, III. 1. g.
968 See above Chapter 5: The Rule of Ne Bis In Idem and Courts of NSAGs, III. 1. f.
969 See above Chapter 5: The Rule of Ne Bis In Idem and Courts of NSAGs, III. 1. h.

courts of NSAGs not as a necessary war crime conduct but as an additional tool in the enforcement of law during armed conflict.[970]

33. To conclude, 'systemic integrity of international law' demands that legally established courts of NSAGs pursuant to pertinent IHL provisions find corresponding recognition in pertinent ICL provisions.
34. If courts of NSAGs adhere to the pertinent statutory requirements, they should have a *locus standi* in IHL and ICL for the limited purpose of exercising criminal jurisdiction during armed conflict.

970 See above Chapter 5: The Rule of Ne Bis In Idem and Courts of NSAGs, III. 1. h.

References

Bibliography

ACLED, 'Conflict Watchlist 2023 - Kurdish Regions: High Risk of Violent Escalation and Domestic Turmoil' (Armed Conflict Location & Event Data Project (ACLED), 2023) <https://acleddata.com/conflict-watchlist-2023/kurdish-regions/> accessed 14 November 2023.

----, 'Middle East Regional Overview: The Regional Implications of the Israel-Gaza Conflict' (Armed Conflict Location & Event Data Project (ACLED) 2023) <https://acleddata.com/2023/11/08/regional-overview-middle-east-october-2023-the-regional-implications-of-the-israel-gaza-conflict/> accessed 25 November 2023.

AI, Amnesty International Report 2022/23: The state of the world's human rights (Amnesty International, 27 March 2023).

Akande Dapo, 'Classification of Armed Conflicts' in Saul Ben and Akande Dapo (eds), The Oxford Guide to International Humanitarian Law (1st edn, Oxford University Press 2020).

Al-Abdullah Muaz, 'The State of Syria: Q2 2022 - Q3 2022' (Armed Conflict Location & Event Data Project (ACLED), 2022) <https://acleddata.com/2022/12/01/the-state-of-syria-q2-2022-q3-2022/> accessed 16 November 2023.

Al-Ali Zana, 'New Social Contract establishes one region in northeast Syria' North press agency (Raqqa 28 August 2023) accessed 22 November 2023.

Alkaff Syed Huzaifah Bin Othman and Yussof Nurulhuda Binte, 'An Overview of the Syrian Conflict' (2016) 8 Counter Terrorist Trends and Analyses 8-11.

Allison Michael E. and Alvarez Alberto Martín, 'Unity and Disunity in the FMLN' (2012) 54 Latin American Politics and Society 89-118.

Ambos Kai (ed), Rome Statute of the International Criminal Court - Article-by-Article Commentary (4th edn, C.H. Beck, Nomos, Hart 2022).

Amoroso Alessandro Mario, 'Should the ICC Assess Complementarity with Respect to Non-state Armed Groups?' (2018) 16 Journal of International Criminal Justice 1063-1091.

Anderson Jon Lee, Guerrillas (1st edn, Abacus 1992).

Anderson Keilin and Sinclair-Blakemore Adaena, 'Ne bis in idem, nulla poena sine lege and Domestic Prosecutions of International Crimes in the Aftermath of a Trial at the International Criminal Court' (2021) 21 International Criminal Law Review 35-66.

André Klip and Wilt Harmen Van der, 'The Netherlands and *non bis in idem*' (2002) 73 Revue Internationale de Droit Pénal 1091-1137.

ARC, Neuvième Conférence Internationale de la Croix-Rouge Tenue à Washington du 7 au 17 Mai 1912, Compte-rendu (The American Red Cross, 1912).

Arjona Ana, 'Civilian Cooperation and Non-Cooperation with Non-State Armed Groups: The Centrality of Obedience and Resistance' (2017) 28 Small Wars & Insurgencies 755-778.

----, Rebelocracy - Social Order in the Colombian Civil War (1st edn, Cambridge University Press 2016).

----, 'Wartime Institutions: A Research Agenda' (2014) 58 Journal of Conflict Resolution 1360-1389.

Arjona Ana, Kasfir Nelson and Mamiplly Zachariah, 'Introduction' in Mampilly Zachariah C., Kasfir Nelson and Arjona Ana (eds), Rebel Governance in Civil War (1st edn, Cambridge University Press 2015).

Arraf Jane, ',Revenge Is For The Weak': Kurdish Courts In Northeastern Syria Take On ISIS Cases' NPR (20 May 2019) <https://www.npr.org/2019/05/29/727511632/revenge-is-for-the-weak-kurdish-courts-in-northeastern-syria-take-on-isis-cases> accessed 20 October 2021.

Aust Helmut Philipp, 'Die Anerkennung von Regierungen: Völkerrechtliche Grundlagen und Grenzen im Lichte des Falls Venezuela' (2020) 80 ZaöRV 73-99.

AW, Violations of Fair Trial Guarantees by the FMLN's Ad Hoc Courts, Report (Americas Watch, 1990).

Bandarage Asoka, The Separatist Conflict in Sri Lanka: Terrorism, Ethnicity, Political economy (1st edn, Routledge 2009).

Bangerter Olivier and Amstel Nelleke van, 'A collection of codes of conduct issued by armed groups' (2011) 93 International Review of the Red Cross 483-500.

Bassiouni Mahmoud C., 'Human rights in the context of criminal justice: identifying international procedural protections and equivalent protections in national constitutions' (1992) 3 Duke Journal of Comparative & International Law 235-297.

Beken Tom Vander, Vermeulen Gert and Ongena Thérèse, 'Belgium - Concurrent National and International Criminal Jurisdiction and the Prinicple ,ne bis in idem'' (2002) 73 Revue Internationale de Droit Pénal 811-848.

Bellal Annyssa, 'Central African Republic: From Conflict to Chaos and Back Again?' in Casey-Maslen Stuart (ed), The War Report - Armed Conflict in 2013 (1st edn, Oxford University Press 2014).

----, 'What Are ,Armed Non-State Actors'? A Legal and Semantic Approach' in Heffes Ezequiel, Kotlik Marcos D. and Ventura Manuel J. (eds), International Humanitarian Law and Non-State Actors: Debates, Law and Practice (1st edn, Asser Press 2020).

---- (ed), The War Report - Armed Conflict in 2017 (1st edn, Geneva Academy of International Humanitarian Law and Human Rights 2018).

Bernard Diane, '*Ne bis in idem* - Protector of Defendants' Rights or Jurisdiction Pointsman?' (2011) 9 Journal of International Criminal Justice 863-880.

Berti Benedetta, 'Violent and Criminal Non-State Actors' in Draude Anke, Börzel Tanja A. and Risse Thomas (eds), The Oxford Handbook of Governance and Limited Statehood (1st edn, Oxford University Press 2018).

Bianchi Andrea (ed), Non-State Actors and International Law (1st edn, Routledge 2016).

Bockel Bas van, 'The ‚European' *Ne Bis in Idem* Prinicple, Substances, Sources, and Scope' in Bockel Bas van (ed), Ne Bis in Idem in EU Law (1st edn, Cambridge University Press 2016).

---- (ed), Ne Bis in Idem in EU Law (1st edn, Cambridge University Press 2016).

Börzel Tanja A., Risse Thomas and Draude Anke, 'Governance in Areas of Limited Statehood: Conceptual Clarifiactions and Major Contributions of the Handbook' in Draude Anke, Börzel Tanja A. and Risse Thomas (eds), The Oxford Handbook of Governance and Limited Statehood (1st edn, Oxford University Press 2018).

Böse Martin, 'The Transnational Dimension of the *ne bis in idem* Principle and the Notion of *res iudicata* in the European Union' in Böse Martin, Bohlander Michael, Klip André and Lagodny Otto (eds), Justice Without Borders - Essays in Honour of Wolfgang Schomburg (1st edn, Brill Nijhoff 2018).

Böse Martin, Bohlander Michael, Klip André and Lagodny Otto (eds), Justice Without Borders - Essays in Honour of Wolfgang Schomburg (1st edn, Brill Nijhoff 2018).

Bothe Michael, Partsch Karl Josef and Solf Waldemar A., New Rules for Victims of Armed Conflict: Commentary on the Two 1977 Protocols Additional to the Geneva Conventions of 1949 (2nd edn, Martinus Nijhoff 2013).

Brown Darryl K., Turner Jenia I. and Weisser Bettina (eds), The Oxford Handbook of Criminal Process (1st edn, Oxford University Press 2019).

Bugnion François, 'Guerre juste, guerre d'agression et droit international humanitaire' (2002) 84 International Review of the Red Cross 523-546.

----, '*Jus ad bellum, jus in bello* and non-international armed conflicts' (2003) 6 Yearbook of International Humanitarian Law 167-198.

Byrne Hugh, El Salvador's civil war : a study of revolution (1st edn, Lynne Rienner Publishers 1996).

Cammett Melani, Diwan Ishac, Richards Alan and Waterbury John, A Political Economy of the Middle East (4th edn, Routledge 2018).

Carrillo-Suarez Arturo, 'Hors De Logique: Contemporary Issues in International Humanitarian Law as Applied to Internal Armed Conflict' (1999) 15 American University of International Law Review 1-150.

Carter Linda E., 'The Principle of Complementarity and the International Cirminal Court: The Role of Ne Bis in Idem ' (2010) 8 Santa Clara Journal of International Law 165-198.

Casey-Maslen Stuart (ed), The War Report - Armed Conflict in 2013 (1st edn, Oxford University Press 2014).

Cassese Antonio, 'The Geneva Protocols of 1977 on the Humanitarian Law of Armed Conflict and Customary International Law' (1984) 3 UCLA Pacific Basin Law Journal 55-118.

----, International Criminal Law (3rd edn, Oxford University Press 2013).

----, International law (2nd edn, Oxford University Press 2005).

Cassese Antonio, Gaeta Paola and Jones John R.W.D. (eds), The Rome Statute of the International Criminal Court: A Commentary (1st edn, Oxford University Press 2002).

Castrén Erik, Civil War (1st edn, Suomalainen Tiedeakatemia 1966).

CICR, Dixième Conférence Internationale de la Croix-Rouge Tenue à Gèneve du 30 au 7 Avril 1921, Compte-rendu (Comité International Croix Rouge, 26 March 1921).

----, Rapport Général du Comité International de la Croix-Rouge sur son activité de 1912 à 1920 (Comité International Croix Rouge, 30 March 1921).

Clapham Andrew, 'Detention by Armed Groups under International Law' (2017) 93 International Law Studies 1-43.

----, Human Rights Obligations of Non-State Actors (1st edn, Oxford University Press 2006).

----, 'The Limits of Human Rights in Armed Conflicts and Other Situations of Armed Violence' in Fassbender Bardo and Traisbach Knut (eds), The Limits of Human Rights (1st edn, Oxford University Press 2019).

----, War (1st edn, Oxford University Press 2021).

Clapham Andrew, Gaeta Paola and Sassòli Marco (eds), The 1949 Geneva Conventions - A Commentary (1st edn, Oxford University Press 2015).

Clooney Amal and Webb Philippa, The Right to a Fair Trial in International Law (1st edn, Oxford University Press 2021).

Coggins Bridget L., 'Rebel Diplomacy: Theorizing Violent Non-State Actors' Strategic Use of Talk' in Ana Arjona Nelson Kasfir, and Zachariah Mamiplly (ed), Rebel Governance in Civil War (1st edn, Cambridge Universtiy Press 2015).

Conway Gerard, '*Ne Bis in Idem* in International Law' (2003) 3 International Criminal Law Review 217-244.

Coracini Astrid Reisinger and Tallgren Immi, 'Art. 20 - *Ne bis in idem*' in Ambos Kai (ed), Rome Statute of the International Criminal Court - Article-by-Article Commentary (4th edn, C.H. Beck, Hart, Nomos 2022).

Crawford James and Brownlie Ian, Brownlie's principles of public international law (9th edn, Oxford University Press 2019).

Cullen Anthony, The Concept of Non-International Armed Conflict in International Humanitarian Law (1st edn, Cambridge Unversity Press 2010).

----, 'The Definition of Non-International Armed Conflict in the Rome Statute of the International Criminal Court: An Analysis of the Threshold of Application Contained in Article 8(2)(f)' (2008) 12 Journal of Conflict and Security Law 419-445.

David Eric, 'Internal (Non-International) Armed Conflict' in Clapham Andrew and Gaeta Paola (eds), The Oxford Handbook of International Law in Armed Conflict (1st edn, Oxford University Press 2014).

David Éric, Principes de droit des conflits armés (6th edn, Bruylant 2019).

Desessard Laurent, 'France - Les compétences criminelles concurrentes nationales et internationales et le principle ne bis in idem' (2002) 73 Revue Internationale de Droit Pénal 913-940.

Dienstein Yoram, Non-International Armed Conflicts in International Law (2nd edn, Cambridge University Press 2021).

Draper GIAD, 'Humanitarian Law and Internal Armed Conflicts' (1983) 13 Georgia Journal of International and Comparative Law 253-278.

Draude Anke, Börzel Tanja A. and Risse Thomas (eds), The Oxford Handbook of Governance and Limited Statehood (1st edn, Oxford University Press 2018).

Ekman Mikael and Meyer William D., Rule of Law Assessment Report: Syria 2021 (International Legal Assistance Consortium, 2021).

Espinosa Nicolás, 'Entre la justicia guerrillera y la justicia campesina ¿Un nuevo modelo de justicia comunitaria? La Macarena, Meta, estudio de caso' (2003) 0 Revista Colombiana de Sociología 117-145.

Essen Jonte van, 'De Facto Regimes in International Law' (2012) 28 Utrecht Journal of International and European Law 31-49.

Fassbender Bardo and Traisbach Knut (eds), The Limits of Human Rights (1st edn, Oxford University Press 2019).

Fleck Dieter, 'The Law of Non-International Armed Conflict' in Fleck Dieter (ed), The Handbook of International Humanitarian Law (4th edn, Oxford Universtiy Press 2021).

---- (ed), The Handbook of International Humanitarian Law (4th edn, Oxford University Press 2021).

Fortin Katharine, The Accountability of Armed Gorups under Human Rights (1st edn, Oxford University Press 2017).

----, 'The Procedural Right to a Remedy When the State has Left the Building? A Reflection on Armed Groups, Courts and Domestic Law' (2022) 14 Journal of Human Rights Practice 387-414.

Frowein Jochen A, 'De Facto Regime', Max Planck Encyclopedia of Public International Law (MPEPIL) (2013).

Gaasbeek Timmo, 'Bridging troubled waters? Everyday inter-ethnic interaction in a context of violent conflict in Kottiyar Pattu, Trincomalee, Sri Lanka' (Thesis, Wageningen University 2010).

Gani Jasemine K. and Hinnebusch Raymond (eds), Actors and Dynamics in the Syrian Conflict's Middle Phase - Between Contentious Politics, Militarization and Regime Resilience (1st edn, Routledge 2022).

Gartner Irene, 'Austria - Concurrent National and International Criminal Jurisdiction and the Prinicple ‚ne bis in idem'' (2002) 73 Revue Internationale de Droit Pénal 787-809.

Gilley Bruce, The Right to Rule: How States Win and Lose Legitimacy (1st edn, Columbia University Press 2009).

Ginsburg Tom, 'Rebel Use of Law and Courts' (2019) 15 Annual Review of Law and Social Science 495-507.

Giustozzi Antonio, Empires of Mud: Wars and Warlords in Afghanistan (1st edn, Hurst 2009).

Goodman Ryan, 'Authorization versus Regulation of Detention in Non-International Armed Conflicts' (2015) 91 International Law Studies 155-170.

Grand Catherine C. Le, 'The Colombian Crisis in Historical Perspective' (2003) 28 Canadian Journal of Latin American and Caribbean Studies / Revue canadienne des études latino-américaines et caraïbes 165-209.

Greenwood Christopher, 'The Relationship between ius ad bellum and ius in bello' (1983) 9 Review of International Studies 221-234.

Groussot Xavier and Ericsson Angelica, 'Ne Bis In Idem in the EU and ECHR Legal Orders - A Matter of Uniform Interpretation?' in Bockel Bas van (ed), Ne Bis in Idem in EU Law (1st edn, Cambridge University Press 2016).

Guillaume Gilbert, 'Terrorism and International Law' (2004) 53 International and Comparative Law Quarterly 537-548.

Gunter Michael (ed), Routledge Handbook on the Kurds (1st edn, Routledge 2018).

Hassanein Ahmed Samir, 'Physical and Legal Inability under Article 17(3) of the Rome Statute' (2015) 15 International Criminal Law Review 101-123.

Heffes Ezequiel, 'Administration of justice by armed groups: Some legal and practical concerns'(Humanitarian Law&Policy Blog, 22 November 2018) accessed 27 May 2021.

----, Detention by Non-State Armed Groups under International Law (1st edn, Cambridge University Press 2022).

----, 'Detentions by Armed Opposition Groups in Non-International Armed Conflicts: Towards a New Characterization of International Humanitarian Law' (2015) 20 Journal of Conflict and Security Law 229-250.

----, 'The establishment of courts by armed groups: what is the legal basis?'(Humanitarian Law&Policy Blog) accessed 27 May 2021.

----, 'Generating Respect for International Humanitarian Law: The Establishment of Courts by Organized Non-State Armed Groups in Light of the Principle of Equality of Belligerents' (2016) 18 Yearbook of International Humanitarian Law 181-201.

----, 'The Responsibility of armed opposition groups for Violations of International Humanitarian Law: Challenging the State-Centric System of International Law' (2013) 4 Journal of International Humanitarian Legal Studies 81-107.

----, 'Responsible Rebels: Exploring Correlations Between Compliance and Reparations in Non-International Armed Conflicts' (2022) 14 Journal of Human Rights Practice 415-433.

Heffes Ezequiel, Kotlik Marcos D. and Ventura Manuel J. (eds), International Humanitarian Law and Non-State Actors: Debates, Law and Practice (1st edn, Asser Press 2020).

Heffes Ezequiel and Somer Jonathan, Inviting non-state armed groups to the table - Report (ODI, December 2020).

Heller Kevin Jon, 'Could a Non-State Actor Challenge Admissibility?'(OpinioJuris, 19 August 2012) accessed 12 October 2022.

Henckaerts Jean-Marie and Doswald-Beck Louise, Customary International Humanitarian Law Volume I: Rules (1st edn, Cambridge University Press 2005).

Hobden Steve, 'El Salvador: Civil war, civil society and the state' (2000) 3 Civil Wars 105-120.

Holmes John T., 'Complementarity: National Courts versus the ICC' in Cassese Antonio, Gaeta Paola and Jones John R.W.D. (eds), The Rome Statute of the International Criminal Court: A Commentary (1st edn, Oxford University Press 2002).

Howard Lise M., 'United Nationals Observer Mission in El Salvador (ONUSAL)' in Koops Joachim A., Tardy Thierry, MacQueen Norrie and Williams Paul D. (eds), The Oxford Handbook of United Nations Peacekeeping Operations (1st edn, Oxford University Press 2015).

HRW, Under Kurdish Rule - Absuses in PYD-run Enclaves of Syria, Report (Human Rights Watch, 18 June 2014).

----, War Without Quarter: Colombia and International Humanitarian Law, Report (Human Rights Watch, 1998).

Huang Reyko, The Wartime Origins of Democratization - Civil War, Rebel Govern-nacne, and Political Regimes (1st edn, Cambridge University Press 2016).

Hyeran Jo, Compliant Rebels: Rebel Groups and International Law in World Politics (1st edn, Cambridge University Press 2015).

IACHR, Annual Report of the Inter-American Commission on Human Rights 1990-1991 (Inter-American Commission on Human Rights, 22 February 1991).

IACtHR, Joint Law Report 2019: African Court on Human and Peoples' Rights, European Court of Human Rights and Inter-American Court of Human Rights).

ICRC, Armed Conflicts Linked to Disintegration of State Structures - Preparatory document drafted by the International Committee of the Red Cross for the first periodical meeting on international humanitarian law (International Committee Red Cross, 19-23 January 1998).

----, Commentary of 1987 Protocol Additional to the Geneva Convention of 12 August 1949, and relation to the Protection of Victims of International Armed Conflicts (Protocol I), 8 June 1977 (International Committee of the Red Cross 1987).

----, Commentary of 1987 Protocol Additional to the Geneva Conventions of 12 August 1949, and relating to the Protection of Victims of Non-International Armed Conflicts (Protocol II), 8 June 1977 (International Committee of the Red Cross 1987).

----, Commentary of 2016 on Convention (I) for the Amelioration of the Condition of the Wounded and Sick in Armed Forces in the Field (International Committee of the Red Cross 2016).

----, Draft Revised or New Conventions for the Protection of War Victims (International Committee Red Cross, May 1948).

----, The Geneva Conventions of August 12, 1949: Analysis for the use of National Red Cross Societies (ICRC 1950).

----, Report of the XVIth International Red Cross Conference (International Committee Red Cross, June 1938).

----, Report on the Work of the Conference of Government Experts for the Study of the Conventions for the Protection of War Victims (International Committee Red Cross, 14-26 April 1947).

----, Report on the Work of the Preliminary Conference of National Red Cross Societies for the study of the Conventions and of various Problems relative to the Red Cross (International Committee Red Cross, 26 July - 3 August 1946).

----, Revised and New Draft Conventions for the Protection of War Victims - Texts Approved and Amended by the XVIIth International Red Cross Conference (International Committee Red Cross, May 1948).

----, Role and Activities of the Red Cross in time of Civil War (International Committee Red Cross, June 1938).

Janik Ralph, 'Putin's War against Ukraine: Mocking International Law'(EJIL:Talk!, 28 February 2022) accessed 8 March 2022.

Jentzsch Corinna, 'Auxiliary Armed Forces and Innovations in Security Governance in Mozambique's Civil War' (2017) 19 Civil Wars 325-347.

Joseph Sarah and Castan Melissa, The International Covenant on Civil and Political Rights: Cases, Materials, and Commentary (3rd edn, Oxford University Press 2013).

Jung Harald, 'The Civil War in El Salvador' (1982) Boletín de Estudios Latinoamericanos y del Caribe 5-13.

Kalyvas Stathis N., The Logic of Violence in Civil War (1st edn, Oxford University Press 2006).

Kamalendran Chris, 'The inside story of „Eelam Courts"' Sunday Times (Sri Lanka) (8 December 2002) <https://sundaytimes.lk/021208/news/courts.html> accessed 24 June 2021.

Kasfir Nelson, 'Rebel Governance - Constructing a Field of Inquiry: Definitions, Scope, Patterns, Order, Causes' in Mampilly Zachariah C., Kasfir Nelson and Arjona Ana (eds), Rebel Governnace in Civil War (1st edn, Oxford University Press 2015).

Katman Filiz and Muhammad Dilshad, 'Tracing Kurdish Politics in Syria and its Prospects' in Gani Jasemine K. and Hinnebusch Raymond (eds), Actors and Dynamics in the Syrian Conflict's Middle Phase - Between Contentious Politics, Militarization and Regime Resilience (1st edn, Routledge 2022).

Khalaf Rana, Governing Rojava - Layers of Legitimacy in Syria, Research Paper (Chatham House, The Royal Institute of International Affairs, December 2016).

Khalil Aldar, 'Syrian Kurds Are Not the PKK' Foreign Policy (15 May 2017) <https://foreignpolicy.com/2017/05/15/syrias-kurds-are-not-the-pkk-erdogan-pyd-ypg/> accessed 18 November 2023.

Klabbers Jan, '(I Can't Get No) Recognition: Subjects Doctrine and the Emergence of Non-State Actors' in Bianchi Andrea (ed), Non-State Actors and International Law (1st edn, Routledge 2016).

Klamberg Mark, 'The Legality of Rebel Courts during Non-International Armed Conflicts' (2018) 16 Journal of International Criminal Justice 235-263.

Kleffner Jann K, 'The collective accountability of organized armed groups for system crimes' in André Nollkaemper Harmen van der Wilt (ed), System Criminality in International Law (1st edn, Cambridge University Press 2009).

Kleffner Jann K., Complementarity in the Rome Statute and National Criminal Jurisdictions (1st edn, Oxford University Press 2008).

----, 'The law and policy of complementarity in relation to 'criminal proceedings' carried out by non-state organized armed groups' in Stahn Carsten and El-Zeidy Mohamed M. (eds), The International Criminal Court and Complementarity - From Theory to Practice (1st edn, Cambridge Universtiy Press 2011).

Kleinert Lukas, 'Recognition of a Taliban Government ?: A Short Overview on the Recognition of Governments in International Law'(Völkerrechtsblog, 8 September 2021) accessed 29 October 2021.

Knapp Michael, Flach Anja and Aybôga Ercan (eds), Revoultion in Rojava: Democratic Autonomy and Women's Liberation in Syrian Kurdistan (1st edn, Pluto Press 2016).

Koops Joachim A., Tardy Thierry, MacQueen Norrie and Williams Paul D. (eds), The Oxford Handbook of United Nations Peacekeeping Operations (1st edn, Oxford University Press 2015).

Krasner Stephen D. and Risse Thomas, 'External Actors, State-Building, and Service Provision in Areas of Limited Statehood: Introduction' (2014) 27 Governacne: An International Journal of Policy, Administration, and Institutions 545-567.

----, 'External Actors, State-Building, and Service Provision in Areas of Limited Statehood: Introduction' (2014) 27 Governance 545-567.

Krause Matthew, 'Northeastern Syria: Complex Criminal Law in a Complicated Battlespace'(Just Security, 28 October 2019) accessed 20 October 2021.

Krieger Heike, 'International Law and Governance by Armed Groups: Caught in the Legitimacy Trap?' (2018) 12 Journal of Intervention and Statebuilding 563-583.

---- (ed), Inducing Compliance with International Humanitarian Law - Lessons fron the African Great Lakes Region (1st edn, Cambridge University Press 2015).

Kubicki Leszek, 'Pologne - Les compétences criminelles concurrentes nationales et internationales et le principle ne bis in idem ' (2002) 73 Revue Internationale de Droit Pénal 1037-1050.

Kunz Josef L., 'The Laws of War' (1956) 50 American Journal of International Law 313-337.

Lambin Julie, 'Mexico: Armed Gang Violence Sliding Into Armed Conflict?' in Bellal Annyssa (ed), The War Report - Armed Conflicts in 2017 (1st edn, Geneva Academy of International Humanitarian Law and Human Rights 2018).

Lauterpacht Hersch, 'The Limits of the Operation of the Law of War' (1953) 30 British Yearbook of International Law 206-243.

----, Recognition in international law (1st edn, Cambridge University Press 1947).

Law Jonathan (ed), A Dictionary of Law (10th edn, Oxford University Press 2022).

Lawrence Thomas Joseph, The principles of international law (1st edn, Littleton, CO: F.B. Rothman 1987).

Ledwidge Frank, Rebel Law - Insurgents, Courts and Justice in Modern Conflict (1st edn, Hurst&Company 2017).

Levi Margaret and Sacks Audrey, 'Legitimating beliefs: Sources and indicators' (2009) 3 Regulation & Governance 311-333.

Loyle Cyanne E., 'Rebel courts and rebel legitimacy' (2023) International Politics 1-18.

----, 'Rebel Justice during Armed Conflict' (2021) 65 Journal of Conflict Resolution 108-134.

Mampilly Zachariah C., 'Performing the Nation-State: Rebel Governance and Symbolic Processes' in Mampilly Zachariah C., Kasfir Nelson and Arjona Ana (eds), Rebel Governance in Civil War (1st edn, Cambridge University Press 2015).

----, Rebel Rulers Insurgent Governance and Civilian Life during War (1st edn, Cornell University Press 2011).

Mampilly Zachariah C., Kasfir Nelson and Arjona Ana (eds), Rebel Governance in Civil War (1st edn, Cambridge University Press 2015).

Mandel Michael, 'Aggressors' Rights: The Doctrine of ‚Equality between Belligerents' and the Legacy of Nuremberg' (2011) 24 Leiden Journal of International Law 627-650.

Mao Zedong, Selected Military Writing of Mao Tse-Tung (Foreign Languages Press 1963).

McGee Thomas, "'Rojava': Evolving Public Discourse of Kurdish Identity and Governance in Syria' (2022) 15 Middle East Journal of Culture and Communication 385-403.

McGoldrick Dominic, Rowe Peter and Donnelly Eric (eds), The Permanent International Criminal Court: Legal and Policy Issues (1st edn, Hart Publishing 2004).

Mégret Frédéric, 'Detention by Non-State Armed Groups in NIACs: IHL, International Human Rights Law and the Question of the Right Authority' in Heffes Ezequiel, Kotlik Marcos D. and Ventura Manuel J. (eds), International Humanitarian Law and Non-State Actors: Debates, Law and Practice (1st edn, Asser Press 2020).

Melzer Nils, ICRC Interpretative Guidance on the Notion of Direct Participation in Hostilities under International Humanitarian Law (1st edn, International Committee of the Red Cross 2009).

Meron Theodor, 'The Humanization of Humanitarian Law' (2000) 94 The American Journal of International Law 239-278.

Mettraux Guénaël, The Law of Command Responsibility (1st edn, Oxford University Press 2009).

Meyer Frank, 'Complementing Complementarity' (2006) 6 International Criminal Law Review 549-583.

Meyrowitz Henri, Le Prinicipe de L'égalité des belligérants devant le droit de la guerre (1st edn, Éditions A. Pédone 1970).

Milanovic Marko, 'What is Russia's Legal Justification fur Using Force against Ukraine?'(EJIL:Talk!, 24 February 2022) accessed 8 March 2022.

Moir Lindsay, 'The Concept of Non-International Armed Conflict' in Clapham Andrew, Gaeta Paola and Sassòli Marco (eds), The 1949 Geneva Conventions - A Commentary (1st edn, Oxford University Press 2015).

----, The law of internal armed conflict (1st edn, Cambridge University Press 2002).

Munir Muhammad, 'The Layha for the Mujahideen: an analysis of the code of conduct for the Taliban fighters under Islamic Law' (2011) 93 International Review of the Red Cross 81-102.

Neff Stephen C., Hugo Grotius - On the Law of War and Peace (1st edn, Cambdrige University Press 2012).

Niyo Joshua Joseph, 'Non-State Armed Groups and the Power to Detain in Non-International Armed Conflict' (2020) 53 Israel Law Review 3-33.

Nollkaemper André and Wilt Harmen van der (eds), System Criminality in International Law (1st edn, Cambridge University Press 2009).

Noortmann Math, Reinisch August and Ryngaert Cedric (eds), Non-State Actors in International Law (1st edn, Bloomsbury 2017).

Nuridzhanian Gaiane, 'Ne Bis In Idem in Article 20(3) of the Rome Statute and Non-State Courts' (2019) 18 The Law & Practice of International Courts and Tribunals 219-239.

Nuzov Ilya, 'Post-Conflict Justice: Extending International Criminal Responsibility to Non-State Entities' in Ventura Ezequiel Heffes Marcos D. Kotlik Manuel J. (ed), International Humanitarian Law and Non-State Actors: Debates, Law and Practice (1st edn, Asser Press 2020).

Offstein Norman and Aristizábal Carolina, 'An Historical Review and Analysis of Colombian Guerrilla Movements: FARC, ELN and EPL' (2003) Revist Desarrollo y Sociedad 99-142.

ONUSAL, Third report of the United Nations Observer Mission in El Salvador (United Nations Observer Mission in El Salvador 19 February 1991).

Oppenheim Lassa and Lauterpacht Hersch (eds), International Law: A Treatise (7th edn, Longmans, Green and Co 1952).

Osiel Mark J., 'Why Prosecute - Critics of Punishment for Mass Atrocity' (2000) 22 Human Rights Quarterly 118.

Paddelford Norman J., International law and diplomacy in the Spanish civil strife (1st edn, Macmillan 1939).

Pararajasingham Illayathamby, 'Thamil Eelam - a de facto State: Tamil Eelam Legal System'(TamilNet, 30 October 2003) accessed 27 May 2021.

Paust Jordan J., 'Armed Opposition Groups' in Noortmann Math, Reinisch August and Ryngaert Cedric (eds), Non-State Actors in International Law (1st edn, Bloomsbury 2017).

Pegg Scott, International Society and the De Facto State (1st edn, Ashgate 1998).

Pejić Jelena, 'Status of armed conflicts' in Wilmshurst Elizabeth and Breau Susan (eds), Perspectives on the ICRC Study on Customary International Humanitarian Law (1st edn, Cambridge University Press 2007).

Pena Mario Aguilera, 'Claves y Distorsiones Del Régimen Disciplinario Guerrillero' (2013) 26 Análisis Político 45-62.

----, 'Las guerrillas marxistas y la pena de muerte a combatientes. Un examen de los delitos capitales y del "juicio revolucionario": An Analysis of Capital Crimes and "Revolutionary Courts-martial"' (2014) 41 Anuario Colombiano de Historia Social y de la Cultura 201-236.

Pictet Jean S., Commentary on the Geneva Convention (I) for the Amelioration of the Condition of the Wounded and Sick in Armed Forces in the Field (International Committe of the Red Cross 1952).

----, Commentary on the Geneva Convention (III) relative to the Treatment of Prisoners of War (International Committee of the Red Cross 1960).

----, Commentary on the Geneva Convention (IV) relative to the Protection of Civilian Persons in Time of War (International Committee of the Red Cross 1958).

Pisani Mario, 'Italie - Le prinicple ne bis in indem au niveau internationa et le procédure pénale italienn' (2002) 73 Revue Internationale de Droit Pénal 1017-1029.

Pita María Del Mar Díaz, 'España, Informe sobre el principio non bis in idem y la concurrenciade jurisdicciones entre los tribunals penales españoles y los tribunales penales internacionales' (2002) 73 Revue Internationale de Droit Pénal 873-899.

Podder Sukanya, 'Understanding the Legitimacy of Armed Groups: A Relational Perspective' (2017) 28 Small Wars & Insurgencies 686-708.

Poels Alexander, 'A Need for Transnational Non Bis In Idem Protection in International Human Rights Law' (2005) 23 Netherlands Quarterly of Human Rights 329-348.

Portillo-Gonzales Esther, 'FMLN Reflections, 20 Years Later: An Interview With Nidia Díaz' (2012) NACLA Report on the Americas 55-57.

Promotion Frente Farabundo Martí para la Liberación Nacional. Secretariat for the and Rights Protection of Human, The Legitimacy of Our Methods of Struggle (FMLN 1988).

Provost René, 'FARC Justice: Rebel Rule of Law' (2018) 8 UC Irvine Law Review 227-274.

----, Rebel Courts: The Administration of Justice by Armed Insurgents (1st edn, Oxford University Press 2021).

Quintin Anne, The Nature of International Humanitarian Law - A Permissive or Restrictive Regime? (1st edn, Edward Elgar 2020).

Rastan Rod, 'What is a 'case' for the purpose of the rome statute?' (2008) 19 Criminal Law Forum 435-448.

RIC, Bringing ISIS to justice - Towards an international tribunal in North East Syria (Rojava Information Center, 14 March 2019).

Richards Joanne, An Institutional History of the Liberation Tigers of Tamil Eelam (LTTE), Working Paper (Graduate Institute of International and Development Studies - Centre on Conflict, Development and Peacebuilding, November 2014).

Risse Thomas and Stollenwerk Eric, 'Legitimacy in Areas of Limited Statehood' (2018) 21 Annual Review of Political Science 403-418.

Rodenhäuser Tilman, Organizing Rebellion: Non-State Armed Groups under International Humanitarian Law, Human Rights Law, and International Criminal Law (1st edn, Oxford University Press 2018).

Rowe Peter, 'War Crimes' in McGoldrick Dominic, Rowe Peter and Donnelly Eric (eds), The Permanent International Criminal Court - Legal and Political Issues (1st edn, Hart Publishing 2004).

Ryngaert Cedric, 'Non-State Actors: Carving out a Space in a State-Centred International Legal System' (2016) 63 Netherlands International Law Review 183-195.

Ryngaert Cedric and Meulebroucke Anneleen Van de, 'Enhancing and Enforcing Compliance with International Humanitarian Law by Non-State Armed Groups: an Inquiry into some Mechanisms' (2012) 16 Journal of Conflict and Security Law 443-472.

Saab Bilal Y. and Taylor Alexandra W., 'Criminality and Armed Groups: A Comparative Study of FARC and Paramilitary Groups in Colombia' (2009) 32 Studies in Conflict & Terrorism 455-475.

Safferling Christoph, Towards an International Criminal Procedure (1st edn, Oxford University Press 2001).

Sandoz Yves, Swinarski Christophe and Zimmermann Bruno (eds), Commentary on the Additional Protocols of 8 June 1977 to the Geneva Conventions of 12 August 1949 (1st edn, International Committee of the Red Cross and Martinus Nijhoff 1987).

Sassòli Marco, 'Taking Armed Groups Seriously: Ways to Improve their Compliance with International Humanitarian Law' (2010) 1 Journal of International Humanitarian Legal Studies 5-51.

Sassòli Marco, Carr Susan and Bouvier Antoine A., How does law protect in war? Vol. I (2nd edn, International Committee of the Red Cross 2006).

Sassòli Marco and Shany Yuval, 'Should the obligations of states and armed groups under international humanitarian law really be eqaul?' (2011) 93 International Review of the Red Cross 425-442.

Saul Ben, 'Legislating from a Radical Hague: The United Nations Special Tribunal for Lebanon Invents and International Crime of Transnational Terrorism' (2011) 24 Leiden Journal of International Law 677-700.

Saul Ben and Akande Dapo (eds), The Oxford Guide to International Humanitarian Law (1st edn, Oxford University Press 2020).

Savelsberg Eva, 'The Kurdish PYD and the Syrian Civil War' in Gunter Michael (ed), Routledge Handbook on the Kurds (1st edn, Routledge 2018).

Schaack Beth Van, 'Finding the Tort of Terrorism in International Law' (2008) 28 Review of Litigation 382-478.

Schabas William A., The International Criminal Court: A Commentary on the Rome Statute (2nd edn, Oxford University Press 2016).

----, An Introduction to the International Criminal Court (6th edn, Cambridge University Press 2020).

Schabas William A. and Zeidy Mohamed M. El, 'Art. 17 - Issues of admissibility' in Ambos Kai (ed), Rome Statute of the International Criminal Court - Article-by-Article Commentary (4th edn, C.H. Beck, Hart, Nomos 2022).

Schlichte Klaus and Schneckener Ulrich, 'Armed Groups and the Politics of Legitimacy' (2015) 17 Civil Wars 409-424.

Schlögel Anton, 'Civil War' (1970) 10 International Review of the Red Cross 123-134.

Schmelzle Cord and Stollenwerk Eric, 'Virtuous or Vicious Circle? Governance Effectiveness and Legitimacy in Areas of Limited Statehood' (2018) 12 Journal of Intervention and Statebuilding 449-467.

Schoiswohl Michael, '*De Facto* Regimes and Human Rights Obligations - The Twilight Zone of Public International Law?' (2003) 6 Austrian Review of International and European Law Online 45-90.

Schomburg Wolfgang, 'Germany, concurrent national and international criminal jurisdiction and the principle ‚ne bis in idem'' (2003) 73 Revue Internationale de Droit Pénal 941-964.

Schwab Regine, 'Insurgent courts in civil wars: the three pathways of (trans)formation in today's Syria (2012-2017)' (2018) 29 Small Wars & Insurgencies 801-826.

Shapiro Martin, Courts: A Comparative and Political Analysis (1st edn, The University of Chicago Press 1981).

Shastri Amita, 'The Material Basis for Separatism: The Tamil Eelam Movement in Sri Lanka' (1990) 49 The Journal of Asian Studies 56-77.

Shultz Richard H., Farah Douglas and Lochard Itamara V., Armed Groups: A Tier-One Security Priority, Report (USAF Institute for National Security Studies, September 2004).

Silva Kingsley De, A History of Sri Lanka (1st edn, C. Hurst & Company 1981).

Sivakumaran Sandesh, 'Courts of Armed Opposition Groups: Fair Trials or Summary Justice?' (2009) 7 Journal of International Criminal Justice 489-513.

----, The Law of Non-International Armed Conflict (1st edn, Oxford University Press 2012).

Somer Jonathan, 'Jungle justice: passing sentence on the equality of belligerents in non-international armed conflict' (2007) 89 International Review of the Red Cross 655-690.

----, 'Opening the Floodgates, Controlling the Flow: Swedish Court Rules on the Legal Capacity of Armed Groups to Establish Courts'(Ejil: Talk!, 10 March 2017) accessed 27 May 2021.

Spadaro Alessandra, 'Punish and Be Punished?' (2020) 18 Journal of International Criminal Justice 1-30.

Stahn Carsten and El-Zeidy Mohamed M. (eds), The International Criminal Court and Complementarity - From Theory to Practice (1st edn, Cambridge Universtiy Press 2011).

Stewart Megan A., 'Civil War as State-Making: Strategic Governance in Civil War' (2017) 72 International Organization 205-226.

Stewart Megan A. and Liou Yu-Ming, 'Do Good Borders Make Good Rebels? Territorial Control and Civilian Casualties' (2017) 79 The Journal of Politics 284-301.

Stokke Kristian, 'Building the Tamil Eelam State: Emerging State Institutions and Forms of Governance in LTTE-Controlled Areas in Sri Lanka' (2006) 27 Third World Quarterly 1021-1040.

Stokke Kristian and Ryntveit Anne Krisit, 'The Struggle for Tamil Eelam in Sri Lanka' (2000) 31 Growth and Change 285-304.

Stollenwerk Eric, 'Measuring Governance and Limited Statehood' in Draude Anke, Börzel Tanja A. and Risse Thomas (eds), The Oxford Handbook of Governance and Limited Statehood (1st edn, Oxford University Press 2018).

Stuckenberg Carl-Friedrich, 'Double Jeopardy and Ne Bis in Idem in Common Law and Civil Law Jurisdictions' in Brown Darryl K., Turner Jenia I. and Weisser Bettina (eds), The Oxford Handbook of Criminal Process (1st edn, Oxford University Press 2019).

Swinnen Lucas, The Syrian Civil War: A Never-Ending Story?, IFF Working Paper Online (Institute of Federalism, March 2023).

Terpstra Niels and Frerks Georg, 'Governance Practices and Symbolism: De facto sovereignty and public authority in 'Tigerland'' (2018) 52 Modern Asian Studies 1001-1042.

Thompson Peter G., Armed Groups - The 21st Century Threat (1st edn, Rowman & Littlefield 2014).

UN, Diplomatic Conference of Plenipotentiaries of an International Criminal Court (United Nations, 13 September 1996).

----, Diplomatic Conference of Plenipotentiaries of an International Criminal Court (United Nations, 15 June - 17 July 1998).

----, 'Secretary-General Says Russian Federation's Recognition of ‚Independent' Donetsk, Luhansk Violate Ukraine's Sovereignty, Territorial Integrity'(United Nations, 23 February 2022).

----, Verification Mission in Colombia, Report (United Nations Secretary General, 27 December 2021).

----, Yearbook of the International Law Commission (1st edn, 1994).

----, Yearbook of the International Law Commission (1st edn, 1996).

Villiger Mark, Commentary on the 1969 Vienna Convention on the Law of Treaties (1st edn, Martinus Nijhoff 2009).

Walther Olivier and Pedersen Patrick Steen, 'Rebel fragmentation in Syria's civil war' (2020) 31 Small Wars & Insurgencies 445-474.

Weber Max, 'Die drei reinen Typen der legitimen Herrschaft' in Winckelmann Johannes (ed), Gesammelte Aufsätze zur Wissenschaftslehre (7th edn, Mohr Siebeck 1988).

Wehberg Hans, The Outlawry of War (1st edn, Carnegie Endowment for International Peace 1931).

Weinstein Jeremy M., Inside Rebellion: The Politics of Insurgent Violence (1st edn, Cambridge University Press 2006).

Welle Deutsche, 'Russia recognizes independence of Urkaine separatist regions' Deutsche Welle (21.02.2022) <https://www.dw.com/en/russia-recognizes-independence-of-ukraine-separatist-regions/a-60861963> accessed 8 March 2022.

Werle Gerhard and Jeßberger Florian, Principles of International Criminal Law (4th edn, Oxford University Press 2020).

Wickham-Crowley Timothy P., 'The Rise (and Sometimes Fall) of Guerrilla Governments in Latin America' (1987) 2 Sociological Forum 473-499.

Wickramasinghe Nira, Sri Lanka in the Modern Age: A History of Contested Identities (2nd edn, Hurst and Company 2015).

Willms Jan, 'Courts of armed groups - a tool for inducing higher compliance with international humanitarian law?' in Krieger Heike (ed), Inducing Compliance with International Humanitarian Law - Lessons fron the African Great Lakes Region (1st edn, 2015).

Wilmshurst Elizabeth and Breau Susan (eds), Perspectives on the ICRC Study on Customary International Humanitarian Law (1st edn, Cambridge University Press 2007).

Wilson Heather, International law and the use of force by national liberation movements (1st edn, Clarendon Press 1990).

Winckelmann Johannes (ed), Gesammelte Aufsätze zur Wissenschaftslehre (7th edn, Mohr Siebeck 1988).

Wissenschaftliche Dienste Deutscher Bundestag, Die Wiederaufnahme eines durch rechtskräftiges Urteil abgeschlossenen Strafverfahrens zuungunsten des Angeklagten aufgrund neuer Erkenntnisse - Überblick über die Rechtslage im Ausland, 31 January 2019).

----, Die Wiederaufnahmen von Strafverfahren zuungusten des Beschuldigten aufgrund nachträglich veränderter Beweislage - Überblick über die Rechtslagen in ausgewählten Ländern, 3 March 2022).

Wolfrum Rüdiger and Philipp Christiane E., 'The Status of the Taliban: Their Obligations and Rights under International Law' (2002) 6 Max Planck Yearbook of United Nations Law 559-601.

Wright Georg Henrik von, Norm and Action: a logical enquiry (1st edn, Routledge 1963).

Wright Quincy, 'The Outlawry of War and the Law of War' (1953) 47 The American Journal of International Law 365-376.

Zegveld Liesbeth, The Accountability of Armed Opposition Groups in International Law (1st edn, Cambridge University Press 2002).

Zisser Eyal, 'Syria - from the six day war to the Syrian civil war' (2017) 44 British Journal of Middle Eastern Studies 545-558.

List of Statutes and International Instruments

African Charter on Human and Peoples' Rights, Organization of African Unity Doc. CAB/LEG/67/3 rev.5, 21 I.L.M 58 (1982) 21 October 1986.

African Union Convention for the Protection and Assistance of Internally Displaced Persons in Africa (Kampala Convention), 6 December 2012.

Agreement between the Governments of the States of the Benelux Economic Union, the Federal Republic of Germany and the French Republic on the gradual abolition of checks at their common borders (Schengen Agreement), Official Journal L 239, 22/09/2000 P. 0013-0018, 14 June 1985.

American Convention on Human Rights, UN Treaty Series Vol. 1144 No. 17955, 22 November 1969.

Charter of Fundamental Rights of the European Union, Official Journal of the European Union 2012/C 326/02, 1 December 2009.

Charter of the United Nations, UN Treaty Series Vol. XV, 24 October 1945.

Convention (I) for the Amelioration of the Condition of the Wounded and Sick in Armed Forces in the Field, neu, UN Treaty Series Vol. 75 No. 970, 12 August 1949.

Convention (II) for the Amerlioration of the Condition of Wounded, Sick and Shipwrecked Members of Armed Forces at Sea, neu, UN Treaty Series Vol. 75 No. 971, 12 Augsut 1949.

Convention (III) Relative to the Treatment of Prisoners of War, neu, UN Treaty Series Vol. 75 No. 972, 12 August 1949.

Convention (IV) Relative to the Protection of Civilian Persons in Time of War, neu, UN Treaty Series Vol. 75 No. 973, 12 August 1949.

Convention for the Amelioration of the Condition of the Wounded and Sick in Armies in the Field, 27 July 1929.

Convention Implementing the Schengen Agreement of 14 June 1985 between the Governments of the States of the Benelux Economic Union, the Federal Republic of Germany and the French Republic, on the Gradual Abolition of Checks at their Common Borders, EUR-Lex Doc. No. 42000A0922(01), 19 June 1990.

Convention on the Prohibition of the Development, Production and Stockpiling of Bacteriological (Biological) and Toxin Weapons and on Their Destruction, UN General Assembly Resolution A/RES/2826 (XXVI), 26 March 1975.

Convention on the Prohibition of the Development, Production, Stockpiling and Use of Chemical Weapons and on Their Destruction, UN Security Council Resolution A/RES/58/52, 29 April 1997.

Convention on the Protection of Cultural Property in the Event of Armed Conflict, UN Treaty Series Vol. 249 No. 3511, 14 May 1954.

Convention on the Rights of the Child, UN Treaty Series Vol. 1577 No. 27531, 20 November 1989.

Convention Relative to the Treatment of Prisoners of War, 27 July 1929.

Council Framework Decision of 13 June 2002 on the European arrest warrant and the surrender procedures between Member States, Doc. No. 2002/584/JHA, 13 June 2002.

Council of Europe, Protocol No. 7 to the Convention for the Protection of Human Rights and Fundamental Freedoms, European Treaty Series No. 117, 22 November 1984.

Draft Articles on Responsibility of States for Internationally Wrongful Acts, 2001.

Draft Code of Crimes Against the Peace and Security of Mankind, Yearbook of International Law Commission 1996, Vol. II, December 1996.

Draft Comprehensive Convention on International Terrorism, UN Doc. A/C.6/56/WG.1/CRP.3, 19 October 2001.

European Convention on Human Rights, Council of Europe Treaty Series No. 5, 3 September 1953.

Federal Political Department Bern, Final Record of the Diplomatic Conference of Geneva of 1949 Vol. I, 24 October 1968.

Federal Political Department Bern, Final Record of the Diplomatic Conference of Geneva of 1949 Vol. II, 16 October 1978.

Federal Political Department Bern, Official Records of the Diplomatic Conference on the Reaffirmation and Development of International Humanitarian Law Applicable in Armed Conflicts 1974-1977, 2 February 1979.

Final Agreement to End the Armed Conflict and Build a State and Lasting Peace - Colombia Peace Agreement, 24 September 2016.

Hague Convention (X) for the Adaption to Maritime Warfare of the Principles of the Geneva Convention, 18 October 1907.

International Convention for the Suppression of the Financing of Terrorism, UN Doc. 38349, 10 April 2002.

International Covenant on Civil and Political Rights, UN Treaty Series Vol. 999 No. 14668, 16 December 1966.

The Kellogg-Briand Pact, 27 August 1928.

Optional Protocol to the Convention on the Rights of the Child on the Involvement of Children in Armed Conflict, UN General Assemby Resolution A/RES/54/263, 25 May 2000.

Protocol Additional to the Geneva Conventions of 12 Augsut 1949, and Relating to the Protection of Vicitims of International Armed Conflicts, UN Treaty Series Vol. 1125 No. 17512, 8 June 1977.

Protocol Additional to the Geneva Conventions of 12 August 1949, and Relating to the Protection of Victims of Non-International Armed Conflicts, UN Treaty Series Vol. 1125 No. 17513, 8 June 1977.

Protocol to the African Charter on Human And Peoples' Rights on the Establishment of an African Court on Human and Peoples' Rights, Organization of African Unity (OAU), 10 June 1998.

Rome Statute of the International Criminal Court, UN Treaty Series Vol. 2187 No. 38544, 1 July 2002.

Second Protocol to The Hague Convention of 1954 for the Protection of Cultural Property in the Event of Armed Conflict, UN Treaty Series Vol. 2253 No. 3511, 26 March 1999.

Statute of the International Court of Justice, UN Treaty Series Vol. XV, 26 June 1945.

Statute of the International Criminal Tribunal for Rwanda, UN Doc. S/RES/955, 8 November 1994.

Statute of the International Criminal Tribunal for the Former Yugoslavia, UN Doc. S/25704, 3 May 1993.

United Nations General Assembly Resolution 68/262 (on the territorial integrity of Ukraine), UN Doc. A/RES/68/262, 1 April 2014.

United Nations General Assembly Resolution 217 A (III), Universal Declaration of Human Rights, 10 December 1948.

United Nations General Assembly, Peace Agreement (between the Government of El Salvador and the FMLN), UN Doc. A/46/864, 30 January 1992.

United Nations Security Council Resolution 693 (on the establishment of the United Nations Observer Mission in El Salvador), 20 May 1991.

United Nations Security Council Resolution 1566 (concerning threats to international peace and security caused by terrorism), UN Doc. S/RES/1566, 8 October 2004.

United Nations Security Council, Agreement on Human Rights (San Jose Agreement), UN Doc. A/44/971/S/21541, 16 August 1990.

United Nations Security Council, Geneva Agreement, UN Doc. A/46/551/S/23128, 9 October 1991.

United Nations Working Group on Arbitrary Detention, Communication addressed to the Government of Peru, Opinion No. 27/2000, 14 September 2000.

Vienna Convention on the Law of Treaties, UN Treaty Series Vol. 1155 No. 18232, 27 January 1980.

ECtHR, Guide on Article 4 of Protocol No. 7 to the European Convention on Human Rights: Right not to be tried or punished twice (Council of Europe 2022).

United Nations Human Rights Committee, General Comment No. 32 on Art. 14: Right to equality before courts and tribunals and to a fair trial, CCPR/C/GC/32, 23 August 2007.

List of Cases

ICJ

ICJ, Allegations of Genocide Under the Convention on the Prevention and Punishment of the Crime of Genocide (Ukraine v Russian Federation), Order, 16 March 2022.

ICJ, Military and Paramilitary Activities in and against Nicaragua (Nicaragua v United States of Amercia), Judgment, 27 June 1986, ICJ Reports 1986.

ICJ, Military and Paramilitary Activities in and against Nicaragua (Nicaragua v United States of America), Jurisdiction of the Court and Admissibility of the Application, Judgment, 26 November 1984, ICJ Reports 1984.

ICC

ICC, Prosecutor v Abdallah Banda Abakaer Norain et al., Decision of the plenary of the judges on the „Defence Request for the Disqualification of a Judge“ of 2 April 2012, 5 June 2012, Case No. ICC-02/05-03/09-344-Anx.

ICC, Prosecutor v Ahmad Al Faqi Al Mahdi, Judgment and Sentence, 27 September 2016, Case No. ICC-01/12-01/15.

ICC, Prosecutor v Al Hassan Ag Abdoul Aziz Ag Mohamed Ag Mahmoud, Trial Judgment, 24 June 2024, Case No. ICC-01/12-01/18-2594-Red.

ICC, Prosecutor v Al Hassan Ag Abdoul Aziz Ag Mohamed Ag Mahmoud, Rectificatif à la Décision relative à la confiramtion des charges portées contre Al Hassan Ag Abdoul Aziz Ag Mohamed Ag Mahmoud, 13 November 2019, Case No. ICC-01/12-01/18-461-Corr-Red.

ICC, Prosecutor v Al Hassan Ag Abdoul Aziz Ag Mohamed Ag Mahmoud, Transcript of Confirmation of Charges, 17 July 2019, Case No. ICC-01/12-01/18.

ICC, Prosecutor v Germain Katanga and Mathieu Ngudjolo Chui, Judgment on the Appeal of Mr. Germain Katanga against the Oral Decision of Trial Chamber II of 12 June 2009 on the Admissibility of the Case, 25 September 2009, Case No. ICC-01/04-01/07 OA 8.

ICC, Prosecutor v Germain Katanga and Mathieu Ngudjolo Chui, Reasons for the Oral Decision on the Motion Challenging the Admissibility of the Case (Article 19 of the Statute), 16 June 2009, Case No. ICC-01/04-01/07-1213-tENG.

ICC, Prosecutor v Jean-Pierre Bemba Gombo, Decision on the Admissibility and Abuse of Process Challenges, 24 June 2010, Case No. ICC-01/05-01/08-802.

ICC, Prosecutor v Jean-Pierre Bemba Gombo, Decision Pursuant to Article 61(7)(a) and (b) of the Rome Statute on the Charges of the Prosecutor Against Jean-Pierre Bemba Gombo, 15 June 2009, Case No. ICC-01/05-01/08-424.

ICC, Prosecutor v Jean-Pierre Bemba Gombo, Judgment on the appeal of Mr Jean-Pierre Bemba Gombo against Trial Chamber III's „Judgment pursuant to Article 74 of the Statute", 8 June 2018, Case No. ICC-01/05-01/08 A.

ICC, Prosecutor v Jean-Pierre Bemba Gombo, Judgment pursuant to Article 74 of the Statute, 21 March 2016, Case No. ICC-01/05-01/08-3343.

ICC, Prosecutor v Mahmoud Mustafa Busayf Al-Werfalli, Second Warrent of Arrest, 4 July 2018, Case No. ICC-01/11-01/17.

ICC, Prosecutor v Saif Al-Islam Gaddafi and Abdullah Al-Senussi, Decision on the admissibility of the case against Abdullah Al-Senussi, 11 October 2013, Case No. ICC-01/11-01/11-466-Red.

ICC, Prosecutor v Saif Al-Islam Gaddafi and Abdullah Al-Senussi, Judgment on the Appeal of Libya against the decision of Pre-Trial Chamber I of 31 May 2013 entitled „Decision on the admissibiltiy of the case against Saif Al-Islam Gaddafi", 21 May 2014, Case No. ICC-01/11-01/11-547-Red.

ICC, Prosecutor v Saif Al-Islam Gaddafi, Decision on the ‚Admissibility Challenge by Dr. Saif Al-Islam Gaddafi pursuant to Articles 17(1)(c), 19 and 20(3) of the Rome Statute', 5 April 2019, Case No. ICC-01/11-01/11-662.

ICC, Prosecutor v Saif-Al Islam Gaddafi and Abdullah Al-Senussi, Decision on the admissibility of the case against Saif Al-Islam Gaddafi, 31 May 2013, Case No. ICC-01/11-01/11-344-Red.

ICC, Prosecutor v Simone Gbagbo, Public redacted Decision on Côte d'Ivoire's challenge to the admissibility of the case against Simone Gbagbo, 11 December 2014, Case No. ICC-02/11-01/12.

ICC, Prosecutor v Thomas Lubanga Dyilo, Decision on the Prosecutor's Application for a Warrant of Arrest, 10 February 2006, Case No. ICC-01/04-01/06-8.

ICC, Prosecutor v Thomas Lubanga Dyilo, Decision on the Prosecutor's Application for a warrant of arrest, Article 58, 10 February 2006, Case No. ICC-01/04-01/06.

ICC, Prosecutor v Thomas Lubanga Dyilo, Judgment pursuant to Article 74 of the Statute, 14 March 2012, Case No. ICC-01/04-01/06.

ICC, Prosecutor v William Samoei Ruto et al., Judgment on the appeal of the Republic of Kenya against the decision of Pre-Trial Chamber II of 30 May 2011 entitled „Decision on the Application by the Government of Kenya Challenging the Admissibility of the Case Pursuant to Article 19(2)(b) of the Statute", 30 August 2011, Case No. ICC-01/09-01/11 OA.

ICC, Prosecutor v. Thomas Lubanga Dyilo, Decision on the confirmation of charges, Case No. ICC-01/04-01/06.

ICC, Prosescutor v Alfred Yekatom and Patrice-Edouard Ngaissona, Decision on the Yeaktom Defence's Admissibility Challenge, 28 April 2020, Case No. ICC-01/14-01/18.

ICC, Situation in Georgia, Corrected Version of „Request for authorisation of an investigation pursuant to article 15", 16 October 2015, ICC-01/15-4-Corr, 17 November 2015, Case No. ICC-01/15-4-Corr2.

ICC, Situation in Georgia, Decision on the Prosecutor's request for authorization of an investigation, 27 January 2016, Case No. ICC-01/15-12.

ICC, Situation in Georgia, Seperate Opinion of Judge Péter Kovács, 27 January 2016, Case No. ICC-01/15-12-Anx-Corr.

ICC, Situation in the Islamic Republic of Afghanistan, Decision Pursuant to Article 15 of the Rome Statute on the Authorisation of an Investigation into the Situation in the Islamic Republic of Afghanistan, 12 April 2019, Case No. ICC-02/17-33.

ICC, Situation in the Republic of Kenya, Decision Pursuant to Article 15 of the Rome Statute on the Authorization of an Investigation into the Situation in the Republic of Kenya, 31 March 2010, Case No. ICC-01/09-19-Corr.

ICC, Situation on the Registered Vessels of the Union of the Comoros, the Hellenic Republic and the Kingdom of Combodia, Decision on the request of the Union of the Comoros to review the Prosecutor's decision not to initiate an investigation, 16 July 2015, Case No. ICC-01/13.

SCSL

SCSL, Prosecutor v Sam Hinga Norman, Decision on Preliminary Motion Based on Lack of Jurisdiction (Child recruitment), 31 May 2004, Case No. SCSL-2004-14-AR72(E).

ICTY

ICTY, Prosecutor v Anto Furundžija, Judgment, Case No. IT-95-17/1.

ICTY, Prosecutor v Dario Kordić and Mario Čerkez, Appeals Judgement, 17 December 2004, Case No. IT-95-14/2-A.

ICTY, Prosecutor v Dusko Tadić aka „Dule", Decision on the Defence Motion for Interlocutory Appeal on Jurisdiction 2 October 1995, Case No. IT-94-1-AR72.

ICTY, Prosecutor v Dusko Tadić aka „Dule", Trial Judgment, 7 May 1997, Case No. IT-94-1-T.

ICTY, Prosecutor v Dusko Tadić, Appeals Judgement, 15 July 1999, Case No. IT-94-1-A.

ICTY, Prosecutor v Fatmir Limaj et al., Trial Judgement, 30 November 2005, Case No. IT-03-66-T.

ICTY, Prosecutor v Kupreškić et al, Judgment, 14 January 2000, Case No. IT.95-16-T.

ICTY, Prosecutor v Ljube Boškoski and Johan Tarculovski, Trial Chamber Judgment, 10 July 2008, Case No. IT-04-82-T.

ICTY, Prosecutor v Milorad Krnojelac, Judgment, 15 March 2002, Case No. IT-97-25-T.

ICTY, Prosecutor v Milorad Krnojelac, Judgment, 17 September 2003, Case No. IT-97-25-A.

ICTY, Prosecutor v Mucić et al., Trial Judgement, 16 November 1998, Case No. IT-96-21-T.

ICTY, Prosecutor v Ragoljub Kunarac et al., Appeals Judgement, 12 June 2002, Case No. IT-96-23/1-A.

ICTY, Prosecutor v Ramush Haradinaj et al., Trial Judgement, 3 April 2008, Case No. IT-04-84-T.

ICTY, Prosecutor v Sefer Halilović, Judgment, 16 November 2005, Case No. IT-01-48-T.

ICTY, Prosecutor v. Enver Hadzihasanovic and Amir Kubura, Judgement, 15 March 2006, Case No. IT-01-47-T.

ICTY, Prosecutor v. Mrkšić et al., Trial Judgement, 27 September 2007, Case No. IT-95-13/1-T.

ICTY, Prosecutor v. Slobodan Milošević, Decision on Motion for Judgement of Acquittal, 16 June 2004, Case No. IT-02-54-T.

ICTR

ICTR, Prosecutor v Georges Anderson Nderubumwe Rutaganda, Judgement and Sentence, 6 December 1999, Case No. ICTR-96-3-T.

ICTR, Prosecutor v Jean-Paul Akayesu, Trial Judgment, 2 September 1998, Case No. ICTR-96-4-T.

ICTR, Prosecutor v Joseph Nzabirinda, Judgment, 23 February 2007, Case No. ICTR-2001-77-T.

ICTR, Prosecutor v Laurent Semanza, Decision, 31 May 2000, Case No. ICTR-97-20-A.

ICTR, The Prosecutor v Nahimana et al., Appeals Judgment, 28 November 2007, Case No. ICTR-99-52-A.

ECJ

ECJ, Aalborg Portland A/S and Others v Commission of the European Communities, Judgment, 7 January 2004, Case Nos. C-204/00 P, C-205/00 P, C-211/00 P, C-213/00 P, C-217/00 P, C-218/00 P.

ECJ, Åklagaren v Hans Åkerberg Fransson, Judgment (Grand Chamber), 26 February 2016, Case No. C-617/10.

ECJ, Criminal proceedings against Filomeno Mario Miraglia, Judgment, 10 March 2005, Case No. C-469/03.

ECJ, Criminal proceedings against Hüseyin Gözütok and Klaus Brügge, Judgment, 11 February 2003, Case Nos. C-187/01, C-385/01.

ECJ, Criminal proceedings against Leopold Henri Van Esbroeck, Judgment, 9 March 2006, Case No. C-436/04.

ECJ, Criminal proceedings against M, Judgment, 5 June 2014, Case No. C-398/12.

ECJ, Criminal proceedings against Norma Kraaijenbrink, Judgment, 18 July 2007, Case. No C-367/05.

ECJ, Criminal proceedings against Zoran Spasic, Judgment, 27 May 2014, Case No. C-129/14 PPU.

ECJ, Jean Leon Van Straaten v Staat der Nederlanden and Republiek Italië, Judgment, 28 September 2006, Case No. C-150/05.

ECJ, Stefano Melloni v Ministerio Fiscal, Judgment (Grand Chamber), 26 February 2013, Case No. C-399/11.

ECtHR

ECtHR, Case of Aviso Zeta AG v Austria, Judgment, 21 June 2018, Application No. 5734/14.

ECtHR, Case of Campbell and Fell v The United Kingdom, Judgment, 28 June 1984, App. Nos. 7819/77, 7878/77.

ECtHR, Case of Cyprus v Turkey, Judgment, 10 May 2001, Application No. 25781/94.

ECtHR, Case of Engel and Others v The Netherlands, Judgment, 8 June 1976, Application Nos. 5100/71, 5101/71, 5102/71, 5354/72, 5370/72.

ECtHR, Case of Franz Fischer v Austria, Judgment, 29 May 2001, Application No. 37950/97.

ECtHR, Case of Gradinger v Austria, Judgment, 23 October 1995, Application No. 15963/90.

ECtHR, Case of Ilaşcu and others v Moldocia and Russia, 8 July 2004, Application No. 48787/99.

ECtHR, Case of Morice v France, Judgment, 23 April 2015, Application No. 29369/10.

ECtHR, Case of Oliveira v Switzerland, Judgment, 30 July 1998, Application No. 25711/94.

ECtHR, Case of Sergey Zolotukhin v Russia, Judgment, 10 February 2009, Application No. 14939/03.

ECtHR, Gudmundur Andri Ástrádsson v Iceland, Judgment, 1 December 2020, Application No. 26374/18.

ECtHR, Korbely v Hungary, Judgment, 19 September 2008, Application No. 9174/02.

ECtHR, Leo Zand v Austria, Decision, Application No. 7360/76.

ECtHR, Pandjikidzé and Others v Georgia, Judgment, 27 October 2009, Application No. 30323/02.

ECtHR, Savino and Others v Italy, Chamber Judgment, 28 April 2009, Application Nos. 17214/05, 20329/05 and 42113/04.

ACtHPR

ACtHPR, Armand Guehi v United Republic of Tanzania, 7 December 2018, Application No. 001/2015.

ACtHPR, Sebastien Germain Ajavon v Republic of Benin, Judgment (Merits), 29 March 2019, Application No. 013/2017.

ACtHPR, Wilfred Onyango Nganyi & 9 others v United Republic of Tanzania, Judgment, 18 March 2016, Application No. 006/2013.

IACtHR

IACtHR, Apitz Barbara et al. ("First Court of Administrative Disputes") v Venezuela, Judgment, 5 August 2008, Case No. Series C No. 182.

IACtHR, Case of Almonacid-Arellano et al. v Chile, Judgment, 26 September 2006, Case No. Series C No. 154.

IACtHR, Case of Barreto Leiva v Venezuela, Judgment, 17 November 2009, Case No. Series C No. 206.

IACtHR, Case of Castillo Petruzzi et al. v Peru, Judgment, 30 May 1999, Case No. Series C No. 52.

IACtHR, Case of Loayza-Tamayo v Peru, Judgment, 27 November 1998, Case No. Series C No. 33.

IACtHR, Case of Nadege Dorzema et al. v Dominican Republic, Judgment, 24 October 2012, Case No. Series C No. 251.

IACtHR, Case of Reverón Trujillo v Venezuela, Judgment, 30 June 2009, Case No. Series C No. 179.

Inter-American Commission on Human Rights, Juan Carlos Abella v Argentina, 18 November 1997, Case No. 11.137 OEA/Ser.L/V/II.98 doc. 6 rev.

IACtHR, The Rochela Massacre v Colombia, Judgment, 11 May 2007, Case No. Series C No. 163.

UNHRC

UNHRC, Andrés Felipe Arias Leiva v Colombia, Decision, 27 July 2018, Comm. No. 2537/2015.

UNHRC, Juan Almirati Nieto v Uruguay, Decision, 25 July 1983, Comm. No. 92/1981.

National Courts

Kammergericht Berlin, Anrechnung von Freiheitsentziehung im Ausland, Judgment, 23 April 2021, Case No. (6) 2 StE 6/20-3 (2/20).

House of Lords, Government of the Republic of Spain v Arantzazu Mendi, Judgment, 23 February 1939, Case No. L.R. 1939 A.C. 256.

Supreme Court of the United States, Hamdan v Rumsfeld, Secretary of Defense et al., Judgment, 29 June 2006, Case No. 05-184.

Stockholms Tingsrätt (Swedish Discrict Court), Prosecutor v Omar Sakhanh Haisam Sakhanh, Judgment, 16 February 2017, Case No. B 3786-16.

Svea hovrätt (Swedish Appeal Court), Prosecutor v Omar Sakhanh Haisam Sakhanh, Judgment, 31 May 2017, Case No. B 2259-17.

Högsta domstolen (Swedish Supreme Court), Prosecutor v Omar Sakhanh Haisam Sakhanh, Judgment, 20 July 2017, Case No. B 3157-17.

The High Court of Justice Queen's Bench Division, Serdar Mohammed v Ministry of Defence, Judgment, 2 May 2014, Case No. 2014 EWHC 1369 (QB).